The Center for Japanese and Korean Studies at the University of California at Berkeley is the unifying organization for faculty members and students interested in Japan and Korea, bringing together scholars from many disciplines.

The Center's major aims are the development and support of research and language study. As'part of this program the Center sponsors a publication series of books concerned with Japan and Korea. Manuscripts are considered from all campuses of the University of California as well as from any other individuals and institutions doing research in these areas.

RECENT PUBLICATIONS OF THE CENTER FOR
JAPANESE AND KOREAN STUDIES

HARUHIRO FUKUI
Party in Power: The Japanese Liberal-Democrats and Policy-making. 1970

ALBERT M. CRAIG and DONALD H. SHIVELY, Editors
Personality in Japanese History. 1971

RICHARD RUTT
The Bamboo Grove: An Introduction to Sijo Verse. 1971

Conspiracy

at Matsukawa

Published under the auspices of
The Center for Japanese and Korean Studies
University of California, Berkeley

Conspiracy

at Matsukawa

CHALMERS JOHNSON

University of California Press, Berkeley, Los Angeles, London

1972

University of California Press
Berkeley and Los Angeles, California
University of California Press, Ltd.
London, England

Copyright © 1972, by
The Regents of the University of California

Library of Congess Catalog Card Number: 73–161998
International Standard Book Number: 0–520–02063–4
Designed by James Mennick
Printed in the United States of America

To
Robert A. Scalapino
Teacher, Colleague, Friend

"War puts its questions
stupidly, peace mysteriously."

Malraux, *Anti-Memoirs*

Preface

IN STUDYING the biggest criminal conspiracy case of postwar Japan, I have tried to follow a method similar to that used by Georges Simenon's celebrated detective and student of society, Chief Inspector Maigret of the Paris Police. Maigret's cases usually break down into three phases. "In nearly all of his cases," writes Simenon, "Maigret came to this period of floating, during which, as his colleagues used to whisper, he appeared to be brooding. In the first stage—that is, when he suddenly found himself face to face with a new world, with people he knew nothing about—it was as if he were breathing in the life around him, mechanically, and filling himself with it like a sponge. . . . At the moment he had absorbed a quantity of impressions, a whole jumble of images, of phrases, of words of varying importance, of startled looks, but he did not yet know what to do with them all." [1] Finally comes Maigret's narrowing down to those suspects with motive and opportunity and his devastat-

1. Georges Simenon, *Maigret's Pickpocket*. Quoted with the permission of Hamish Hamilton Ltd., London, and Harcourt Brace Jovanovich, Inc., New York.

ing interrogations of them—sessions which combine the suspect's
anxiety, Maigret's own force of character, sandwiches and beer
from the Brasserie Dauphine, and a complete, psychologically
valid reconstruction of the criminal act.

Unfortunately I am not Maigret, and it looked for awhile
as if my "floating period" would go on forever. Partially this was
because of the sheer size of the cast of characters and the documents they produced. The Matsukawa case had twenty defendants, five courtroom battles (including two before the Supreme
Court of Japan), and thousands of pages of testimony; the defense appeal to the Supreme Court, prepared by some 241 lawyers, itself runs to fifteen thousand pages. A study of Matsukawa
involves reading approximately seventy-five volumes of court records, eleven volumes of newspaper clippings, as many boxes of
archives from the American occupation of Japan as one has the
energy to plow through, and possibly a hundred novels, movie
scenarios, propaganda booklets, and independent studies. All of
this material, except the occupation archives, is in the Japanese
language.

In addition to these materials on the case itself, one must be
familiar with twenty-five years of Japanese political history, the
postwar Japanese trade union movement, the vicissitudes of the
Japanese Communist party, the changes in American policy during the occupation of Japan, the complexities of the emerging
half-Japanese, half-American procedures for administering criminal justice, and the milieu in which the Matsukawa case itself
arose—namely, Tōhoku, or the great northern third of the main
Japanese island of Honshu. It is impossible to make an exhaustive
study of the Matsukawa case, as I was warned before I began by
my friend and invaluable helper, Murata Shirō, proprietor of
the Murata Bookstore near Gakugei University Station on the
Tōyoko Line in Tokyo. The attempt, however, affords an exhil-
arating departure from the high plane of generalities at which
foreigners often study social and political change in postwar
Japan.

Although my method has been copied after Maigret's, my
subject is different. I shall not try to "solve" the Matsukawa case

(although I cannot refrain from continuing the speculation on whether clandestine American agents sabotaged the train at Matsukawa), and I shall often go farther afield from the crime itself than Maigret would find necessary. This is because the Matsukawa case is not fiction and because it occurred in a society about which I do not have a native's knowledge. The chief justification for reading the Matsukawa materials today is the insights that the longest, most complex political-legal-economic cause célèbre of postwar Japan offers into the great questions of how the world's third industrial power got where it is. The Matsukawa case suggests that the process of change in Japan was rather more complex than veterans of the American occupation or ideologically committed Japanese might think.

I have many individuals and agencies to thank for assisting me. The Director of the National Diet Library in Tokyo gave me permission to microfilm the eleven-volume file on the Matsukawa case in his Newspaper Clipping Room (Shimbun Kiri-nuki Shitsu). Mr. Yutani Eiji of the East Asiatic Library, University of California, Berkeley, bought seventy-five volumes of court records for me to use. Murata Shirō performed his usual miracles in finding me esoteric items such as Murata Daizō, et al., *Matsukawa jiken wa kurisuchan ni totte nani o imi suru ka* (*What is the Meaning of the Matsukawa Case for a Christian?*) (Miyagi Prefecture, 1954). Mr. Joseph Avery and Mrs. Sally Ortan of the National Records Center, Suitland, Maryland, were unfailingly resourceful in helping me locate relevant parts of the archives left by the Supreme Commander for the Allied Powers (SCAP).[2]

2. I should add that all of the SCAP Archives I have read were unclassified or previously declassified. In accordance with the procedures made available under Executive Order 10816 I applied to the Secretary of the Army for "access for historical purposes to classified defense information"—that is, to still classified SCAP Archives—in order to be able to offer at least the negative proof that there is no evidence in the SCAP Archives that members of the occupation had anything to do with the Matsukawa case. On October 29, 1969, I received a letter from Major General Kenneth G. Wickham, the army's adjutant general, telling me that my application had been received but that "because of the foreign

The Center for Japanese and Korean Studies, University of California, Berkeley, made available the funds with which I hired my friend and colleague Kim Yong-mok as a research assistant. His work was, as in the past, of an exceptionally high standard, including his interview in Tokyo with Sugiura Saburō, head of the Matsukawa Defendants Association, on November 7, 1969. Professor Masumi Junnosuke of Tokyo Metropolitan University has helped me in numerous ways during my study trips to Japan since 1961. Evelyn Bingham Prosser drew the maps contained in this book. Most important, Sheila Johnson, my wife, accompanied me on a ten-mile walk through the Fukushima countryside during our on-the-site investigation in June of 1968, and she has been my companion throughout the difficult passages, both literal and literary, encountered in this case.

All Japanese names in this book are given in the Japanese manner, surname followed by given name. Translations from Japanese are entirely my responsibility. Errors of fact or vagaries of interpretation should also be charged exclusively to my account.

C. J.

Berkeley, California
March 1971

---

relations aspects of your topic, the application is being coordinated with the Department of State." I never again heard from him or anyone else in the government. This official discourtesy was not wholly unexpected or unwelcome. If access to classified archives had been granted, I would have had to submit my manuscript to the Army for vetting—which I did not want to do. Nonetheless, I cannot say that I have exhaustively searched the SCAP Archives for answers to the Matsukawa puzzle.

Contents

Chapter 1

A Severed Arm on the Railroad Tracks

LIKE any other big city, Tokyo is made manageable for the people who live there by its districts, comparable to Manhattan's upper and lower, east and west "sides" or Paris's "quarters." The Japanese capital, the world's largest city, is dominated by its railroad stations—Tokyo, Shimbashi, Shinagawa, Shibuya, Shinjuku, Ikebukuro, and Ueno—which form a great circle of districts around the Imperial Palace in the center of the city. Ueno is Tokyo's Gare du Nord, its opening to the northern environs and the terminus for long-distance trains serving Tōhoku, the northeast third of the island of Honshu.

Early on the morning of July 6, 1949, motorman Shiina Toshio left Ueno station driving the last interurban train of the night for the northern suburb of Matsudo. Shortly after passing through North Senju station in the old part of Tokyo near the Sumida and Arakawa rivers, he noticed the mangled body of what he believed to be a woman alongside the tracks. At his next stop, Ayase, he notified the assistant stationmaster, who went immediately to the little-frequented stretch of railway tracks, situated at the curve where two main lines intersect, not far from a prison, in the Gotanno Minami section of Adachi ward. It was an unlikely place for a suicide but a most suitable site for a murder.

The body had been run over by a train at 12:20 A.M., the time indicated on its shattered wristwatch, and was disfigured beyond recognition. It was not a woman but a man, later identified by calling cards and a railroad pass spread over the hundred yards the body had been dragged. He was Shimoyama Sadanori, age forty-nine, president of the Japanese National Railroads, who only two days earlier had handed out dismissal notices to 37,000 railroad employees—part of 102,000 workers he intended to fire during the month of July—and who was one of the men whose name most often appeared on the front pages of Japanese newspapers during the first half of 1949.

The cause of Mr. Shimoyama's death has never been established—there is some evidence that he may have been dead when his body was placed on the tracks—although interest in the case has never flagged. Twenty years later the Association to Study the Shimoyama Case (Shimoyama Jiken Kenkyū Kai) was going strong, and several national magazines carried the latest sallies of former police officials and interested parties in the ongoing verbal war over whether he was murdered (and by whom, including possibly authorities of the United States occupation of Japan) or had committed suicide. More significantly perhaps, during October 1968 the press revealed that Prime Minister Satō had ordered three scenes cut from a color documentary film that the Prime Minister's Office had produced to commemorate the centenary of the Meiji Restoration, Japan's debut in 1868 as a modern nation. One of the cut scenes showed a severed arm, allegedly belonging to Shimoyama, lying on a railroad track. His mysterious death nineteen years earlier seemed to remind the official viewers too strongly that the Japanese "success story" was not without its darker aspects.

Shimoyama's death in 1949 was only the beginning of a bloody summer in Japan. A little more than a week later, on July 15, an unmanned electric train with its operating handle tied down drove out of control into the suburban Mitaka station west of Tokyo, derailed, and killed six people standing on the platform. The government subsequently indicted ten persons on a charge of train sabotage resulting in death—which itself carries the death penalty in Japan. All ten were members of the National Railroad Workers' Union (NRWU) and nine were prominent Communists. The Mitaka case disappeared from the headlines only on June 7, 1967, when Judge Higuchi Masaru of the Tokyo High Court denied a retrial to Takeuchi Keisuke, the only defendant still under a sentence of death for the crime since August 11, 1950, on the grounds not that Takeuchi was in fact guilty but that the case had become moot since he had died in prison on January 18, 1967.

The biggest case of 1949 was still to come. A month after the Mitaka incident, on August 18, 1949, the *Asahi shimbun,* Japan's leading newspaper, carried the headlines: PASSENGER TRAIN OVERTURNED, A SECOND "MITAKA INCIDENT." On the same day Masuda Kaneshichi, Chief Cabinet Secretary to Prime Minister Yoshida, said to the press that this new incident was like the Mitaka case in that both were caused by Communist terrorists. This third political crime occurred not in Tokyo but some 168 miles north of Tokyo, in the rural prefecture of Fukushima. At 3:09 on the morning of August 17, passenger train number 412 from Aomori on the northern tip of Honshu was proceeding south, bound for Ueno. The train had left Fukushima city, the prefectural capital, only a few minutes before, when it had come onto the Northeast Main Line (Tōhoku Honsen) of the Japanese National Railroads. It carried some 630 passengers. Just south of the hamlet of Kanayagawa and slightly more than a mile north of the village of Matsukawa, in a lovely wooded valley surrounded by hills and planted in paddy rice, the locomotive suddenly derailed and overturned.

As the firebox came back on them and the boiler burst, engineer Ishida Shōzo, age forty-nine, and locomotive fireman Itō Toshiichi, age twenty-seven, were killed instantly. The assistant engineer, Mogi Masaichi, age twenty-three, lived for a few minutes, long enough to gasp to Abe Gorō, the train's conductor, that "the train was sabotaged." And indeed it was.

Virtually the only thing that all parties to the Matsukawa case agree upon is that this train wreck was no accident. The "fishplates" or "tie plates" (in Japanese, tsugime-ita) which join the rails together had been removed in at least two places, numerous spikes holding the rails to the ties had been pulled up, and the outside rail in the gently curving section of track where the wreck occurred had been moved some thirteen feet out of place. Numerous learned books and innumerable polemical ones have been written in Japan on the subject of how many men would have been required to do the job in the time available since the last train had passed, and even on whether or not it was possible for any man, no matter how strong, to loosen the nuts holding a railroad fishplate using only a foot-long monkey wrench, the tool found along with a crowbar at the site of the wreck. Numerous learned judges have themselves tried their hands at sabotaging a railroad track in the prescribed manner, just to see if it could be done. The conclusion that all these books, articles, and experts hold in common is that somehow, some group of men did in fact take apart the tracks of the Northeast Main Line and they did so in a very short period of time.

The Matsukawa incident resulted in what one authority has called "the biggest cause célèbre in the history of law suits in Japan." The state indicted twenty people, nineteen men and one woman, charging them with conspiracy to violate and actual violation of article 126, paragraphs 1 and 3, of the Penal Code of Japan—to wit, "A person who upsets or destroys a train or electric car actually containing persons shall be punished with penal servitude for life or not less than three years. . . . A person, who by committing a crime mentioned in the preceding . . . paragraph . . . causes the death of another, shall be punished with death or penal servitude for life." Although in 1963 all of the defendants were judged innocent of the crime, twenty years after the wreck occurred the case still remained before the Japanese courts in the form of suits against the government for damages. This case altered the lives of several hundred Japanese citizens; made numerous writers and publicists famous; involved Communist China, the Soviet Union, and the United States in the domestic affairs of Japan; and shook postwar Japanese democracy in the form of serious charges against government officials. Above all, it brought the unpleasant word *detchi-age* ("frame-up") into daily political discussion and contributed to the radicalization of left-wing politics in Japan.

The Shimoyama, Mitaka, and Matsukawa cases are as familiar to Japanese adults as the Alger Hiss, Rosenberg, and J. Robert Oppenheimer cases are to American adults. Any Japanese college student of the fifties or sixties could tell a stranger the essential facts of each of these cases, and he probably participated at some time in one or another of the huge rallies, marches, and vigils that attended the Matsukawa trials. I propose in this book to explore the Matsukawa case in its full detail, although I shall refer to the other two cases, and to many other cases not yet mentioned, as part of the Matsukawa story. My purpose is not, however, merely forensic curiosity or sensation-mongering. The Matsukawa case is important in its own right, for some reasons that have already been mentioned and others that will become clear later on. But I propose not only to make a study of the Matsukawa case but also to make of Matsukawa a case study of three fundamental aspects of social change in postwar Japan: the occupation itself, the role of trade unions in Japan's spectacular economic recovery, and the Americans' efforts to "democratize" Japanese ideas of criminal justice.

The Matsukawa case was symptomatic of, and at the same time dramatically made manifest, the single most damaging contradiction of the American occupation of Japan (1945–1952)— that is, the Americans' failure to harmonize their democratic reforms with Japan's need for economic recovery from the war. Not only did the Americans fail to integrate these two objectives, they also helped create through their democratic reforms conditions which made it doubly difficult later for them to correct their earlier mistake. Specifically, during 1948, when the Americans finally decided to try to get Japan's economy back on its feet, they had to couple their new policies with a frontal attack—the so-called red purge—on Japan's Communist-dominated trade unions, unions whose very existence and whose Communist domination depended in large measure on earlier occupation policies. This reversal of basic policy, and the way in which it was carried out, continues to the present day to influence Japanese political life.

"Japan's American interlude," as Kawai Kazuo has so aptly called it, was a most unusual and even ambiguous enterprise that deserves much greater attention from historians than it has received thus far.[1] It was surely the most successful of the various policies the United States has pursued in east Asia over the past twenty-five years. However, when one begins to study what it actually accomplished and how it did so, one is drawn to the conclusion that although many right things were done, they were almost invariably done for the wrong reasons.

My approach to the occupation is "revisionist," not in terms of disputing its favorable outcome for Japanese-American

1. Kawai, Kazuo, *Japan's American Interlude* (Chicago, 1960), is the best general analysis of the occupation written in English.

relations or the present-day Japanese level of living, but certainly in terms of its administration and its advertisements. Other scholars have been struck by "the smoothness and efficiency of Japan's postwar transition to democracy" and by the "smooth and cooperative quality of the postwar political transition in Japan." [2] In this book, evidence is presented for the opposite point of view. It has been said that General MacArthur was properly fearful of sponsoring another Weimar regime in Japan—a regime disliked and ridiculed by the population because its authority came solely from the approval of the conqueror. He avoided doing so, but the fact is that he came dangerously close to producing what he sought to avoid.

The basic contradiction of occupation policy, democratization versus economic recovery, had diverse origins. In part it derived from wartime propaganda and the attitudes associated with total war (i.e., war in which all civilians are mobilized and treated like belligerents). The Japanese themselves helped foster attitudes of national superiority and retribution by their conduct of the war, but by the end of the war the Americans fully reciprocated the attitude of national self-righteousness. Thus, as Supreme Commander for the Allied Powers (SCAP) officials note in one of their official but as yet unpublished histories, "In accordance with the view that the disaster which had befallen Japan was of her own making, the Basic Directive for Postsurrender Military Government in Japan stated that the Supreme Commander was in no way to assume any responsibility for the economic rehabilitation of Japan, the strengthening of her economy, or the maintenance of any particular standard of living." [3] It is to General MacArthur's credit that he did not implement this directive literally.

2. Robert E. Ward, "The Potential for Democratization in Prewar Japan," in John D. Montgomery and Albert O. Hirschman, eds., *Public Policy* (Cambridge, Mass., 1968), XVII, 141, 143.
3. SCAP, *History of the Nonmilitary Activities of the Occupation*

There were other roots to the contradiction between the victors' desire to democratize Japan and the Japanese need to achieve economic recovery and growth. The Allies themselves were divided; some had good reasons for wanting to punish the Japanese (e.g., the Filipinos), and others had imperial and ideological reasons for wanting to exploit the Japanese (e.g., the Soviets). The Americans were also divided between old China hands and old Japan hands, and between Americans with socialist inclinations and Americans with capitalist inclinations.[4] However, the basic source of the contradiction was a fundamental lack of knowledge about Japan in both a sociopolitical and an intelligence-collecting sense. The intelligence error became obvious with Japan's early surrender. Japan had already been more effectively beaten than the Americans realized when, at Yalta, they made significant concessions in the Far East in order to bring the USSR into the war. The atomic bombs probably hastened the end of the war, but they were militarily only the coup de grâce; fire bombs and submarine warfare against Japan's shipping had already produced more casualties than the atomic weapons did and had reduced Japan's war machine to a shell. However, a revised intelligence estimate of Japan's strength did not register in time to affect initial postsurrender policy. Thus, faulty intelligence influenced the occupation by excluding from serious consideration the possibility that if economic recovery were not seriously undertaken the Americans would have to feed the Japanese—which is exactly what happened.

American lack of cultural and political understanding of

---

of Japan (Tokyo, 1952), 55 volumes, mimeographed. Classification removed from all but a few volumes by Executive Order 10501. Microfilmed by the World War II Records Division, National Archives and Records Service. The quotation is from Monograph No. 47, "The Heavy Industries," p. 3. These histories will be cited hereafter in this book by monograph number and title.

4. See Harry Emerson Wildes, *Typhoon in Tokyo* (New York, 1954).

Japan was more profound and less easily corrected; it lay behind the occupation's positive policies of "democratization." On January 12, 1950, in a National Press Club speech, Dean Acheson argued that "throughout our history the attitude of Americans toward the peoples of Asia had been an interest in them not as pawns in the strategy of power or as subjects for economic exploitation, but simply as people. . . . Trade was a very small part of American interest in the Far East, and it was a very small part of American interest in trade." [5] To any unbiased observer this is a broadly accurate generalization, particularly when the American record is compared with that of other non–east-Asian nations. It should also be added, however, that part of the historical American interest in Asians as people was as objects for missionary activity, precisely because they belonged to an entirely different culture. China was long the focus of the greatest American missionary efforts, and early American occupation policies in Japan strongly suggest the reappearance of the old American missionary fervor.

How else explain certain of General MacArthur's statements about the Japanese and the impact of the occupation on them? For example, on May 5, 1951, the then recently retired Supreme Commander for the Allied Powers said to the United States Senate:

> Tucked away there in the North Pacific, they [the Japanese] had little or no realization of how the rest of the world lived. They had evolved a feudalistic system of totalitarianism which had produced results which were almost like reading the pages of mythology. . . . They are like all orientals. They have a tendency to adulate a winner, and to have the most supreme contempt for a loser. . . . There was an enormous vacuum created there [in Japan as

5. *Present at the Creation* (New York, 1969), p. 356.

a result of the defeat], in which the Anglo-Saxon system of decency, fair play, and justice came into play.

They probably would have followed us and adopted many of our policies and criteria, merely because of what I have explained [i.e., the alleged tendency of orientals to "adulate a winner"]; but the more accustomed they became to our system of life—they watched us carefully—they were struck enormously by the spirituality of the American home. . . .

If the Anglo-Saxon was say forty-five years of age in development, in the sciences, the arts, divinity, culture, the Germans were quite as mature. The Japanese, however, in spite of their antiquity measured by time were in a very tuitionary condition. Measured by the standards of modern civilization, they would be like a boy of twelve as compared with our development of forty-five years.

The German was quite as mature as we were. Whatever the German did in dereliction of the standards of modern morality, the international standards, he did deliberately. . . . But the Japanese were entirely different. There is no similarity. One of the great mistakes that was made was to try to apply the same policies which were so successful in Japan to Germany, where they were not quite so successful, to say the least.[6]

6. U.S. Senate, 82nd Congress, 1st Session, Hearings before the Committee on Armed Services and the Committee on Foreign Relations, *Military Situation in the Far East* (Washington, 1951), pp. 310–313. It is possible to imagine "the spirituality of the American home" having a different effect on the Japanese than General MacArthur thought. What Kennan saw in Germany could also be observed in Tokyo: "I had been twice in Germany since the termination of hostilities. Each time I had come away with a sense of sheer horror at the spectacle of this horde of my compatriots and their dependents camping in luxury amid the ruins of a shattered national community, ignorant of the past, oblivious to the abundant evidences of present tragedy all around them, inhabiting the very same sequestered villas that the Gestapo and SS had just abandoned,

That these remarks did not arise merely in the course of a senatorial "bull session" but actually reflected official views is made clear by John Bennett, who served as a member of the occupying forces, and who characterized SCAP's image of Japanese society thus: "The Japanese were seen as highly intelligent but amoral humans, not to be trusted and in need of stern authoritarian guidance." [7]

It is not my intention to belittle the opinions of either General MacArthur or American missionaries. Today MacArthur is probably more admired in Japan than he is in the United States; and many Japanese of widely different political positions credit him with preserving the Japanese Imperial institution and with saving the country from a much harsher occupation, including possible partition into separate Allied zones, which the Soviet Union advocated. Nor would it be accurate to imply that General MacArthur made all occupation policies. His views are important because they established guidelines for the kind of occupation it

---

and enjoying the same privileges, flaunting their silly supermarket luxuries in the face of a veritable ocean of deprivation, hunger, and wretchedness, setting an example of empty materialism and cultural poverty before a people desperately in need of spiritual and intellectual guidance, taking for granted—as though it were their natural due—a disparity in privilege and comfort between themselves and their German neighbors no smaller than those that had once divided lord and peasant in that feudal Germany which it had been our declared purpose in two world wars to destroy." George F. Kennan, Memoirs (1925–1950) (New York: Bantam ed., 1969), p. 452.

7. John W. Bennett and Ishino, Iwao, Paternalism in the Japanese Economy (Minneapolis, 1963), p. 25. The idea that occupation policy derived at least in part from American missionary impulses has some grounding in fact. On April 6, 1964, the Reverend Billy Graham, preaching at the "Mayor's Prayer Breakfast" at the Waldorf-Astoria Hotel in New York, said that General MacArthur had once told him he turned down an offer by Emperor Hirohito to make Japan a Christian nation. "General MacArthur, Mr. Graham said, told of rejecting the proposal in favor of asking the American people to send 10,000 Christian missionaries to evangelize Japan." New York Times, April 7, 1964.

would be—"a stupendous but improvised social experiment which used an empire and 74,000,000 people as its laboratory materials" [8]—and because they suggest clues to why it came out the way it did.

American missionary and quasi-missionary activities, from nineteenth-century evangelists to the Peace Corps, have arisen primarily from an excess of domestic idealism; rarely, however, have they been informed by any coherent theory of cultural relativism. Conversion, development, modernization, or whatever the goal, was usually equated with change toward the American way of life. It is significant that General MacArthur specifically uses a metaphor of "development" in talking about change in Japan; other SCAP officials use the term "modernization" together with "democratization" in speaking of reforms in the legal field.[9] But the meanings they gave these terms are clear examples of the implicit equation of "modern" with one's own society, in this case the United States—an elementary error against which every teacher of social science warns his college freshmen. This is not to say that using the United States as a model is necessarily a bad idea; the Soviet Union certainly interpreted its tutelary role as the implanting of Soviet communism in the territories it occupied after the war. The fact that "democratization" was implicitly understood as "Americanization" in Japan does, however, alter the kinds of questions that one must ask about the occupation. One becomes less interested in whether trade unions, fair trade commissions, and land reform actually do promote democracy and more interested in the specific influence of American institutions on the evolving Japanese democratic consensus.

To put the matter bluntly, SCAP officials were ordered to "democratize" Japanese society without having any clear idea of what "democratization," abstractly and in a culture-free for-

8. Wildes, *Typhoon in Tokyo,* p. 1.
9. SCAP Monograph No. 14, "Legal and Judicial Reform," p. 50.

mulation, might entail or what the end result might look like. They therefore tried to Americanize Japanese society—America being a stable, functioning (and victorious) example of democracy. This simplified matters a good deal—one needed to know something about America, not Japan—and it saved a good deal of abstruse thinking about whether there might be any economic prerequisites of democracy, since this problem is not central to American democratic theory. It should be repeated that American policies for the occupation had diverse sources, including the nature and outcome of the war, faulty intelligence estimates, and ideological proclivities of American leaders at the time. It should also be added that different policies of the occupation sprang from different mixes of these various intentions and that no summary statement can do justice to the actual events. Nonetheless, the contents of the policies that figure directly in the Matsukawa case—economic recovery only after the attempt at "economic democratization," police reform, promotion of a democratic trade union movement, guarantees of civil liberties, and reform of criminal procedure—all were influenced by an orientation more attuned to American practice than to either an abstract notion of democracy or an understanding of what was likely to work in Japan.

In September 1945 the Americans occupied a country physically and spiritually gutted. With defeat and the loss of its colonies Japan not only was unable to feed, clothe, house, and employ its wartime home population, but it also had to absorb some five million demobilized servicemen and returnees from former colonial areas. This addition to the labor force was equivalent to a ten-year natural increase in the fifteen to fifty-nine age group at the rate which prevailed between 1914 and 1935.[10] Although the postwar indexes of industrial production

10. Yamamura, Kozo, *Economic Policy in Postwar Japan* (Berkeley and Los Angeles, 1967), p. 153.

(see table 1) do not indicate Japan's misery in trying to meet its population's needs, they do reveal how long the Japanese economy took to regain even the levels of the 1930s. Only during the last quarter of 1950, four months after the outbreak of the

TABLE 1

INDEXES OF INDUSTRIAL PRODUCTION: 1946–1950

(1932–1936 = 100)

1946	. . . . 33.1
1947	. . . . 40.2
1948	. . . . 58.1
1949	. . . . 77.2
1950	. . . . 95.1

SOURCE: SCAP Monograph No. 29, "Working Conditions," Appendix I.

Korean War, did industrial production begin to surpass the levels of the mid-thirties, when of course the population was smaller (October 1950: 108.4; November 1950: 110.5; December 1950: 115.0).

The American response to these conditions was hardly helpful. As George Kennan puts it, "In the face of this situation the nature of the occupational policies pursued up to that time [the summer of 1947] by General MacArthur's headquarters seemed on cursory examination to be such that if they had been devised for the specific purpose of rendering Japanese society vulnerable to Communist political pressures and paving the way for a Communist takeover, they could scarcely have been other than what they were." [11]

Postwar Japanese leaders, who in the past had opposed the aggressive policies of the militarists, saw the situation ironically.

11. Memoirs, pp. 396–397.

Prime Minister Yoshida, who actually led Japan through her period of recovery, writes in his memoirs: "Prince Konoye said during an audience with the Emperor towards the end of the Pacific War that, defeat then being imminent, one of the most serious results to be feared in the event of any mismanagement in bringing the conflict to a close was a Communist revolution. It is in a way ironical that, after we had surrendered to the U.S. Forces in order to avoid such a disaster, one of the first acts of the occupation authorities was, if not actually to favor Communism, at least to adopt an exceptionally lenient attitude towards Japan's Communists." [12]

Of course this was not what the Americans thought they were doing; they thought they were just being democratic. The first official act of democratization by the occupation—the Civil Liberties Directive of October 4, 1945—was to free all so-called political prisoners: 439 "thought offenders" imprisoned under the 1928 amendment to the Peace Preservation Law, 17 persons under preventive detention, 39 spy suspects, and 2,016 persons under "protection and surveillance." [13] Communists were not specially favored in this civil liberties directive, but they were included in the groups covered by the directive; and the occupation authorities bent over backward in their definition of a political prisoner. For example, two of the most prominent postwar Communist leaders, Miyamoto Kenji and Hakamada Satomi, had been sentenced to life imprisonment in the early thirties for torturing to death a Communist suspected of being a police agent. Both men were released in October 1945, and as late as March 1947 the Legal Section of SCAP-GHQ was defending

12. Yoshida Shigeru, *The Yoshida Memoirs* (Cambridge, Mass., 1962), p. 225.
13. SCAP Monograph No. 14, "Legal and Judicial Reform," p. 8. Slightly different figures are given in Monograph No. 11, "Development of Political Parties," p. 76.

their release, saying that torture was sometimes unavoidable in a movement of this kind and that they had been in fact political prisoners.[14]

Japan's freed Communist leaders were remarkable organizers of men and fully committed to creating a new political and economic order in Japan. In addition to their own talents, they were often welcomed and trusted by the people because they were virtually the only group who could claim not to have been tainted by the militaristic mistakes of the past. They immediately took charge of the new labor movement that SCAP was encouraging, and generally speaking, they probably offered the most effective leadership the Japanese labor movement has ever had. As Ayusawa Iwao, former director of the International Labor Organization office in Tokyo, recalls: "While Communist members on the Labor Relations Commission were bitterly critical on most matters, they were always punctual and present at meetings. They studied the subjects under discussion with remarkable thoroughness to substantiate their criticisms, often more thoroughly than other members. Their seriousness of purpose and self-sacrificing dedication were impressive and sobering to other members. We might add that SCAP in the early stages of the occupation did not merely tolerate but welcomed the participation of Communists in such important bodies as the central and local labor relations commissions." [15] Unfortunately for Japan,

14. See the letter of March 26, 1947, from Howard Meyers, Legal Section, SCAP-GHQ, to the Chief, Government Section, in the SCAP Archives, National Records Center, Suitland, Maryland, Legal Section files, box 1500. (Materials from this source will be cited hereafter under the general title "SCAP Archives," by the unit in which they originated, and by the number of the box in which they are stored.) For a discussion of the so-called "Red Lynching Case" of 1933, in which Miyamoto and Hakamada were implicated, see George M. Beckmann and Okubo, Genji, *The Japanese Communist Party, 1922–1945* (Stanford, Calif., 1969), pp. 144–145.

15. *A History of Labor in Modern Japan* (Honolulu, 1966), p. 251.

the Communists were ultimately undone by their single greatest weakness, their subservience to the orders and interests of foreign Communist leaders. In retrospect the chief Communist contribution to the miracle of Japan's economic recovery and growth was to discredit the postwar trade union movement's economic as well as its political activities, thereby contributing comparatively low wage levels to Japan's rebuilding efforts.

It is a controversial question whether the Americans should have been quite so liberal in their definitions of political prisoners and in acting on their unquestioned beliefs that everything done by Japan's prewar and wartime governments was fascistic and against the public interest. The allies in World War II had a right to punish Japanese violators of international law, and as victors they might even be expected, within reason, to create and apply some new international law ex post facto. Whether the occupation's measures of what has been called psychological disarmament were an inevitable or appropriate or laudable outcome of total war is a question that goes beyond the scope of this study. What seems clear, however, is that the release of a large group of ideologically committed revolutionaries into a wartorn and defeated society without any efforts to rebuild the economic foundations of that society resembled less a prescription for "democratization" or "psychological disarmament" than one for revolution and counterrevolution.[16]

The occupation did have policies for the Japanese economy;

16. The phrase "psychological disarmament" is used by Dr. Alfred C. Oppler, former chief of the Legislation and Justice Division, Legal Section, SCAP-GHQ. Oppler writes: "The modern type of treatment of the occupied nation by the conquering authority assertedly aims at far broader objectives when compared to military occupations of the past. It no longer restricts itself to disarming the enemy from a purely military and technical point of view, but is designed to prevent him from future aggression by what may be termed as psychological disarmament." "The Reform of Japan's Legal and Judicial System Under Allied Occupation," *Washington Law Review* XXIV:3 (August 1949), 290.

it too was to be psychologically disarmed and rebuilt as a "democratic economy." [17] SCAP took as its model an idealized image of a freely competitive American economy, one maintained by governmental antitrust intervention in the public's interest, and it accepted a good deal of the neo-Marxist theory that capitalist munitions makers promote imperialist expansion. Therefore SCAP came up with four main policies in the economic field: elimination of so-called Zaibatsu control (i.e., financial concentration), deconcentration of economic power generally, elimination of private control organizations (comparable to cartels), and the promotion of "fair trade practices." The last objective involved the creation of a Fair Trade Commission, which was to supervise the economy and prevent the reappearance of a new alliance between big business and government by seeing to it that businesses did not become too big.

Regardless of whether these were good or bad objectives, or whether there were better means to have achieved them (including the use of non-American models such as a socialized or nationalized economy), or whether the Americans' economic theories made sense in view of Japan's dependence on international trade—the policies that were actually pursued inhibited all but the most desultory economic activity. War devastation, disrepair, misuse of equipment, and the departure of Korean and Formosan labor were disruptive enough to the economy; the freezing of assets and the designation of a company as a likely target for reorganization (the occupation-created Holding Company Liquidation Commission made such "designations" *before* a company was investigated) brought most enterprises to a standstill until the uncertainty was over. Combined with SCAP's policy of making Japan pay reparations in kind immediately after the war to previously occupied nations (a policy whose publica-

17. The term "democratic economy" is used by SCAP officials in Monograph No. 25, "Deconcentration of Economic Power," p. 13.

tion alone stopped virtually all maintenance on capital equipment), the program to democratize the economy soon became one of uneconomic democratization. As Yamamura puts it, "During the initial phase of the program, SCAP was able to dissolve the Zaibatsu, impose a rigid Anti-Monopoly Act, overhaul the tax system, and so on, because the possible impact of these measures on economic recovery and growth was ignored." [18]

It did not take the Americans long to figure out that something was wrong with their policies. For one thing, they had to pay out $400 million annually to feed the Japanese people. Their policies also exposed Japan to a spiraling inflation, a black market, continuous strikes, government loans to businesses just to meet payrolls, corruption, and a general lowering of popular morale —ideal conditions from the point of view of the Japanese Communist party. The Americans therefore reversed themselves. They gave up on at least the third and fourth of their objectives: Japanese were allowed to organize their economy in ways that differed from the free competition model and to create a Ministry of International Trade and Industry, which soon eclipsed the Fair Trade Commission as the primary public arbiter of what was and was not permissible economic activity.

The actual reversal of basic policy—which involved making economic recovery first priority when it had not even been on the list of priorities to begin with—came about slowly and for reasons that are still highly controversial. Most of the numerous reasons and rank-orderings of reasons that have been offered to explain it reflect more the ideological commitment of the authors than the actual history of the time. Shinobu Seisaburō, for example, argues that the Americans, scared by the Communist advances being made in China, sought economic recovery in order to make Japan into a forward American military base, an "unsinkable aircraft carrier" (fuchin kūbo), to use the language

18. *Economic Policy*, p. 173.

of the time. He also suggests that the Americans wanted to get Japan's steel production up in order to meet world shortages caused by the capitalist nations' rearmament and that foreign capitalists wanted to aid Japanese enterprises in which they held investments (such as General Electric's alleged aid to the Tokyo Shibaura Electric Company—or Tōshiba, as it is more commonly known—one of the firms that plays a leading role in the Matsukawa case).[19]

These are the standard leftist explanations accepted by a majority of Japanese historians. As a further example, Shiota Shobei, writing in the journal Rekishigaku kenkyū (The Journal of Historical Studies), asserts: "The Matsukawa case was a part of the oppression of the labor unions by American imperialism in the face of the great change in the situation in Asia following the Chinese revolution. American imperialism wanted to build an anti-Communist military base in Japan by encouraging the revival of Japanese monopoly capitalism and by aiding the militarist reorganization of the Japanese economy; it regarded the labor unions as the great obstacle to this purpose." [20] The Communists view these events in the same way except that they add the Marxist factor that the Americans were "forced" to reverse economic democratization because of a depression back home and the consequent need of capitalists in the United States to obtain profits through imperialism.[21]

19. Sengo Nihon seiji shi (A History of Postwar Japanese Politics) (Tokyo, 1967), III, 920–1010, particularly 928 and 948–949.

20. "Matsukawa jiken tōji no Fukushima kenka no rōdō undō," (The Labor Movement in Fukushima Prefecture at the Time of the Matsukawa Case), Rekishigaku kenkyū, No. 224 (October 1958), 47.

21. See, e.g., Matsukawa Undō Shi Hensan Iinkai (The Committee to Compile the History of the Matsukawa Movement), ed., Matsukawa undō zenshi (Complete History of the Matsukawa Movement) (Tokyo, 1965), p. 46. Cf. Zen'ei (Vanguard), No. 150, "rinji zōkan" (special issue) (January 1959), "Matsukawa no shinjitsu" (The Truth of Matsukawa), passim. Zen'ei is the official theoretical journal of the Japanese Communist Party Central Committee.

Unquestionably, American leaders in Washington and Tokyo were responding in part to domestic American criticism of the occupation. Some newspaper editors in the United States were calling SCAP's economic policies a "New Deal" operation, while others were charging that the occupation's programs would make Japan a permanent economic ward of the United States. Senator William F. Knowland denounced the economic reforms as "socialistic" in the Congressional Record.[22] Within Japan occupation authorities seemed most concerned about the fact that the economic reforms were providing fertile conditions for the growing Communist domination of the trade unions, with consequent political strikes and the exploitation of economic stagnation for political purposes.

SCAP did not oppose union political activities. On the contrary, SCAP labor officials hoped that the trade unions would evolve and coalesce into something like the British Labour party, and they often wrote as if they were more interested in the educational functions of unions than in their economic ones. For example, a SCAP document of 1948, entitled "Organization and Structure of Trade Union Movements," explains: "One of the functions of the trade union movement in Japan is, as it has proven to be in other countries, to serve as a training school for youth, men, and women. If the trade union is operated in a democratic manner, if it serves the entire membership, every member of the trade union will, through participation in the trade union, learn to think, to speak, and to act in a democratic manner." [23] SCAP's real problem with the unions was not that they were political but that the Communists, not being plagued

22. See Chicago Tribune, September 18, 1947; Newsweek, December 1, 1947; and Congressional Record, Vol. 93, No. 168, December 19, 1947, pp. 11809–11811.

23. SCAP Archives, Economic and Scientific Section, SCAP-GHQ, in Civil Affairs Section, Tōhoku Civil Affairs Region, box 2612. Also see SCAP Monograph No. 28, "Development of the Trade Union Movement," p. 31.

by the same factional rivalries as the non-Communist labor leaders, had been able to capture control of the labor movement and were running it in a decidedly undemocratic manner. Many SCAP leaders thus came to recognize that economic democratization and the payment of reparations, which they acknowledged to have been "a significant deterrent to production," [24] were feeding workers' grievances and undercutting another important democratization program—namely, the trade union movement.

The official reason given for the reversal in economic policy was that it was too costly to the American taxpayer. On January 6, 1948, speaking in San Francisco, Secretary of the Army Kenneth C. Royall said that the United States could not be expected to provide relief indefinitely for occupied areas and stressed the importance of making Japan self-supporting as soon as possible. On April 7, 1948, Undersecretary of the Army William Draper officially announced that the United States was abandoning much of its program to deconcentrate the Japanese economy. The most significant element underlying all these decisions was of course the development of the Cold War and, specifically, the emergence on the Chinese mainland of a Communist revolutionary movement that was anti-American, pro-Soviet, and likely to win. It still took considerable time in Japan to turn things around. Industry did not begin to respond until two further changes were made: the United States had to overcome Allied pressures and stop dismantling factories for reparations (something it did not do until May 12, 1949), and SCAP had to demonstrate to industrialists through words, actions, legislation, and pressure on the Japanese government that a manager who stood up to the unions on either economic or anti-Communist grounds was not going to be attacked as antidemocratic, or arrested in violation of one or another trade union law, or purged as a fascist or a militarist. This latter requirement

24. SCAP Monograph No. 47, "Heavy Industries," p. 9.

SCAP fulfilled during 1949—when the Matsukawa incident took place as the biggest of innumerable whirlpools in the ensuing riptide.

By the beginning of 1949 SCAP was committed to Japan's economic recovery, but it was not SCAP's new policies that actually got the economy moving upward. SCAP's so-called reverse course of 1949 stopped inflation and stabilized the yen at the international rate of exchange it enjoyed until mid-1971, but it did so at the cost of a recession in Japan, a sharp rise in unemployment, and some of the harshest working conditions during 1949 and 1950 since the end of the war five years earlier. Thousands of workers were fired in order to lower unit costs (over one hundred thousand in the National Railroads alone), between twelve thousand and twenty-two thousand Communist trade unionists were summarily dismissed in the "red purge," the stock market average declined from 150 to 101 during the first quarter of 1950, and stock sales fell from ¥40,367 million in 1949 to ¥22,587 million in 1950. Stabilization rather than economic growth was what SCAP had managed to achieve. The actual credit for economic growth—which, paradoxically, contributed more to Japanese democracy than any other dynamic element—goes less to SCAP's policies than it does to international factors (chiefly the Korean War), the discipline and frugality of the Japanese worker, Japan's minimal expenditures on arms or public works, and the cordial relations that developed informally between the United States and Japan as a by-product of the occupation.

The Korean War was in many ways the equivalent for Japan of the Marshall Plan. Between June 1950 and 1954 the United States spent close to $3 billion in Japan for war and war-related supplies. This *tokuju keiki*, or "tokuju boom" (from the name of the United States procurement orders, called "special needs," or *tokubetsu juyō*), overcame the depression caused by economic stabilization and started the economy on its upward course. The tokuju boom saved the regime of Prime Minister Yoshida from almost certain discredit as a Japanese Hoover Administration and saved the United States occupation from possible charges of monumental bungling. But it was not the tokuju boom alone that got things going. Equally important, the onset of growth coincided with the nadir of the postwar labor movement; workers were pleased to get a job at all and to put the five previous years of hardship behind them. They did not ask for high wages or even for wages tied to increases in output, and they did not get them. Savings in wages thus added to the investment funds needed for more growth.

The trade union movement in Japan has yet to recover fully from the events of 1949. Incidents like the Shimoyama, Mitaka, and Matsukawa cases turned the public against the unions, and even many rank and file members came to harbor deep suspicions of union leadership. At the same time SCAP policies decimated the leadership of enterprise unions, the predominant kind in Japan, by prohibiting full-time union officials from receiving salaries or offices from the company. Enterprise unions in small firms could thus no longer afford a full-time union official. The major non-Communist trade union federation that emerged from the struggle, Sōhyō, committed itself politically to the Socialist party, but it did not become an effective voice for labor's economic rights. Sōhyō engaged instead in an endless internal Marxist argument over how and when the socialist apocalypse would occur in Japan, and, economically, it betrayed many of the signs of a labor aristocracy—ignoring its organizing tasks, tolerating management's exploitation of a class of "temporary employees" (some of them permanently employed as temporaries, without fringe benefits, seniority, or other union rights) amounting to as much as 10 percent of the labor force in manufacturing firms of five hundred or more employees, and accepting gross inequities in the national wage picture in different industries.

Today this union situation constitutes some of the unfinished business of the Japanese economy. Although Japan is third in the world in terms of its industrial output, it has yet to reach that level in terms of per capita income. SCAP's promotion of trade unions after the war created a labor movement that was stronger than any prewar workers' organization, but it never came up to standards that prevail in other industrialized countries, either economically or politically. In the long run the subsequent weakening of the labor movement in 1949 may have been a blessing in disguise, for it removed one potential obstacle to growth. Certainly Yoshida thought so; he had never had any enthusiasm for SCAP's labor reforms anyway. "The zeal of the occupation," he writes in his memoirs, "was never . . . more apparent than in connection with this question of the liberation of the nation's workers. And the evil effects of that fact are still being felt in my country today." [25] However, during and after 1949 the zeal of the occupation was directed against the trade union movement and toward creating conditions in which the workers helped pay for economic recovery. The Matsukawa case dates from these dark days of the occupation, and it related directly to the economic goals and policies of the occupation. Its study reveals some of the human and social costs of Japan's economic growth, which, ironically enough from the point of view of the occupation's fundamental objectives, has become the greatest bulwark and sustainer of the democratization of Japan.

As a criminal case the Matsukawa incident also affords many insights into the cardinal democratic reforms of the occupation —namely, the Constitution of 1947, the reform of criminal procedure, and the changing positions of police and procuracy in

25. *The Yoshida Memoirs*, p. 211. See also Robert A. Scalapino, "Labor and Politics in Postwar Japan," in W. W. Lockwood, ed., *The State and Economic Enterprise in Japan* (Princeton, N.J., 1965), pp. 669–720.

postwar Japan. SCAP's "humanization" of the Japanese emperor was probably its single most significant act of democratization— or at least so many Japanese scholars believe.[26] The new constitution and the other reforms it made necessary, however, were SCAP's most important positive policies for building democracy in Japan.

Before commenting on these reforms and the light the Matsukawa case throws on them, one caveat must be entered. As Arthur von Mehren puts it: "Discussions, both Japanese and Western, tend to proceed in terms of dichotomies: the Anglo-American and Continental European legal systems, modern and premodern Japan, and Japanese and non-Japanese elements. . . . Such contrasts are useful in exposition and often suggestive. But, unless used with caution and a full awareness that they were not formulated with special reference to the development of contemporary Japanese law, these dichotomies may obscure a much more complex reality—a law that is a unique and specifically Japanese product arising from all the circumstances of Japanese life." [27] Another dichotomy that the student of SCAP's criminal law reforms must avoid is the tendency to see their eventual fate as either trivial or tragic. After 1952 Japan altered through legislation and practice many of SCAP's reforms, and numerous *ayamatta saiban* ("mistrials")—of which the Matsukawa case is an excellent example—were in the forefront of national political controversy. These cases were not trivial, either for the people involved in them or for Japan, but neither were they tragic in terms of their total impact on Japan. Japan has not "reverted" to prewar authoritarianism, nor has it failed to evolve in a democratic direction. After the occupation ended, the Japanese learned a great deal about how SCAP's reforms worked in prac-

26. See, e.g., Ishikawa Hiroyoshi, *Nihonjin no shakai shinri* (The Social Psychology of Japanese) (Tokyo, 1965), pp. 80–81 and passim.
27. *Law in Japan*, Arthur T. von Mehren, ed. (Cambridge, Mass., 1963), p. 188.

tice, rejecting some of them and altering others. This process is continuing in Japan today. The Matsukawa case reveals some of the grave weaknesses in the structure SCAP bestowed on Japan, but it is much too early to come to any firm conclusions about where the process of change and adaptation of the reforms will end.

SCAP approached reform of the police and criminal justice systems in much the same way it approached reform of the economy: it assumed initially that the existing practices were beyond salvation; it then decided that an entirely new set of democratic institutions had to be installed; and finally it imported wholesale from the United States the institutions that prevailed there. These reforms differed from those for the economy, however, in that they were not reversed during the course of the occupation and they were much more desperately needed.

During the militarist and wartime periods (roughly 1931 to 1945), Japan's criminal law was in awful shape. The militarists, having entered politics through assassination and having fanned the flames of emperor worship and ultranationalism in order to justify their own insubordination, fostered a general climate of illegality. This, combined with repressive laws making "dangerous thoughts" a criminal offense and virtual collaboration between police, procurators, and judges (for reasons both of political conviction and of timidity), reduced to a shambles the system of criminal justice that had been introduced during the Meiji era. Most corrosive of all, the police commonly resorted to torture in obtaining confessions, and the judiciary closed their eyes to it. The leftist attorney and distinguished legal theorist Masaki Hiroshi cites the use of torture during the war as conclusive evidence for him of the complete corruption of the Japanese judiciary.[28]

28. *Chikaki yori* (Tokyo, 1964), pp. 427–429. See also pp. 351–378. *Chikaki yori* was an important monthly critical magazine published by

Corruption is a relevant concept here. The hardest task in evaluating the occupation's reforms is to make an accurate diagnosis of the social maladies that they were intended to correct. If the prewar judiciary was corrupt, a thorough purge might have sufficed to correct it; a totally new system of criminal justice would not have been indicated. On the other hand, if the abuses which were so common in Japanese courts during the thirties and early forties were inherent in the system itself, then the system would have to be changed. Even if change were called for, it is not immediately clear what the new system should look like— perhaps the American system would do, but possibly an older Japanese system would have been better.

Prewar Japan's legal system had enjoyed a relatively unpoliticized trial period of about forty years. During the Meiji era, in 1889, the Japanese government promulgated a Western-style constitution, and during the succeeding decade it borrowed from France and Germany its six basic legal codes, including its penal code and code of criminal procedure. Japan's purpose in importing these foreign laws was to demonstrate its "modernity" in the eyes of Western nations and thereby end the humiliating Western insistence on extraterritoriality for Europeans residing in Japan. These laws had no more basis in indigenous thought and practice than had the laws imposed after 1945 by a foreign conqueror.

Nonetheless, the Continental European codes did grow roots in Japan, and the new Japanese judiciary, made up of accomplished students of Continental jurisprudence, did nourish the imported laws into domestic growth. The landmark case for the modern Japanese judicial system, its own *Marbury v. Madison*, was the Ōtsu decision of 1891. A Japanese policeman attempted to murder the Russian crown prince, then on an official visit to Japan and passing through the town of Ōtsu. The government

Masaki between April 1937 and October 1949. This volume, published by Kōbundō, brings together many outstanding articles from it.

sought to placate Russia by demanding the death penalty for the policeman even though the maximum penalty specified for the offense by the penal code was life imprisonment. The Supreme Court resisted the enormous official pressure and imposed a life sentence, not the death penalty. The result was the legitimation of judicial independence in Japan. As Takayanagi writes, "The inclusion in the [Meiji] Constitution of an institution quite foreign to the Japanese scene [the Supreme Court] provided the foundation on which a tradition of judicial independence very quickly emerged. The Ōtsu judgment remains the most valuable tradition of the Japanese judiciary. Whatever their shortcomings, Japanese judges since then have scrupulously guarded their independence, and the nation has reposed implicit confidence in their integrity and their freedom from corruption, although of course not everyone always likes their decisions." [29]

Seventy years after the Ōtsu decision, in August 1961, its tradition was again invoked in the press after the Sendai High Court's not-guilty verdict in the Matsukawa case had renewed controversy over whether or not the Japanese judiciary was independent. Miyazawa Toshiyoshi, emeritus professor of constitutional law at Tokyo University and himself no stranger to police repression in the thirties, defended the Sendai verdict. "Ever since the Ōtsu case," he wrote, "I have firmly believed that the tradition of judicial independence has been established within our courts." [30]

What, then, happened to Japan's courts and their traditions during the militarist era? Corruption was part of the problem. Perhaps most important, the development of the "legal consciousness" of the population—its *hō ishiki*, in Kawashima's terms[31]—had not kept pace with the development of the cadre

29. Takayanagi Kenzō, "A Century of Innovation: The Development of Japanese Law, 1868–1961," in *Law in Japan*, p. 10.

30. *Asahi shimbun*, August 9, 1961.

31. Kawashima Takeyoshi, *Nihonjin no hō ishiki* (Legal Consciousness of Japanese) (Tokyo, 1967).

of practitioners. Change in popular understanding had unquestionably occurred since the Tokugawa period, when the Japanese vocabulary lacked even the word for "right" (or *kenri*: the term was introduced in late Tokugawa as a translation of the Dutch word *recht*), but mass attitudes had not changed enough to provide real social support for the judiciary against the forces of backlash and reaction. Judges themselves had often had to bow to this fact. In prewar Japan not only did they make compromises between legal norm and practice, but their doing so was praised as evidence of their flexibility.[32]

Given the relative social visibility and isolation of the prewar judiciary, when the militarists came to power and used the weapon of extreme bureaucratic centralization against all dissenters, the judiciary collapsed and a police state emerged. Japanese judges—like all Continental judges—were civil servants and therefore subject to economic and bureaucratic pressures from an unscrupulous Ministry of Justice. The professors of Continental jurisprudence and the judiciary did not give up without a fight, however; Minobe Tatsukichi became famous in the course of his resistance to the militarists' interpretation of the Meiji Constitution which put them beyond all legal and political restraints.[33] Nevertheless, by 1945, Japan's independent judiciary had become extinct.

It is doubtful that occupation leaders knew much at all about the traditions of the Japanese courts. Certainly they were unable to conceive of militarism or fascism or reactionary politics in a culture-free formulation as political maladies that might occur in any social system under identifiable circumstances. SCAP diagnosed that what was wrong with Japanese justice was that it derived from Continental European sources and—fully consistent with much vulgar American legal ideology—concluded

32. Ibid., p. 45.
33. See Frank O. Miller, *Minobe Tatsukichi, Interpreter of Constitutionalism in Japan* (Berkeley and Los Angeles, 1965).

that Continental procedures were virtually equivalent to the methods of a police state.[34] Throughout the occupation, official writers harped on the alleged horrors of the Continental preliminary investigation (in Japan, the *yoshin*), on the tendency of procurators to rely on confessions rather than build circumstantial cases, on the fact that procurators sat in the courtroom at the same level as the judges while the defendant and his lawyer sat down below (suggesting that these Americans had never been in a French or German courtroom to see the same scene), and on the alleged inherent unfairness of putting the discovery of truth before the "due process of law."[35] There is no question that these typical Continental, semi-inquisitorial procedures were

34. Compare the following remarks by Ronald L. Goldfarb, a Washington attorney, writing in favor of preventive detention in a national newspaper: "No doubt, one reason for widespread, instinctive reactions against preventive detention is that it sounds like something it is not meant to be. Other countries that practice an inquisitorial form of criminal investigation condone a police practice of arrest for investigation (called in some places preventive detention) which is anathema to the sense and spirit of our accusatorial criminal justice system. Senator Ervin made this haunting comparison when he described recent proposals as reminiscent of 'devices in other countries that have been tools of political repression' and a 'facile police state tactic.' " *New York Times Magazine*, March 1, 1970, p. 28. Even Herbert L. Packer is not entirely free of an Anglo-American bias in labeling the alternative to a "due process" model the "crime control" model. See "Two Models of the Criminal Process" in his brilliant study *The Limits of the Criminal Sanction* (Stanford, Calif., 1968), pp. 149–173.

35. For example, in one of its official histories SCAP wrote, "The new Code banned the pernicious system of 'interrogation of the accused,' the core of the old criminal procedure, which tended to attach too much importance to confessions by regarding the accused as an object of investigation rather than as a party to the case." SCAP Monograph 14, "Legal and Judicial Reform," p. 47. Richard B. Appleton, one of the drafters of the new Code of Criminal Procedure, refers to "the former lamentable situation in Japan, where it was true more often than not that prosecution was based upon confessions wrung from the accused by means of irresponsible detention and severe grilling lasting for months or even years, during the secret preliminary examination, which resembled a

abused in Japan during the militarist era, but SCAP never demonstrated that they were intrinsically unjust or that Anglo-American adversary procedures, in which the judge plays virtually no part in investigating a case or in eliciting the facts in the courtroom, were a sine qua non of democratic criminal justice.

The Continental and Anglo-American traditions of criminal procedure are both compromises and both have recognized strengths and weaknesses. As Sybille Bedford has observed:

> In the trial courts [in Germany] two things stand out. One, not unexpectedly, is the overwhelming preponderance of cases in which guilt is a foregone and confessed conclusion, the other the enlightened mildness guilt is dealt with. . . . I don't mean to suggest that people who admitted guilt were in fact innocent. Any British jury would have convicted every single one of them in ten minutes on the case presented. The point is that in Britain the prosecution could seldom have presented so complete a case; under our rules those people would have had a rather better chance of getting away with it (just as, conversely, some innocent persons would have been filtered out in Germany at an earlier stage and spared a trial). The question is whether this more ample evidence has or has not been unfairly or oppressively obtained.[36]

Evidence can be obtained oppressively under any legal system, but so long as the judiciary is independent and not corrupt, oppression is no more a part of Continental than of Anglo-American procedures. Fairness, however, is an entirely different matter. "The sporting spirit," writes Bedford, "the notion of the law as

---

medieval inquisition." "Reforms in Japanese Criminal Procedure under Allied Occupation," *Washington Law Review* XXIV:4 (November 1949), 416.

36. *The Faces of Justice* (New York, 1961), pp. 162–163.

a game of skill with handicaps to give each side a chance, is entirely absent on the Continent." [37]

There are several features of the Continental tradition that the Japanese find congenial. They have argued that entrusting the determination of facts and motive to skilled and experienced judges rather than leaving it to a "courtroom battle" or a jury engenders greater trust in the outcome. They also feel that the broad discretion of prosecuting officials to institute prosecutions or not usually works out in favor of persons who are not criminals and do not belong in criminal courts. In Japan, among the criminal cases in 1957 handled by procurators, only 46.1 percent resulted in prosecution; in 1958 the figure was 50.2 percent. However, of those eventually prosecuted almost all are convicted. Japanese also believe that the right of prosecution appeal is fair and avoids miscarriages of justice wherein the guilty go free on technicalities, and that the greater responsibility exercised by the procuracy over the police reduces the degree of discretionary power put in the hands of the police.

Regardless of the merits and weaknesses of the two systems, by 1945 the Continental system had already been implanted in Japan and had been found congenial with Japanese society and values. Its continued congeniality to Japanese is suggested by the fact that despite the wholesale revision of Japanese laws, the occupation does not seem to have radically altered what Japanese expect their system of criminal justice to do. For example, the rate of acquittals in Japanese criminal courts in 1938 was 0.985 percent, while the rate in England in 1933 was 15.2 percent and in the United States in 1935, 25.6 percent. In 1960 the Japanese rate was virtually unchanged, 0.49 percent, and the highest all-time rate of acquittals in Japan was reached in 1949—1.76 percent. To take a different example, although the Constitution of 1947 says that "No person shall be convicted or punished in

37. Ibid.

cases where the only proof against him is his own confession" (art. 38, par. 3), in 1963 the Supreme Court of Japan reported: "The average number of witnesses called per case in recent years is roughly two. This number may appear extremely small at first sight, but in connection with this we must remember that in most cases handled by the District Courts, the accused have confessed to the alleged offenses (around 77% thereof), which rendered the examining of witnesses superfluous." [38]

These examples are intended, not to suggest that nothing has changed in Japan, but to suggest rather that after the occupation Japan adjusted its new Anglo-American procedures to fit domestic requirements—and in the direction of the country's Continental heritage. The Americans actually tried to transform entirely the old procedures of criminal justice, and they did so with the intention of supplanting the Continental-derived procedures with the Anglo-American system. Richard B. Appleton, one of the attorneys of the SCAP Legal Section directly responsible for reform of criminal procedure, writes: "This series of reform laws adopted in 1948 [particularly the new Code of Criminal Procedure, Law Number 131 of 1948, passed by the Diet on July 5, 1948, and enforced from January 1, 1949] introduced into Japanese criminal procedure for the first time institutions and ideas derived from the Anglo-Saxon rather than the Continental system." [39] Dandō Shigemitsu, Japan's leading authority on the new Code of Criminal Procedure and one of the academicians SCAP consulted in drafting it, remarks that the code "was born as a hybrid of the Continental and Anglo-Saxon systems." [40] Even the official SCAP monograph on legal reform

38. Supreme Court of Japan, *Outline of Criminal Justice in Japan* (Tokyo, 1963), p. 30.
39. Appleton, p. 407.
40. Cited by Alfred C. Oppler, "Courts and Law in Transition," *Contemporary Japan* XXI:1–3 (May 1952), 23. Cf. Dandō, *Japanese Criminal Procedure*, B. J. George, Jr., trans. (South Hackensack, N.J., 1965), pp. 12–18.

acknowledges that the new Anglo-American procedures did not have "social force" behind them.[41]

The actual procedure through which SCAP rewrote the Code of Criminal Procedure was complex and has sometimes been misrepresented by SCAP officials. Alfred C. Oppler, former chief of the Legislation and Justice Division of the Legal Section, SCAP-GHQ, liked to point out in his various reports and public articles that SCAP never issued a so-called SCAPIN—that is, a SCAP Instruction, or a direct order to the Japanese Government based on its acceptance in surrender of the Potsdam Declaration—in the legal field. "Instead, SCAP views ordinarily were set forth and differences threshed out at conferences and round-table discussions," committee meetings which Oppler says were characterized by nothing more than "the feeling of an international fellowship among jurists who have in common the ardent concern for the improvement of a law." "To be sure," he acknowledges, "there remains a nucleus of a conservative or, one may say, reactionary group, particularly among the ministerial bureaucracy and the older judges, who are opposed and hostile to any idea or institution not fully Japanese. But, on the whole, the occupation has resulted in a great eagerness of Japanese jurists to acquaint themselves or to improve their familiarity with Anglo-Saxon law." [42]

SCAP did consult Japanese in the drafting of the new Code of Criminal Procedure, and it is quite true that several Supreme Court justices and academics did themselves propose or support various reforms, notably the Habeas Corpus Law. It is also true that the conferences which considered the draft Code of Criminal Procedure included representatives of all the various groups concerned and that "complete freedom of argument and discussion" appeared to prevail, judging from the official records of

41. SCAP Monograph No. 14, "Legal and Judicial Reform," p. 112.
42. Ibid., p. 45; Oppler, *Washington Law Review*, pp. 302–305 (see n. 16 above).

those conferences.[43] But there are two major obstacles—one procedural and the other constitutional—to a belief that reform of criminal procedure came about primarily on the initiative of the Japanese.

First of all, occupation leaders seem to have overestimated the degree to which "collegiality" existed or could exist between occupier and occupied. John Bennett is perceptive in noting that his Japanese colleagues were usually the most Westernized Japanese and that the other Japanese members of his staff tended to be deferential and even obsequious.[44] No SCAPIN may ever have been issued in the legal field, but it is hard to accept the implication that representatives of SCAP's Government Section and Legal Section did not speak with full authority in their meetings with Japanese jurists.

For example, at a meeting in 1947 concerning the new procurator's law, Ministry of Justice officials said that public opinion would not favor separation of procuracy and police because it would increase the independence and power of the police in investigations, and that the people placed greater confidence in the public procurator than they did in the police. To this Oppler replied that "strong guarantees against . . . [police] excesses had been included in the new Constitution" and that

43. SCAP Archives, Legal Section, box 1530. The following Japanese attended the conferences held at Government Section, SCAP-GHQ, concerning the new Code of Criminal Procedure: (a) representatives of the Attorney General's Office: Kiuchi Tsunenori, assistant to the attorney general; Kunimune Sakae, director of the Prosecution Bureau, Attorney General's Office; (b) representatives of the Supreme Court: Mano Tsuyoshi, justice; Shima Tamotsu, justice; (c) representatives of the Public Procurator's Office: Hashimoto Kanzō, procurator of the Supreme Public Procurator's Office; Baba Yoshitsugu, procurator of the Tokyo District Public Procurator's Office; (d) representatives of Bar Associations: Ebashi Katsuo, lawyer; Maruyama Densaku, lawyer; (e) scholars: Dandō Shigemitsu, professor, Tokyo University; Saitō Kinsaku, professor, Waseda University. SCAP Archives, Legal Section, box 1529.

44. Bennett and Ishino (see n. 7 above), p. 18.

decentralization of the police being an objective of the occupation, the police and the procuracy would be separated whether the Ministry of Justice liked it or not.[45] Similarly, when Japanese representatives, particularly those whom Oppler regularly referred to as "ministerial bureaucrats," [46] objected that various reforms did not square with Japanese values or practice (e.g., cross-examination), Oppler was inclined to say that "an attempt should be made at reform now, regardless of the difficulties which would be imposed on officials. Reforms are always troublesome, and decisive action at times is necessary." [47] Also, when Japanese demurred at a proposed reform, representatives of Government Section present at the meetings, who usually took a more hard-nosed attitude than Legal Section officials, would often deliver a little impromptu lecture on American civics. The Japanese then accepted the reform.

Reforms were not merely drafted by SCAP and then implemented; they had to be passed by the Japanese Diet. And here, even in the general climate of reform and criticism of the past that prevailed in après guerre Japan, debate was often sharp. SCAP had to issue orders to the prime minister in order to have articles 73–76 of the old penal code deleted by the Diet; they covered the crimes of lese majesty, and the Diet did not want to abolish them. Similarly, the Diet eliminated entirely from the penal code the crime of adultery rather than accept SCAP's demand that men should be held equally liable with women for the offense. In Japan today adultery is grounds for divorce but it is not a crime.

45. Oppler memo "Legal Reform and Police Organization," February 11, 1947, SCAP Archives, Legal Section, box 1500.

46. For example, Oppler writes, "In opposing the traditional conservatism of the ministerial bureaucrats, we repeatedly were supported by the judges of the Supreme Court." Memo of March 18, 1947, in SCAP Archives, Legal Section, box 1500.

47. Memo of April 19, 1948, SCAP Archives, Legal Section, box 1530.

The second reason why the Code of Criminal Procedure had to be entirely reformed was that the Constitution of 1947 demanded it, and the constitution was *not* written in consultation with Japanese. The constitution was written by the Government Section of SCAP, translated into Japanese, and forced on the Diet after the Japanese themselves had vacillated over producing an acceptable draft of their own.[48] This is not to say that the constitution has not gained innumerable adherents in Japan today; some of the more charitable Japanese analysts even recognize that if SCAP had not taken forceful action in this area, Allied pressure on SCAP to abolish the Imperial institution and establish a republic probably would have been overwhelming.[49] The viability and strength of this document, one of the most liberal constitutions in the world, is a subject that goes beyond the present discussion. The point is that the constitution was written two years before the criminal procedure code was revised (Oppler's meetings on the code took place between April 13 and May 5, 1948, whereas the constitution became the fundamental law of the land on May 3, 1947), the constitution itself introduced Anglo-American principles into Japanese law, and the constitution forced the review and revision of all existing substantive and procedural law. Article 98 (1) asserts that "no

48. Some scholars contend that the Constitution of 1947 was the fruit of American-Japanese cooperation, but this interpretation is based on the considerable Japanese support the constitution gained after it was promulgated and the belief that the Japanese government liked SCAP's draft but preferred to have SCAP assume the responsibility for overturning the Meiji Constitution. For an analysis that accepts this view and that is basically a paean to the occupation, see Robert E. Ward, "Reflections on the Allied Occupation and Planned Political Change in Japan," in R. E. Ward, ed., *Political Development in Modern Japan* (Princeton, N.J., 1968), pp. 477–535, particularly 510–512.

49. See Kainō Michitaka, *Hōritsu, sono hi sono tsuki* (The Law, Day by Day and Month by Month) (Tokyo, 1957), p. 99. Professor Kainō (Tokyo Metropolitan University) holds the view that "after the war the Japanese Government tried desperately to preserve the old Constitution."

law, ordinance, imperial rescript or other act of government, or part thereof, contrary to the provisions hereof, shall have legal force or validity."

The Japanese Constitution is American in inspiration and even in wording—for example, the people's "right to life, liberty, and the pursuit of happiness" is declared to be the supreme consideration in legislation and other governmental affairs (art. 13). Its articles 31 to 39 made the old Continental criminal procedures instantly obsolete, and they guaranteed a judicial warrant for arrest (art. 33), the privilege of counsel and immediate information of charges to be given to accused persons (art. 34), a warrant for searches and seizures (art. 33), the prohibition of torture and cruel punishments (art. 36), the right to a speedy trial and exclusion of confessions obtained by duress (art. 38), and the exclusion of double jeopardy (art. 39). It was in order to secure these rights in the criminal process that SCAP officials set about recasting all of the 500-plus articles of the Code of Criminal Procedure.

The new code established a vast series of procedural safeguards to guarantee the constitutional rights of the accused—chiefly by bringing Anglo-American adversary methods into the Japanese courtroom. The results were not encouraging. As Tanabe observes:

> Lacking experience, Japanese lawyers were clumsy amateurs in the examination of witnesses. Their questions were apt to be inept and time-consuming; it was said that the examination of a witness by a lawyer took twice as long as examination by a judge. For a while after 1948, many lawyers simply read aloud the written "topics" and asked a witness to answer yes or no. The gross leading question was very common. Cross-examination, though frequently used, was often a mere repetition of the direct examination or was unduly argumentative. For many lawyers, cross-examination was a vehicle for arguing the falsity or error of the testimony

rather than a vehicle for eliciting additional testimony and for testing the witness' credibility. Objections to improper or irrelevant questions were rarely made, for not only were lawyers unaccustomed to objecting but each had an interest in being able to pose freely leading and "fishing" questions. Older lawyers frequently felt personally insulted by an opponent's objection. Even after the 1956 changes regulated objections and rulings in detail, these difficulties persisted. . . . Judges tended to be lax in prohibiting improper questions. The lack of training in the new rules of evidence made judges hesitate when quick rulings were required. Moreover, trained under the Continental system of "free evaluation," the judges were naturally inclined to be rather generous in permitting questions that would be considered improper in the American practice; they satisfied themselves by discounting the evidential value of the answers. Some judges adopted the passive policy of waiting for counsel to object, which seldom actually occurred.[50]

In addition to abolishing preliminary hearings and all the other informal, inquisitorial aspects of the old system, the new Code of Criminal Procedure prohibited the public procurator from sending to the court along with the charge the records of the investigation by the police and his own office as well as pieces of evidence. The intent was of course to prevent prejudgment of the case before evidence was presented in open court. Ironically, if the old procedure had been followed, the Matsukawa defendants would not have spent so many years behind bars. It was, in fact, an old-fashioned judge employing a judicial investigation of the prewar type who eventually got them off.

On January 1, 1949, the new Code of Criminal Procedure

50. Tanabe Kōji (District Court judge), "The Process of Litigation: An Experiment with the Adversary System," in *Law in Japan*, pp. 102–103.

went into effect, and before the year was out the Matsukawa case had become the first major capital case to be tried under its procedures. That a case like Matsukawa should have come up during the code's first year was unlucky—both for the government officials who were trying to apprehend those responsible for the sabotage and for the twenty individuals who were arrested and charged with the crime. It was not simply that the code was new and unfamiliar; in addition, the defendants were accused of conspiracy, a notoriously difficult charge to prove even in an American court staffed with the most experienced personnel. The Japanese knew how to deal with conspirators under the old code, but they found it frankly puzzling under the new one. Also, the crime and the first trial took place in rural Japan; in 1949, the judges and procurators of the Fukushima District Court were not exactly familiar with American law and procedures, and they had not participated in SCAP's Tokyo law seminars.

Another complicating element was the status of the police. Wholly uncoordinated with the reform of criminal procedure because carried out by different sections within SCAP, reform of the police was one of the clearest examples of SCAP's mechanically copying American institutions. Two American expert missions visited Japan and recommended police reform. One was led by Lewis J. Valentine, former police commissioner of New York City, and the other by Oscar Olander, former commissioner of the Michigan State Police. Based on their reports, SCAP ordered the Japanese police divided into two different and only tenuously connected organizations. For cities of five thousand or more population SCAP set up locally controlled and locally financed police forces, and for all other areas a national police force—the so-called National Rural Police (NRP). The occupation wanted to eliminate the highly centralized police of wartime Japan—even though probably the only aspect of wartime police activity that most Japanese did not object to after the war was its centralization. Under the new structure, the national force could not operate where local control was in effect except when invited to do so. Yoshida used the big cases of 1949 to illustrate what he thought was wrong with the scheme:

> Riots were occurring in different prefectures throughout Japan, to which acts of violence were added a number of cases of train wrecking and the discovery of the dead body of the president of the Japan National Railways on a railroad track in the suburbs of Tokyo on the eve of the announcement by him of a substantial reduction in railway personnel. I called in Mr. Noboru Saito [Saitō Noboru], who was then head of the national police, and asked why he did not go to the scene of these incidents and assume direction of operations, only to be told that the national police could not intervene unless the local police requested their aid.[51]

As things developed, Japanese cities were unable to pay for their police, and the numerous local civilian police commissions (called public safety commissions) could not raise the necessary funds from almost nonexistent local sources. By 1950 the reform had already begun to be reversed as one city after another voted to give up local control. Immediately after the end of the occupation, the ruling conservative party recentralized the police, preferring to find some other way to prevent or control police excesses than atomization of the forces themselves. Nevertheless, during 1949, the reform was in full effect, adding structural debilitation to the spiritual malaise and general popular dislike the police had to endure in postwar Japan. On top of these strains, police leadership was badly disorganized; all former Tokkō (Special Higher Police, sometimes called the Thought Police) and many senior police officials had been purged.

In a 1959 round-table discussion, a group of *Mainichi* reporters who had covered the Matsukawa case from its beginning laughingly recalled members of the Fukushima NRP arriving

51. *The Yoshida Memoirs*, p. 177.

at the scene of the wreck driving their old charcoal-burning car. At the time, these Tokyo journalists felt, the Fukushima police were only good for investigating "chicken and daikon stealing" (a daikon is a kind of Japanese radish, about a foot and a half long and shaped like a carrot).[52] Because Matsukawa was a big case with major political implications and the local forces were inadequate, a good deal of prefectural and outside NRP brass came in to assist the investigation. The resultant muddle has always been embarrassing to police and procurators. Throughout the fourteen years that the Matsukawa case was in the courts, unbelievably important new clues kept turning up in procuracy warehouses, and to the very end police officials in charge of the case could not remember who first discovered the crowbar and wrench—the two most important items of material evidence in the case—at the scene of the crime. At least some of the responsibility for this confusion must be laid at the door of the SCAP police reforms.

There are many other facets to the Matsukawa case. It triggered the entire "criticism of the courts" (saiban hihan) controversy of the mid-1950s, resulted in charges being brought against some very prominent police and procuracy officials, caused one Supreme Court justice to disqualify himself from hearing the case when it first came before the Grand Bench, and resulted in innumerable feuds in the magazines among members of Tokyo's literary intelligentsia. As a vignette of the Cold War, it abounds in "fellow travelers" and "front organizations," and it illustrates the extraordinarily maudlin and sentimental quality of Communist propaganda at the time. Perhaps typical of the entire case, while the fourth trial of the Matsukawa defendants was under way within the Sendai High Court building, thousands of extras were milling around outside, shouting slogans and carrying red flags for the left-wing propaganda movie The Matsukawa Case. They were supposed to be reenacting the anger

52. Sandē mainichi, August 23, 1959.

of the people when the second trial's verdict had been delivered some seven years earlier.

Even though the Matsukawa case had both political and theatrical aspects, it remains most significant as a criminal case. The late and distinguished novelist and literary critic, Hirotsu Kazuo, Japan's most important commentator on the case, always tried in his writings to portray the case as a miscarriage of justice, even though he himself was far from successful in remaining free of the case's political entanglements. As a criminal case, Matsukawa bears the same relationship to the evolution of the Japanese Constitution that any case at Old Bailey does to the English Constitution. "The development of criminal law," writes F. T. Giles, "is closely linked up with the evolution of constitutional government. Theories of constitutional usage are often crystallized by cases actually occurring in the courts, particularly the criminal courts. The struggle which fills so many pages of English history between the forces of common law and Parliament on the one hand and monarchs bent on despotism on the other was largely a conflict for the rights of the subject when he came into collision with the State; and these rights never came into such high relief for all to see as they did when the individual was charged with some definite offence." [53]

In studying Matsukawa as a criminal case the reader should be forewarned against coming to any premature conclusions about the motive for the crime or the guilt or innocence of the accused; it was for making just such mikomi sōsa ("investigations based on hypotheses") that the most serious critics have condemned the police. "The facts appeared to point in one direction," writes Sybille Bedford. "They nearly always do until one's heard the other side." [54] The Matsukawa case came before the courts of Japan on questions of fact rather than law five times, including once before the Supreme Court's Grand Bench (twelve

53. The Criminal Law (Baltimore: Penguin ed., 1961), p. 14.
54. The Faces of Justice, p. 19.

justices in this case) and once before the Supreme Court's First Petty Bench (criminal), composed of four justices in this case. A grand total of twenty-five Japanese judges voted on the case; their combined opinions add up to twelve guilty and thirteen innocent. However, three Supreme Court justices voted twice, having been involved both times that the case came before the court. When their double votes are subtracted, there remains a total of twenty-two different individual judges rendering their judgments on the guilt or innocence of the defendants in the Matsukawa case; and they divide eleven to eleven.

In September 1963, after the Supreme Court had finally and definitively thrown out the convictions of all twenty defendants, several enterprising reporters went around the country, as they had numerous times before, interviewing legal authorities, individuals involved, witnesses, and relatives of the victims killed in the wreck. Locomotive engineer Ishida's widow, Ishida Tsugi, was quoted as saying, "Have we gone on waiting for fourteen years to end up not knowing who the true criminals are? . . . What am I to report at the graveside of my husband?" [55] This book is an attempt to provide some answers to her questions, perhaps not the ones that she wants or deserves, but the only ones that are available any longer, more than two decades after the crime itself.

55. *Nihon keizai shimbun* (eve. ed.), September 12, 1963.

Chapter 2

Time, Place, and Manner

IN HIS celebrated novel *The Spy Who Came in from the Cold*, John Le Carré used the metaphor of a small Renault car caught between two huge lorries to symbolize some of the human perils of people caught between the two major protagonists of the Cold War. In occupied Japan, the actual drivers of the lorries were the Japanese government and the highly politicized leadership of the trade unions, both of whom were in turn dispatched on their routes by the Supreme Commander for the Allied Powers (SCAP) on the one hand and by the Japanese Communist party on the other. The occupants of the Renault were primarily Japan's industrial workingmen. Ever since February 1, 1947, when SCAP had prohibited a revolutionary general strike called by the Communist-dominated unions, the two lorries had been proceeding on a collision course. During 1949 they collided, with the government and the Americans coming out of it only slightly dented, but with the unions and the party sustaining major damage. Although this book is mostly about

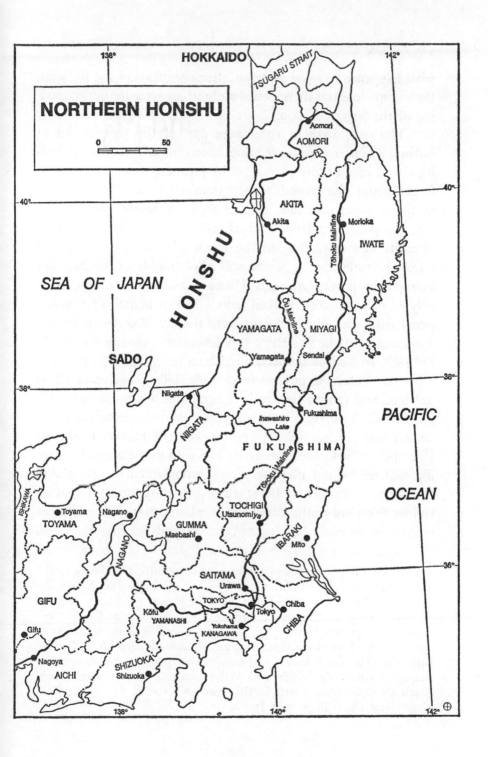

what happened to some representative occupants of the Renault, their story does not make sense without an accurate understanding of the larger collision.

The years 1948 to 1950 were part of the postwar era of *butsujō sōzen,* a phrase meaning approximately "confused feelings" and used twenty years later by Japanese who would like to forget about the period rather than study it. Inflation was rampant, wages were low, wildcat strikes were the order of the day, the police regularly stopped trains to seize the goods that peasants were smuggling to the black market, and several odd crimes occurred that Japanese still have trouble explaining. For example, on January 26, 1948, Hirasawa Sadamichi, a respectable fifty-six-year-old artist, walked into a Tokyo branch of the Imperial Bank dressed as a doctor from the health department and announced that he was there to administer a cholera vaccine to the staff. Instead he induced all sixteen people present to drink a potion containing potassium cyanide, killing twelve of them outright, and robbed the bank, allegedly to buy presents for his girl friend.[1] Two years later, in July 1950, an apprentice priest named Hayashi, age twenty-one, burned the famous Kinkakuji (Temple of the Golden Pavilion) in Kyoto to the ground, claiming that he did not like the people who visited the place and that he was disturbed by his stuttering. During the same year an eighteen-year-old youth robbed Nihon University of ¥1.9 million in payroll funds; when caught he replied in English, "Oh,

1. The Teigin (Imperial Bank) case bears three similarities to the Matsukawa case: (1) it has never been convincingly solved; (2) defenders of Hirasawa were indicted for manufacturing evidence and for perjury in another of Japan's extremely long litigations; and (3) suspicions have been raised linking the Teigin case with occupation personnel, just as in the Matsukawa case. See, e.g., Matsumoto Seichō, *Nihon no kuroi kiri* (The Black Mist over Japan) (Tokyo, 1962), which contains chapters on both the Teigin and Matsukawa cases. Matsumoto's book, which we shall consider later in this book, was one of the two or three biggest best sellers in postwar Japan.

mistake," and the phrase became a standard part of Japanese slang. It was a period that seems hardly believable in light of Japan's achievements and contributions to the world over the succeeding two decades.

Part of the problem was that during 1948 most Japanese urban workers were employed without really doing any work. Despite the new liberal political climate brought about by the introduction of democracy into every area of social life, there was an air of unreality that pervaded the entire economy. In early 1948, SCAP had decided to promote economic recovery rather than economic democratization, but in order to implement any economic growth policies at all both SCAP and the Japanese had to come to grips with one of the fundamental problems Japan inherited from the war, namely, surplus labor. It seems odd in the 1970s to speak of surplus labor in Japan, since today there is a labor shortage. But what was happening in the period 1948 to 1950 was a basic socioeconomic shift in the characteristics of the Japanese population, a shift that helped provide the large, urbanized labor force on which Japan's recovery and growth were subsequently based. During the late 1940s and early 1950s, Japan brought home its armies and colonialists to settle in the cities and also saw the beginning of the great migration from the countryside to the cities that continues to the present time. Japan's cities doubled and tripled in size, providing the concentrations of labor that fulfilled one prerequisite for Japan's becoming, during the 1960s, the world's third industrial power.

During 1948 this process was in its infancy. Huge numbers of people were jamming the cities, a result of both demobilization and migration, but these workers were not yet harnessed to the world's fastest growing industrial economy, for it did not then exist. They were not unemployed, however. Since the end of the war Japanese enterprises and the government itself had sat benignly waiting for the Americans to finish stripping factories for reparations and to reorganize the corporate structure in a democratic manner. While waiting, not only did they not lay off workers, but they hired their full assigned quotas of returnees from the war. Payrolls were met through the simple device of borrowing from commercial banks, from the government, or from the Reconstruction Bank (established at the beginning of 1947), which was supposed to supply capital, not payroll funds. The lenders in turn obtained their money from inflation, which was barely held under control by loans on the average of $400 million annually from the Americans to the Japanese government. Japanese businessmen did not think that this was the proper way to run a firm, but they had no choice. On the one hand, SCAP would not let them discharge workers while reorganization was in progress; on the other hand, the powerful new trade unions enforced labor contracts which virtually prohibited layoffs. In 1949, SCAP broke this logjam; the resulting retrenchment has often been called SCAP's reverse course, but it should more properly be understood as a Japanese "management offensive."

The national railroads illustrate some of these problems perfectly. On April 1, 1948, the Japanese National Railroads (JNR) had 610,486 employees, including 1,600 full-time union officials carried on the government payroll. (By contrast, in 1970 the two main government railroad unions had only 340,000 members serving a vastly expanded system, and this figure was still considered far too large.) The cost of this labor force was staggering. The JNR showed a deficit for fiscal year 1949–50 of ¥50 billion, and it could not raise passenger fares because of the low wage levels prevailing throughout the economy, although it did double freight rates that year.

There were many reasons for this featherbedding. First, the railroads were desperately short of modern equipment; for example, manpower was used at this time to shunt freight cars for loading and unloading. Similarly, since only about 1,400 kilometers of the 19,000-kilometer system were electrified, the employment of a full complement of locomotive firemen and staff was required to supply coal throughout the system. Today the system is entirely electrified. Second, the personnel employed had an extremely low level of efficiency. During the war large numbers of women and minors had been employed on the railroads, and as late as 1948 an investigation revealed that about eight thousand women were still engaged in night work, that about two thousand women performed hazardous duties, and that about nine thousand male employees were under sixteen years of age, all of which constituted violations of the new Labor Standards Law that became effective on May 1, 1948. SCAP had hoped that the Labor Standards Law, which prohibited women and minors from doing very hard work, would cut about forty thousand workers from the JNR payroll, but this did not happen until strict enforcement of the law was ordered during 1949. Third, the JNR had been obliged by the government to absorb 183,411 repatriates, of whom it actually hired 168,651 without releasing any of their female or underage wartime replacements. Some of these repatriates were malnourished or infirm because of war service.

Fourth, the paternalistic ethos of Japanese labor-management relations inclined the JNR to provide lifelong job security for its employees. This is a very important sociological factor, although it should not be overstated; the unions (the National Railroad Workers' Union was the largest in the country) also guaranteed that workers would not be laid off and that union officials would be there to see to it that they were not. Thus article 45 of the JNR labor agreement concluded on February 21, 1947, provided that one full-time union official be carried on the payroll for each five hundred union employees, plus five hundred full-time union employees to perform the administrative duties of the union headquarters and district councils; and article 66 provided that management would not discharge any employee once he was placed on the regular payroll except when charges of criminal actions or criminal negligence had been proved against him. These provisions were outlawed by the Japanese National Railways Law (Law No. 256, dated December 20, 1948, and in effect from June 1, 1949) which set up the JNR as a governmental corporation and which institutionalized collective bargaining on the national railroads. However, this piece of legislation was itself part of the "reverse course" and bitterly opposed by the unions.

Fifth, and finally, democratization and the improvement in labor standards had lowered the workweek by about 25 percent. In 1936 station and platform workers in rural areas put in ninety-one hours of duty per week and operating employees sixty hours. The figures for 1948 were sixty-six and forty-five hours respectively.

The combination of these five factors produced a railroad system with 610,000 employees and a ¥50 billion deficit, two of the problems that the Japanese government would have to solve if it were to lead the economy toward reconstruction and growth. The long-range solution was modernization and increased labor productivity, but the immediate need was to lay off the excess labor in order to obtain funds for investment. More important, railroads were only one—if an acute—sector in which extreme featherbedding existed; similar conditions prevailed to a greater or lesser extent throughout the entire economy and civil service.

Both SCAP and the Japanese government had long been aware of the need to overcome these problems, although they tended to see them more in terms of controlling inflation and promoting export industries than in terms of excess labor as such. As the *Asahi* noted editorially on February 20, 1949, all postwar cabinets had promised a 30 to 50 percent reduction in at least the bloated governmental personnel rolls, but every effort to effect a reduction invariably proved to be perfunctory or, worse, produced precisely the opposite effect. The nation now demanded, said *Asahi*, a retrenchment in public finances and a balanced budget.

Nothing had as yet been done, of course, because of the great political liabilities any government would incur in taking the lead in firing people, as well as because responsibility was actually, if not in law, divided between the Japanese government and SCAP, and because the government was not forced to act so long as the Americans kept pouring in loans. Clearly, it was therefore up to SCAP to supply the leverage.

On July 22, 1948, General MacArthur began to implement the prior American decisions to reorient priorities in Japan in favor of economic growth. He sent a letter, famous today as the MacArthur Letter (Ma shokan), to Prime Minister Ashida telling him, in effect, that the trade union honeymoon was over and that, specifically, government workers were going to be treated differently from labor in general. Among other things, they were no longer to be allowed to strike. MacArthur's letter resulted in the enactment of three new laws, all of them bitterly contested during 1949 by the trade unions: the Japanese National Railways Act, the Japanese Monopoly Public Corporation Act, and the Public Corporation and National Enterprises Labor Relations Act. These laws, together with the revision of the basic National Public Service Law itself, brought employees who were paid out of the public treasury firmly under the control of the ministries and laid the foundations for the big firings of 1949. The Ma shokan was only the start, however.

On December 19, 1948, General MacArthur sent another letter to the Japanese prime minister, this time setting forth a so-called Nine Point Economic Stabilization Program for the economy as a whole. It ordered a balanced budget for the next fiscal year, no matter how many people had to be laid off, and aimed at two economic improvements: stopping the so-called Reconstruction Bank inflation by curtailing the bank's loans, and attracting foreign investment (in order to relieve the critical shortage of capital) by establishing an official exchange rate. Although foreign capital eventually came to Japan primarily as a by-product of the Korean War and not through foreign private investment, MacArthur's policies did at least fulfill the *financial* prerequisites of economic growth. Nothing happened at once in response to the December letter, however, except for a flurry of discussion in the press. A general election was coming up on January 23, 1949, and government leaders tended to sit on their hands until they found out who was going to have to implement —and take responsibility for—this new program. Even after the election General MacArthur would have to do a lot more than send a letter before he could get government and industrial leaders to start fighting with the trade unions.[2]

The leaders of the trade unions were not at all defensive in the face of these new measures. Everyone in Japan was aware that economic reconstruction was not purely an economic problem and that the economic situation offered important political opportunities; least of all did the Japanese Communist party see the situation in purely economic terms. The party began to think that the year 1949 might somehow hold a Communist revolution in Japan as well as in China. Despite the setback on February 1, 1947, when SCAP had canceled the general strike, the Communists had managed with great success to turn the trade union movement into an instrument of revolutionary agitation. During April 1948, for example, the Communist-inspired strike of the Tōhō movie company became so fierce that United States Army tanks had to be called in to get the fired strikers out of the studios. Moreover, now that general strikes were likely to produce intervention by the occupation, the Communists resorted throughout 1947 and 1948 to widely dispersed "piston strikes" and wildcats. A memo of December 22, 1947, from the Military Government Team in Sendai to SCAP reported that on December 15 out of eight passenger and eleven freight trains scheduled

2. For the text of MacArthur's letter of December 19, 1948, setting forth the Economic Stabilization Program, see SCAP Monograph No. 28, "Development of the Trade Union Movement," appendix 9.

to go from Aomori to the south, only three passenger and three freight trains could be operated. The reason given was wildcat strikes in the roundhouses following a visit to Tōhoku by Tokuda Kyūichi, secretary general of the Communist party.[3]

SCAP was fully aware of the gains being made by the Communists, and in fact much of the pressure for a reorientation of economic policy among occupation leaders arose from a desire to combat the Communists rather than from purely economic considerations. Reports poured in from Military Government teams all over the country. On August 20, 1948, for example, Major George J. McDermott, commander of the Fukushima Military Government Team, reported an "expression of fear on the part of prefectural and municipal governments [and] civic and business leaders that Communism is making incursions to the extent of threatening the prefectural economic structure and future welfare of the general public" and that "Communistic influences are steadily gaining strength in the government operated railway, postal, and communications unions." Similarly, on August 17, 1948, the Fukushima team reported to Tōhoku Military Government headquarters in Sendai that through a rigged election the Communists had won four out of five official positions on the Fukushima Prefectural Labor Union Council. One of the new vice-chairmen of the council and also a party member, Suzuki Makoto, would appear again a year later as a defendant in the Matsukawa case.[4]

Communist propaganda of this period was not aimed exclusively at economic difficulties, although it did exploit them above all others. The party also appealed to Koreans, especially in a prefecture like Fukushima where many of them worked in the coal mines, and to the families of servicemen still detained in the Soviet Union. Of the 408,729 Japanese prisoners of war SCAP estimated to be in Siberian camps, the first large con-

3. SCAP Archives, Tōhoku Civil Affairs Region, box 8769.
4. Reports of August 17 and 20, 1948, in ibid., box 2571.

tingent was not repatriated until June 1949. Until that time the Japanese Communist party claimed to be negotiating with the USSR for their release and urged a vote for the party as a way of wooing the Russians and getting the men home sooner. In all speeches of this period the Japanese Communists also identified themselves with the Chinese Communist revolution and argued that it represented the wave of the future in Asia.

SCAP's alarm over the growing strength of the Communists was undoubtedly based on many factors other than an analysis of the concrete situation itself. In reading the occupation archives, one cannot avoid the conclusion that many Americans had taken on some of the worst prejudices of the Japanese toward the Koreans, fearing them and believing all of them to be Communists. Similarly, some insignificant incidents tended to get blown up into signs of Communist influence, such as two boys in Fukushima beating up an American soldier after he had driven over their peddler's cart with his jeep. Also the development of the domestic anti-Communist movement in the United States made its influence felt among military officers in Japan. One of the first and most important calls within the occupation for action against the Communists came from Major General Charles W. Ryder, commanding general of the Ninth Corps with jurisdiction over the Tōhoku region. In a letter dated October 13, 1948, addressed to Lieutenant General Walton H. Walker, commanding general of the Eighth Army, and later widely circulated throughout SCAP, General Ryder wrote:

> The approach of the Occupation Forces toward the problem of Communism in Japan is in need of immediate revision and clarification. On the one hand we find ourselves bound to act in the best interests of the United States Government in handling of the Communist problem and on the other hand, we, as an occupying force, are committed to the sponsorship of a democratic form of government in

Japan—a form of government foreign to the tastes, experiences, and desires of the Japanese people and a form of government in which we must foster complete freedom for all parties if we are to succeed in our purpose.

The United States Government is presently engaged in a thorough house-cleaning of all branches of government to ferret out and remove Communists and Communist sympathizers from public office. . . . Can we, then, maintain Japan as an oasis in which Communism may flourish, with our active or passive support, in direct opposition to the stated position of the United States Government? . . . The answer is an emphatic NO because to do so is to impose additional burdens on an already over-burdened America. . . .

While it is not advocated that members of the Occupation Force be encouraged or permitted to enter into public debates with or engage in open denunciation of any political party, it is recommended that the present rigid hands-off policy be modified to permit military government to:

(a) Give active support to groups and organizations whose honest aims and objectives are directed toward the elimination of minority control within the labor movement and government.

(b) Publicize, through labor unions and other organized groups, the benefits and attendant rights and responsibilities of democratic trade unionism. . . .[5]

In fact, something like what General Ryder advocated was already under way within the labor movement with SCAP's quiet encouragement. Following the abortive general strike in early 1947, a movement developed within the National Railroad Workers' Union (NRWU), one of the most militant and Com-

5. Copies of General Ryder's letter can be found in ibid., box 2571, and many other files scattered throughout the SCAP Archives.

munist dominated of all the unions, against its Communist leadership. Arguing that the union was being used by a small group of extremists for purely political purposes, the dissidents demanded fair elections and greater participation by the rank and file in policy making. By November 1947 this right-wing faction organized itself as the NRWU Anti-Communist League (Kokutetsu Hankyō Renmei), and in February of the following year it managed to establish nuclei of its organization within most of the unions affiliated with the Communist-dominated Industrial Congress (Sanbetsu Kaigi) labor federation. Despite vigorous opposition from the federation's Communist leadership, on February 24, 1948, these dissident labor leaders formed the Industrial Congress Democratization League (Sanbetsu Minshūka Dōmei, most commonly known by its acronym, Mindō) for the expressed purpose of eliminating "minority control" within the trade union movement.[6]

At the Sanbetsu convention in November 1948, the Communists denounced the Mindō factions as strikebreakers, scabs, and lackeys of SCAP and expelled them from the federation. Nonetheless, throughout 1949 Mindō continued to grow, gaining as many as 913,000 members. It was eventually discredited because of its strong SCAP backing. A new labor federation, Sōhyō (General Council of Trade Unions of Japan), came into being on March 11, 1950, with support from the Labor Section of SCAP, but was opposed to either Communist party or Mindō leadership of the union movement. Mindō had, however, played an important role in the formation of Sōhyō by raising the issue of Communist domination and making it a point of discussion within unions.[7]

6. Furuya Tetsuo, "Matsukawa jiken ni itaru hankyō ishiki no dōin ni tsuite" (On the Arousing of Anti-Communist Consciousness Leading up to the Matsukawa Case), *Rekishigaku kenkyū*, No. 224 (October 1958), p. 43; and Shinobu, *Sengo Nihon seiji shi*, III, 941–942.

7. Takano Minoru, who became the director general of Sōhyō in

SCAP began the year 1949 relatively confident that it now had workable policies for stopping the inflation and for starting Japan's economy on an upward trend. Its primary problems were to force the government to carry out the policies and to keep the reaction from the unions in check—something for which it hoped the Mindō factions would prove useful. Communism was perceived as a danger, but not as an immediate or uncontrollable threat; and at least a part of the anti-Communist sentiment within SCAP (sentiment the very existence of which contrasted markedly with SCAP's attitude during 1946 and 1947) was based on the growing anti-Communist movement in the United States. This calm situation changed on January 23, the day of the general election. Prime Minister Yoshida's Liberal party was returned to power, but the Communist party jumped from four to thirty-five seats in the Diet, the largest parliamentary strength it ever enjoyed, before or since.[8]

Both the Americans and the Communists overreacted to

1951, explains Sōhyō's origins as follows: During 1949 Mindō split the trade union movement on anti-Communist grounds thereby making it impossible for labor to present a united front against SCAP's "reverse course" and industry's "management offensive." However, Mindō itself was discredited in the course of the year because management exploited its legitimate anti-Communist activities to attack and weaken the union movement as a whole. Beginning in the summer of 1949, officials of the Labor Section of SCAP realized that the anti-Communist campaign was becoming antiunion and therefore shifted their support to union leaders who were not affiliated with either the Communists or Mindō. At least the Labor Section of SCAP was never opposed to a strong union movement, only to one dominated by Communists. Thus, by the end of 1949, SCAP's Labor Section was giving strong support to the Preparatory Committee for Sōhyō. See Takano's book, Nihon no rōdō undō (The Japanese Labor Movement) (Tokyo, 1958), pp. 81–97.

8. The Communists held four seats in the House of Representatives during the Fourth National Diet (December 1, 1948 to December 23, 1948); thirty-five seats in the Fifth National Diet (February 11, 1949 to May 31, 1949); and thirty-six seats in the Sixth National Diet (October 25, 1949 to December 3, 1949).

this development. The Communist gain in strength came about chiefly because the Socialist party, which had briefly led a coalition government during 1947 and 1948, had been discredited in a wave of corruption scandals at the end of its administration, and many regular Socialist voters cast their ballots for the Communists (just as they did twenty years later in the general election of December 1969). The election did not represent a glacial shift of popular attitudes to the Communist cause. SCAP became alarmed, however, and from that point on, the economic stabilization program acquired, sotto voce, a definitely anti-Communist secondary purpose. Layoffs were necessary to get the economy on its feet, but it was also decided that Communists should be earmarked as one major category to be laid off. The following year even this muffled approach was dropped; the program became known openly as the "red purge."

The Communists themselves, through their shrill propaganda, did much to fan the flames of SCAP's alarm. Of the three major political crimes of 1949, the Shimoyama, Mitaka, and Matsukawa cases, two have never been solved (Shimoyama and Matsukawa), and the courts finally held a single man responsible for the Mitaka wreck rather than a group of Communist conspirators. No evidence exists to prove that these crimes were carried out on Communist party orders. Nevertheless, Communists were involved in a very large number of violent disturbances during the year (as we shall see), and they *talked* as if they were about to launch open, armed struggle within the country. If the Communists had the right to speak about revolution in the public press, their political enemies also enjoyed the right to try to discredit them by suggesting that the Communists were resorting to violence. Whether or not the Communists actually ordered the carrying out of acts of sabotage and terrorism, they led a great many people to think that they had.

Communist party strategy was in a highly anomalous state during 1949. Since the end of the war, the party had been pursuing a policy calling for "peaceful revolution" in Japan, primarily through labor organization and the winning of a parliamentary majority. Even though Stalin, during 1947, had swung the international Communist movement in a more left-wing, militantly anti-American direction, the Japanese party had been allowed to retain its peaceful façade, thereby avoiding a direct confrontation with SCAP. And, as we have seen, in January 1949 this peaceful approach paid off handsomely at the polls in terms of the greatest electoral legitimation the Japanese party ever acquired. Nevertheless, time was running out on the "lovable party" line. The following year, in January 1950, Stalin thunderously criticized the Japanese Communist party and ordered it to undertake a direct struggle against the Americans, a policy which served Stalin's global interests (although not those of the party in Japan) and which led to SCAP's crushing the Japanese Communist movement. Of more lasting consequence, the open revelation of the party's subordination to Moscow discredited it in the eyes of the public for a decade, and even today the Japanese Communist party remains extremely fearful of appearing to follow the orders of either Moscow or Peking.

The year 1949 was the last year of the "lovable party" line, but the line was not quite what it had been during 1946 or 1947. Tension with SCAP was high, and the international situation, particularly the revolution in China, seemed to be flowing in the Communists' favor. Party secretary general Tokuda could not resist following up his party's recent favorable showing at the polls with some highly optimistic theses on the imminence of revolution in Japan. At a series of plenary meetings of the central committee, held shortly after the elections, Tokuda talked at great length about the significance of the Chinese revolution for Japan, about the worldwide crisis of monopoly capitalism, and about the need for a "summer offensive" (*kaki kōsei*) to stop SCAP's economic stabilization program. He even put forward a "September revolutionary thesis" (*kugatsu kakumei setsu*) which vaguely implied that a "people's government" would come into existence in Japan during September.[9] His main purpose in all this was to establish a "united front" with the Socialists and other leftist groups on the basis of which a dramatic change in government might take place but which in any case would enhance the strength of the overall Communist mass movement. There is no evidence that he was calling for a revolutionary uprising by the Communists alone, and it seems probable that in lauding the Chinese Communists' tactics he had in mind their use of a united front with non-Communist groups rather than their reliance on guerrilla warfare.

Whatever Tokuda and other top leaders had in mind, his line was open to misinterpretation, particularly by two groups: the police and his own followers. Unquestionably the police took him at his word and maintained constant vigilance throughout the year against "Communist excesses." When serious incidents did occur, the police automatically believed that their worst

9. See, in particular, Aochi Shin, "1949 nen no rekishi, Matsukawa jiken no jidai-teki haikei" (The History of 1949, Background of the Era of the Matsukawa Case), Chūō kōron, No. 860 (special issue) (September 1959), p. 99, where Tokuda, Yamada Munemutsu, and others are quoted concerning the "September revolutionary thesis." See also Ichinose Masayuki, Nihon kyōsantō (The Japanese Communist Party) (Tokyo, 1954), pp. 133–149; "Matsukawa jiken o kyūmei suru" (Survey of the Matsukawa Case), Shūkan asahi, November 29, 1953, "tokushū" (special edition); and Asahi shimbun, September 12, 1963. Takano observes that "Sanbetsu, under the influence of the Communist party, advocated waging local struggles in order to overthrow the Yoshida regime. Nosaka Sanzō [one of the Japanese Communist party's three top leaders in this period] agitated the labor movement by arguing that the Yoshida regime would face a grave crisis during the summer of 1949; that a new [Communist] regime would be born in China; that a people's government would be established after Yoshida's fall; and that a people's regime composed of the Socialist, Communist, and Labor-Farmer parties would be possible even under the occupation. Tokuda Kyūichi claimed that it was possible to overthrow the Yoshida regime by September [1949]." Nihon no rōdō undō, p. 83.

fears had been confirmed and retaliated directly against party members. As for the members themselves, many of them knew nothing about the national situation other than that a great elec-' toral victory had been won and what they read in *Akahata* (*Red Flag*). Following the election the party newspaper was saying things like "This general election indicates that the mass of the people . . . have a firm determination to make revolution," and "If the working class will fight in accordance with party policy, we shall be able to combine regional [trade union] councils, including [patriotic] Liberal Party members, into an anti-government struggle and thereby launch a great united front of national defense [against American capitalists and the Yoshida traitors]. . . . This is exactly the kind of revolution that would lead to setting up a people's government." [10]

Tokuda himself took to the hustings following the election to tell the people that the situation was favorable to the Communists. On February 23, 1949, he spoke outside the Fuji Bank in Fukushima city, referring constantly to China, the People's Liberation Army, and its amazing victories. He predicted that SCAP and its agent, the Yoshida government, would soon fire 30 percent of the employees of the Japanese National Railroads and the postal and communications services, singling out the poor for discharge and retaining "lackeys and loafers." He also argued that the real purpose behind United States aid and the economic stabilization program was the American colonialization of Japan. The Communist answer to these grim predictions was to be a united front behind the Communist party, leading perhaps to a "peaceful revolution." [11]

Tokuda failed miserably in his efforts to secure allies and to

10. January 25, 1949, and April 29, 1949, as quoted by Shinobu, *Sengo Nihon seiji shi*, III, 939, 953.

11. SCAP Archives, Tōhoku Civil Affairs Region, box 2571. Memo from Captain Jack Miller, adjutant, Fukushima Military Government Team.

broaden the party's mass base; no major group, least of all the Socialists, joined the party's proposed united front. But according to several Japanese commentators, he did succeed in convincing some of his less sophisticated followers that a revolution was imminent. Among the allegedly simple (*soboku na*) Communists of Fukushima, for example, many held firmly to the September revolutionary thesis; and some local leaders of the National Railroad Workers' Union went so far as to draw up lists of railroad supervisory positions and to assign people to them for use when the people's government was set up.[12] During the course of 1949, when conservative Diet members started to identify the strikes, demonstrations, and criminal violence of June and July as "preliminary skirmishes of the Communist revolution" and called for a national anti-Communist movement, some local Communists may have decided to make their own contributions to the coming apocalypse.[13] At least this is one, relatively charitable, conclusion in view of the lack of hard evidence that the Communist party's central committee either changed its basic "peaceful revolution strategy" or ordered the rank and file to engage in armed struggle and sabotage. There are, however, other aspects to the matter, which we shall return to later.

It was in this postelection climate of militant labor opposition and Communist thinking-out-loud about revolution that SCAP began seriously to implement its economic stabilization program. Occupation leaders were well aware that it was not going to be easy to get the government to move vigorously on the economic front. Both the Shidehara and first Yoshida administrations in 1945 and 1946 had promised a 50 percent cut in government personnel, but the opposite had actually occurred. Government personnel classed as "officials" had risen from 226,-

12. *Shūkan asahi*, November 29, 1953; *Asahi shimbun*, September 12, 1963.
13. Furuya, *Rekishigaku kenkyū*, No. 224, p. 45.

915 (plus 43,056 overseas officials) on March 31, 1945, to 590,-108 four years later. The Ashida administration had tried to reduce overstaffing but to no avail, and the Yoshida government elected in January 1949 had *not* run on a platform of strong retrenchment. In fact, one of SCAP's most severe problems was that in pushing through the economic stabilization program it would force Yoshida to reverse his campaign promises and might gravely weaken him politically. In order to cause the government to cut personnel, balance the budget, stop subsidizing industry payrolls, and stop pleading for more American loans, SCAP clearly would have to bring up some big guns. And this it did.

Five days after the election, on January 28, 1949, Secretary of the Army Kenneth C. Royall left Washington for Japan, bringing with him a group of financial and economic experts to assist SCAP and the Japanese government in "combatting inflation and working out markets for Japanese goods." Although such a mission probably should have been sent to Japan three or four years earlier, the one that came in the spring of 1949 certainly left its mark on the country. Royall, who came along chiefly to stress the importance of the mission, stayed only a short time. The mission itself was known as the Dodge mission, after its leader, Joseph M. Dodge, a Republican, the president of a Detroit bank, former deputy to Secretary of State Marshall at the London Council of Foreign Ministers, head of the United States delegation to the Austrian Treaty Commission in Vienna, and chosen in 1952 to assist President-elect Eisenhower in selecting his new cabinet. One of Dodge's several contributions to Japanese history was his name, which he left as the most common Japanese appellation for the tumultuous year 1949—namely, the year of the "Dodge line" (*Dojji rain*) or, more graphically, the "Dodge whirlwind" (*Dojji sempū*).

Dodge arrived in Tokyo on February 1 and stayed until April 30. He was assisted by Paul M. O'Leary, dean of the School of Business and Public Administration of Cornell University;

A. H. Stephen, financial specialist from Rutgers University; Orville J. McDiarmid, foreign exchange expert from the State Department; and two more Ph.D.'s, W. E. Reid and William W. Diehl. Dodge himself was given the rank of minister in order to stress the importance the United States government attached to his mission and to allow him to negotiate directly with the Japanese government. Upon its arrival in Tokyo, however, the Dodge mission proceeded very slowly; and the Japanese, aware that something was up, tested the water by putting forward a few plans of their own in the economic field.

Yoshida was in a difficult position. His conservative rivals in the Democratic party could not decide whether to support him as part of a conservative anti-Communist front or to allow Yoshida's Liberals to take the blame for retrenchment in the hope that the Democrats would profit politically in the next election. The issue and the conservatives' response to it (the Democratic party split over the economic stabilization program) was typical of a pattern of political coalitions that has prevailed in Japan ever since.

Yoshida's first chore was to name a minister of finance—a highly unpopular job during 1949—and after the opening of the Fifth Diet on February 11, he named Ikeda Hayato, himself to become one of the most popular premiers of Japan in the 1960s. Dodge and Major General William F. Marquat, chief of the Economic and Scientific Section of SCAP-GHQ, had already told Yoshida that they wanted a balanced budget for the coming fiscal year (in Japan, April 1 to March 31) and that they expected to look it over personally before the Diet passed it. On February 10, Yoshida visited MacArthur himself, as he had done many times in the past, and found that this time he would not be able to pull an end run around lesser SCAP officials—in this case, Dodge. He therefore gave the bad news to Ikeda: cut expenditures as ruthlessly as possible, consistent with political survival.

On February 23, Yoshida and Ikeda got the cabinet to approve a mildly deflationary budget, one that still included some ¥69 billion to ¥84 billion worth of subsidies to industry and that relied on American loans; and on March 1, Ikeda set out to negotiate approval of his budget with SCAP-GHQ. Dodge thought the budget did not go far enough and decided to put a little political pressure of his own on the Yoshida cabinet. On March 7, he made his first public statement since his arrival in Japan, and it shook the Japanese government to its core. "Japan is operating a rigged economy," Dodge said. "Japan's economy is walking on stilts, one leg of which is built on external aid from the United States and the other on internal subsidies." [14] The place to stop inflation, he argued, was at its source: in the government. The only solution to Japan's economic difficulties was not more United States aid but increased production, lower costs, and greater exports. In any case, there was not going to be any more United States aid unless all subsidies were stopped.

Generally speaking, editorials in the press supported Dodge, saying that it was time to cut enterprises free from government support and let them sink or swim. On March 12, Dodge's position was reinforced by a white paper from the government's own Economic Stabilization Board. It said that Japan was living off foreign loans, and that the economy needed to cut labor costs and to stress exports over domestic consumption needs. Yoshida squirmed under this pressure, and throughout March a succession of government and political leaders paid calls on Dodge at SCAP and asked for leniency in the stabilization program. None was forthcoming. Finally, on March 31, Washington sweetened the pill by announcing a $100 million loan, provided Japan accepted the economic stabilization budget.

Three days later Yoshida capitulated. In an address to both houses of the Diet he asked for "economic patriotism" on the

14. *Nippon Times*, March 8, 1949.

part of his countrymen and presented a balanced budget, the first since the end of the war and one which both reduced the governmental payroll and raised taxes. The issue during April then became to make the Diet itself swallow what the government had already accepted. On April 15, Dodge spoke publicly for the second and final time: Japan had been "living beyond its means. . . . There seems to be astonishingly little comprehension among the Japanese people of the real situation of their country." A balanced budget, said Dodge, was not a party but a national issue. A balanced budget should have been included in the plank of every political party. The next day, Saturday, April 16, the House of Representatives passed Yoshida's deflationary budget.

Dodge stayed on a few more weeks in order to see the new international exchange rate for the yen go into effect on April 25, 1949. It is to Dodge's credit that this rate (¥360 = US$1) remained stable until August of 1971. On April 30, Dodge himself sailed for the United States, and in May the "Dodge storm" began.

The government itself had to fire about 30 percent of its employees in order to live within the new budget; and private industry, no longer able to meet payrolls out of subsidies, also began massive layoffs. During May the Diet was preoccupied with the single most important piece of legislation implementing the Dodge line—namely, the "Law for the Fixed Number of Personnel in Administrative Organs" (Gyōsei kikan shokuin teiin hō, commonly known simply as the Teiin Hō)—which went into effect on May 31, 1949.[15] This law, bitterly opposed in the Diet, set ceilings on the numbers of employees in all branches of government service, including the government railroads (which became a separate government corporation on June 1, 1949). The government estimated that there were approximately

15. SCAP Monograph No. 13, "Reorganization of Civil Service," (unpaged), microfilm frames 559–563.

618,000 railroad employees on January 1, 1949, and the Teiin Hō fixed the railroad ceiling at 506,734, thus necessitating a cut during 1949 of approximately 100,000 workers. Altogether somewhere upwards of two million private and government employees were laid off during 1949; the Teiin Hō alone saved the government ¥7 billion annually in wages.

The passage of the budget and the launching in earnest of the economic stabilization program brought a flurry of activity to SCAP. On May 16, 1949, the Civil Transport Section (Rail) froze all employment by the Japanese National Railroads; and Robert T. Amis, acting chief of the Labor Division, went into almost daily discussions with President Shimoyama of the JNR on how to bring about the personnel cuts. Amis indicated to Shimoyama that in the latter's relations with the unions the size of the work force was not a negotiable issue and that he should consult the unions on the criteria and means of personnel reduction. Meanwhile, on June 24 and 25, 1949, a conference of all regional labor-relations officers in Japan was held in Yokohama. It was pointed out at the conference that approximately ninety-five thousand railroad workers would be discharged during the month of July; and plans were laid to pay unemployment insurance, to get employers needing workers to send requests to the labor exchanges, and to provide public works employment on a local basis for those unable to find a job. The actual orders for railroad layoffs, based primarily on seniority, went out in two waves: thirty-seven thousand were fired on July 4, and sixty-five thousand on July 14.

The situation in private industry was similar. Nippon Muden (wireless) fired 1,200 out of 3,600 employees; Japan Victor Recording Company let go 700 out of 2,300 employees; Adachi Denki fired 1,000 of its 1,700 workers; and Daidō Seikō (steel) laid off 2,600 out of its 9,800 workers.[16] All of the Com-

16. Aochi Shin reports that Daidō Steel fired 3,500 employees (44

munist-dominated Sanbetsu unions were hard hit in these layoffs, but they concentrated their counterattack on one major firm, seen as a test case for private industry as a whole—namely, the Tokyo-Shibaura Electric Company, or Tōshiba, one of the big three (together with Hitachi and Mitsubishi) of the Japanese electrical manufacturing industry. Tōshiba was at the heart of the Dodge storm in private industry, just as the JNR was among the government enterprises; and both Tōshiba and the JNR are central to the Matsukawa case since all twenty defendants were former employees of either one or the other organization.

During 1949, Tōshiba, with its twenty-nine thousand employees, was in double trouble. Its company union, noted for the ferocity of its labor offensives, was on the warpath as a result of the layoffs; and at the same time, SCAP was still trying to "deconcentrate" the corporation. Back in July 1948, as SCAP began to shift its priorities toward economic reconstruction, the Holding Company Liquidation Commission (HCLC) had removed 225 from the original group of 325 companies designated as targets for deconcentration. But Tōshiba was not one of them; in fact, Tōshiba was one of the last big firms to come under the original occupation policies for the "democratization of the economy." The HCLC did not make its final recommendations with regard to Tōshiba until January 25, 1949, when the company was ordered to divest itself of twenty-seven of its forty-three plants scattered around Japan. The HCLC acknowledged that many of these factories were war damaged, but it felt that if all of them were rebuilt the company would then possess a dangerous concentration of power in the electrical industry. Several concessions were made, however: out of the twenty-seven factories over which it was to relinquish control, Tōshiba was allowed to turn fourteen into small subsidiary com-

percent), Nihon Denki 3,500 (35 percent), Oki Denki 2,800 (42 percent), and Hitachi 5,500 (percentage not known). *Chūō kōron*, No. 860 (September 1959), p. 95.

panies, to make one over into a laboratory, and to sell the remainder. (The Tōshiba plant at Matsukawa was one of those to
be converted into a subsidiary of the main corporation.) This
action, together with a deconcentration order against Hitachi,
brought the three main electrical manufacturers to approximately
equal strength.

The Federation of Tōshiba Trade Unions (Tōshiba Rōdō
Kumiai Rengō Kai), created in March 1948 with headquarters
at Tsurumi, Tokyo, is described by Shiota as "the most militant
among civilian industries." [17] It was affiliated nationally with the
Sanbetsu federation, and although the rank and file were far
from being all Communists, its leadership was completely Communist. Between October 1946 and February 1947, the Tōshiba
unions had led a long strike against the company, and the federation's leadership was always willing to use its forces to assist other
strikes, as it did in the Tōhō movie strike, which produced a
clash with occupation forces.

The union's fierce opposition to the company was partly
ideological. Tōshiba had been affiliated with the biggest of the
Zaibatsu—namely, Mitsui—and before the war General Electric
in the United States held 24 percent of the company's shares.
When, during 1948, a vice-president of General Electric came
to Japan for an inspection tour of Tōshiba, the company asked
that he be given a friendly welcome by the workers. Instead, the
union concluded that here was firm evidence of international
collusion between monopoly capitalists and met the General
Electric man with a strike and red flags. Although during 1948
Tōshiba had hoped to obtain capital from General Electric, the
American firm turned it down. Nevertheless, the workers saw
much of the Dodge-line reorganization as a plot to make Tōshiba
an attractive firm for General Electric investment. In this they
were partly right (in the sense that Dodge did hope to attract
foreign capital), and indeed by 1960 International General Elec-

17. *Rekishigaku kenkyū*, No. 224 (October 1958), p. 48.

tric (USA) was once again the largest shareholder in Tōshiba, controlling 7.16 percent of the shares. The second and third largest shareholders were Dai-Ichi Life Insurance (4.04 percent) and the Daiwa Bank (3.48 percent).[18] Needless to say, General Electric's share of the stock did not amount to a controlling interest; generally speaking, ownership of Japanese corporations in the postwar era was greatly broadened over the prewar period as a result of occupation policies.

One further ideological goad to the union was the fact that the president of Tōshiba, Ishizaka Taizō, was one of the biggest chōrō ("elders," i.e., VIP's) of Japanese finance. In addition to heading Tōshiba, he later took on the chairmanship of Arabian Oil Development, Japan Atomic Energy, and the Dai-Ichi Life Insurance Company; and in 1951, Prime Minister Yoshida named him a member of the committee to consider alterations in occupation reforms after the Americans left. Twenty years later, he headed Expo 70, the first world's fair ever held in Asia. Ishizaka was part of the establishment and exactly the kind of person the Japanese Communists did not like.

The Tōshiba unions were chosen by their Communist leadership to make a major test case out of the occupation-directed economic reforms. SCAP estimated that Tōshiba had twelve thousand excess employees, and the company acknowledged a surplus of seven thousand. With the final settlement of its case before the HCLC in January, Tōshiba began its firings, either from the main company itself or from the fourteen new satellite companies being set up during the year. All together, at least four thousand Tōshiba employees, approximately 18 percent of the company's work force, were let go during the summer of 1949, many of them union officials. The unions took the view that these firings were illegal and in violation of their existing contracts. However, since SCAP had amended the basic labor

18. Yamamura, *Economic Policy in Postwar Japan*, p. 117, table 27.

law, making it illegal for companies to pay full-time union officials out of company funds (rather than union dues), the company took the view that the old contracts, guaranteeing union officials a job, were null and void and went to court against the unions. In response to this the unions struck or, in some cases, took over the factories.

The situation at the Kamo works of Tōshiba in Niigata Prefecture was in many ways typical of conditions prevailing throughout the corporation. This factory, constructed in 1942, manufactured electrical appliances. During its peak production period, in 1944, it employed 1,160 workers, and at the end of the war it had 1,100 employees on its payroll. After the war a factory union was organized, which was Communist dominated from its inception. On December 3, 1948, the manager, unable to meet his payroll because of the poor financial condition of the company, retired 197 workers with two months' retirement pay. The union claimed that this was a violation of its contract and demanded that the severances be negotiated. The manager refused to negotiate and instead went into hiding.

At this point the union instituted something peculiar to postwar Japanese trade unionism—namely, seisan kanri ("production control"), or the physical takeover of the plant by the union, which continues to manufacture and sell the plant's product. It was a union tactic, since outlawed by the courts, designed both to make labor's point against management and to demonstrate that industries could be operated without a managerial class. Seisan kanri was resorted to often in the postwar period, most spectacularly in the Yomiuri newspaper strike which lasted from October 1945 to June 1946. In the case of the Niigata factory of Tōshiba, the workers took over the plant and manufactured and sold goods valued at ¥10 million. On March 26, 1949, the company finally gained an injunction against the union, and on June 3, the Niigata District Court rendered a firm decision in favor of management. On June 17, court bailiffs, accompanied by 240 policemen, recaptured the factory from the union and arrested 143 workers. The factory was reopened on June 28, with a work force entirely purged of Communists.

Not all Tōshiba disputes resulted in *seisan kanri*, nor were all settled so early in the year. There is no question but that the Communist party made Tōshiba a special target for attack, partly because Tōshiba's firings were greater in scale and allegedly more callous in terms of severance pay than other companies. The SCAP archives contain several directives of the Japanese Communist party's central committee, intercepted by G-2 (Eighth Army counterintelligence), ordering all-out offensives against Tōshiba, including a call on July 6, 1949, for a "joint struggle," which says: "The center of this joint struggle shall be the National Railroad, All-Japan Communications, and Tōshiba unions, and *force shall be used*." [19] On March 31, 1949, the union had called a strike of all the main company plants, and as we shall see, by August the firings and union retaliation had filtered down to the reorganized satellites, such as the Tōshiba electric-motor works at Matsukawa, Fukushima.

Needless to say, if the Tōshiba unions retaliated against the Dodge storm, the National Railroad Workers' Union, the largest and one of the most Communist-influenced unions in the country, also took action. However, the situation here was complicated by the fact that the NRWU was split, owing to the presence of the original Mindō faction in its midst and the fact that it governed a nationwide industry. As early as September 1946, Japanese National Railroads management had tried to discharge some seventy-five thousand employees but had been forced to back down in the face of a threatened strike. From that time until 1949 conditions within the nation's rail transportation system had become increasingly chaotic; and on July 19, 1948, the Civil Transportation Section (Rail) of SCAP-GHQ had written

19. SCAP Archives, Tōhoku Civil Affairs Region, box 2610, "Labor File."

that the JNR was "apparently helpless to cope with the situation." [20]

The railroads seemed to mirror all of the nation's postwar problems. Trains were frequently robbed; black marketeers moved their supplies by rail, sometimes with the connivance of local stationmasters; and the union, fragmented into hundreds of different locals, was torn between protecting the workers' rights and protesting real grievances and the Communist leadership's desire to use the workers and their grievances to further the party's political ambitions. During 1947, the Ministry of Transportation created a Public Safety Bureau (i.e., police) in order to try to cope with robberies and black market activities; and this bureau, with sections at the division and subdivision levels, deputized more than eight thousand stationmasters, conductors, and assistant conductors, giving them limited police authority.

Some of the robberies were spectacular. On May 13, 1947, on the Sanyō Main Line in the Hiroshima Division, a group of armed robbers jammed the automatic signal system and stopped passenger train number 974. They then rushed the freight car, making off with large quantities of medical supplies and cotton fabric. On April 5, 1947, on the Hokuriku Line between Niigata and Tokyo, some sixty robbers boarded the train and robbed passengers all night long while the train was under way. The robbers ultimately left the train without interference at Ōmiya, on the approaches to Tokyo. As late as January 25, 1949, Mr. Kawahara, director of the Public Safety Bureau, reported to G-2 that a gang of about eight thousand demobilized soldiers, Koreans, and gangsters was operating in the Shizuoka subdivision. This gang attacked trains in three groups, some boarding trains and throwing down goods, others picking the goods up along the tracks, and still others transporting the loot to the urban black

20. SCAP Archives, box 8769, file entitled "Labor."

market. As we shall see much later, a couple of nighttime thieves walking along the tracks in Fukushima played their part in the Matsukawa case.

Robberies were only a minor headache for the Japanese National Railroads, however, compared to its union situation. The National Railroad Workers' Union (Kokutetsu Rōdō Kumiai), with its 618,000 members, was headed by a central committee which during the first half of 1949 was divided between sixty extremely militant Communists or left-wing radicals allied with them, and fifty-seven Mindō moderates. Below the national level, as of December 31, 1948, there were 1,537 semiautonomous locals, some of them exclusively Communist-led, some Mindō-led, and some split. The key to Communist control of the union was the strategic placement of Communists in leadership positions throughout the union structure. Given the large numbers of Communists in the union, the party was as important a channel for transmitting instructions as the official union institutions. The NRWU as a whole was the nation's largest union, and it was not affiliated with any federation until 1950, when it adhered to Sōhyō.

The structure of the locals paralleled that of the railroad itself. In 1949, the JNR system was made up of 19,877.2 working kilometers and was divided into nine major geographical divisions for administrative purposes: Tokyo, Nagoya, Osaka, Hiroshima, Shikoku, Moji, Niigata, Sendai, and Sapporo which were then further divided into forty-seven subdivisions. For example, the Sendai Division, serving Tōhoku (and of primary concern to us in this book), had four subdivisions—Fukushima, Sendai, Morioka, and Aomori—with 52,783 employees as of June 1, 1949, operating 429 stations, two main lines—the Tōhoku and Ōu—and six feeders—the Jōban, Banetsu-west, Senseki, Rikuu-east, Ōkoku, and Senzan. Sendai's total working trackage at the time was 2,014.3 kilometers. Generally speaking, a union local (bunkai) existed at every level of the system as well as in each roundhouse, marshaling yard, and large station. Federations of locals, called "branches" (*shibu*) were organized in every city with more than one local and on a prefecture-wide basis.

The Fukushima Subdivision, smallest in the Sendai Division (with 424.1 kilometers compared to Sendai's 600.1, Morioka's 556.1, and Aomori's 434.0), was completely dominated by Communists, although its total union strength had not even a simple majority of Communists. On August 20, 1948, the Fukushima Military Government Team reported to its Tōhoku headquarters in Sendai the results of an opinion survey that had been administered among employees in the Fukushima Subdivision of the NRWU. The total numbers questioned and the survey methods were not reported, but the findings offer some insights into rank and file opinion. To the question "Speaking as a citizen do you think that the activities of your union are sound and beneficial to the entire country?" 85 percent of the replies were no. The team further reported that during the first half of 1948 the NRWU local in Kōriyama city, Fukushima prefecture, had voted 161 to 101 to exclude Communists from official positions in the union but that this vote had had no effect on the composition of the local's leadership.[21] However, these statistics may help to explain the Fukushima rank and file's conspicuous lack of support for the Matsukawa defendants after their arrests, a subject to which we shall return.

The National Railroad Workers' Union, a huge, heterogeneous, trade union giant, in some localities highly political, in others markedly conservative, reacted to the Dodge line in many different ways. On April 26, 1949, four days before Dodge left Japan, the Sixth National Convention of the NRWU ended with a decided swing to the left. Despite the fact that Mindō was active within the NRWU, where it had first come into being as a reaction against the union's Communist leadership, Mindō del-

21. SCAP Archives, Tōhoku Civil Affairs Region, box 2571.

egates to the convention were unable to hold out against Communist calls for active opposition to the forthcoming layoffs. Thus, during May, the NRWU central committee strongly petitioned the Diet to increase the railroad budget and to reject the Dodge-Yoshida scheme to cut manpower. When the Teiin Hō came into effect on May 31, the union's leadership knew that threats and petitions were not going to work, and it turned to other measures.

The first reaction occurred in the Tokyo Division and produced one of the more bizarre incidents of the entire year, namely, the People's Streetcar case. On June 9, 1949, President Shimoyama of the Japanese National Railroads personally fired nineteen conductors working in the city of Yokohama and in nearby Chiba prefecture who had refused to conform to new, tighter working schedules. In retaliation the Yokohama local of the NRWU carried out the first instance of *seisan kanri* ("production control") in the transportation sector: for the next two days operators and conductors took over the streetcars and interurban trains in and around Yokohama and operated them as "people's streetcars," collecting fares and retaining them in special union accounts. At the same time the Chiba local called a strike, which happened to delay some SCAP trains as well as interrupt the regular service. As a result SCAP intervened directly. Robert Amis of the Labor Division ordered Shimoyama and the central committee of the NRWU to stop the strike forthwith, and as in the February 1, 1947, general strike, the union immediately complied with SCAP's order. To do otherwise was to risk arrest and trial before an American military court for resisting the occupation of Japan. The Japanese government arrested forty-seven NRWU members in Yokohama and sixteen in Chiba and eventually convicted most of them of the crime of obstructing business (Penal Code art. 234), in two of the most riotous political trials of 1949 and 1950.

SCAP and the Japanese government both were infuriated

by these incidents, and Chief Cabinet Secretary Masuda lashed out in the press, calling them political strikes and condemning Communist influence in the unions. At a conference at GHQ on June 26, MacArthur himself cautioned General Marquat, chief of the Economic and Scientific Section, that labor problems in transportation vitally affected the rehabilitation of Japan's economy. On the same day, General Courtney Whitney, chief of the Government Section, personally telephoned the Civil Transportation Section (CTS) "stating that CTS must advise the railroad officials to proceed vigorously with their curtailment program and that any backsliding from their program would strengthen the union's position and cause the railroad officials to lose face." [22] Clearly SCAP had sighted the enemy—the union—and was advancing to meet him.

SCAP's intervention in the People's Streetcar case warned the NRWU leadership that occupation authorities would not tolerate strikes in response to the Dodge line. This fact undoubtedly influenced the meeting of the NRWU central committee which began on June 23, 1949, at the beach resort of Atami. At that meeting the central committee beat back moderate proposals for legal protests against past and anticipated firings and, on the motion of the Communist faction, resolved to employ "continuous, illegal, bloody, regional strike tactics" [23]—that is, wildcat-appearing violent sit-ins, kangaroo courts, and work stoppages in dispersed areas throughout the country rather than throughout the whole system at once. The resolution defended these methods by saying that the layoffs would endanger the safety of railway operations, would contribute to poor maintenance of equipment, and would reduce the workers to such poverty that they would be unable to perform their duties properly. The resolution did not clearly advocate sabotage, but

22. SCAP Archives, box 8770, file entitled "Labor Policy."
23. Takano, Nihon no rōdō undō, p. 83. See also Aochi Shin, Chūō kōron, No. 860 (September 1959), p. 97.

it came close enough to doing so for the judges in the first
Matsukawa trial to cite the Atami resolution as a probable motive
for the crime.[24]

Sabotage—or the suspicion of it—undertaken on a local, ad
hoc basis, was in the air. Years later the *Shūkan asahi* magazine
referred to the period beginning in April 1949 and lasting
through 1952 as the "era of railroad terror." [25] Conservative
politicians and the press harped on sabotage and unquestionably
exaggerated its prevalence. Out of twenty-six "major" train accidents on the Japanese National Railroads between September
1945 and July 1951, SCAP concluded that only two—the
Mitaka and Matsukawa cases—were proven cases of sabotage.[26]
Leftist historians of the period also argue that, beginning in June
1949, the JNR decided to report every stone placed on a track
by a small boy and that these new reporting standards account for
the rise in the official sabotage statistics. They allege that management's reason for publicizing incidents of sabotage was to alienate
the public from the unions in preparation for the firings.[27] Whatever the case may be, the official—and widely disseminated—
statistics did shoot up markedly (table 2). Judged either on the
basis of these figures or by SCAP's two confirmed cases, the year
1949 was Japan's all-time worst for railroad sabotage, with July
being the worst month, with 1,574 cases.

Two cases, not described by SCAP as sabotage but interpreted that way by Japanese investigators, were widely discussed
in the press and bear a remarkable resemblance to the Matsukawa
case. One occurred in Fukushima, the other in Ehime prefecture

24. Fukushima Chihō Saibansho (Fukushima District Court), *Matsukawa jiken dai-isshin hanketsu* (Matsukawa Case First Trial Verdict
(Fukushima, January 12, 1951), p. 8.
25. *Shūkan asahi*, September 27, 1963.
26. SCAP Archives, box 8769, file entitled "JNR Accidents."
27. Cf. Furuya Tetsuo, *Rekishigaku kenkyū*, No. 224 (October
1958), p. 44.

on the island of Shikoku—a rural province like Fukushima and also like Fukushima an area of considerable Communist strength. The first case occurred on April 27, 1948, a year before the Dodge storm, when a train derailed and overturned near Niwazaka sta-

TABLE 2

RAILROAD SABOTAGE INCIDENTS, 1939–1950

Period	Reported cases
1939–1945	ca. 400 per annum
1946	721
1947	1,069
1948	1,478
1949	4,577
1950	4,106

SOURCES: (1) Furuya Tetsuo, "Matsukawa jiken ni itaru hankyō ishiki no dōin ni tsuite" (On the Arousing of Anti-Communist Consciousness Leading up to the Matsukawa Case), *Rekishigaku kenkyū* (The Journal of Historical Studies), No. 224 (October 1958), p. 44; (2) *Shūkan asahi* (Weekly Asahi), November 29, 1953; and (3) Kokka Chihō Keisatsu Honbu Keiji-bu Sōsa-ka (National Rural Police Headquarters, Criminal Affairs Division, Investigation Section), *Bōgaihan no sōsa* (Investigation of Sabotage Crimes) (Tokyo, 1952), pp. 1–127.

tion on the Ōu Main Line (which connects Aomori and Fukushima via Akita). The engineer and his assistant were killed, and a nineteen-year-old boy riding in the locomotive was severely injured and later died. It may only be a coincidence, but this wreck occurred between the second and third stations from Fukushima city on the Ōu Main Line (i.e., between Niwazaka and Akaiwa), whereas the Matsukawa wreck took place between the second and third stations from Fukushima on the Tōhoku Main Line (i.e., between Kanayagawa and Matsukawa). In the Niwazaka case, Japanese police investigators concluded that the tracks had been sabotaged, but the case was never solved. The second case occurred on May 9, 1949, on a remote section of the Yosan Line near the city of Matsuyama. Again the tracks appeared to have been sabotaged, and a passenger train was overturned and three people were killed. After an investigation for a year and a half the case was dropped as unsolved. Only five days before this accident, on May 4, an unsuccessful attempt to sabotage the Yosan Line using dynamite was reported to JNR headquarters.

Whatever the cause of these incidents, SCAP, the Japanese government, and the Japanese people were alarmed by them and by numerous other instances, reported in the press, of jammed switches, rocks placed on tracks, and the malfunctioning of rolling stock. On June 28 the Public Security Bureau of the railroad issued an emergency order directing subordinate units to report all cases of sabotage, large or small; and on June 30, President Shimoyama stated, "Some railway incidents are the result of playful acts by grammar school children, but others are evidently the work of professionals well acquainted with the operations of the JNR. Some cases have occurred in areas known for the presence of radicals, suggesting that these incidents were politically motivated." [28] In his Fourth of July speech, General MacArthur himself, after reviewing sixteen thousand occupation troops, seemed to be alluding at least in part to the criminal incidents occurring within the country when he described communism as "international outlawry."

One other incident occurred on the eve of implementation of the Dodge line in the railroads that may or may not be related but that certainly shocked the nation. On June 27, 1949, a large contingent of the Japanese prisoners of war held in Soviet Siberia since 1945 returned home. Some two thousand men aboard the *Takasago Maru* arrived at the Japan Sea port of Maizuru, but many of the families who came to meet them were bitterly dis-

28. Quoted in Yoshihara Kōichirō, *Matsukawa jiken no shin hannin* (The True Criminals of the Matsukawa Case) (Tokyo, 1962), p. 11.

appointed by the reunion. Headlines in the *Nippon Times* told the story: USSR SENDS BACK POW's SATURATED IN RED DOCTRINE. REPATRIATES STUN THOSE WELCOMING THEM BY SHEER RUDENESS. The returnees started singing the "Internationale" as the ship entered the harbor, and upon going ashore, they ignored their families and instead staged a demonstration, pledging to join the Japanese Communist party. All along the rail line from Maizuru to Kyoto, Communist unionists held rallies to welcome home their brethren from the land of socialism. With all this going on, it crossed the minds of both SCAP and the Japanese police that there just might be a saboteur or two among these repatriates, who had obviously been handpicked by the Soviets for early return because of their superior performance in Communist ideology.

On July 1, 1949, orders went out to each railroad division giving the numbers to be fired (in Japanese, *kubikiri*, literally "decapitated") on July 4. According to the instructions, discharges were to be made using the criteria of (a) inefficiency and (b) lack of seniority. In the first round 37,000 were let go, including 9,658 in the Sendai Division; and on July 14, the second series of cuts began, totaling 65,000 throughout the country and about 20,000 in the Sendai Division. The Labor Relations Division of the Tōhoku Civil Affairs Region noted in its "Staff Notes and Unit History Report" that "on 16 July the Liaison Section of the Sendai Railroad Division reported that the majority of discharges had already been effected and that generally everything was quiet and orderly. [It was] *also stated that the radical and influential Communists were among those first being discharged* and that those next discharged were mostly young workers because they had the least seniority." [29] The official directives did not say anything explicit about firing Communists, but

29. SCAP Archives, Tōhoku Civil Affairs Region, box 2602, italics added.

the Tōhoku military government officers knew that this was one objective of the campaign and noted down their local results accordingly.

Both series of firings were punctuated by extremely serious incidents—the death of JNR president Shimoyama immediately following the first cut, and the Mitaka wreck the day after the second. Shimoyama was last seen by some seventeen witnesses at about ten o'clock on the morning of July 5; he was standing near the entrance to the subway that stops within the basement floor of the Mitsukoshi department store in Nihombashi, Tokyo. He had left his home shortly after eight o'clock, driven by his chauffeur in the Buick automobile assigned to him as president of the National Railroads. His schedule that morning included a ten o'clock staff meeting with Kagayama Yukio, vice-president of the JNR, and other senior officials concerning the firings that had begun the day before, and a meeting about eleven o'clock with Lieutenant Colonel D. R. Changnon,[30] director of the Rail Transportation Division, Civil Transportation Section, SCAP-GHQ, and members of his staff. According to later reports, Changnon, in uniform and allegedly wearing a pistol, had visited Shimoyama the evening before at his home and urged him to show no hesitation in carrying out the firings, particularly with

30. Some confusion exists about the spelling of this officer's name. The novelist Uno Kōji in his sensational (and important) book on the Matsukawa case *Yo ni mo fushigi na monogatari* (The Strangest Story in the World) (1953) writes it in *katakana* as "Shagunon" and in roman letters as "Chagnon" (p. 78). Uno's usage is followed by most other Japanese writers. The spelling I have used in this book is based on the "SCAP Telephone Directory, Tokyo, July 1, 1949," a copy of which is available in the SCAP Archives. Some writers also confuse Changnon with Lt. Col. J. Y. Cannon, who was alleged to have headed a special SCAP counterintelligence unit (known in Japanese as the Kyanon Kikan, the "Cannon Organization"). There is no evidence, however, to suggest that Colonel Changnon had any other duties than as director of the Rail Transportation Division, Civil Transportation Section, SCAP-GHQ. We shall return to this matter later in this book.

regard to Suzuki Ichizō (since 1955 an alternate member of the Japanese Communist party's central committee) and other Communist leaders within the top directorate of the National Railroad Workers' Union.

All of the members of Shimoyama's staff, including Kagayama, his successor as JNR president, reported that he had been under incredible pressure during the previous few weeks. He was a popular figure within the railroad and was also known to have had very friendly relations with occupation officials. In the days preceding the first firings, he had received innumerable letters from railroad workers pleading their special cases and asking not to be put out of work. Shimoyama was not described as particularly strong-willed or as doing much more, in carrying out the firings, than following orders from his superiors in the Ministry of Transportation and in SCAP. He seemed more devoted to operating the railroad than to making it operate profitably. Thus nobody was surprised when on the morning of July 5, Shimoyama—known to have dreaded attending both of his scheduled meetings—did not show up. Some thought that he might have gone into hiding until the furor over the firings died down; others conjectured that he might be visiting his mistress.

In any case his chauffeur testified that on the morning of July 5, Shimoyama gave him various directions and then countermanded them—first to go to JNR headquarters, then to the Chiyoda Bank (the cover name of the Mitsui Bank during the occupation), and finally to the Mitsukoshi department store. The driver last saw him entering Mitsukoshi. Shortly after midnight the following morning his body was found on the Jōban Line tracks in northern Tokyo. He had either lain down himself or been laid with his neck on one track and his feet on the other. He was run over by a freight train originating from the Tabata marshaling yard in northern Tokyo, and his body was almost completely dismembered.

Shimoyama's remains were delivered to Professors Kuwashima Naoki and Furuhata Tanemoto of the Department of Forensic Medicine, Tokyo University Medical School, for autopsy. On July 6 they concluded that Shimoyama was dead when his body was run over, chiefly on the basis of the relatively slight amount of bleeding in evidence. Professor Furuhata went so far as to fix the time of death as between 9:00 and 10:00 P.M., July 5, using methods he had developed in experiments with animals. This conclusion was strongly attacked and denounced by Professor Nakadate Hisahira of Keiō University Medical School, also an authority on legal medicine, but who was not present at the autopsy. Nakadate contended that the heavy rain on the evening of July 5 plus the intense shock of being hit by a train (with a resulting drastic lowering of blood pressure) accounted for the apparently bloodless corpse. In effect the Tokyo University professors argued that Shimoyama had been murdered and then placed on the tracks, whereas the Keiō observer believed that Shimoyama had committed suicide by placing himself on the tracks. Thus began a controversy that continues to this day.

Different branches of the Metropolitan Police and the procurators divided over the murder theory versus the suicide theory. The entire controversy was even carried into the Diet, and on September 20 the House of Representatives began an investigation into the case. As for the official record, on July 6 the police announced that Shimoyama had been murdered, but they subsequently reversed themselves after the complete police investigation report had been either stolen from police headquarters or sold by an insider to the press and published in the February and March 1950 issues of the magazines Kaizō and Bungei shunjū. This report, the so-called Shimoyama White Paper, supported the conclusion that Shimoyama had committed suicide, and the police ultimately endorsed that conclusion.

Opinion concerning the Shimoyama case has varied over the years, and it has always been the subject of heated controversy. During the Dodge-line period conservative opinion generally held that Shimoyama had been murdered (probably by disgruntled NRWU Communists), and leftist groups sought to show that he committed suicide because of remorse over his responsibility for the firings. Twenty years later the positions had become reversed. With the development of anti-Americanism among Japanese radical groups, left-wing publicists now suggest that Shimoyama was murdered—by agents of Colonel Changnon and SCAP (for the alleged motives of discrediting the unions and bringing in a tougher president)—while conservatives are sure that he did, in fact, commit suicide, having been driven to the breaking point by the Dodge line.

During 1968, after the statute of limitations on the Shimoyama case came into effect, a group of left-wing professors and writers formed the Association to Study the Shimoyama Case, and the following year they published the single most important book on the incident: *Shiryō Shimoyama jiken* (*Documents of the Shimoyama Case*).[31] The historical materials gathered in this book do not in themselves prove either the suicide theory or the murder theory; but, ironically, one of the compilers of the volume, Satō Hajime, a former defendant in the Matsukawa case, who after his release from prison had been given a job by the Shimoyama Association, came to the personal conclusion that Shimoyama committed suicide. Since this view was unacceptable to his sponsors, Satō had to resign from the association. Today he remains 95 percent convinced of the suicide theory, reserving

31. Tokyo: Misuzu Shobō, 1969. The founders of the Association to Study the Shimoyama Case included: Nambara Shigeru, former president of Tokyo University; Numada Inejirō, professor of Tokyo Metropolitan University; Unno Shinkichi, Director of the Japanese Human Rights Committee; Kuwabara Takeo, professor of Kyoto University; Dandō Shigemitsu, a Tokyo University authority on criminal law; Saeki Chihiro, an Osaka lawyer; Matsumoto Seichō, reporter and writer of detective stories; Hirotsu Kazuo, the leading publicist on the Matsukawa case; Kinoshita Junji, playwright; and Shiota Shobei, professor of Tokyo Metropolitan University.

5 percent for the possibility that not Americans but railroad workers in the Tabata marshaling yard kidnapped and murdered Shimoyama.[32] We shall return to these speculative theories and their influence much later in this book. For now it is only necessary to remember that during 1949 the police, the press, and much of the public believed that President Shimoyama had been murdered—and by Communist trade unionists.

The Mitaka case, which followed the second series of layoffs in mid-July, seemed to confirm the government's contention that the Communists had adopted murderously violent tactics in resisting economic stabilization. Shortly after 9 o'clock on the evening of July 15, an electric train used in the Tokyo Division's interurban service drove out of control, with its operating levers tied down, into a platform of waiting passengers at suburban Mitaka station, killing six people and wounding twenty. All of Japan, particularly the government and the press, seemed to shout their disgust at this outrage; and the police mobilized a massive task force drawn from all over the country to produce

32. For Satō Hajime's views, see "Wrestling with the Shimoyama Case," *Mainichi shimbun*, June 12, 1969. Other sources on the Shimoyama case consulted for this section, in addition to *Shiryō Shimoyama jiken*, are: (1) Aochi Shin, *Gendaishi no magarikado* (Turning Points in Modern History) (Tokyo, 1959), particularly chap. 9, "Shimoyama sōsai no kaishi" (The Mysterious Death of President Shimoyama), pp. 229–256; (2) Matsumoto Seichō, "Shimoyama kokutetsu sōsai bōsatsu ron" (The Murder Theory of [the Death of] JNR President Shimoyama) in *Nihon no kuroi kiri*, pp. 41–102; (3) Matsumoto Seichō, "Saisetsu: Shimoyama kokutetsu sōsai bōsatsu ron (Reexamination: The Murder Theory of [the Death of] JNR President Shimoyama), *Gendai*, August 1969, pp. 96–116 (this article is a reply to Mr. Sekiguchi Yoshizō, former police official of the Tokyo Metropolitan Police Board and author of the original "Shimoyama White Paper," who had written a long article supporting the suicide theory, attacking Matsumoto, and insinuating that Matsumoto was a Communist); and (4) "Kore ga Shimoyama jiken shinsō da?" (This Is the Truth of the Shimoyama Case?), *Sandē mainichi*, June 15, 1969, pp. 46–50, which presents essentially the case of police official Sekiguchi.

quick results. Within a month indictments were obtained against ten NRWU members, nine of them Communist union leaders, based on the confession of Takeuchi Keisuke, a railroad employee discharged in the manpower reductions.

The outcome of the Mitaka case differed from either the Shimoyama or Matsukawa cases. After an uproarious trial, which was continuously disrupted by Communist demonstrators and observed in the courtroom by members of G-2 and the CIC (the Eighth Army's and SCAP's counterintelligence services respectively), the Tokyo District Court in August 1950 found no evidence of conspiracy and released all the defendants but Takeuchi, who had confessed. The court concluded that he alone had committed the crime in an act of insane revenge for having been fired, and it sentenced him to life imprisonment. When the case was reviewed on appeal, the Tokyo High Court sustained the verdicts of innocent for the nine Communists but increased Takeuchi's sentence to death. His appeal to the Supreme Court against the death penalty was denied in June 1955.

Within a year after its occurrence the Mitaka case thus lost much of its political significance because of the release of the alleged conspirators. From 1950 on, its interest lay primarily in the personal struggle of Takeuchi to gain his freedom. In 1956 he began proceedings intended to show that he had an alibi (he claimed to have been in the bathhouse of the Mitaka railroad yard at the time of the wreck) and that his confession had been obtained by force. He made little progress in these efforts, and his appeal was still pending when, on January 18, 1967, he died of a brain disease in Sugamo Prison. Like the Shimoyama case, however, the Mitaka case had a great impact on Japanese politics during its first year, the period during which the public naturally took it as evidence of Communist terrorism. Even after the nine Communists were released, many policemen and a segment of the public continued to believe that they were guilty and that the police had been inept in gathering evidence against them. This

attitude prevailed because of the example of the Matsukawa case
—where railroad sabotage and Communist conspiracy to commit
sabotage were both charged and sustained in the courts.

The effects of these two cases on the National Railroad
Workers' Union was dramatic. On July 15, the day of the second
round of firings, thirteen Mindō members of the NRWU central
committee walked out of the central strike committee meeting
that had adopted by a vote of 17 to 14 a resolution warning the
government that serious trouble would result because of the layoffs. Three days later the Japanese National Railroads fired the
seventeen Communist central-committeemen who had voted for
the resolution; and on July 22, the Mindō faction reconvened the
NRWU central committee without its Communist members.[33]
This was the beginning of the end of Communist control of the
NRWU but it was not yet the end. The railroad workers' locals,
like the enterprise unions prevailing throughout Japan, were semi-
independent of their national governing body, and those with
Communist cells were still capable of receiving and acting on
orders from the Japanese Communist party.

The Shimoyama and Mitaka incidents both took place dur-

33. Takano, *Nihon no rōdō undō*, pp. 84–85; and SCAP Archives,
box 8769, file entitled "Labor." The Communist faction within the
NRWU central committee was headed by Suzuki Ichizō and Ii Yashirō;
the Mindō leaders were Saitō Tetsuo, Hoshika Kaname, and Kikukawa
Takao, all of them associates of the famous recanted Communist, Nabe-
yama Sadachika. Suspicion of the Communists during July 1949 was so
great that Suzuki Ichizō was banned from attending JNR president
Shimoyama's funeral (Aochi Shin, *Chūō kōron*, no. 860, pp. 96–98).
Concerning the public's response to the People's Streetcar, Shimoyama,
and Mitaka cases, SCAP concluded, "While the Communists were not
proven to have instigated or to have caused all these incidents, public
opinion linked them to each. Public support or sympathy for the party
plummeted" (SCAP Monograph No. 11, "Development of Political
Parties," pp. 84–85). Given such attitudes among the public, it was relatively easy for SCAP in late July to see to it that the JNR fired the leading Communists within the NRWU's central committee.

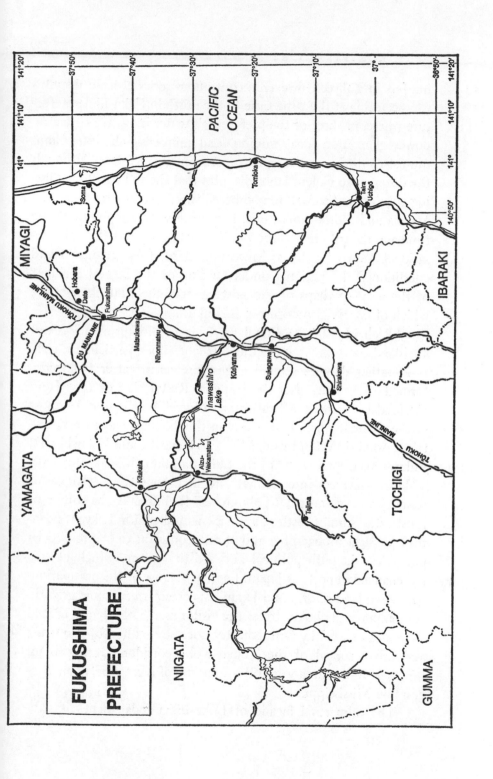

FUKUSHIMA PREFECTURE

ing July in Tokyo. However, a continuous series of labor disputes was occurring at the same time to the north in Fukushima prefecture where, in three of the prefecture's major industries—electric power generation, coal mining, and railroads—absolute Communist control over the trade unions remained intact. Although the dozen or so violent labor disputes that shook Fukushima during 1949 are not so well remembered twenty years later as are the Mitaka and Shimoyama cases, they were widely reported at the time and contributed to the public reaction against the two sensational Tokyo incidents. More important, they led up to and conditioned the national understanding of the biggest incident of the year—perhaps of the postwar era—the Matsukawa case, which of course also occurred in Fukushima.

"Rich island," the literal meaning of "Fukushima," is not an island, nor was it until quite recent times particularly rich. It is, rather, Japan's second largest prefecture, after Hokkaido, formed a few years after the Imperial Restoration of 1868 from the feudal provinces of Iwashiro and Iwaki. As the southernmost of the six prefectures that make up the Tōhoku (northeast) district (Aomori, Akita, Iwate, Miyagi, Yamagata, and Fukushima), Fukushima displays most of the traits traditionally associated with Tōhoku—severe winter climate, relative poverty and backward economic development (Tōhoku was traditionally the source of prostitutes, sumō wrestlers, and ricksha pullers for Tokyo), beautiful physical topography, and strong conservative or premodern proclivities in both political and artistic culture. Much of this has changed in postwar Japan. Largely because of the occupation-sponsored land reform and Japan's spectacular economic growth, contemporary Tōhoku strikes the visitor as a "rich island" indeed —an area of wealthy farm country not yet engulfed by the smog and urban sprawl of the Tokyo–Kobe corridor. During 1949, however, Fukushima was still something of a cross between Oregon and Mississippi.

The calm rural façade of Fukushima today belies its turbulent past. Shōji Kichinosuke, a leftist historian, argues that since the Meiji Restoration there have been three major periods of governmental repression directed against workers and peasants: the suppression of the so-called people's rights movement (*jiyū minken*) during the 1880s, the period following the rice riots of 1918, and the period from the aborted general strike of 1947 until the end of the Dodge line.[34] Whether any or all of these periods were ones of "repression of workers and peasants," it is worth noting that in two of them, the first and the last, Fukushima prefecture played a significant part.

The so-called Fukushima Incident of 1882 was a major event in the political development of early modern Japan. It occurred during a period of broad public dissatisfaction with official corruption and apparent policy failures of the fifteen-year-old Meiji government as well as demands for "civil rights and free elections" by political rivals of the Meiji leaders—a period not unlike that in many contemporary new nations a decade and a half after the onset of "nation building." The Meiji government responded initially with repressive measures, ultimately with the promulgation of a constitution (1889).

During 1882 Fukushima was torn by a series of local riots and mob actions protesting economic conditions, although the government believed that these riots were instigated by the Jiyūtō (the Liberal party)—not so much a political party as a factional grouping of the main political opponents of the ruling oligarchs. The governor of Fukushima prefecture, Mishima Michitsune, a stern administrator from Satsuma in the far south and after 1885 feared and disliked because of his reputation as superintendent general of the Tokyo Metropolitan Police, was quoted at the time of the Fukushima riots as saying that he "would not

34. "Matsukawa jiken zenshi oboegaki, 1949 nen ni okeru Fukushima kenka no rōdō tōsō" (Notes on the Prehistory of the Matsukawa Case, Labor Struggles in Fukushima Prefecture during 1949), *Rekishi hyōron* (History Review), No. 52 (February 1954), p. 30.

even put the Jiyūtō in as high a category as firesetting thieves" and that one of the reasons he had been made governor of Fukushima was to stamp out the Jiyūtō.[35] This he tried to do, employing extremely repressive measures against the people, including increased taxation and forced labor.

Because of his policies Governor Mishima was scathingly denounced in the Fukushima Assembly by one of the great liberals of the Meiji era, Kōno Hironaka (1849–1923), a native of Fukushima. As a result of his stand Kōno was arrested and imprisoned for "riotous sedition," but it is his name that is cherished today while Governor Mishima is commonly recalled as a tyrant. Some eighty-six years later, during 1969, Sugiura Saburō, leader of the Matsukawa Defendants Association, commented that "since the early Meiji era Fukushima has been known for its militant opposition to governmental power" and indicated that he thought he and the other former defendants were in the tradition of Kōno Hironaka.[36]

As a matter of historical record, however, Fukushima over the past century has been characterized more by powerless poverty than by labor militancy. During the depression years of 1933 and 1934, for example, the practice of poor peasants selling their children into virtual indentured slavery was widespread in Tōhoku. It disappeared during the war, but in 1948 the first postwar traffic in children was exposed in Tochigi prefecture, bordering directly on Fukushima to the south. During 1948 and

35. Quoted by Robert A. Scalapino, Democracy and the Party Movement in Prewar Japan (Berkeley and Los Angeles, 1953), p. 104.

36. Interview with Sugiura Saburō by Kim Yong-mok, November 7, 1969, at the offices of the Matsukawa Jiken Zenkoku Renraku Kaigi (National Liaison Congress for the Matsukawa Case), Tokyo. Concerning the Fukushima Incident of 1882 and its background, see Kobayashi Seiji and Yamada Akira, Fukushima-ken no rekishi (The History of Fukushima Prefecture) (Tokyo, 1970), pp. 178–210; and Masumi Junnosuke, Nihon seitō shi ron (On the History of Japanese Political Parties) (Tokyo, 1965), I, 213–373.

1949 child-selling also reappeared in the Aizu and Shirakawa districts of Fukushima.

Child traffickers offered about ¥10,000 ($28) to parents as payment in advance on three- to seven-year labor contracts for children, who usually became farm hands for rich farmers, or prostitutes, or employees in textile factories. On January 19, 1949, the press reported that twenty-five hundred teenage children had been sold during the previous year in Tōhoku, and a year later, on February 27, 1950, the chief of the Fukushima Labor Standards Bureau filed a report concerning the sale of several children in Aizu and Shirakawa for work in Sano city, Tochigi prefecture, a textile center. The child trafficker's profit was reported as ¥500 to ¥1,000 ($1.40 to $2.80) per head. Although the government and SCAP fought the practice, it did not end until after economic recovery. The reason was simple: during 1949 and 1950 Fukushima had the next to lowest income level in Tōhoku (Yamagata had the lowest), the average take-home pay being between ¥7,500 and ¥8,000 per month (about $21 to $24).

As of September 1, 1950, the population of Fukushima stood at 2,065,559, of whom 216,388 constituted the industrial work force (mining and manufacturing but exclusive of agriculture) employed in 15,180 enterprises. Of this industrial labor force, 51,803 were women and 22,719 were minors, reflecting the large number of silk and textile plants in the prefecture. The main industries at the time were coal mining, textiles, chemicals, sawmills and lumbering, electric power generation, and manufacturing.

In terms of economic geography, Fukushima, 68 percent of which is covered with forests, is divided vertically into three main natural districts. The eastern district along the Pacific Ocean has a comparatively mild climate favorable to farming and fishing. The economy of the southern county of this coastal district, named Ishiki, is dominated by the city of Taira, center of the Jōban mining region. In and around Taira during 1949 there were sixty-seven mines, the three biggest being the Jōban, the Dai Nippon, and the Furukawa. Ishiki-gun (county) also contained the largest numbers of Communist party voters in the prefecture.

The central part of Fukushima lying along the Tōhoku Main Line of the JNR contains the cities of Fukushima, Nihonmatsu, Kōriyama, and Shirakawa, and is a thriving region for silk reeling, cotton spinning, and manufacturing. Most farmers in this region engage in the profitable sidelines of sericulture and stock breeding. The prefecture as a whole and particularly this area is noted for weaving *habutae* silk and for the manufacture of plain silk cloth for export as handkerchiefs. Central and western Fukushima were and are today known also for a number of beautiful mountain spas and hot-springs resorts, a sizable portion of the prefecture being given over to national parks.

The third region of the prefecture, the mountainous west, was described by the *Nippon Times* of February 24, 1949, as an "area pervaded by feudalism." Aizu-Wakamatsu city is famous for its lacquerware, and the valley in which it is located is the prefecture's main rice-producing area. Forest products are also important in the west. Most important of all, however, is the generation of hydroelectric power for a good part of Honshu, particularly at the huge Inawashiro Lake powerhouses. During 1949 and 1950 the members of the Inawashiro locals of Densan (Electrical Industry Workers' Union), who operated the big generators of Nippatsu (Japan Electric Power Generation and Transmission Company) and the facilities of nine Haiden (electricity distributing) companies, were nationally famous as the hardest of hard-core Communists. It was physically dangerous to be an electrical worker at Inawashiro and not be a Communist in the days before the red purge, and both SCAP and the Japanese government were always worrying about the situation because of the capacity of Densan to cut off electrical power to the northern third of the nation.

Many Japanese writers have characterized Fukushima during

1949 as a veritable hotbed of Communism. Shiota Shobei says that the Communist party had a strong following in the area, and the Asahi shimbun recalled Fukushima as "a vanguard of the labor movement." Sugiura, himself a Communist, testifies that the prefectural NRWU branch, the Inawashiro electrical workers, and the coal miners at Taira were all led by militant Communists and that most of the rank and file believed that a revolution was due in September of 1949, although his own union, the Matsukawa local of the Tōshiba union, was not particularly militant until it came under attack from management.[37] Military Government officials watched the situation closely, and according to Shiota, Major (later Lieutenant Colonel) George J. McDermott, commander of the Fukushima Military Government Team, regularly called in Takeda Hisashi and Suzuki Makoto, leaders of the NRWU in Fukushima and both destined to become defendants in the Matsukawa case, to threaten them with military courts-martial and deportation to Okinawa if they continued to give him trouble.[38]

No doubt the trade unions were Communist dominated, but it appears in retrospect that the prefecture's problems were due

37. Shiota, Rekishigaku kenkyū, No. 224 (October 1958), p. 47; Asahi shimbun, September 12, 1963; Sugiura interview, November 7, 1969. Aochi Shin is closer to the truth when he writes: "As to the situation in Fukushima prefecture in this period [the summer of 1949], the Japanese Communist party held strong positions in the Inawashiro Lake electrical industry unions, in the Jōban coal mines, and in the JNR union at Fukushima, although the prefecture as a whole had a low degree of consciousness. With the labor unions as nuclei, the Japanese Communist party organized peasant unions and the general public into [what it called] organizations of enterprises to defend local industry (kyōdo sangyō bōei jigyō soshiki) against the Dodge line and the Yoshida administration. In response, the prefectural government concentrated the police power of the six Tōhoku prefectures into Fukushima." Chūō kōron, No. 860, p. 98.

38. Shiota, op. cit., p. 48. See also Matsukawa Undō Shi Hensan Iinkai, ed., Matsukawa undō zenshi (Complete History of the Matsukawa Movement) (Tokyo, 1965), pp. 50–51.

as much to real economic grievances as to Communist subversion. One reason why the size of the Communist party was consistently overestimated was the presence of large numbers of Koreans in Fukushima, many of whom had been brought to Japan during 1939 to replace conscripted coal miners.[39] Most Japanese and a good many SCAP officials tended to equate Koreans with communism. Actually the available figures suggest that the party was a definite minority, and certainly today Fukushima is anything but a Communist stronghold.

On January 23, 1950, an election was held in Fukushima prefecture to elect a successor to former Governor Ishihara Kanichirō, who resigned to run in the House of Councilors by-election of December 24, 1949, and its results reveal the approximate size of the Communist electorate. On election day official polling inspectors estimated the population of the prefecture at approximately 2,030,000, of whom approximately 1,030,000 were eligible voters. The actual number registered was 1,007,847 (475,248 male and 532,599 female, reflecting the effects of the war), and the actual number who cast votes was 722,833. Of these 11,298 ballots were declared invalid. Ōtake Sakuma of Yoshida's conservative party was elected with 386,357 votes, while Suzuki Yoshio of the Socialist party garnered 287,-851. The Communist candidate, Hirata Yoshio, supported in his campaign by visits to the prefecture of several famous Communist leaders, made a poor showing with 37,327 votes. Coal-rich Ishiki county with its capital at Taira gave Hirata most of his votes.

Later in the year, on September 12, 1950, officials of SCAP's Civil Affairs Section, Tōhoku Civil Affairs Region (headquartered in Sendai, the most important city of Tōhoku), combined intelligence reports with election statistics to estimate Communist strength in the whole region. The results are shown

39. See Richard H. Mitchell, The Korean Minority in Japan (Berkeley and Los Angeles, 1967), pp. 79, 84.

in table 3. Even these statistics should be seriously questioned; their chief value lies in their relative magnitudes, indicating as they do that Fukushima had absolutely more Communists than any other Tōhoku prefecture even though it was the most populous.

TABLE 3

COMMUNISTS IN TŌHOKU, 1950

Prefecture	Population (approx.)	Registered Japanese Communist party members	Sympathizers (approx.)
Miyagi	1,722,000	872	22,606
Iwate	1,424,000	852	31,350
Aomori	1,395,000	946	23,186
Akita	1,317,000	1,345	30,622
Yamagata	1,315,000	1,266	14,029
Fukushima	2,065,000	1,359	34,427

SOURCE: SCAP Archives, Tōhoku Civil Affairs Region, box 2601.

One further factor in estimating the "Communist menace" in Fukushima should be mentioned. As a rural and conservative prefecture, its leaders did not suffer radicals lightly, and almost all labor disturbances were routinely laid to Communist influence and the activities of Communists. Some leftist writers also find it significant that Masuda Kaneshichi, Prime Minister Yoshida's Chief Cabinet Secretary, who two days after the Matsukawa wreck declared that it "had the same ideological undercurrent as the Mitaka case" thereby virtually insuring that the police would find Communists responsible for it, was a former governor of Fukushima prefecture. Of course, it is also possible that he was correct. He certainly had good reason to jump to that conclusion.

Throughout the first half of 1949 Fukushima witnessed a rising tide of violent labor incidents, which culminated in the

Taira and Matsukawa cases. The situation had begun to deteriorate at the end of 1948 when the chronically depressed coal industry began to cut excess and unskilled labor permanently from its payrolls, particularly in and around Taira city. This led to repeated clashes between police and Tanrō (Japan Federation of Coal Miners' Unions) and to frequent interventions by the Fukushima Military Government Team, an arm of the Eighth Army rather than of SCAP, to maintain order when the capabilities of the police were overburdened. Although the military government teams scattered around the country had officially only supervisory powers (rather than the ability to set policy), they were often closer to the Japanese people—where SCAP policy ultimately had to be implemented—than were the great "democratizers" sitting in Tokyo. However, the military government teams also had a remarkable ability to blunder into situations they did not fully understand.

After the first of the year SCAP had increased the size of the CIC (counterintelligence) detachment at Sendai and had established subdetachments at Wakamatsu, Kōriyama, and Taira in order to provide better intelligence on trends in the labor movement. At the same time, during February, the Fukushima prefectural government gave the Japanese police new powers to control demonstrations through passage of a "public peace ordinance" (kōan jōrei), an action that was bitterly opposed by labor and the Communist party and that led to demonstrations outside the prefectural assembly. Labor also, whether on the orders of the Communist party is unclear, joined together coal miners with railroad workers and electrical employees for the purpose of presenting the agents of the Dodge line with a united front. They did not plan a general strike, but they did plan to "struggle" against policies the Communists told them were designed to colonize Japan for America and which in any case would certainly make their harsh lives even more difficult.

The opening shot came on June 27 and 28 when the factory

union of Mitsubishi Seikō (steel), located in Aizu-Wakamatsu city, seized the plant manager and subjected him to a kangaroo court. Although the workers had genuine grievances, this particular action had all the earmarks of Communist revolutionary plotting, since it seemed to be a protest less against firings and low wages than against the revival of capitalism as such.

Two days later the scene shifted to the prefectural capital, Fukushima city. A mob some 330 strong occupied the visitor's gallery of the Prefectural Assembly building and hung six big red flags over the balcony and generally created an uproar. The chairman demanded that they leave, and then called the police. Four persons were arrested for violation of the "public peace ordinance." In the course of clearing the hall the police discovered that most of the participants came either from the National Railroad Workers' Union or from the Matsukawa factory of the Tōshiba Electric Company. This caused them to suspect that the "demo" involved collusion among Communist-dominated unions. When, on the same day, the news started to come in from Taira, they had no doubt about it.

Although not as well known as the Shimoyama, Mitaka, and Matsukawa cases, the Taira incident of June 30, 1949, was the closest thing to actual insurrection that occurred in Japan during 1949. Before it was over the "Taira incident" actually affected the cities of Sendai, Fukushima, Kōriyama, Uchigō, Nihonmatsu, Aizu-Wakamatsu, and Yumoto, in addition to the city of Taira. The Fukushima Military Government Team provided the spark that set it off, but the actual causes went much deeper. The true cause was the dismissal during June of 143 out of 500 members of the Yagō Coal Mine Workers' Union in Taira, including its chairman and vice-chairman, both of whom belonged to the Communist party. These fired workers were looking for a vent for their anger in a city already sullen and frustrated by economic conditions when members of the Fukushima Military Government Team arrived on a "routine inspection trip." The SCAP

Archives contain descriptions of what ensued from the chief of the Taira police and from Captain Jack Miller, adjutant of the Fukushima Military Government Team; and while they both agree in outline, there are interesting differences of nuance between them.[40]

It seems that back in January the Communist party had petitioned the police of Taira to put up a public bulletin board in front of Taira railroad station and that this request had been granted. (According to the police version the applicant for the bulletin board permit simply indicated that the sign was to be used for advertising, and the Iwaki District Committee of the Japanese Communist party took it over after it was erected.) This bulletin board was a wooden structure of the type seen around most Japanese railroad stations of the time to which were attached copies of Akahata, "wall newspapers," and Communist party notices. When officials of the Fukushima Military Government Team drove into the square in front of the station, they observed a fairly sizable crowd standing in front of the sign reading items on it and they concluded that it constituted an obstruction and a hazard to traffic. The permit for the bulletin board was not due to expire until July 24, but according to the police chief, the Fukushima Military Government Team told him to tell the people responsible for the sign to remove it (Captain Miller says that he requested that the sign be moved to another location). In any case, after the military visitors had left Taira, the chief of police told the local Communist party committee chairman to get rid of the bulletin board. He refused, saying that such an order was a violation of the occupation's directives

40. Police report: SCAP Archives, SCAP-GHQ, Government Section, Central Files, box 2975, file entitled "Fukushima Labor Disputes, 1949"; Miller report: SCAP Archives, Tōhoku Civil Affairs Region, box 2603, file entitled "Legal and Government." Miller's report, dated August 5, 1949, is in the form of a letter to Tōhoku Civil Affairs Region Headquarters in Sendai.

banning official interference with the activities of political parties.

About 3:00 P.M. on June 30, fifty to sixty Communists gathered, allegedly to protect their bulletin board, and then marched on the police station, where a free-for-all fistfight with thirty policemen developed. Hearing of the fight, an alleged four hundred miners rushed to join it, and the police were easily over-come. The police station was occupied, draped in red flags, and declared to be the office of the "people's police." The mob then entered the cell block, released two Communists, locked up the regular police, and stole the one and only usable firearm, a pistol, allowed by occupation authorities to be in the hands of the Taira police. By 10:00 P.M. the occupiers had broken all the windows in the place and they then withdrew.

This contrctemps was bad enough, but it was what ensued in other cities that really bothered the authorities. Upon hearing of the seizure of the Taira police station, the Fukushima Military Government Team and prefectural officials immediately wired to Fukushima, Sendai, and other cities asking for armed National Rural Police to recapture it. In all of these places, however, the National Railroad Workers' Union instantly launched a "move-ment to stop the advance of police reinforcements to Taira." At Nihonmatsu railroad workers opened the switches, and at Kōri-yama a crowd of four hundred workers rushed to the police sta-tion and surrounded it, preventing anyone from leaving. In Sendai the most spectacular event occurred. About two hundred armed cadets of the National Rural Police Academy marched to the railroad station to board a special train for Taira. However, the NRWU first stoned the train, then pulled the engineer down from his locomotive and locked the car doors from the inside to prevent rescuers from gaining access. When the police were finally transferred to trucks, the railroad workers used the rail-road's communications system to order the gates at railroad grade crossings closed all along the way to Taira, thereby blocking road traffic. Needless to say, by the time the reinforcements got to Taira there was nothing to do but let the local policemen out of their cells.

This amateur revolution-making backfired badly on the Communists. On July 2, the chief of the Fukushima National Rural Police, Arai Yutaka, stated to the press that insurrectionary conditions existed in both Fukushima city and Wakamatsu and that he was prepared to declare a state of emergency in the whole prefecture. He also retained in Fukushima the National Rural Police reinforcements sent from Sendai in order to deal with still another outbreak of violence. On July 2, two days before the first round of Japanese National Railroads firings, a large group of railroad workers from the Fukushima branch and local of the NRWU marched on the office of the Japanese National Railroads superintendent for the Fukushima Subdivision, dragged this official down the stairs, and tried to obtain from him a definite promise that "absolutely nobody will be fired" (*kubikiri wa zettai ni shinai*). The workers occupied the superintendent's office for twenty-four hours until armed police removed them and arrested ten, including Suzuki Makoto, Takeda Hisashi, Honda Noboru, and Okada Toramatsu, all of whom were subsequently indicted as conspirators in the Matsukawa case. The police also took this occasion to raid the offices of the NRWU, where they obtained a good deal of information that became quite useful to them six weeks later. As a result of this incident Prime Minister Yoshida threatened to declare a state of emergency throughout the nation.

The turmoil, however, did not stop. On July 6, Shimoyama's mangled body was discovered; and on July 7, the Fukushima railroad workers made the headlines again. At Date railroad station in the northern suburbs of Fukushima city, on the Tōhoku Main Line, about thirty railroad workers took justice into their own hands. They maintained that the stationmaster and his assistant had been confiscating black market rice and then releasing it for shipment only after a bribe had been paid. Accordingly, the railroad men held a kangaroo court and beat their two prisoners. On July 16, the police arrested twenty-one NRWU members for this act, including once again Saitō Yuki, Takeda Hisashi, and Okada Toramatsu, all leaders of the railroad union in Fukushima and all fired in the manpower cuts. More important in retrospect, the police also arrested a nineteen-year-old chimpira (an "urchin," or juvenile delinquent), Akama Katsumi, who had worked, until he was fired, as a member of a JNR track-maintenance gang. Akama was released on August 1, when the union put up his ¥10,000 bail; and this turned out to be important, for it involved Akama with the union leadership. Before the year was out Akama Katsumi would have become nationally famous as the key to breaking the Matsukawa case.

At least 280 people, virtually all of them Communists, were arrested in the four main Fukushima incidents that preceded the Matsukawa case—the Prefectural Assembly Red Flag case (Kenkai Akahata Jiken), the Taira case, the Fukushima Subdivision Superintendent's Office case (Fukkan Jiken), and the Date Station case. Those arrested for involvement in the Taira incident were charged with sedition, and of all these cases it was the Taira incident and its coordinated activities that most alarmed the Diet and the public. The Diet created a special investigating committee, chaired by Hanamura Shirō (later to become minister of justice in the Hatoyama cabinet), and this committee on July 27 concluded that these incidents had been instigated by the Communists and that they had been field tests of the party's new violent tactics. This was the first time in postwar Japan that a legal political party had been openly blamed for fomenting social unrest. It was not, however, an unpopular conclusion. The press repeated it daily in front-page articles and editorially, and the people accepted it as the most plausible explanation. There is, moreover, virtually no doubt that Communists were in fact responsible for carrying out these actions. The question is whether they also engineered the big one yet to come.

At the same time that the Fukushima NRWU and the coal miners were reacting violently to the layoffs, the relatively small factory of Tōshiba, located south of Fukushima city at Matsukawa, had also had its troubles. The workers there did not know what was going to happen to them now that the parent company was both reorganizing under the orders of the Holding Company Liquidation Commission and trying to cut back its payroll in order to become more efficient. Sugiura Saburō, head of the local union, believed that the Matsukawa plant was going to be closed. As a matter of fact the Matsukawa works were in the process of being reconstituted as an independent satellite (kokaisha, literally "child company") of Tōshiba. This reorganization was finally completed on February 21, 1950, when the Matsukawa plant took on the only barely disguised new name Kitashiba Electric Company (Kitashiba Denki K. K.), capitalized at ¥15 million, and manufacturing electric appliances and motors.[41] Only the "tō" of Tōshiba, meaning "east," had been changed to "kita," meaning "north," and no Japanese had any doubt that the new firm was closely affiliated with Tōshiba, as in fact it was and is today.

The manpower cut in preparation for this reorganization was carried out, like many others, in July of 1949. The Tōshiba plant at Matsukawa had only 318 employees in its company union, and on July 15 the management passed out dismissal notices to 32 workers. Over the ensuing month negotiations continued between management and the union over this cut, and on August 16, the union voted to carry out a one-day protest strike the following day. It was not a very militant union, but its leader, Sugiura Saburō, was a Communist party member, and he was also one of the 32 who had been fired. As things turned out, however, neither supervision of the one-day strike nor losing his job would

41. SCAP Monograph No. 25, "Deconcentration of Economic Power," appendix 1-B, "Final Reorganization of the Tokyo Shibaura Electric Company."

be of much concern to Sugiura. For on August 17 something happened that would affect him for the rest of his life. Early on the morning when the Tōshiba plant was scheduled to be shut down by a strike, and only a mile up the tracks toward Fukushima from the factory, the Matsukawa incident took place.

Chapter 3

Matsukawa

A GENERATION and more ago attacks on and sabotage of trains were a familiar device of political extremists, just as airplane hijackings and bomb explosions became during the 1960s and 1970s. During August 1931 in Germany, for example, the destruction of the Frankfurt–Berlin express on which Chancellor Heinrich Brüning was supposed to be riding led to violent recriminations against the Communist party, which allegedly had ordered it. Similarly, in the Far East, Japanese military conspirators blew up the train of Chang Tso-lin in 1928 in order to replace him as their Manchurian puppet, and in 1931 they used the destruction of the tracks of the South Manchurian Railroad at Mukden as a pretext for their seizure of all of northeast China. It was not until after World War II that it was proven that the Japanese Army itself had masterminded both of these incidents. The Matsukawa case thus constitutes another famous instance of political train-wrecking, and its perpetrators, like those of its predecessors, are not necessarily to be discovered among those individuals with the greatest opportunity and most apparent motive for carrying it out.

The reconstruction of the crime presented in this chapter is based on the confessions of eight of the twenty workers indicted by the procurators, particularly the confession of Akama Katsumi on the actual execution of the sabotage, and of Ōta Shōji on the conspiracies that preceded it.[1] Juridically speaking, these confessions have no probative value—that is to say, they are not true. All of the defendants in the case have been judged not guilty by the Japanese courts, and this renders their confessions null and void. Nonetheless, courts do not decide historical truth, and those who study history are obliged only to record and try to understand courtroom verdicts, not necessarily to believe them. It is possible that the actions described in this chapter never took place; it is also possible that they did. In any case, this chapter describes the way most Japanese saw the case for more than a decade, and even today the most ardent supporters of the Matsukawa defendants—the thousands of Communists, fellow travelers, trade unionists, and students who make annual on-site inspections of the miles of railroad track between Fukushima and Matsukawa—use copies of the "Akama Confession"

1. I have relied primarily on the complete collection of all pretrial statements of the defendants compiled in 1961 for the Sendai retrial. See Sendai Kōtō Saibansho Dai Ichi Keijibu (Sendai High Court, First Criminal Affairs Division), *Matsukawa jiken sashimodoshi-shin kōhan shiryō* (Matsukawa Case Retrial Documentary Materials), *Kōhan mae hikokunin kyōjutsu chōsho* (Record of Defendants' Pretrial Depositions) (Sendai, 1961), Vol. I (487 pp.). Other useful collections include: (1) Matsukawa Jiken Shiryō Kankō Kai (Committee to Publish the Materials of the Matsukawa Case), "Akama hikoku no jihaku" (Defendant Akama's Confession), *Matsukawa jiken shiryōshū* (Collected Materials on the Matsukawa Case), No. 2 (Tokyo, April 1, 1954) (381 pp.); and (2) (Same source), "Ōta jihaku to sono kaibō" (The Ōta Confession and Its Dissection), *Matsukawa jiken shiryōshū*, No. 5 (Tokyo, June 1, 1955) (244 pp.). For other related materials consulted, see the Bibliography.

(after 1963 with the words "so called" in front of it) as a guide-book to the case's many memorable spots and landmarks.[2]

Before turning to a reconstruction of the crime based on Akama's and Ōta's confessions, a brief sketch of the twenty defendants may help the reader to keep track of the case's many participants. There are four distinct groups among the accused: a total of nine leaders of the Fukushima prefectural branch and the Fukushima city local of the National Railroad Workers' Union (NRWU); Akama Katsumi, a juvenile delinquent; a total of nine leaders and members of the Tōshiba Matsukawa factory union; and Satō Hajime, a representative of the Federation of Tōshiba Unions, who arrived in Matsukawa on August 11, 1949, from Tokyo to assist in the struggle against the layoffs. The ages given are those at the time of arrest.

RAILROAD WORKERS

Takeda Hisashi, age thirty-one: A native of Fukushima, Takeda had been an employee of the Japanese National Railroads since 1938, except for two and a half years served in the army during World War II. On September 15, 1948, he was elected chairman of the executive committee of the NRWU's Fukushima prefectural branch (*shibu*), having jurisdiction over the three NRWU locals (*bunkai*) in the prefecture, those at Fukushima city, Kōriyama, and Wakamatsu. On July 20, 1949, he was fired by the Japanese National Railroads (JNR), and on July 21 he was arrested for his part in the occupation of the Fukushima

---

2. See, for example, Aichi Ken Matsukawa Jiken Taisaku Kyōgikai (Aichi Prefecture Matsukawa Case Countermeasures Council), *Me de miru Matsukawa jiken, Akama jihaku o chūshin to shite* (The Matsukawa Case Before One's Eyes; According to the Akama Confession) (Nagoya, 1959); and Sōhyō (The General Council of Japanese Labor Unions), *Matsukawa jiken genchi chōsa no tebiki* (Guidebook to the Matsukawa Case On-site Inspection) (Tokyo, 1957).

Subdivision superintendent's office earlier that month. On August 4, he was released on bail, and he returned immediately to active leadership of the railroad workers in the prefecture. He was a member of the Japanese Communist party.

Suzuki Makoto, age twenty-nine: Suzuki, who had worked for the railroad without interruption since 1937, was chief of the Fukushima city local of the NRWU and simultaneously chairman of the Japanese Communist party committee for the district in which Fukushima city is located.

Okada Toramatsu, age twenty-three: Okada held the key posts of chief secretary to the NRWU prefectural branch and chief secretary of the Fukushima Regional Trade Union Congress, the federation representing all unions in the prefecture. Like Takeda and Suzuki, he was out on bail during August, having been arrested in the Superintendent's Office case.

Abe Ichiji, age twenty-six: A full-time clerk for the NRWU branch and local, Abe had worked for the railroad since 1939. Like other railroad defendants, his active railroad experience was as a freight dispatcher and station ticket-collector rather than in a job requiring technical skills.

Ninomiya Yutaka, age twenty-eight: He was one of twelve members of the executive committee that directed the NRWU in Fukushima prefecture (of the twelve executive committee members, five—Takeda, Okada, Ninomiya, Honda, and Saitō— were indicted in the Matsukawa case). After being fired by the JNR on July 4, Ninomiya got a job with the Fukushima office of the Northeast Cultural Sales Company (Tōhoku Bunka Shōji K. K.) of Sendai, a general sundries and supplies distributing firm. Takeda found the job for him.

Honda Noboru, age twenty-three: Honda was young enough to have served only two months in the navy before the war ended. He was a postwar graduate of the railroad dispatcher's school in Sendai. Within the union he was a member of the branch executive committee and chief of the Education and Propaganda Section.

Saitō Yuki, age twenty-nine: Also a member of the branch executive committee and head of the union's Cultural Section, Saitō had had considerable war experience and was receiving outpatient care from the railroad hospital for malaria at the time of his arrest. Few details of his past are known because he alone, of all the defendants, consistently told the police, procurators, and judges to mind their own business and delivered harangues against "Yoshida fascists," "American imperialists," and so forth, during his interrogations. His statements in court and his later appeal documents reveal a man of considerable anger and of rather more deeply held Communist convictions than those of many other defendants.

Takahashi Haruo, age twenty-five: A railroad worker throughout the war, particularly on the Ōu line, Takahashi had been married only a little more than a year and had a five-months-old daughter at the time of his arrest. He was working at Niwazaka station and was a member of the Fukushima local when he was fired in the first JNR personnel cut. There was one other matter in Takahashi's past—the fact that he had been mildly crippled in a railroad mishap—which was to become crucial to the Matsukawa case several years after the first trial, but this was not public knowledge during 1949.

Katō Kenzō, age nineteen: A former telegrapher in the Fukushima superintendent's office, Katō was perhaps the best educated of the railroad defendants. After being laid off in the first reduction in force, he went to work as an assistant to Okada Toramatsu in the prefectural labor federation. His job was to write for and deliver Rōdō sensen (Labor Front), the organ of Sanbetsu, to the various union offices in the Fukushima area. Because of his inside knowledge of train scheduling up and down the Tōhoku Main Line, he is said to have played a key role in the conspiracy.

AKAMA

Akama Katsumi, age nineteen: Born in Fukushima on August 13, 1930, Akama at the age of five accompanied his parents to Manchuria where his father had taken a job with the South Manchurian Railroad. In 1938, his parents sent him back to Fukushima to receive a standard education and to live with his grandmother, Akama Mina, who also played an important part in the Matsukawa case. After graduating from elementary school in March 1945, Akama continued to live with his grandmother in the Kuroiwa section of southern Fukushima city. Kuroiwa, the site of a minor Buddhist temple, was soon to become famous throughout Japan because of what allegedly took place at the temple on the night of August 16, 1949.

From 1945 until July 4, 1949, when he was fired, Akama worked as a common laborer for the Nagaigawa Track Maintenance Crew of the JNR. This unit was responsible for care of the Tōhoku Main Line track between the Nagaigawa Signal Station and Kanayagawa, near Akama's home and also just directly north of the site of the Matsukawa wreck. During 1949 his father, who had returned from Manchuria, was working in a local factory, and his mother was a school cook. Akama himself, after the railroad let him go, got a job in a bakery. At the time of his arrest he was under suspicion for rape, indicted for participating in the Date station kangaroo-court case, and awaiting indictment for theft. He did not know personally, and was unknown to, the leaders of his NRWU local until August 1, 1949, when they put up the money to bail him out of jail following the Date incident. He was not a member of the Communist party.

TŌSHIBA WORKERS

Sugiura Saburō, age forty-eight: The head of the factory union at Tōshiba's Matsukawa plant, Sugiura was the oldest and most mature of all the defendants and soon became their natural leader during the long years in prison. Some younger defendants have suggested that he had an *oyabun-kobun* ("fictive parent-child") relationship with both his union followers and his fellow defendants—that is, the sort of leader-follower relationship that characterized some criminal gangs and labor bosses in both pre-war and postwar Japan and that has been strongly criticized by modern Japanese as "feudalistic."

Sugiura was born in Tokyo, March 25, 1901, and was studying for college entrance exams when, in 1923, he was called up for compulsory military service. He never returned to college but rather, in 1925, went to work for the old Shibaura Manufacturing Company in Tokyo before it merged with Tokyo Electric to become the modern Tōshiba. He worked continuously for Tōshiba until the company fired him on August 9, 1949. In 1945, he transferred from Tokyo to Matsukawa, and in March 1946 he became head of the local union. His local consisted of 318 employees, of whom 32 were let go in the company's 1949 reorganization, including himself. Sugiura was not a longtime Communist, having joined the party only in February 1949, although twenty years later he liked to suggest that it was their "iron discipline" as Communists that saw the defendants through their ordeal. Differing from most of the other defendants, Sugiura was not a native of Tōhoku and today lives in Yokohama.

Ōta Shōji, age twenty-three: Vice-chairman of the Matsukawa plant union, Ōta was Sugiura's deputy. There is some evidence that Ōta was not very stable emotionally, and although his confession was crucial to the prosecution's case, it was so inconsistent and confused that it is unlikely it could ever have stood up in court without the confessions of Akama and others to reinforce it.

Satō Shiroji, age twenty-three: A native of Fukushima, Satō worked at the Yokosuka Naval Shipyard and studied electrical machinery in Yokohama during the last years of the war. After returning to Matsukawa in 1946, he was employed at Tōshiba and became a member of the union's executive committee. He was not fired in the company's personnel reduction.

Ōuchi Shōzō, age eighteen: An undistinguished Tōshiba employee from nearby Nihonmatsu, Ōuchi was fired by the company on August 12. He, together with Sugiura, Ōta, and Hamazaki, had applied to join the Japanese Communist party in early 1949 after being encouraged to do so by Suzuki Makoto of the NRWU and by Satō Shiroji of their own union.

Hamazaki Futao, age twenty: Hamazaki, who had moved from Tokyo to Matsukawa during 1944, was a graduate of a Tokyo electrical trade school located in the Hitotsubashi district of the capital. He worked at the Tōshiba plant from 1944 until he was let go on August 15, 1949. He was a candidate member of the Japanese Communist party.

Kikuchi Takeshi, age eighteen: A native of Fukushima, Kikuchi worked at Tōshiba Matsukawa from May 1946 until August 15, 1949, when he was fired. He had participated in the Prefectural Assembly Red Flag incident and was a member of the Communist youth organization. On September 18, 1949, he was investigated by the police for the alleged theft of ten packets of cigarettes from the Tōshiba plant workers' dormitory, where he lived. He was released on September 18, and was rearrested on October 8 as an accomplice in the Matsukawa case.

Nikaidō Takeo, age twenty-four: A highly skilled electrician, Nikaidō joined the main plant of Tōshiba in Tsurumi (Tokyo), in May 1940 when he was only fifteen years old. He transferred to Matsukawa in October 1947. A member of the Japanese Communist party since August 1948, he was fired by the company a year later, on August 13, 1949. Together with Nikaidō Sonoko, he was charged with participation in the train-wrecking conspiracy and also with framing false alibis for the Tōshiba participants.

Nikaidō Sonoko, alias Sasaki Sonoko, alias Yokoya Sonoko, age twenty-five: The sole woman defendant, Nikaidō Sonoko was not related in any way to Nikaidō Takeo. She was born on

March 20, 1924, in Hokkaido and received at birth her true father's name of Sasaki. When she was three years old her mother and father were permanently separated, and she was raised by her mother. When Sonoko was fourteen, her mother remarried, and Sasaki Sonoko adopted the family name of her stepfather, Nikaidō, the name she was using at the time of her arrest. As one of the unforeseen outcomes of the great political trials of the early 1950s, Nikaidō Sonoko met and married Yokoya Takeo, one of the freed Communist party defendants in the Mitaka case. They met in 1950, when Yokoya came to Fukushima to give comradely encouragement to the Matsukawa defendants in their struggle against the police, and they were married three years later, in January 1953, while Sonoko was out on bail. Their life together has not been easy; as a "Mitaka defendant" Takeo found it hard to get work, even though exonerated by the courts, and this cloud over his reputation was compounded by his marriage to a "Matsukawa defendant." Today they have two sons and are living in Kunitachi, a suburb of Tokyo.

At the time of the Matsukawa wreck Nikaidō Sonoko had been fired from her secretarial job at Tōshiba but was continuing in her concurrent position as secretary of the plant union. According to her own statements, she joined the Communist party in February 1949 after being deeply moved by a speech given by the party's secretary general, Tokuda Kyūichi, that month in Fukushima. She participated in both the Prefectural Assembly Red Flag and JNR Superintendent's Office incidents and was known to the police as a radical.

Kobayashi Genzaburō, age twenty: A member of the Tōshiba plant union and an apprentice machine operator, Kobayashi was born and raised in Matsukawa. He was too young to have served in the war, though his elder brother was killed in combat. Kobayashi was not among the thirty-two fired in the Tōshiba reorganization.

SATŌ HAJIME

Satō Hajime, age twenty-eight: Generally speaking, biographies of workingmen are not particularly edifying, since the chief thing that workers do is to spend their lives working at their jobs. This was not true of Satō Hajime, however. He was the most intellectually aware and insightful of the twenty Matsukawa defendants, and his involvement in the case turned him into an accomplished writer. Of his many published works two stand out: an autobiography that was included in a collection of five distinguished autobiographies entitled *Warera Taishōkko* (*We, Children of the Taishō Era*)—the other contributors were Nakasone Yasuhiro, a member of the cabinet in the 1960s and 1970s; Mori Mitsuko, an actress; Ishii Hisashi, a stockbroker; and Minakami Tsutomu, a novelist—and a book, entitled *Hikoku* (*Defendants*), which is perhaps the most revealing thing written about the lives of the Matsukawa defendants during their fourteen-year court battle.[3] Although the Matsukawa case changed his life and brought him close to death, either on the gallows or from the tuberculosis he suffered in prison, Satō Hajime not only endured those bitter years but commented on them with candor and courage.

Born December 10, 1921, in Ibaraki prefecture, Satō received only an elementary education in Tokyo and at the age of sixteen went to work for Hitachi Precision Instruments, transferring two years later to Tōshiba. During the war he served two years in the navy in Hokkaido and Karafuto as a communications specialist. From February 1946 until July 28, 1949, the date on which he was fired, Satō worked at the Tsurumi plant of Tōshiba, located in the heavy industrial area between Tokyo and Yokohama. From the beginning of 1947 he was both a mem-

3. *Hikoku* (Tokyo: Heibonsha, 1958); *Warera Taishōkko* (Tokyo: Tokuma Shoten "Human Books," 1961).

ber of the executive committee of the Tsurumi factory union and a national committeeman on the executive board of the Federation of Tōshiba Unions, whose headquarters were also located at Tsurumi. When the Tōshiba layoffs began in July 1949, Satō argued strongly within the national committee that an organizer should be sent to assist the workers at the Matsukawa plant. Although he knew nothing of the situation at Matsukawa and had only met Sugiura briefly at union conferences, Satō got the job because other union leaders more familiar with the Matsukawa plant were ill. When he arrived at Matsukawa station on August 11, 1949, he realized that he did not even know where the factory was. On asking directions, he was astonished to learn that it was immediately adjacent to the station, a mere two-minutes' walk. While Satō was none too familiar with the labor situation at Matsukawa, company officials and the police were all too aware of his arrival—of the presence of an "outside agitator" in their midst—as Satō would soon discover. He was, of course, a member of the Japanese Communist party, although he claims always to have held certain basic mental reservations about the program of the party.

These twenty individuals were the defendants in the Matsukawa case; they may or may not have been the people responsible for planning and executing the wrecking of passenger train number 412 on the morning of August 17, 1949. The courts have decided that they were not, but the accuracy of that verdict is a question we shall delay until much later in this book. Of the twenty, eight—Akama, Hamazaki, Ōta, Kobayashi, Kikuchi, Ōuchi, Katō and Nikaidō Sonoko—confessed to the crime or otherwise made extremely damaging statements to the police.

Fifteen of the defendants were regular members of the Japanese Communist party, and four others, Hamazaki, Kobayashi, Ōuchi, and Kikuchi, had a candidate-member or youth-league affiliation; only Akama was not a Communist. All of the railroad workers and all but Satō Shiroji and Kobayashi among the Tōshiba workers had been recently fired (Abe Ichiji had been let go by the JNR a year before the wreck). Even though occupation authorities had stated that lack of seniority and incompetence were to be the main criteria in laying off excess workers, it is clear that within this group many were fired only because they were union leaders and Communists. By 1950, SCAP had acknowledged that purging the union movement of Communists was an objective equal to economic reconstruction and was openly describing its campaign as the "red purge." During 1949, however, the removal of Communists was an important, but still unstated, lesser included goal of the economic stabilization policies. Communists were being fired because it was thought, on good evidence, that they were manipulating the union movement in order to foment revolution. The sabotage at Matsukawa seemed to confirm this point of view: who else but Communist revolutionaries would threaten the lives of innocent passengers in order to make a political point? As Sybille Bedford has said, "All the evidence seemed to point in a certain direction." Let us therefore see what the evidence—the confessions—revealed.

During the first weeks of August 1949, the offices of the Fukushima branch of the NRWU were the scene of much hectic, if also deeply frustrated, activity. Occupying an old frame building situated on the southeast corner of the railroad yard of the Fukushima city station, the branch headquarters provided desks for its own staff as well as for the Fukushima city local of the NRWU, the prefectural trade union congress, and the Fukushima branch of the Democratic Youth League, in addition to housing a conference table and several cots for use by night-duty station and train crews. Back in April the NRWU national convention had resolved that laid-off railroad workers would be retained as members of the union, and the men in Fukushima who had lost their jobs in July continued to call at the union office, seeking information on the campaigns to resist economic

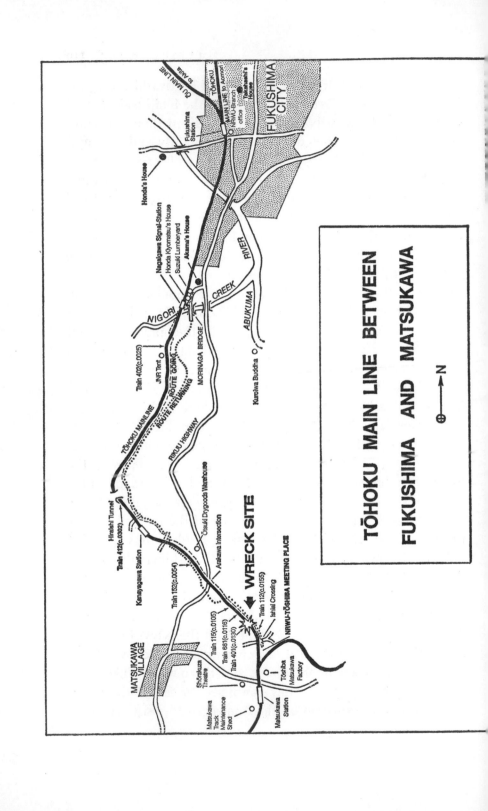

TŌHOKU MAIN LINE BETWEEN
FUKUSHIMA AND MATSUKAWA

N

retrenchment, repaying bail money if they had been arrested in one of the earlier demonstrations, talking about the police's blaming the Communist party for the Mitaka wreck, or just having a cup of tea and gossiping with their comrades about the hard times.

In these daily gatherings there was a good deal of ominous muttering and loose talk. For example, a former railroad official in a conversation with Takeda Hisashi and Suzuki Makoto on August 5 recalled Suzuki's saying, "Before long there's likely to be a big accident." Similarly a man who came around collecting for newspaper subscriptions remembers union men saying to him, "Be on the lookout. Before long we'll come up with something big." Most witnesses who came forward after the Matsukawa wreck with stories of this kind said that they thought the remarks probably reflected the workers' deep grievances rather than a determination to resort to sabotage.

The railroad workers contended that they were suffering at the hands of the Yoshida government and SCAP because of ideological and political differences, not because of Japan's economic needs, and they said that they wanted either reinstatement or revenge. Moreover, they believed the NRWU executive committee's propaganda that budget cuts on the railroad would endanger safety and lead to accidents, and they were therefore always telling visitors from the press about declining maintenance, hazardous conditions, and so forth. During August they were also mad about the police reprisals for the demonstration at the railroad subdivision superintendent's office and the Date station incident. The workers thought that arrests for these actions, particularly the charge of sedition in the Taira case, were illegal and that they themselves had done nothing more than exercise the rights so loudly proclaimed by SCAP as theirs in a "democratic" Japan. As for the Date incident, they argued that this was merely an instance of the union taking care of two of its own members, the stationmaster and his assistant, who were corrupt.

Thus, a vague desire to *make* the prediction about the danger of accidents come true may already have existed when, on August 12, something happened to galvanize the prefectural NRWU leadership into renewed action. Watanabe Ikuzō, vice-chairman under Takeda of the union's branch committee and one of the key men in the Fukushima labor movement, was arrested and jailed by the Kōriyama city police for violating the public peace ordinance. He had only been released from jail on August 4 (together with Takeda and others) after having been arrested for participating in the seizure of the superintendent's office, and this new arrest seemed a certain sign that the police had it in for him. On the morning of the twelfth Takeda Hisashi called a conference at branch headquarters to discuss Watanabe's arrest and the actions that had to be taken to obtain his release. In attendance at this conference were branch executive committeemen Saitō Yuki, Honda Noboru, and Ninomiya Yutaka, plus the Fukushima local's chairman, Suzuki Makoto, the union's chief clerk, Abe Ichiji, and the regional union federation's secretary, Okada Toramatsu.

These seven men decided to put up some more of the union's diminishing funds to bail out Watanabe and also to launch a counterattack against their supposed oppressors. Suzuki Makoto, who emerges from the Matsukawa confessions as the leader of the conspiracy on the railroad side, proposed that they engineer a train wreck similar to the one that had occurred at Mitaka, and that they either try to frame local Mindō leaders for it or, failing that, make certain that they themselves would not be held responsible. Such a wreck, he argued, would show the police and the government that they could not arrest railroad union leaders and still keep the trains running. As "propaganda of the deed" it might also contribute to the forthcoming peaceful revolution being announced by the Communist party. All the others present agreed with Suzuki's proposal, but felt that careful planning and nonrailroad allies would be needed to bring it off. They suggested approaching the union at Tōshiba's Matsu-kawa plant—which had cooperated before with the NRWU in protest demonstrations—to request the assistance of some of its members. From evidence obtained later in the confessions of lesser Tōshiba participants, it seems that Suzuki, who was con-currently chairman of the Fukushima district committee of the Japanese Communist party, was probably able to assure his rail-road colleagues at this meeting that Sugiura, head of the union at Tōshiba, would respond favorably to such a request. Suzuki and Sugiura, who knew each other through the party and whom the prosecution would accuse of being the two masterminds be-hind the conspiracy, had apparently discussed before August 12 the desirability of an action of the sort now recommended.

The railroad workers' meeting broke up with a decision to meet again the following day with a Tōshiba representative present. Immediately after this meeting on the morning of August 12, Abe Ichiji telephoned to the Matsukawa plant and reached Sugiura. This was the first of the "liaison conspiracies" (renraku bōgi), the crucial gatherings that linked the two entirely separate unions into the plot to wreck a train. Abe simply asked Sugiura to come to the union offices at Fukushima station around noon on the following day for an important meeting. He did not say what the meeting was about.

At this time Sugiura was extremely busy at the Tōshiba plant. He was engaged in almost daily collective bargaining ses-sions with management over the layoffs, and he was preparing for demonstrations and a possible strike in response to the layoffs and for the eventuality that Tōshiba might decide to shut down the Matsukawa works altogether. In addition he had an organizer from his national union headquarters present in Matsukawa to help and advise (perhaps also to observe) him, namely, Satō Hajime, who had arrived on August 11. On top of all this Sugiura was quite disturbed by his knowledge that the Tōshiba plant managers were in contact with the Fukushima police and with

SCAP's CIC (Counter-Intelligence Corps), and that they were apparently ready to call for police assistance if the union should offer the slightest resistance to the personnel cuts. Sugiura had already posted union lookouts to warn him of the possible approach of the police.

MATSUKAWA CASE CONSPIRACY MEETINGS *
(According to the Prosecution in the First Trial)

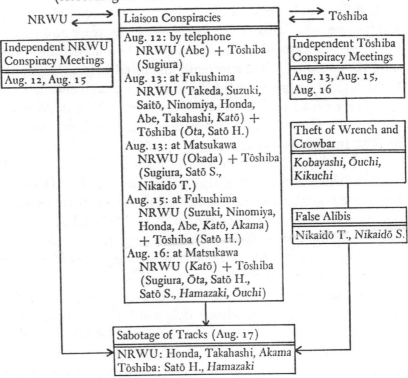

NRWU ⇄	Liaison Conspiracies	⇄ Tōshiba
Independent NRWU Conspiracy Meetings	Aug. 12: by telephone NRWU (Abe) + Tōshiba (Sugiura)	**Independent Tōshiba Conspiracy Meetings**
Aug. 12, Aug. 15	Aug. 13: at Fukushima NRWU (Takeda, Suzuki, Saitō, Ninomiya, Honda, Abe, Takahashi, *Katō*) + Tōshiba (*Ōta*, Satō H.)	Aug. 13, Aug. 15, Aug. 16
	Aug. 13: at Matsukawa NRWU (Okada) + Tōshiba (Sugiura, Satō S., Nikaidō T.)	**Theft of Wrench and Crowbar**
		Kobayashi, *Ōuchi*, Kikuchi
	Aug. 15: at Fukushima NRWU (Suzuki, Ninomiya, Honda, Abe, *Katō*, Akama) + Tōshiba (Satō H.)	**False Alibis**
	Aug. 16: at Matsukawa NRWU (*Katō*) + Tōshiba (Sugiura, *Ōta*, Satō H., Satō S., *Hamazaki*, *Ōuchi*)	*Nikaidō T.*, *Nikaidō S.*

Sabotage of Tracks (Aug. 17)
NRWU: Honda, Takahashi, Akama
Tōshiba: Satō H., *Hamazaki*

* Italics = defendants who made confessions.

When Abe Ichiji called from Fukushima, Sugiura said that he could not get away but that he would send a substitute. In fact, he sent two: his second-in-command at Matsukawa, Ōta Shōji, and his new associate from the ultraradical Tōshiba union headquarters, Satō Hajime. According to Ōta's later confessions, on the morning of the thirteenth he and Satō caught a train from Matsukawa (the time of this train is controversial) and attended the meeting called for noon that day by the NRWU leaders. Others present were Takeda, Suzuki, Saitō, Ninomiya, Honda, Abe, Takahashi Haruo, Katō Kenzō, and a man who was not a railroad worker, Honda Yoshihiro, the Fukushima correspondent for *Akahata* (*Red Flag*), the newspaper of the Communist party. Okada Toramatsu, who had attended the previous day's session, was not present for reasons that will become clear in a moment.

Takeda began the meeting by saying that Yoshida's policies were ruining the country and that the government would willingly allow the masses to starve to death. "What means of retaliation do we who've been laid off have against Yoshida's policies?" he asked (these direct quotations are recorded in Ōta's confessions). Suzuki answered, "The [Communist] party is trying to pin the Mitaka wreck on Mindō. If we're also able to wreck a train and put the blame on Yoshida's policies we'll win the esteem of all our [party] comrades." Others agreed that here was a proposal for meaningful retaliation against the ruling capitalist class: cause a wreck similar to the one that had occurred at Mitaka. The conspirators settled on it in principle and decided to meet again two days later to draw up a detailed plan of action and to make assignments to the people who would be asked to carry out the actual sabotage. Meanwhile, Ōta and Satō were to report back these decisions to Sugiura and to begin lining up some of the men that would be required. The meeting broke up with Saitō swearing them all to lifelong secrecy.

Okada did not attend the August 13 "liaison conspiracy" because he had to go to Kōriyama on union business. En route, however, he stopped off at Matsukawa about 1:00 P.M. and communicated directly with Sugiura on what had obviously already been agreed upon by the NRWU leaders. Okada met with Sugiura, Satō Shiroji, and Nikaidō Takeo (all three members of

the union's executive committee) in the union office, a small
building located within the Tōshiba plant grounds between the
large Yasaka dormitory, where many employees ate and lived, and
a modest Shintō shrine called Yasaka Jinja, situated on a small
hill directly behind the factory to the east. He told them about
the idea of derailing a train and obtained their assent to cooperate
in carrying it out. Sugiura allegedly entered into the conspiracy
because he thought that such an incident would distract the
police and keep them so preoccupied that they would not have
time to interfere in the Tōshiba struggles. According to all
accounts, he genuinely believed that management would try to
have him and any others who joined him arrested if the union
called a strike.

About two o'clock that same afternoon and immediately following the talk between the Tōshiba union leaders and their
visitor from the railroads, Nikaidō Takeo called Hamazaki, Ōuchi,
Kobayashi, and Kikuchi to the union office. These young workers
were the ones selected by the senior plotters on the Tōshiba side
to obtain the required tools and to help in actually sabotaging
the tracks. Nikaidō spoke directly to them about the plan to
wreck a train and asked for their participation, to which they
assented by nodding their heads. The confessers did not remember clearly later whether Okada and Sugiura were still present in
the room when this request was made to them, but they believed
that they were. Ōuchi later said that he was "dragged into this
case because I was a member of the Japanese Communist party
and had to listen to Sugiura and other leaders," and Hamazaki
strongly implied that Sugiura played the role of oya ("fictive
parent") in relations with his younger employees. Kikuchi explained his involvement this way: "I was taken into this conspiracy by accident. Back in April I had stolen some cigarettes
from Itō Hana, a woman cook at Yasaka dormitory who is a
friend of Sugiura's. I had also stolen some tools from the factory.
Sugiura knew all about these incidents, and I felt I was picked

to participate in the conspiracy because of the things I'd done. I had to say 'yes' to anything Sugiura told me to do." Kobayashi, who had not been fired by Tōshiba, said that he simply went along with his close friends, particularly Hamazaki.

About 5:30 that evening (August 13), Ōta and Satō returned from Fukushima and closeted themselves with Sugiura in Yasaka dormitory. They reported on the meeting at NRWU headquarters, and Sugiura in turn told them of Okada's visit and his decision to participate in the plot. Sugiura told Satō that he would have to attend the August 15 meeting by himself because Ōta would be needed at Matsukawa for the major collective bargaining session scheduled for that date. Sometime later that evening Satō Hajime and Nikaidō Takeo conferred about Nikaidō's progress in selecting other men for the conspiracy. During the following day, August 14, Satō followed up Nikaidō's initial invitation to Ōuchi with a little persuading of his own because the latter seemed to be wavering in his decision to participate.

On the same day (August 13) that the Tōshiba union leaders began selecting the Matsukawa contingent for the conspiracy, Abe Ichiji, the railroad workers' chief clerk, went recruiting in Fukushima. In order to sabotage the railroad tracks the plotters needed at least one man who knew something about tracks or who had some experience working on them. Abe thought he knew just the right man: Akama Katsumi, a former member of the JNR's Nagaigawa Track Maintenance Unit, who was indebted to the union local because it had put up ¥10,000 for his bail after he was arrested in the Date station case. Akama himself says in one of his confessions that it was his inability to repay the bail money that established the union's hold over him. Abe sent for Akama on the thirteenth and told him to be at the branch headquarters at about 11:00 A.M. on August 15. Akama agreed to come.

The "liaison conspiracy" meeting on August 15 was the most important of the series since it actually set the conspiracy in motion. When Akama arrived at the NRWU offices shortly after eleven o'clock, he found Suzuki, Ninomiya, Honda, Abe, and Katō already seated, examining a railroad schedule. Suzuki chaired the meeting. Abe spoke first to Akama, explaining to him that the date they had chosen for the wreck, the next to last night of the Bon matsuri ("Bon festival," described below), would produce so many suspects for the police that nobody would think that railroad workers had done it. He then asked Akama to participate in the sabotage activities. Akama confessed later that he wanted to say no (iya) but could not because of his indebtedness to the union; he therefore replied to Abe, "I'll go along" (ikimasu).

The date that they had already selected for the wreck was sometime after midnight the following night, August 16–17. This was right at the end of the three-day (August 15–17) Bon festival, the annual Buddhist All Souls' Day, or festival of the dead, which, together with New Year's, is one of the two most important holidays in Japan. Bon is a time when families hold reunions, visit ancestral graves, and offer up prayers and food before ancestral tablets. More important for the plotters' purposes, one of the nights of Bon is also the occasion for lively community dances and carnivals, normally attracting many residents to the local temples, particularly in rural areas. In 1949 the Bon festival fell on the night of August 16; and in southern Fukushima city its site was a locally well-known Buddhist temple. This temple, situated in the suburb of Kuroiwa, near the house of Akama's grandmother and also not far from the Nagaigawa Signal Station on the Tōhoku Main Line, is not particularly distinguished artistically but it does possess a locally prized Buddhist statue and provides the usual pleasant green park of most Japanese temples.[4]

4. Kuroiwa's Buddhist effigy is of the Boddhisattva "Kokūzō" (in Sanskrit, Ākāśagarbha) and is locally known—and identified in the Matsukawa case records—as the Kuroiwa Kokūzō. It is situated in a temple

The NRWU conspirators had chosen the time well. The festival of the Kuroiwa Buddha would attract farmers from all over, certainly from Kanayagawa and Matsukawa, and they would spend a good deal on food and drink that night (some local farmers were getting from ¥230 to ¥240 per shō—1.8 liters—for black market rice sent up to Tokyo, and their purses were full). In addition to the festival at the temple, there were student dramatic productions, and a girls' revue troupe—something fairly rare in the countryside—was playing at a small theatre opposite Matsukawa station. It thus seemed likely that there would be enough people making their way home after midnight early on the morning of August 17 that the police would not connect a train wreck with railroad workers. Indeed, the police anticipated that there would be people walking through the countryside on the night of August 16–17 and had set up a special guard post in a tent at the railroad crossing at the southern end of the Nagaigawa Signal Station in order to help people across the Tōhoku Main Line tracks. This tent would prove to be more important than the police realized at the time.

The site chosen for the wreck was also apt. The stretch of Tōhoku Main Line track about midway between Kanayagawa and Matsukawa is distinguished by two important properties: it curves, which is ideal for a derailment, and there are virtually no houses in this quiet valley. The conspirators believed that this was a good place for their sabotage because it was far enough out in the countryside for the police to suspect local residents returning from the festival rather than city dwellers, and because it provided a spot where the saboteurs could work unobserved. Akama was familiar with the territory, and both the NRWU group and the Tōshiba group could reach it fairly easily.

---

named Manganji (Temple of the Fulfillment of a Vow), and both the temple and the Kokūzō are located beside the Abukuma River. To avoid too many names for the same place, we shall use only the phrase "Kuroiwa Buddha" in referring to the site of the Bon festival.

Although they had been studying a train schedule when Akama arrived at the meeting, the plotters left the actual choice of which train to derail until the following day. They had to choose the one that gave them the greatest amount of time between its arrival on the scene and the passage of the previous train in which to rip up the tracks; and they wanted to see the final railroad schedule for August 16–17, including possible cancellations of trains, before deciding. Katō was assigned the mission of passing the word to Tōshiba the following day on the train finally selected.

At about 11:30 in the course of the meeting, Honda turned to Akama and said that they had to pick a meeting place for those who were going to the sabotage site from Fukushima. Akama suggested, "How about the Sugitsuma Agricultural Cooperative, which is near my place?" "OK," said Honda, "we'll meet tomorrow night at midnight, behind the Sugitsuma Coop, right next to the Suzuki lumber yard." [5] Suzuki Makoto also repeated to Akama a point he had been stressing throughout the meeting, "You've got to have a firm alibi for tomorrow night." After this exchange Akama concluded that he was being dismissed by his union superiors, and he left the NRWU offices to return home and think about his alibi.

It was about noon, after Akama had left, when Satō Hajime arrived from Matsukawa. He had had a busy morning. A final collective bargaining session had begun at the plant at about 10:30, and his presence had been required. Nine workers, including himself and led by Sugiura and Ōta, had represented the union in these negotiations, while across the table sat the factory manager, Mr. Washimi Seizō; the head of the Manage-

5. Sugitsuma is a very common name for places and institutions in the Fukushima area. In about A.D. 1180 Sugitsuma Yukinobu built a castle on the site of present-day Fukushima, called Sugitsuma-jō, and the name continues to be used to this day. Akama himself graduated from Sugitsuma Elementary School.

ment Section, Mr. Nishi Hajime; and Nishi's deputy, Mr. Suwa Shin'ichirō. (The names of these men, particularly the last, would become household words throughout Japan within the decade.) The local managers were also backed up in these negotiations by representatives from the Tōshiba Company at Tsurumi. Satō Hajime had spoken up in these sessions and was only able to slip out of the bargaining room unnoticed at about 11:05 A.M. for the short walk to Matsukawa station in order to catch the 11:15 train to Fukushima. It was the only train that would enable him to make the noon meeting at the NRWU offices.

After Satō joined the group, the decisions on time and place were explained to him, and the group then went on to make final selections of the actual participants. Akama had, of course, already been selected; his technical knowledge, acquaintance with the area, and obligation to the railroad union leaders were the only reasons he had been recruited. The other saboteurs chosen from the NRWU side were executive committee member Honda Noboru, who would actually be in command of the saboteurs at the site, and Takahashi Haruo, who did not attend the August 15 meeting, but who had been present on August 13. He was out of town on the fifteenth, having taken his wife and daughter to visit his wife's parents in Yonezawa, Yamagata prefecture, as part of the Buddhist holidays. He returned to Fukushima on the afternoon of August 16, and he and his wife attended the Bon festival at Kuroiwa that evening. Why he was chosen and the circumstances under which he was informed of the rendez-vous site for the night of the sixteenth were never made clear. Presumably he and Honda were picked as early as the thirteenth, and it would have been relatively easy for one of the railroad leaders to have briefed him on the final decisions after his return on the following afternoon.

The Tōshiba side was asked to provide two men for the actual sabotage party (in addition to the three railroad workers) and also to bring along the tools. Satō was told by the railroad workers that these tools should be stolen from the Matsukawa Track Maintenance Unit's shed on the west side of the Tōhoku Main Line tracks at Matsukawa station. Satō replied that he would pass all these instructions along to Sugiura, who would actually choose the Tōshiba men who were to participate. The final item on the agenda was Suzuki's instruction and warning to everyone concerned to establish an alibi for the night of August 16–17. Satō then returned to Matsukawa to confer with Sugiura.

At about 5:30 P.M. on August 15, the Tōshiba union leaders (Sugiura, Satō Hajime, and Ōta) met privately at Yasaka dormitory to discuss the assignments given to them at the morning's meeting. Sugiura picked Satō himself and Hamazaki as actual track saboteurs and decided that Ōuchi, Kobayashi, and Kikuchi would be given the job of stealing the tools. The three conspirators talked at some length about the need to establish alibis, and Sugiura indicated that he would take care of that matter on the following day. When Satō had finished telling about the plans laid at Fukushima that morning, Sugiura filled Satō in on developments at Matsukawa. The collective bargaining negotiations had failed, and all thirty-two Tōshiba workers who had received dismissal notices were now off the payroll as far as the company was concerned. Sugiura had called a general meeting of the union for 2:00 P.M. the following day (August 16) at which time he would recommend a strike vote. The timing of these events appeared to be working out well, thought Sugiura. If the rank and file did decide on a strike, the wreck would take place some time during the night of August 16–17, thereby hindering the police from concentrating their forces on the seventeenth for use against the strikers. Later on the night of the fifteenth, at about 10:30, Satō spent some time in Yasaka dormitory talking with Hamazaki and Kobayashi. He told them of the importance of the planned action and put further pressure on them in terms of their loyalty to the Communist party and the union to try to insure their cooperation.

Everyone at the Matsukawa plant was up early on the morning of August 16. There was a union executive-committee meeting at nine o'clock followed at once by an expanded conference of the struggle (i.e., agitation and strike) committee. The whole staff was busy making posters and printing handbills that opposed the layoffs, and then seeing to it that they were delivered to nearby cities. Some outsiders came by to help—for example, Katō Kenzō, who after being fired by the JNR had gone to work as an assistant in the prefectural union congress. On the sixteenth he was at the Matsukawa plant all afternoon and evening, providing what assistance he could as well as offering the backing of the prefectural federation for the local union's fight against Tōshiba. (Katō was not the only railroad worker lending a hand at the Matsukawa plant on the sixteenth; Yabe Kan'ichirō, head of the NRWU local at Wakamatsu, was also there from 1:00 P.M. until 9:00 P.M.)

At two o'clock Sugiura convened the general meeting of the union in Yasaka dormitory with about 230 members of the rank and file in attendance. Satō Hajime delivered a long fiery speech to the gathering, and Katō Kenzō also attended. The workers themselves were divided about what to do, and the meeting dragged on interminably. Finally, at 8:30 P.M. the meeting ended with a decision to go out on strike for one day (August 17) to protest Tōshiba's allegedly callous firing of thirty-two workers who had done nothing themselves to warrant losing their means of livelihood. After the meeting some members of the staff and executive committee went back to work making new handbills and prepared to post and distribute them the following morning at Matsukawa and Fukushima stations.

Ten minutes after the close of the general meeting, about 8:40 P.M., Sugiura and Katō Kenzō took Satō Hajime, Satō Shiroji, Ōta, Hamazaki, and Ōuchi aside into a private room reserved for the union within Yasaka dormitory. There (according to Hamazaki's confession) Sugiura said, "There've been a good many incidents of repression of workers in the present social situation, and I get the feeling that the time has come for us here at Tōshiba to get ours. I think we need some kind of incident to take the police pressure off us, and for this reason I think that the plan to derail a train is a good one." He then told Hamazaki that he was to accompany Satō Hajime on the sabotage mission that night. Hamazaki tried to refuse but was soon persuaded.

After Sugiura had laid out the basic scheme, Katō took over and gave them precise times for their various tasks. Before leaving Fukushima that morning Katō had used his contacts in the subdivision superintendent's office to find out what changes if any had been made in the night's operating schedule. Train number 159, a freight scheduled to pass through the chosen sabotage site at 2:12 A.M., had been canceled. Therefore the target train would be number 412, a long-distance passenger train bound for Ueno. It would reach the derailing point shortly after 3:00 A.M. The train immediately preceding number 412 would be the mixed passenger and freight, number 112, scheduled to go past the site at about two. Therefore, the saboteurs had a maximum of an hour to do their work, and they would have to plan on reaching the site not much later than 2:00 A.M. Obviously, the tools would have to be stolen soon enough to leave time for the Tōshiba participants to pick them up and walk to the scene. After delivering this information, Kato left the Tōshiba plant and returned directly to Fukushima by train.

The Tōshiba conspiracy meeting did not end just then, however. Sugiura kept the men he had gathered in Yasaka dormitory a little longer, and at about 9:30 P.M. sent for Kobayashi and Kikuchi. Apparently the non-Communist workers living in Yasaka took little heed of the continued presence of Sugiura's group in the dormitory, for it was well known that the union's Communist party members held a "cell meeting" after all general meetings of the union. Nevertheless, the manageress of the dormitory did ask them to use the main union office if they were going to have a long meeting, and they therefore had only a short time to confer at 9:30 before clearing out of the residential quarters. With few preliminaries Sugiura told Ōuchi, Kobayashi, and Kikuchi that later that evening they were to walk undetected to Matsukawa station, steal a crowbar and a wrench from the track-repair gang's shed, and then leave them outside on either the east or the west side (the confessions differ on this and many other small points concerning the tool theft) of the union office building. According to Ōuchi, "All those present approved of Sugiura's ideas."

Sugiura also gave precise instructions to everyone on how each man was to establish his alibi. Ōuchi, Hamazaki, Kikuchi, and Kobayashi were ordered to spend the night at the union office, where Sugiura would arrange to have other people present to vouch for them. Satō was told to sleep in Yasaka dormitory, from which he would have to leave and return without being seen by the plant guard. Others without an active part to play were to insure that they were in their homes or the dormitory like good citizens and not at the Bon festival.

When this meeting broke up Sugiura had only one more chore to attend to and then he, too, could return home. At about 10:00 P.M. he asked Nikaidō Takeo and Nikaidō Sonoko to step outside the union office for a moment. There, in the words of Sonoko's confession, "He instructed us to stay overnight at the labor union office without sleeping in order to establish an alibi for the overturning of a train. Nikaidō Takeo showed by the expression on his face that he approved of this. . . . That night Nikaidō Takeo, Hamazaki, Ōuchi, Kikuchi, and I remained at the office making posters and singing revolutionary songs." The plant security guard clearly remembered the sound of several voices singing the "Internationale" in the union office for a good part of the night. He supposed that the people there were preparing for their strike the following day.

TABLE 4

TŌHOKU MAIN LINE TRAIN SCHEDULE BETWEEN
KŌRIYAMA AND FUKUSHIMA

AUGUST 17, 1949
(00:00—03:09 O'CLOCK)

Train[a]	Destination	Fukushima	Kanayagawa[e]	Matsukawa[e]	Kōriyama
402 (S) (passenger express)	Ueno	Arr: 00:10 Dep: 00:19	00:34	00:39	Arr: 01:24 Dep: 01:32
152 (S) (freight)	n.a.[b]	n.a.	00:52	Arr: 00:59 Dep: 01:05	n.a.
115 (N) (passenger)	Aomori	Arr: 01:19 Dep: 01:29	01:07	01:03	Arr: 00:02 Dep: 00:11
681 (N) (locomotive only)	n.a.	n.a.	Arr: 01:20 Dep: 01:56	01:12	n.a.
401 (N) (passenger express)	Akita	Arr: 01:42 Dep: 01:55	01:35	01:29	Arr: 00:37 Dep: 00:46
112 (S) (passenger & freight)	Ueno	Arr: 00:55 Dep: 01:27	01:54	02:00	Arr: 02:45 Dep: 02:54
412 (S) (passenger)	Ueno	Arr: 02:28 Dep: 02:50	03:06	[03:15][d]	[Arr: 04:04 Dep: 04:24]

[a] S = Southbound; N = Northbound
[b] n.a. = not available
[e] Where only one time is shown, the train did not stop but passed through the station at that time.
[d] Times for Matsukawa and Kōriyama are scheduled only. Train did not arrive. Sabotaged after leaving Kanayagawa.
SOURCE: Sendai Kōtō Saibansho Dai Ichi Keijibu (Sendai High Court, First Criminal Affairs Division), *Matsukawa jiken sashimodoshi-shin kōhan shiryō* (Matsukawa Case Retrial Documentary Materials) (Sendai, 1961), Vol. VIII, p. 432; Vol. XII, pp. 12–13.

About 10:30 or 11:00 P.M. (depending on the confession one chooses to accept), Ōuchi, Kobayashi, and Kikuchi slipped singly out of the union office, crossed the railroad tracks, and made their way south along the railroad right of way until they came to the tool shed. It was hard to remain undetected, because a boisterous crowd of men was waiting on the platform for an interurban train—they had been attending the girl revue at the theatre opposite the station. None of these men ever came forward after the wreck, however, and claimed he could identify the three thieves, although a station employee thought he had seen three figures walking beside the tracks at about the right time. At the shed Kobayashi stood watch while Kikuchi and Ōuchi broke in, selected a foot-long monkey wrench and a very heavy crowbar (about four and one-half feet long and used also as a tie gauge to measure the distance between the tracks), and left with Kobayashi carrying the wrench, and Kikuchi and Ōuchi the crowbar between them. A half hour later they were back at the union office with the tools, and Nikaidō Sonoko would later confess that she saw the men leave them outside next to the building.

Together with the tool thieves, Satō Hajime and Hamazaki had also gone to the union office where they had made posters and sung until about the time that the first thief had departed on his mission. Satō had then said good night to Hamazaki, who remained at the office, and ostentatiously went to the dormitory to go to bed. At about 1:30 A.M. he sneaked out again and returned to the union office, picked up the tools and a still somewhat reluctant Hamazaki, crossed the Tōshiba plant property, keeping close to the bordering hill, and began walking north up the tracks of the Tōhoku Main Line. Satō himself carried the foot-long wrench, and Hamazaki, according to his first confession wearing geta rather than Western shoes, carried the heavy crowbar. Since Satō did not know the terrain, before they had gone very far Hamazaki had to take the lead. "While we were walking along the railroad tracks toward Kanayagawa," Hamazaki later confessed laconically, "we met three men coming toward us." Of course he did not know then who they were (never having been in on the key "liaison conspiracies" or fully briefed by Sugiura), but these three men were destined to become very well known to him over the next twenty years.

Akama Katsumi had spent the evening of August 16, 1949, in a less militant way than by making strike posters and singing labor songs. Having worried about his alibi ever since he had been warned on the fifteenth that he had to have one, he had finally come up with a satisfactory solution to the problem: why not work in one of the sales or entertainment booths set up in the Kuroiwa temple grounds for the festival? Among Akama's numerous relatives in the Fukushima area, one, a Mr. Minami, was manager of a local company that had contracted to show movies and lantern slides at the Bon festival. Akama went to see Minami and was signed up as a general helper, projectionist, and assistant candy salesman. On August 16 Akama was at the Kuroiwa temple grounds from 4:00 P.M. on, unloading and setting up equipment, manning the candy booth, and generally making himself useful. Minami and his other assistants certainly remembered Akama's presence. At about 7:30 P.M. Akama returned to his grandmother's house for dinner, and while there, he went to his chest of drawers and took out a pair of old army gloves which he had used when he was working on the railroad. They were distinctive gloves in that he had once had them repaired at a shoe shop with the heavy hemp thread used in shoemaking.

At about nine o'clock he returned to the Kuroiwa temple and worked steadily until eleven, showing lantern slides and selling candy. As seems inevitable in retrospect, Akama met several of his local pals at the festival—youths not known for their devotion to work—and after the dancing began to let up and the crowds to disperse, he wandered around the temple grounds chatting with them in the way nineteen-year-old boys tend to talk. According to his own confession, at about 11:30 P.M. Akama carelessly remarked to Iijima Yoshio and Andō

Sadao, both approximately his own age and longtime friends since grade school days (both also under police suspicion for rape, as was Akama), "There's a good chance that there's going to be a train wreck tonight." [6] Akama recalled that at the time his friends merely said "un" in response to his prediction, a comment that is about as meaningful in Japanese as "oh" would be in English, but they did remember his saying something about a train wreck. This incident would soon become famous in the annals of Japanese courts as "Akama's prophecy." Not long afterward, Akama parted from his friends, said that he was going home, and walked the short distance to the Suzuki lumberyard. Honda and Takahashi were waiting for him when he got there.

Honda had gone to more trouble to set up an alibi than Takahashi had. On the evening of the sixteenth Takeda Hisashi, head of the prefectural NRWU, was carrying out the thirteenth annual Buddhist memorial service (hōyō) for his late father, and he had invited several relatives and union officials—among them Honda, Suzuki, Okada, and Abe—to his home to join him. After the service was finished Takeda brought out big bottles of sake, as is the custom, and he and his guests began a drinking party that would last through the night. Sometime fairly late in the evening Honda claimed to be drunk—"I must be drunk," he said, "because I am seeing two light bulbs"—and Takeda's younger sister, Hisako, volunteered to see him as far as Fukushima station. There he thanked her and went to the NRWU offices, saying to the workers present that he was too drunk to

6. Akama quotes himself in various different ways in his confession statements—e.g., "Komban ressha no dassen de mo aru no de wa nai ka," "Komban atari ressha no dassen ga aru de wa nai ka nā," and "Komban ressha tempuku jiken de mo aru no de wa nai ka"—but they all add up to approximately the same meaning. See Matsukawa Jiken Shiryō Kankō Kai (Committee to Publish the Materials of the Matsukawa Case), "Akama hikoku no jihaku" (Defendant Akama's Confession), Matsukawa jiken shiryōshū (Collected Materials on the Matsukawa Case), No. 2 (Tokyo, 1954), pp. 20, 32, 49.

go home and was going to sleep on one of the night-duty crew's cots. Several workers came forward later to say that executive committeeman Honda spent the night of the Bon festival in the union office sleeping off too much holiday wine.

Takahashi and his wife returned from a visit to her parents' home in Yonezawa at four o'clock on the afternoon of August 16. During the early evening they stopped by an appliance store and priced a sewing machine, and then they went to the Kuroiwa festival and danced. At about 10:30 P.M. they returned to their own home, where they had to pass Takahashi's landlady, Suzuki Setsu, and went to bed. Takahashi's wife later testified that she was in and out of bed all night caring for her five-months-old daughter and that her husband was assuredly in bed with her. However, Mrs. Suzuki, the landlady, said that Takahashi could have come and gone in her house without her knowledge, and she clearly recalled Takahashi's coming downstairs shortly after seven o'clock the following morning and telling her the news about the train wreck.

According to Akama, at midnight on the sixteenth Honda and Takahashi were not in bed either at home or at the union office; instead they were standing about waiting for him in the southern suburbs of Fukushima city, well on their way to Matsukawa. When Akama walked up, they exchanged greetings, and he noticed that his comrades were dressed, just as he was, in white shirts and black pants. The night was rainy but warm, and no one needed a coat. An official of the Fukushima meteorological station later described the weather that night as follows: at 10:00 P.M. the sky was cloudy and at 10:35 rain began to fall. This had changed to a foggy mist by 10:50 and stopped at 11:03, beginning again between 11:45 and midnight. By 1:00 A.M. it was windless and clear, and a bright moonlight began to shine at 1:03. The night remained clear until dawn, at 5:24, but shortly before sunrise at 5:54 weak rain again began to fall and continued intermittently throughout August 17. Akama did not remember the night quite like that; he said that it rained most of the night and that it was quite dark, but this was only one of several relatively minor discrepancies in his confession.

After Honda advised his collaborators that they must take care not to be seen, they set out on foot in Indian file. Unfortunately for them, they were seen almost immediately. As they walked along a typical unpaved Japanese country road they passed the home of Honda Kiyomatsu, where he and some associates were resting and having a cup of tea after doing some repair work on a piece of machinery. By the light of a bright, unshaded light bulb shining from the second story, these late workers saw three figures marching past in column, although they were unable to recognize their faces. A short distance further on the three saboteurs came to the Morinaga bridge over a small tributary of the Abukuma River, aptly called the Nigori, or "Muddy," Creek (it was in fact a stagnant open sewer). On the hike to the scene the walkers did not cross the Nigori via the Morinaga bridge (a wooden structure named after a milk company that built it for its own use), but instead turned right and walked along the creek's banks for about three city blocks, directly to the Nagaigawa Signal Station on the Tōhoku Main Line. There they crossed the tracks and began walking down their western side toward Matsukawa, using the railroad's trestle to get over Nigori Creek.

One of the most controversial points in Akama's confession is what he and his comrades encountered when they came to the normally unguarded grade crossing at the southern end of the Nagaigawa Signal Station (today a regular stop on the Fukushima interurban service and known as South Fukushima). A police tent, open on three sides and with four men in it, had been specially set up there to protect the expected large numbers of festival visitors who would have to cross the railroad tracks that night. There was also a temporarily rigged 60-watt light bulb burning at the spot. In his first confession Akama did not mention the tent, and the guards in the tent stated that they had not seen three men pass at the appointed time. When the police asked Akama about it, he remembered the tent, but said he did not see it until he was quite close, because of its olive drab color —which is odd because of the light bulb and because in subsequent tests the tent and its light could be seen from every direction for more than two hundred yards. Akama merely indicated that he and his companions had skirted the tent without themselves being seen.

Somewhat beyond the signal station, the saboteurs began walking on the railroad itself. The first train they encountered was the Ueno-bound express, number 402, which approached them from the rear. In addition to the tent, another odd omission in Akama's confession is any mention of trains numbered 401 and 402. This is odd because all other trains that were known to have passed are accounted for in his statements. A hypersuspicious observer might be drawn to the fact that trains 401 and 402 were both expresses, and express trains are indicated on official JNR schedules by red cross-hatching across the columns in which their schedules are detailed. A person unfamiliar with railroad practice reading one of these dispatchers' sheets for the first time might conclude that the red cross-hatched trains had been canceled, since they look as if they have been crossed off. If such a person were writing a confession or suggesting one to a prisoner on the basis of a schedule rather than actual experience, he might not include these trains. This is only speculation, however.

Still in the vicinity of the Nagaigawa signal, Akama and company came across still another tent, this one owned by the railroad and occupied for the night by three men belonging to a track-maintenance team. These three men (a subsection chief, a technician, and a laborer) were making routine inspections of the railroad fishplates (the bars that join the rails together). One of them later testified that he saw the shapes of three men pass in the night, but Akama made no mention of this tent in any of his confession statements.

For approximately the next three miles of the six-and-a-half-mile trip (one way) nothing untoward happened. The men marched up and over the short Hiraishi tunnel just north of Kanayagawa, and they gave Kanayagawa station itself a wide berth. They were now getting near the Arakawa intersection— the point where the Tōhoku Main Line crosses the Rikuu National Highway, the main road connecting Fukushima and Matsukawa—a grade crossing manned by a watchman and supplied with gates that were lowered whenever a train passed. Freight train 152 went by at this time, and the hikers stayed in the underbrush, watching the gateman lower and raise the barriers and then reenter his billet. They then crossed the highway and continued on toward the site, now only a short distance away. Just slightly before they reached the spot selected for the sabotage two northbound trains, numbers 115 and 681 (the latter a locomotive only), passed and forced them to take cover. When they reached the sabotage site, however, they had to march on past it, since their collaborators from Tōshiba were nowhere to be seen. It was just beyond the so-called Ishiai crossing (a narrow underpass for an unpaved rural road) and almost within sight of the Tōshiba factory buildings that the NRWU contingent finally came upon Hamazaki and Satō walking toward them.

As the two groups met, Honda said "Good evening" in the rural dialect (oban desu), and was answered with an "oban desu" and with the urban equivalent, "komban wa," from the Tōshiba crew. Akama, who had not met either man, noted in his confession that from this brief verbal exchange he concluded that the man carrying the crowbar (Hamazaki) was from Tōhoku, but that the other, carrying the wrench (Satō Hajime), "used the language of a man brought up in the city." Honda knew the names of the two saboteurs from Tōshiba and mentioned them to Akama, but Akama had forgotten them by the time he confessed. Whatever else was said during this encounter Akama did not record, but it may be guessed that he cursed when he saw the tools. The crowbar was fine, but the wrench was absurdly small for the work it would have to do. Railroad men usually use a fixed-diameter, or "box," wrench to tighten (or loosen) the nuts on a fishplate, but the Tōshiba thieves had stolen a monkey wrench—what the English call a "universal spanner"—and a very small one at that. There was nothing to be done at that hour, however, and the five men therefore set off northward, three of them retracing their steps, toward the chosen site.

They had gone only a short distance when they were all forced to jump off the tracks and crouch down in a culvert right next to the railroad because of the passage of southbound train number 112. This unforeseen incident produced the one and only unequivocal eyewitness in the entire case. Number 112 was a very slow, mixed passenger and freight train, and because of the slight grade southbound in this part of Fukushima and because of the very poor coal in use at the time, it was both drawn and pushed by fore and aft locomotives. Engineer Ōnishi Tsutomu in the rear locomotive saw four or five men wearing white shirts and black pants crouched down alongside the railroad tracks. He fixed the time as between 1:50 and 2:00 A.M., and the place as only a few yards south of where train 412 would be derailed a little more than an hour later. If Ōnishi did not see Honda, Takahashi, Akama, Hamazaki, and Satō, it has never been discovered whom he did see, although he was not able to make out the faces on any of the crouching figures.

At approximately 2:00 A.M. the saboteurs reached the site. They rested for three minutes and then, under Honda's direction, set to work. Akama, the only experienced line-maintenance worker, wielded the crowbar to pull up the spikes that grip the rails to the wooden ties and to remove the chocks, or wedges, that are driven in between the rails and the ties to hold the rail rigid. Working at full speed, he removed spikes and chocks along the outer rail of the curving section of railroad, loosening completely one whole rail about twenty-seven yards long, and about 80 percent of the next rail. He appears to have pulled out between seventy and eighty-five spikes and between twenty and twenty-eight chocks.

More important and more difficult were the fishplates connecting one rail to the next. To remove one set of fishplates it is necessary to pull out four spikes holding the two fishplates (one on either side of the rail ends) to the ties, loosen four nuts on four bolts that go through both fishplates and the rail, hammer on top of the rails to get the bolts out, and then pry off the fishplates. In one experiment conducted in 1958 by a left-wing Matsukawa investigating team, it was found that to loosen nuts on a fishplate tightened with a standard railroad wrench required 2,000–3,000 kg./cm. of pressure, and that a foot-long monkey wrench bent well before this pressure was reached—in the range of 1,000–1,300 kg./cm.[7] It is possible that the fishplate nuts at the sabotage site were easier since they had not been tightened for some time. However, railroad witnesses later testified that they could also have been harder than usual because they might have been rusty.

Hamazaki, Satō, and Takahashi worked on this problem while Honda supervised and occasionally took a turn himself. According to Akama, who looked up once in a while to see how the work was going, the four men by taking turns with the wrench were able to remove both fishplates completely at one place and to start on one bolt on a fishplate on the inside rail (which was an amateurish spot to choose to work, and therefore they did not complete it). Akama's testimony on the number of fishplates removed is perhaps the single most important item in his several

7. Yamaguchi Keiji, "Genchi chōsa sanka-ki" (Record of Participation in On-site Inspection), *Rekishigaku kenkyū* (The Journal of Historical Studies), No. 224 (October 1958), p. 50.

confessions. He said, "I saw that Honda had removed them [two fishplates] in one place completely" (*Honda ga ikkasho kanzen ni torihazushita no o mimashita*), and "We removed fishplates completely in one place" (*Tsugime-ita ikkasho o kanzen ni tori-hazushita*). This was perfectly consistent with the police's finding two fishplates at the scene of the crime the following morning, and it remained so for four years—until two more fishplates turned up in a procuracy warehouse!

The five men worked for twenty to thirty minutes (on the basis of a careful calculation of all evidence the Supreme Court later fixed the time of work at between twenty-three and twenty-seven and a half minutes), and then Honda called a stop. He said (according to Akama), "Let's get out of here. I want a pledge on pain of death that you'll all keep absolutely quiet about this." They then threw their tools as far as possible out into the nearby flooded paddy field and split up, the two from Tōshiba returning to Matsukawa, and the three from the NRWU hiking the much longer distance back to Fukushima. Just as they were about to pass over the Hiraishi tunnel on the return trip, the three former railroad workers saw the ill-fated train number 412 under way toward the south. Akama had the bad taste to ask Honda whether there would be many killed or wounded when the train was derailed. Honda replied, "Probably" (*Ūn, sō da*).

Hamazaki and Satō were back at the Tōshiba plant by 3:00 A.M., before the wreck occurred. Honda, Takahashi, and Akama, however, did not reach the Morinaga bridge over the Nigori Creek until after four o'clock. They were resting on the south bank of the Nigori near the bridge's abutment when a local farmer, Takahashi Tsuruji, came across the bridge pulling a wagon stacked up with night-soil tubs. He testified in court later that he saw the shapes of three men sprawled on the bank.

After this close call the men got up and returned rapidly to the places they were supposed to be that night. Akama stopped on the bridge, pushed one of his gloves into the other, filled them with rocks, and dropped them into Nigori Creek. He then hastened to his grandmother's, entered the room in which another of her grandchildren was sleeping, and woke up Onodera Itsuko, age eleven, his cousin, by pulling her hair. The time was about 4:30 A.M., and he hoped thereby to establish his alibi. The following morning he told his grandmother that he had come home about 1:00 A.M. Takahashi went straight home and presumably climbed into bed with his wife, while Honda went back to sleep at the NRWU offices.

Back down the tracks an hour or so earlier train number 412 was just pulling out of Kanayagawa station headed toward Matsukawa and points south. It carried about 630 passengers and was traveling at forty miles an hour when, at nine minutes past three, on August 17, 1949, it derailed and overturned. The engineer and his two assistants were trapped beneath the locomotive and burned to death; and numerous passengers were injured, three of them seriously. Shortly after the wreck, the Matsukawa village fire siren began to be sounded continuously, and by 4:40 A.M. a railway maintenance crew and civilian guards had left Matsukawa station for the scene. Passengers stood about the train in helpless confusion waiting to be led out of the dark and unfamiliar terrain in which the accident had occurred. The first rescue train was formed at Fukushima station at 4:52 A.M. By the time it arrived the police were on the scene, led by Tamagawa Tadashi, assistant chief investigator of the Fukushima Prefectural Headquarters, National Rural Police. Messages were also being flashed by telephone and telegraph to SCAP's local CIC and to General Headquarters in Tokyo, informing occupation authorities of the wreck.

Unknown to anyone for more than ten years was a virtual eyewitness to the wreck itself. On the nights of August 15 and 16, two burglars had been at work in the area, trying to break into and rob the warehouse of the Ōtsuki Drygoods Company, located on the Rikuu Highway near the Arakawa intersection. On the sixteenth, after they had split up and gone in different directions, one of the two, Murakami Yoshio, was sitting having a smoke near the Ishiai crossing when he heard the sound of a very serious railroad accident shattering the nighttime stillness. Ten years later he and his partner would tell the courts that that was not all they had heard or seen that night, although most Japanese tended to disbelieve what they had to say. (That is another story to be discussed much later in this book.) However, whether the citizen of Japan should or could believe the events described in this chapter became one of the major political issues of the country for the succeeding fifteen years after 1949. As we ponder the same questions in this book it is well to remember that nobody ever doubted at least one fact—namely, that on August 17, 1949, train number 412 of the Japanese National Railroads was derailed and overturned and that some group of individuals caused it to do so by sabotaging the tracks.

Chapter 4

Confession in Japanese Law
and Society

I N DEALING with criminal cases Japanese police, procurators, and judges think of the confession as the "king of
evidence" (*shōko no ō*). It is the decisive element of proof
sought by every procurator before he takes a case into court and
the single most important item determining the reception his
efforts are likely to receive from most Japanese judges when he
gets there. Compared with having a good confession, circumstantial evidence is definitely secondary; and given this preference
for confessions on the part of procurators and judges, it is small
wonder that Japanese policemen are much more attuned to obtaining them than to building "objective" cases. Before the war
virtually all successfully prosecuted criminal cases were based on
the defendant's confession, and even fifteen years after the occupation-sponsored Code of Criminal Procedure came into effect
the rate of convictions based on confessions ran about 75 per-

cent.[1] Confessions dominate Japanese criminal courtrooms for several different reasons, and their persistence is a highly controversial subject both within and outside the country.

Most commentaries on the subject can be grouped into one of two broad schools of thought. The first, associated with radical social critics and Marxist professors in Japan, emphasizes the institutional roots of the reliance on confessions. Theorists of this school see the preference for confessions rising out of the bureaucratization of the judicial system that existed in prewar Japan and the system's indifference to the legal rights of citizens. Procurators sought confessions because of the perils they perceived to a bureaucratic career if they lost a case, and they were reinforced in this attitude by the ideology of Imperial infallibility: it would not do for one of the emperor's agents, say the state procurator, to be found making a mistake. According to this view the prewar Japanese state (allegedly only superficially changed after the war) conducted criminal proceedings in its own interests rather than in the interest of society, and it could and did use its awesome powers to coerce confessions from anyone who fell into its hands.

The second school, associated with analysts deeply impressed by the special qualities of Japan's cultural tradition (including Western sociologists and historians), stresses that Japanese values predispose prisoners to confess to anything that authorities want them to. As Professor Uematsu Tadashi (Hitotsubashi University) has remarked, "Compared with other people Japanese characteristically make confessions easily. . . . Seldom are Japanese

1. Masaki Hiroshi, the chief attorney in the Yakai case (which was almost of equal importance to the Matsukawa case in launching the criticism-of-the-courts movement of the mid-fifties), says that 99 percent of prewar criminal cases were based on confessions. "Jihaku to wa? Saiban to jihaku shimpyōsei" (What is Confession? Trials and the Credibility of Confessions) (round-table discussion), *Sekai*, No. 99 (March 1954), p. 92. For the postwar figures, see Supreme Court of Japan, *Outline of Criminal Justice in Japan* (Tokyo, 1963), p. 30.

suspects able to maintain their own contentions to the last. Not completely free of their feudal consciousness, they cannot maintain their own point of view in the presence of superiors." [2]

Both of these views are partially correct, but serious misconceptions result when one is advanced to the exclusion of the other. The Marxists contend that most confessions are obtained through inducement or torture, and they ignore the fact—encountered by numerous appeal court judges—that many confessions are completely voluntary and may yet be false (and these are not confessions motivated by a desire to protect a relative or friend). On the other hand, an exclusive commitment to the primacy of values in social analysis virtually cuts off all practical investigation of concrete social phenomena. Values do differ from culture to culture, and Japanese values are quite distinctive, but it is bad logic to *begin* any discussion of human behavior with a discussion of values, since, like Freudian psychology, arguments about the uniqueness of values can explain (away) anything. Too often foreign commentators have merely acknowledged confessions in Japanese courts (or paternalism in Japanese industry) with the pseudoprofound observation that the Japanese are different.

Not all Japanese orientations vis-à-vis the courts or the state are that different from Western values. Many Japanese accused of a crime confess because they are poor, just as poor people do in other countries. They realize that they cannot afford the extremely expensive procedure of defending themselves through numerous courts, possibly all the way to the Supreme Court (a process that was so expensive in the Matsukawa case, where the issue was taken to the Supreme Court twice, that it required an international fund-raising effort). Under these circumstances they "cop a plea" of guilty, which usually gets them a reduced sentence or saves their life in a capital case. It will also make the

2. In *Sekai*, No. 99, pp. 103–104.

courts much more likely to release them on bail, the procedures for which are very liberal in Japan, while awaiting trial or appeal. Procurators have often obtained confessions by offering bail for the period between the confession and the verdict. Prisoners rationalize that they can always change their confession when they get in court—which often turns out to be harder to do than they think, and which inevitably angers the procurator and judges. In any case more poor men than rich men confess in Japan, as elsewhere.[3]

Another source of confessions, not unknown in other societies but quite strong in Japan, is "detention reaction," or a sense of despair and resignation at having been arrested. Kawashima believes that this reaction is heightened by the relatively underdeveloped "legal consciousness" of most Japanese and by their knowledge of the administration of justice over the past century.[4] Japanese society has been evolving for only a little more than a hundred years from a rigorously authoritarian and highly stratified social system. The principle that the citizen has rights against government officials is foreign to the traditional culture; moreover, it was not recognized by the government or the fundamental law of the land prior to the end of World War II. One attorney has written that Japanese tend to humble themselves and become docile when confronted by government officials; they are more likely to pray for a friendly judge than try to do battle with the forces arrayed against them.[5]

This propensity is abetted by a relative unfamiliarity with

3. See, e.g., Hara Toshio, *Nihon no saiban* (Japan's Courts) (Tokyo, 1959), pp. 61–70, on *kinryoku* ("the power of wealth").

4. Kawashima Takeyoshi, *Nihonjin no hō ishiki* (Legal Consciousness of the Japanese) (Tokyo, 1967), passim.

5. Koizumi Eiichi, in "Jihaku to wa?" *Sekai*, No. 99, pp. 104–105. Kawashima adds, "While in the West the defense of one's own rights is approved as just and proper, in Japan it is reproached as being selfish, disturbing to the peace, and improperly demanding of personal redress through the use of political power." *Nihonjin no hō ishiki*, p. 32.

the law among the people as a whole and by the fact that legal language in Japan is often much more flexible and ambiguous than it is in other legal systems. Uncertainty as to the actual meaning of a law is so pronounced in Japan that Kawashima concludes that much domestic jurisprudence amounts to casuistry.[6] "The notion that a justice measured by universal standards can exist independent of the wills of the disputants is apparently alien to the traditional habit of the Japanese people. Consequently, distrust of judges and lack of respect for the authority of judicial decisions is widespread throughout the nation."[7] The result of these and other factors is the widespread practice of multiple trials—that is, appeal courts tend to try a case de novo rather than on the specific points of appeal (something that happened twice in the Matsukawa case, in addition to the first trial)—because Japanese like it that way: they do not trust a single trial and only three judges.[8]

Probably the best known of all Japanese values is that of the obligation of loyalty to one's group and the lack of personal individualism (what the Japanese call "egotism"). Nakane Chie has an interesting theory to account for this.[9] She argues that all social groups are determined by the *attributes* of their members and the *frame* in which a given group is located. Attributes are personal qualities, which may be either achieved or ascribed, while frames are situational contexts—for example, "professor" and "student" are attributes, whereas "men of the university" refers to their frame. She believes that the basic values of a social system differ according to the saliency of one or the other

6. *Nihonjin no hō ishiki*, pp. 37–42.
7. Kawashima in *Law in Japan*, Arthur T. von Mehren, ed. (Cambridge, Mass., 1963), p. 50.
8. Uematsu Tadashi, in "Matsukawa jiken: haki-sashimodoshi hanketsu no imi suru mono" (Significant Aspects of the Reversal and Referral Back Verdict in the Matsukawa Case), *Jurisuto* (Jurist) (special extra issue), September 1959, p. 5.
9. *Japanese Society* (Berkeley and Los Angeles, 1970).

element, and that Japan is fundamentally a frame-oriented society. (India, by contrast, where caste divisions predominate, is a good example of an attribute-oriented society.) Japan draws great strength from this property, for example in company unions, where men are drawn together more by the frame of the enterprise than by their possessing a common craft or skill. However, when a man finds himself outside his usual frame of reference or in a situation demanding personal initiative, he may be unable to perform at all. Worse yet, he may perform as if he had entered a new frame, one which has been defined for him by others and in which he may be cast in the role of sacrificial victim.

Thus, for example, a person detained by the police may exhibit a "courtesy bias," a tendency to answer questions put by the police in ways which the respondent believes are cooperative and will please the police. Several of the defendants in the Matsukawa case answered questions about whether the Communist party, Sugiura, or others had paid them to join the train-wrecking conspiracy by saying yes and naming sums from a thousand to several hundred thousand yen. Since no money was found, the procurators summarily threw out this part of their confessions, and the presiding judge in the second trial wrote, "When Inspector Tamagawa casually asked them [the defendants] if they had received any payment, they tried to ingratiate themselves [geigō shite] with him by saying that they had." [10] Miyagi Otoya says that false voluntary confessions are made in criminal cases in order to preserve one's decency (avoiding a scene), to overcome one's sense of inferiority in the face of the police, to avoid the death penalty, out of impulsiveness (setsunashugi)—true particularly of postwar youth, he says—and because "some people cannot resist authority." [11]

10. Matsukawa Jiken Shiryō Kankō Kai, "Matsukawa jiken dai-ni-shin hanketsu zenbun" (Complete Text of the Verdict of the Second Trial of the Matsukawa Case), Matsukawa jiken shiryōshū, No. 3 (Tokyo, 1954), p. 85.
11. In "Jihaku to wa?" Sekai, No. 99, p. 106.

This problem of courtesy bias and lack of individualism extends beyond the tendency to confess. Judge Kumagai of the Tokyo District Court asserts that Japanese, in contrast to Americans, hate with a passion to have to testify unfavorably against a defendant in open court and that for this reason documentary evidence, pretrial depositions, and testimony taken *in camera* have always played a large role in Japanese procedure (even though the admissibility of such evidence was strongly attacked in the postwar Code of Criminal Procedure).[12] As an example of this reluctance to testify publicly, virtually every one of the Tōshiba confessers in the Matsukawa case warned the procurators that they would be unable to maintain their confessions in open court—in the presence of Sugiura and their fellow defendants. They thereby implied to the police, not that these were false confessions, but only that the social pressures would be too great to repeat them. The question remains, however, whether there were social pressures in the police station that caused them to confess in the first place.

Japanese do sometimes confess voluntarily to crimes they did not commit and for reasons more associated with Japanese social structure than with any personal psychopathology or feeblemindedness. Needless to say, this occurs more often among the uneducated or unsophisticated, and any good policeman, procurator, or judge should be able to spot it. Moreover, the values that have been conducive to "courtesy confessions" are rapidly changing, and the figures for the numbers of convictions based on confession decline yearly. The true significance of the general value predispositions that exist within Japanese society to the administration of criminal justice lies in the attitudes, practices, and regulations of the judicial officials: Do they conduct criminal proceedings in such a way that justice results? Or are the

12. Kumagai Hiroshi, in "Matsukawa jiken muzai hanketsu tokushū" (Special Collection on the Matsukawa Case Not-guilty Verdict), *Jurisuto*, No. 239 (December 1, 1961), p. 66.

people both victimized by the authorities and allowed occasionally to victimize themselves?

Unfortunately the prewar record on this score is not very salutary. None of the criminal codes of post-Restoration Japan ever stipulated or implied that a defendant's confession was necessary to his conviction. Instead, the practice of relying on confessions developed gradually over time, beginning with the discovery that confessions could be easily obtained, moving on to a tendency on the part of the prosecuting authorities to utilize them and then to depend on them as their investigating skills declined, resulting finally in virtual demands from the bench in the immediately prewar period that confessions be obtained in most criminal cases. Several factors contributed to this trend. One was simply Japan's having adopted the Continental system of criminal procedure during the period of its legal modernization. Confessions are more common in the Continental than in the Anglo-American practice because of the ease with which a procurator can detain a suspect and the long pretrial investigation which a judge conducts. These semi-inquisitorial sessions often reveal that a suspect is in fact guilty, and he may then prepare a written confession for the judge.

Continental pretrial investigating procedures can be abused, but they are not inherently unjust, nor is the fact that confessions often result from them necessarily a sign that the authorities did anything more to a suspect than invite him to explain the crime, his guilt having already been established and admitted. It is just as common for the pretrial judge to discover that a suspect is innocent and release him forthwith. As Professor Hirano (law, Tokyo University) explains:

> Under the Continental semiaccusatorial system, at successive stages of the inquiry an investigating official and a judge interrogate the suspect or defendant, and each has a considerable opportunity to obtain a statement from him in the

form of a confession or otherwise. In this way, there is provided a direct method of determining those subjective and psychological elements of a crime that often can be definitively proven only by the defendant's statement of them. . . . On the other hand, it is extremely difficult to establish the subjective elements of a crime under the adversary system of criminal procedure, in which an opportunity is only rarely given either to the judge or to the investigating official to interrogate the defendant or suspect. Consequently, in American criminal law substantive criminal proscriptions embody objective elements which are relatively easy to prove, as well as presumptions adverse to the defendant by which the required subjective element may be established.

Japanese jurists prize the subjective quality of the Continental method, and certainly very few Japanese judges oppose the introduction of confessions as such in criminal cases. Hirano continues:

The approach that the sole purpose of punishment is deterrence stands in opposition to that approach which stresses as one leading purpose of punishment the rehabilitation of the offender. This antithesis is ordinarily referred to as the division between the classical and modernist schools of thought on theories of punishment. In Japan, however, this antithesis is often expressed in terms of a conflict between the "objective principle" and the "subjective principle," since the modernist group in Japan stresses the subjective elements of the act as material constituents of the crime.[13]

Thus Japanese judges often will decrease or suspend punishment in cases where it has been determined subjectively that there is

13. Hirano, Ryūichi, "The Accused and Society: Some Aspects of Japanese Criminal Law," in *Law in Japan*, pp. 274–275.

little chance of recidivism, where contrition is shown, or where the crime has little or no antisocial significance. To Japanese the issue is not the desirability of confessions in criminal cases; it is rather whether procurators and judges corruptly misuse the powers entrusted to them to obtain confessions.

There is, however, one further complicating element, the so-called free discretion of the judge. In Japan (both before and after the war) the determination of facts in a case is entrusted to one or more judges rather than to a jury. That is to say, an experienced and professionally trained courtroom expert hears the evidence, and he does not require the elaborate safeguards against hearsay and other questionable forms of evidence that are erected in the American system to insure that a jury is not misled or lied to. According to article 318 of the postwar Code of Criminal Procedure (unchanged from prewar practice), "The probative power of evidence shall be left to the free discretion of a judge or judges."

This means that if you are a defendant you should hope and pray that your judge is honest, independent, and unbiased, because you will have little chance of going free by arguing that the evidence against you was "inadmissible" for one reason or another. Judges cannot, of course, make a capricious decision concerning a defendant's guilt or innocence (article 317 of the current code says, "Findings as to the fact shall be made by evidence"), and the presiding judge must write an extremely long and detailed explication of the evidence to explain his verdict. Nevertheless, verdicts often come down to the point where a judge invokes his "free discretion": he has listened to all the evidence and he thinks the accused is guilty or innocent (Judge Monden invoked it in freeing the Matsukawa defendants, and Chief Justice Tanaka of the Supreme Court cited it as one factor in his judging them guilty).

Under the postwar constitution confessions that have been obtained through torture or prolonged detention are illegal, but the fact remains that judges can still hear such confessions in the courtroom. "Under the old criminal procedure," writes Kainō, "the truthfulness of a confession was more important than the volition with which it was given." [14] Confessions that are coerced may still be truthful, it used to be argued, just as the police may frame up a case against a guilty man. Many Japanese citizens and commentators on the courts fear that some of the old habits have not been eradicated and that judges trained in the prewar tradition are still more interested in "Who did it and why?" than in "How do we know who did it?"

It must be repeated once again that knowing why a crime was committed is often highly desirable from a social standpoint, and that there is nothing inherently unfair about the principle of free discretion—it is, in fact, hard to imagine any other kind of rule prevailing when a panel of judges perform the functions given to a jury in the United States. Moreover, experienced judges are probably much more competent than the average member of a jury in judging when a total stranger is lying to them. If a judge misuses his discretion or is determined to frame a defendant, no rule is going to stop him; the proper remedy is appeal to an honest court. However, in prewar Japan the whole system was stacked against the defendant in such a way that if the judges and procurators wanted to put somebody away—for reasons of state, their own convenience, protection of their personal positions, or maintenance of the prestige of the judiciary —they could do so.

According to the Meiji Constitution of 1889, "The Judicature shall be exercised by the Courts of Law according to law, in the name of the Emperor" (art. 57). Court officials in prewar Japan were wielders of the *Kiku no gomon*, the Chrysanthemum Crest, and as such they were part of the state apparatus of the modernizing Japanese nation, not authorities mediating between

14. Kainō Michitaka, *Hōritsu* (The Law) (Tokyo, 1957), p. 87.

citizens and the representative of organized society in the name of justice. The Chrysanthemum emblem was conspicuously displayed in prewar courtrooms, and its removal after the defeat was considered by many an important measure of reform.

Through the Ōtsu decision (see chapter one) the old Supreme Court had established the principle of judicial independence under the Meiji Constitution, but the judiciary still came under intense pressure to insure that the interests of the state and the ruling class and the interests of justice were never incompatible. Ienaga Saburō writes: "Even though the judiciary was independent, judges in the period of the Meiji Constitution had a strong common identification with procurators as officials of the Emperor. Together with procurators they could not rid themselves of the habit of judging the 'people.' There were also many judges who had a strong psychological resistance to refuting an indictment brought by the procurators and investigating authorities, even when they had not cooperated in framing false charges." [15] A prewar Japanese indicted by the procurators had no reason to expect much help from the judge, and he rarely got any.

In retrospect it should perhaps be observed that the Meiji state was carrying out one of the most extensive and successful campaigns of "modernization from above" the world has ever witnessed. If judges and other officials occasionally sided with the state rather than defended the rights of citizens, Japan was on the whole still a more humane society than many others, notably the nations modernizing under Communist auspices, during comparable periods. What seems worse than officials serving the emperor too loyally was their subservience to the demands of their own bureaucratic careers. Judges and procurators were employees of the Ministry of Justice, and although the minister could not fire them, he could and did decide who should

15. *Saiban hihan* (Criticism of the Courts) (Tokyo, 1959), p. 103.

be promoted and who should be transferred. Procurators who lost cases or judges who went too far in criticizing police methods were very likely to find themselves sitting in Aomori or Okinawa if they did not improve. This condition, not fully overcome among procurators in the postwar world, contributed to collaboration between the judiciary and the procuracy; when necessary both sides could justify such cooperation to themselves in terms of maintaining the Imperial integrity.

Continental procedures, Japanese personal values, the Imperial ideology, bureaucratization of the judiciary, and the capture of the government by the militarists all came together just before the war to produce what Japanese call *kensatsu fassho* ("fascism by the procuracy").[16] Its worst manifestation was the procurator's framing a defendant (for political or personal reasons) by forcibly extracting a confession from him, and the court's acquiescence and even connivance with the procurator in doing this. The possibility that *kensatsu fassho* had not been completely eradicated after the war occurred to some Japanese editorial writers as they commented on the course of the Matsukawa case during the 1950s.[17]

Without ever realizing the full import of confessions within the Japanese system of criminal justice or Japanese society, the Americans during the occupation launched a direct attack on *kensatsu fassho* and particularly on those aspects of it whereby a procurator could obtain a conviction on the basis of a false confession. SCAP officials wrote into the Constitution of 1947 an article prohibiting the use of torture in the administration of justice and another one stipulating that no person could be convicted in cases where his confession was the sole piece of

16. For more complete definitions of *kensatsu fassho*, see Hattori, Takaaki, "The Legal Profession in Japan: Its Historical Development and Present State," in *Law in Japan*, p. 125, n. 50.

17. See, e.g., the regular column "Kiryū" (Currents), in *Yomiuri shimbun*, February 22, 1952.

evidence introduced against him. SCAP also sought to make it much harder for the procuracy and investigating officials to obtain confessions. In the old criminal procedure procurators detained suspects for long periods of time without charging them, often moving their prisoners from one police station to another so that their whereabouts were not even known, and they also commonly arrested and charged suspects with a lesser crime while, in fact, they were interrogating them about a different, more serious crime. The confessions that came out of these incommunicado sessions could rarely be checked by even the most diligent judge, and the prisoner could not, of course, obtain counsel until after he had been formally charged.

The new Code of Criminal Procedure tried to change all that. According to its provisions a police officer can make an arrest only on the basis of a warrant of arrest, and he must immediately inform the suspect of the essential facts of the crime and of his right to select defense counsel (art. 203). If the suspect cannot exonerate himself and is to be charged, he must be transferred to a public procurator within forty-eight hours from the time of his physical apprehension. The procurator gives the suspect another opportunity to explain and either releases him or, within twenty-four hours after receiving him, obtains a warrant of detention from a judge (art. 205). Such warrants can be granted by a court for ten days and renewed only once. Before that time is up formal charges must be filed or the suspect must be released.

These safeguards sound good on paper, but in actual practice the new law allows the procurator to hold a suspect for a total of twenty-three days from apprehension to charge (forty-eight hours plus twenty-four hours plus ten days plus ten days). This is not as long as was possible under the old law, but it is a long enough period of time for most procurators merely to have adapted their procedures to it. There are other safeguards: the Habeas Corpus law, the right of a suspect to an interview with counsel without any official being present (Code of Criminal Procedure, art. 39), and so forth. But there are also escape clauses, provisions that sound very much like the old procedure —for example, judges are allowed to take secret testimony from witnesses prior to a trial when the likelihood exists that such testimony would be contradicted if presented in open court (art. 227). Many of the clauses that the American drafters thought they were allowing in the new code in order to deal with highly unusual situations turned out, in fact, to establish the new (old) norms.

The biggest problem in the whole reform effort lay, not surprisingly, in retraining and changing ingrained habits and attitudes. SCAP recognized the need, but its efforts were really successful only with one major segment of legal officialdom, the judiciary. Judges became fully independent of all other law enforcement agencies, and the Supreme Court set up and managed a new judicial training institute. For police and procurators, however, the major changes were purges of allegedly fascist procurators and police and the bringing of the police under local control—two reforms that did not last even until the end of the occupation. SCAP wrote in its official history of police reform: "The new codes [the Civil Code and the Code of Criminal Procedure] embodied the Anglo-Saxon concept of presumption of innocence until guilt was established by regular court action. The changes required complete reorientation and training of the police in new techniques. In a land where persons had not been able to move freely and where the neighborhood associations made apprehension of suspects easy, the police had never experienced great need for perfecting techniques *to uncover and prepare conclusive evidence of guilt*. Retraining thus became a necessity if the new reforms were to be effective in preserving law and order." [18] Differing from the usual occupation pattern,

18. SCAP Monograph No. 55, "Police and Public Safety," p. 31, italics added.

here was an accurate diagnosis, but the remedy—local control
of the police as in the United States—proved to be totally un-
suitable to Japan.

Police procedure remained almost impervious to change
until the 1960s.[19] Oriented in the past toward continuous and
almost total surveillance of the population, the police normally
tackled a case by rounding up all the people known to them
(usually quite accurately) as potentially capable of committing
the offense and then holding as suspects all those who could not
establish their alibis. These suspects were then interrogated until
the guilty person or group confessed. It does not seem likely that
the police made many mistakes—they knew their own society
too well—but it is equally undeniable that they launched most
investigations on the basis of a hypothesis as to motive. Whenever this hypothesis turned out to be wrong, disaster usually resulted: false confessions were elicited or manufactured, and the
police stuck to them through thick and thin. To do otherwise
would have seriously damaged their prestige. The only real change
in the postwar world was that confessions had to be reinforced
with physical evidence. Too often, it appears, this evidence was
collected with the confession in mind; and evidence that contradicted it was either discarded or ignored. It must also be
pointed out, however, that in the Matsukawa case the police were
acting just after the new Code of Criminal Procedure had come
into effect; they could not legally employ their old methods, and
they did not yet fully understand what was called for under the
new code.

19. Note the comment of Judge Kishi Seiichi, Tokyo District Court:
"The warrant of arrest system in Japan is not serving its intended purpose of providing a judicial check on investigations. Rather the investigating authorities seem to work on the assumption that a warrant of arrest
allows them to take a suspect into custody and force a confession out of
him. In Japan arrest is not the end of an investigation but the beginning."
"Keiji saiban no hansei" (Reflections on Criminal Trials) (round-table
discussion), Jurisuto (special issue), September 1959, p. 55.

Virtually every contemporary commentator on the criminal law in Japan has criticized the tendency of police, procurators, and judges to construct hypotheses in solving criminal cases. Kainō argues, "In Japanese law schools the techniques of discovering facts, which are the most vital points in criminal trials, are not taught at all. Japanese law students are trained to formulate theories, not to make scientific investigations of fact." [20] And Judge Abe Hakaru, in an article, "The Education of the Legal Profession in Japan," observes, "Criminal proceedings such as the Matsukawa and Yakai cases, which centered on disputes concerning the determination of facts, drew strong public attention. The risk of erroneous judgment was sharply described and led many to believe in the necessity of scientific study of the factfinding process." [21] The long reliance on confessions had, of course, contributed to the police's lack of investigative abilities; and as things turned out it took the Matsukawa case and several similar cases to cause them to begin to modify (if not fully abandon) their well-established methods.

Kensatsu fassho no longer exists in Japan, although the police and the public are still arguing with each other (as they should be) about police methods and the kinds of evidence that really satisfy the Japanese mind concerning a suspect's guilt or innocence. As the Matsukawa case makes clear, the reform of criminal procedure by the occupation probably contributed less to the elimination of the old grievances than did SCAP's establishment of freedom of the press and of the right of people to criticize government officials (things that were previously restricted by various laws and forms of censorship). As will also become clear, the Matsukawa case itself is ambiguous with regard to the role played by the police in eliciting confessions and collecting evidence. The government in the end had to pay damages for what looked suspiciously like a police frame-up, and yet no

20. Hōritsu, p. 144.
21. In Law in Japan, p. 179.

court ever found that the confessions obtained by the police were extracted through force. It is possible, though, that in their zeal, or in ignorance of the proper methods, the police actually framed the guilty parties.

Very shortly after train number 412 was derailed early on the morning of August 17, 1949, Assistant Chief Inspector Tamagawa Tadashi of the Fukushima Prefectural Headquarters, National Rural Police (NRP), received a call from SCAP's Counter-Intelligence Corps (CIC) informing him of the wreck. He went directly to the scene by car, arriving sometime between 4:30 and 5:00 A.M., and he was joined there about dawn by three other leading investigators from Fukushima: Anzai Mitsuo, senior procurator of the Fukushima Regional Procuracy; Arai Yutaka, chief of the prefectural brigade of the National Rural Police (and a man who would cover himself with sufficient glory in the Matsukawa case to become, fifteen years later, head of the National Police Agency, the top law enforcement position in Japan); and Honda Izumi, chief of the Criminal Affairs Bureau, prefectural NRP. In the Matsukawa case Tamagawa was always to be the man in day-to-day charge of the investigation, while Anzai and Arai met the press and made the decisions about arrests and indictments. Tamagawa also took the knocks years later when the prosecution's case went sour. By the time of the final Supreme Court verdict settling the case, he was living in Aizu-Wakamatsu city and running a newspaper distributing agency; he said then to the press, "I got a raw deal."

It was still dark when Tamagawa reached the wooded valley north of Matsukawa station where the wreck had occurred. Someone standing nearby told him of huge clouds of steam and boiling water that had poured from the overturned locomotive, and he could see at least one mangled body near the cab. After only a cursory inspection he concluded that the train had been sabotaged—pulled-out spikes were lying all over the site—and he immediately sent squads of his men to the Japanese National Railroads track-maintenance sheds at Matsukawa and Kanayagawa stations to see if any tools had been stolen. Over the years the defense lawyers have been very critical of this order of Tamagawa's, since it suggested to them that he intended to frame railroad workers even before he had found, in the nearby paddy fields, the tools that had actually been used in the destruction. However, Tamagawa was an experienced investigator of train wrecks; he had been in charge of the unsolved Niwazaka case that had occurred a year earlier. He also knew that whoever had carried out the sabotage had to have heavier-duty tools than were commonly available. He therefore merely ordered the immediate investigation of their most likely source.

Sure enough, his men reported back to him that the Matsukawa shed had been broken into and that the crew chief there thought that some tools were missing. By the time this word arrived, a JNR employee named Katō had found the crowbar in the paddy field, and someone else, never to this day identified, came across the wrench. These tools, the ripped-off fishplates, spikes, chocks, and any other pieces of evidence anyone happened to find were simply put in a pile, even though Tamagawa and the other police officials on the scene knew that they should have been treated with greater care. In later police studies and statements, the investigators have always acknowledged that they did a poor job at the scene on the morning of the wreck, but they have also argued in extenuation that they had an impossible task in trying to control the site: it was raining, there were about a thousand passengers and local residents milling around, SCAP and the JNR were clamoring to have the line reopened, and the police did the best they could with inadequate photographic equipment and poorly trained personnel.

As August 17 wore on under a continuous drizzle, some 771 railroad workers arrived to remove the wreck from the right of way. Some twenty-four hours were required to rebuild the railroad tracks, and even then the first train to pass over them, a freight, derailed (but did not overturn), causing a further delay in reopening the single most important rail link between Tōhoku and Tokyo. That afternoon Anzai, Arai, and Honda set up an investigation headquarters at Kanayagawa station and held a press conference: the wreck had been caused by deliberate sabotage as even the untrained eye could see (reporters agreed, and no one has ever doubted it); the tools used for the sabotage had been found; they were probably stolen from the Matsukawa track maintenance shed; it took more than one man to do the job; and engineer Ōnishi of train 112, which was the last train to pass the site prior to the wreck, saw four or five young men in the vicinity. The police promised a speedy conclusion to the case.

Shortly after the news of the wreck reached union headquarters at Fukushima station that morning, the leadership of the National Railroad Workers' Union formed its own "democratic investigating team" and sent it to the site. This union team, with Takeda Hisashi, Honda Noboru, Okada Toramatsu, Ninomiya Yutaka, and Takahashi Haruo as members, immediately got in the hair of the police and aroused their suspicions. The police stopped the union leaders from talking to railroad workers at Matsukawa station and took pictures of all of them. These photographs led directly to the identification and arrest, at 1:30 P.M., of one Yabe Kan'ichirō, the head of the NRWU's Wakamatsu local. It will be recalled that he had spent the afternoon of August 16 attending the Tōshiba factory's strike meeting even though he was wanted by the police in connection with an earlier union demonstration against the railroad in which some official records had been destroyed. Anzai hinted to the press that Yabe was actually being held as a suspect in the train sabotage case, and on the eighteenth all Tokyo papers reported the arrest of a Communist unionist in connection with the Matsukawa case. The issue was allowed to die quietly a few days later when Yabe's alibi for the night of August 16–17 stood up.

If Suzuki and Sugiura actually did mastermind the sabotage, their scheduling of it for the night of the Bon festival and at some distance from Fukushima in order to draw suspicion away from railroad workers flopped miserably. The press immediately took up the theme of "another Mitaka case," and the Tokyo *Asahi* of August 19 ran big headlines saying: FOCUS ON NATIONAL RAILROAD UNION CONNECTION. Its story was based on an interview with Criminal Affairs Bureau chief Honda, in which he made the following points: several former railroad workers had attended the Tōshiba strike meeting on August 16, the police had confirmed that the tools came from a JNR track crew, and a Tōshiba manager had informed the police of a suspicious statement attributed to the wife of Ōta Shōji. According to the *Asahi*, on the morning of August 16 Mrs. Ōta had said to another worker at the Matsukawa plant, "Another Mitaka incident is going to occur this evening." Since Ōta himself had an alibi, this lead did not produce immediate results, but the police were seriously looking into the whole question of union activity and the links between the NRWU and Tōshiba immediately prior to the wreck.

On that same day, August 19, *Akahata* (the organ of the Communist party) charged "frame-up" in its headlines and said that no Communist could possibly be implicated because one of the engineers killed had been a "party sympathizer." However, that same afternoon the government's Chief Cabinet Secretary, Masuda Kaneshichi, released this statement to the press: "This was an even more vicious crime than the Mitaka incident. On August 17 Hayashi Hyakurō, a Communist party member of the Diet, called on me and asked me not to describe this accident as an act of the Communist party. I answered that I understood his point of view but that the ideological trends surrounding this latest incident are the same as in the numerous accidents that took place following the mass layoffs." [22] An

22. *Fukushima mimpō* and *Yomiuri shimbun*, August 19, 1949

official statement such as this carried a lot of weight in Japan at the time, and every newspaper in the nation save those controlled by the Communists echoed Masuda's belief. In Fukushima the police utilized the new anti-Communist climate to raid union offices all over the prefecture and arrest suspects in the Taira and related cases.

Nothing much more happened after that for about a month. Takeda and the Tōhoku Committee of the Japanese Communist party issued statements denouncing Masuda and the Yoshida government and asserting that the union would never have wrecked a train. Anzai and Arai held less frequent news conferences and said nothing more than that the police were working on various leads. Reporters covering the case began to get bored (and a little snide): they filed stories about the incompetence of the police and how they were investigating every urchin and small fry in northern Fukushima. At the Tōshiba plant the one-day strike on August 17 came and went without incident and also without shaking management in its decision to fire thirty-two workers. Sugiura filed a petition with the prefectural labor relations board (a record of which is contained in the SCAP Archives), contending that his firing was illegal and appealing for an order of reinstatement. By the time the board got around to considering it, Sugiura had been arrested, and he therefore accepted his retirement pay while in prison and withdrew his appeal.[23]

Satō Hajime stayed on at Matsukawa until late August and

(both reprinted in Sendai Kōtō Saibansho, Dai Ichi Keijibu, *Matsukawa jiken sashimodoshi-shin kōhan shiryō*, Vol. 14, *Shimbun kiji no utsushi*, pp. 9, 13). See also *Tokyo shimbun*, August 19, 1949.

23. SCAP Archives, Tōhoku Civil Affairs Region, box 2612. See "Fukushima Prefectural Labor Relations Committee, Monthly Report," November 1949 (dated December 6, 1949), p. 2, case 4; and December 1949 (dated January 11, 1950), p. 1, case 2. Sugiura filed his complaint of an unfair labor practice on September 2, 1949; his final retirement from the Tōshiba company was backdated to August 16, 1949.

then returned to Tokyo. Immediately after the wreck he reported it to his union headquarters by telegram, saying that a railroad disaster had occurred but that it had nothing to do with his work. After Satō left, Sugiura attempted to hold the fired employees together in a united front against Tōshiba, but this effort began to collapse during September. Ōuchi Shōzō had long harbored doubts about his Communist party affiliation and Sugiura's leadership, and he had both a paralyzed mother and a younger sister working in a textile mill to worry about. On September 22 he therefore visited the Matsukawa factory, accepted his retirement pay, and resigned from the union. Ōuchi's growing resentment against the party and Sugiura would prove quite useful a few weeks later to a skilled police interrogator who was trying to obtain a statement from him.

The police were keeping the actual course of their investigation to themselves, and they never did reveal the full details of how they broke the case until their internal documents were made public in 1961 at the Sendai retrial. However, in March 1953, National Rural Police Headquarters published a confidential report, entitled A Study of the Matsukawa Case, for the information and education of other police officials. With a preface by Arai Yutaka, this booklet was marked bugaihi ("internal use only"), and each copy was numbered. Years later it figured in the Matsukawa compensation trials and suits against the government, when the plaintiffs attempted to introduce it as evidence of official bad faith in the investigation of the case.[24] This police document offers the most complete explanation of how the case was broken, although even it leaves out one or two never fully revealed details.

24. Kokka Chihō Keisatsu Honbu Keiji-bu Sōsa-ka, ed., Matsukawa jiken no kenkyū (Tokyo, 1953), "Criminal Police Materials Vol. 15." I possess a copy of and have used for this book serial number 849. On the use of this police study in the compensation trials, see Matsukawa Zenkoku Renraku Kaigi (Matsukawa National Liaison Council), comp., Matsukawa tsūshin (Matsukawa Bulletin), No. 147, April 15, 1969.

During 1949 the National Rural Police had a total of 860 police officers in Fukushima prefecture, and Arai assigned 32 of them to work on the Matsukawa case. In addition an unspecified number of officers from the Fukushima Municipal Police were detailed to work with the NRP.[25] Eleven procurators also devoted themselves full time to the investigation, including Yamamoto Isamu and Suzuki Hisanori, who actually prosecuted the eventual defendants in court. Of these procurators, five were borrowed from Osaka, Kobe, Aomori, Akita, and Sendai, and their relative unfamiliarity with Fukushima contributed to some of the difficulties—acknowledged by the police—in getting the confessions into the best possible form for presentation in court. What the police do not admit was that some friction also arose between procurator Yamamoto, who was in charge of the case on the procuracy side, and the procurator brought in from Akita, whose elder brother was a classmate of Anzai's (Fukushima's chief procurator). Yamamoto had been a lawyer in Taiwan during the war, and his alleged airs as a former colonialist, plus the fact that the Akita procurator sometimes used his connections to go directly to Anzai over Yamamoto's head, contributed to poor liaison and confusion in preparing the evidence in the case.[26]

The police and procurators have always claimed that they did not approach the case with any preconceived line of investigation (and they so claimed again in their 1953 booklet),

25. The authorized complement of NRP officers for Fukushima prefecture was 860, and during 1949 it was up to full strength. The authorized number of so-called autonomous police—i.e., locally financed and locally controlled municipal police—for the five cities of Fukushima was 619, but the local police were understrength in every city. The approximate figures of actual staff were: Fukushima city, 129; Kōriyama, 97; Wakamatsu, 90; Taira, 52; and Shirakawa, 32 (total: 400). See SCAP Archives, box 2575, file "Police."

26. See *Nihon keizai shimbun*, October 14, 1949; *Sandē mainichi*, December 20, 1953.

but it is perfectly obvious that they did. The police study of the Matsukawa case devotes several pages to the trade union situation in Fukushima and then concludes: "This objective situation [just described] was both a direct and an indirect cause of the crime, and it later proved to be a key factor in the success of the investigation. Our men, at the beginning of the investigation, made an analysis of this objective situation and thereby gained a general comprehension of the case." [27] The police directed the first stage of their investigation exclusively to checking the prophecy of Ōta's wife, inquiring into Satō Hajime's reasons for being in Matsukawa, asking for alibis from all NRWU leaders, and generally investigating the nature of Communist activity in the unions in Fukushima.

This approach did not turn up anything that would warrant an arrest. It was therefore temporarily set aside while the investigation entered a second stage, one that all Japanese police understood and were completely at home with. About two weeks after the wreck the police began a general check of alibis of everyone they could conceivably imagine might have been involved, holding as suspects anybody who could not establish one. The police reasoned that their only clue was the stolen tools and that it was unlikely that anybody other than a local resident would have known where to steal them. They first singled out for investigation local young hoodlums (furyō seinen), but before they were through, the sweep included about four thousand people—half the population of Matsukawa village.[28] The chief inspectors also tapped some thirty-two known criminals in the Fukushima area, asking them to obtain hearsay information. They wanted to know about all suspicious movements at the Kuroiwa festival or at the girl revue in Matsukawa, mischievous passengers on trains, people who bore a grudge against the railroad, or people who had any kind of record of crimes or threats

27. Matsukawa jiken no kenkyū, p. 11.
28. Sandē mainichi, December 20, 1953.

against people in general or against public property. The police checked every lead for the time and place of the person's whereabouts on the night of August 16 and for his physical capacity to have committed the crime. According to the *Weekly Asahi*, "A state of terror descended on the region around Fukushima city and throughout Adachi county. Tips and information circulated in every house like lice, while youths were formed into groups and brought to confront the inspectors. Rumors fed off rumors." [29]

Reporters for the big Tokyo papers did not think too much of these rural police methods, and they needled the police in their stories. Some reporters wrote that the case was proving to be unsolvable. Despite this skepticism, the newsmen continued to file stories for the back pages of their papers on the various rapists, petty thieves, black marketeers, and people with forged railroad passes who were being caught in the net. In the *Mainichi* of September 12, buried in a small article concerning the arrest for questioning of a former railroad employee with a poor alibi, there was mentioned the arrest of an even more insignificant person: "Also on the tenth the police reported the arrest of Akama Katsumi, age nineteen, of Kuroiwa, Fukushima city, on suspicion of rape. He is a former track maintenance worker of the Nagaigawa track crew." That was all; there was no more reporting in the Tokyo press about the Matsukawa case until September 23. Although the *Mainichi* did not know it, this last arrest was causing a good deal of excitement at investigation headquarters.

Working under Bureau Chief Honda and Assistant Inspector Tamagawa, police sergeant Takeda Tatsuo of the Fukushima Municipal Police had been specializing for two weeks on the alibis of known juvenile delinquents. On or about September 6, one of Takeda's policemen brought in two youths, ages

29. *Shūkan asahi*, November 29, 1953.

nineteen and twenty, who had no alibis for the night of August 16 and one of whose parents had said that she didn't know where her son had been all night. Takeda did not think that these two had anything to do with the wreck, but he questioned them thoroughly anyway. As it happened, they were Iijima Yoshio and Andō Sadao, the two friends Akama had chatted with after the Kuroiwa festival. In the course of his interrogation, sergeant Takeda apparently managed to pick up the name of Kaneko Tsuyoko, a nineteen-year-old girl employed at the big Nittō spinning works in southern Fukushima city, who may or may not have been raped over a year earlier by either Iijima or Andō—or by Akama, their friend, whose name they supplied to the police probably to divert suspicion from themselves (the police have never explained the rape case that ostensibly gave them a hold over Iijima and Andō). Takeda merely recorded this information for later use. What really startled him was their statement that Akama had spoken to them about the likelihood of a train wreck that night, before it had actually occurred.

On September 9, 1949, Takeda arrested Akama and booked him, along with Iijima, Andō, and several other delinquents, on suspicion of rape. This was a patently false arrest—the rape had allegedly taken place in February 1948—but the practice of arresting a suspect on one charge in order to obtain evidence against him on another was very common (until February 26, 1970, when the Tokyo District Court in the case of *Japan v. Tsukamoto* held the practice to be unconstitutional).[30] There is

30. In early 1967 a thirty-two-year-old man, Tsukamoto Kazuo, was arrested on a charge of trespassing and the theft, three years earlier, of a wristwatch. After being held for twenty-three days he confessed to arson in a fire that had occurred on November 29, 1965, the crime that the police had in mind throughout their investigation of him. He was indicted solely on the basis of this confession, and the procurator asked for thirteen years imprisonment. Judge Aizawa Masahige found that Tsukamoto's confession had been unconstitutionally obtained, because the charges

very little likelihood that the police actually intended to bring Akama to trial on rape charges, but they did prepare the case and use the rape threat to scare him. Takeda tricked Miss Kaneko into signing a deposition against Akama by saying to her that Akama had admitted the offense and that the police demanded her cooperation; he then went back to Akama and showed him the complaint she had signed against him. Akama became scared and confused, and then Tamagawa and Takeda together started questioning him about something much more serious—his prediction of the Matsukawa train wreck and how he happened to know about it in advance. Thus began the process of inducing Akama to confess to a capital offense.

Both Tamagawa and Takeda have sworn under oath that they did not beat Akama or otherwise torture him, and Akama has acknowledged this, contending instead that he was subjected to "spiritual torture." The key clue against him was the prophecy reported by Iijima and Andō, which Akama denied even when confronted by the pair. According to the police report, A Study of the Matsukawa Case, he was unable to keep up his denial in the face of the "zeal" (netsui) of the investigators and therefore confessed.[31] It was no doubt a bit nastier than that, although the zeal shown by these particular investigators was not exceptional in Japanese criminal cases of the time.

Later in court Akama claimed that Tamagawa swore to him that he was lying, showed him a fat compendium of laws, and read where he could be thrown into prison for life for telling lies. Tamagawa also threatened to go through with the rape indict-

---

against him had not been explained at the time of his arrest. The judge did not rule out all cases of arrest for one crime and indictment for another, but he held that there must be sufficient evidence of the first crime to warrant arrest in the first place. This decision was unprecedented in Japan. See New York Times, March 1, 1970; Japan Times, February 27, 1970.

31. Matsukawa jiken no kenkyū, p. 27.

ment and "force him to reenact the crime in the courtroom" if he did not tell the truth. Takeda allegedly stuck a dagger under his heart and said he'd kill him on the spot if he kept on lying. Akama said that all of these threats, plus the rape accusation, scared him almost to death, but they were not the things that broke him down. It was the testimony of his grandmother, Akama Mina, age seventy-four. Takeda called her to the police station and obtained her signature on a statement saying that Akama did not return home the night of the Bon festival until after 4:00 A.M. He showed this to Akama, who said later he felt "forsaken by everyone, even my grandmother." The police also added that the Communists were saying that he had done it and urged him to get even with the Communists.

One of the defense attorneys, Kikuchi Yōnosuke of the Sendai Bar Association, said later to the press that Akama was "a big-mouthed delinquent," who was scared by the police because he was out on bail and who, being immature, succumbed to a lot of old police tricks.[32] Judge Monden in the retrial verdict said that he was convinced Akama had simply tried to ingratiate himself with his interrogators by providing concrete answers in response to their hints and leading questions.[33] Suzuki Makoto, one of the defendants, offers a different explanation: "Akama was made to believe that he had been used by the Communist party in the Date station case and that Communist party members were now trying to blame him alone for the Matsukawa wreck. Akama did not fully understand how the bail money for him had been arranged, and he had come to have a grudge against the Communist party."[34] Akama himself seemed to confirm

32. *Shūkan asahi*, November 29, 1953.

33. "Matsukawa jiken hanketsu zenbun, sashimodoshi ato no dai-ni-shin hanketsu" (Complete Text of the Matsukawa Case Verdict, The Decision of the Second Trial Following the Return of the Case), *Hanrei jihō* (Review of Leading Cases), No. 275 (November 11, 1961), p. 55.

34. *Matsukawa jiken kōso shuisho* (Matsukawa Case Kōso [First Instance] Appeal Documents), July 1951, Vol. 1, p. 475.

Suzuki's view, at least according to the earliest explanation he made of his confession, before trial strategy and propaganda considerations became paramount. On October 8, 1949, a *Mainichi* reporter published what was allegedly an inside account of why Akama confessed. Under banner headlines reading I WAS TAKEN IN (*Watakushi wa damasareta*) and A CRIME FOR 10,000 YEN, the reporter explained that Akama was forced to commit the crime by Suzuki Makoto and others because he owed the Communist party ¥10,000 in bail money the party had put up for him after he was arrested in the Date case. His resentment at this party pressure supposedly caused him to confess.

Whatever the case, on September 19, 1949, Akama began to talk. He described the actual execution of the crime, identified Honda and Takahashi as his cosaboteurs from the railroad union, said that two more came from Tōshiba whom he did not know by name, and revealed the names of the participants and what they said in the August 15 conspiracy meeting. Two days later, on the basis of photographs shown him by the police, he identified Satō Hajime and Hamazaki from Tōshiba as the fourth and fifth members of the actual sabotage party. Procurator Yamamoto later told the first court that the police were flabbergasted by these revelations. They had thought that Akama might have made an accurate prediction at the Kuroiwa festival but that he was too insignificant a person actually to have been involved in such a crime. Since he was a member of the union and had been involved in the Date case, he had reason to hang around union headquarters and might have overheard something not intended for him. Being young and irresponsible, he had then revealed it to his friends. Little did they realize, they said, that for a week they had had one of the actual saboteurs in their hands.

Akama's confessions, actually detailed answers to questions, were hurriedly written up, signed by Akama, and carried to procurator Anzai. On September 22, at five o'clock in the morning, six special squads of National Rural Police called at the homes of Honda, Ninomiya, Suzuki, Abe, Takahashi, and Hamazaki in the Fukushima area and took them into custody. In Tokyo at the same time of day NRP officers picked up Satō Hajime at the Tōshiba hostel in Tsurumi and put him on a train under police guard for Fukushima. All of these new arrestees were lodged, along with Akama, in Fukushima Central police station.

The police did not interrogate all the new suspects in the same way that they had Akama. Generally speaking, they just got basic facts from the union leaders and looked for a weak link among the people now in their hands on which to concentrate. Hamazaki appeared promising. One line of argument with him was that the others arrested were saying that he alone had done it and that the Communist party was trying to pin the blame on him, just as it had done to Takeuchi in the Mitaka case, in order to save its leaders. This approach was also working with Akama, who continued to confess, draw maps, explain details, and so forth, having been told that "Honda is saying that you forced him to go along"—a not very creative use of the ancient "prisoner's dilemma." Hamazaki was not tortured or beaten; perhaps there was a little *jūdō*, which all police enjoyed and practiced a good deal, but nothing serious, "with implements," as the press of the time put it. All major authorities on the case, with the exception of later propagandists, agree that Tamagawa was too experienced for that.

Hamazaki confessed what he knew, which allowed the police to penetrate the conspiracy at the Tōshiba plant. At ten o'clock on the morning of October 4, procurator Anzai and police chief Arai held a news conference to announce the second series of arrests in the Matsukawa case, which had been made that morning, again at five o'clock. This new batch included Sugiura, Satō Shiroji, Ōuchi, Ōta, and Kobayashi, bringing to a total of thirteen the suspects thus far apprehended. The press was jubilant about all of this, and a great deal of evidence from the confessions was released to reporters at this time. Most newspapers had already concluded that the confessions were accurate when one of Akama's gloves was found in Nigori Creek; the headlines read: CREEK DRAGGED IN ACCORDANCE WITH AKAMA'S CONFESSION; DISCARDED GLOVE DISCOVERED. It was several years before anybody even raised the question whether the recovered glove was actually Akama's.

Among the Tōshiba suspects, Ōta, Ōuchi, and Kobayashi all confessed, leading to the arrests of Kikuchi on October 8 and of Nikaidō Takeo and Nikaidō Sonoko on October 16. Kikuchi and Nikaidō Sonoko also confessed to their interrogators that they had been involved. On October 10 procurator Anzai decided to indict eight of his suspects. As he explained to the *Asahi*, the twenty-day detention period allowed under the new Code of Criminal Procedure was about to run out, and although he did not think the case was yet in perfect shape, he had to go ahead. He did reassure the press that in addition to Akama's confession, the confessions of Hamazaki, Ōuchi, and Kobayashi all tended to agree with the emerging picture of conspiracy, tool theft, and actual commission of the crime. Therefore, he had filed formal complaints against Akama and the first seven arrested, charging them with violation of article 126 of the Penal Code (destruction of trains) and naming them all as "coprincipals" under article 60 ("Two or more persons who act jointly in the commission of a crime are all principals").

The Japanese law of coprincipals is not exactly the same as the Anglo-American law of conspiracy, and generally speaking the Japanese use the term "coprincipal" (*kyōdō seihan*) in preference to "conspirator" in official translations. As Professor Hirano explains:

> The Japanese Penal Code divides accomplices into coprincipals, instigators, and accessories. . . . An instigator is

punished within the same statutory limits as provided for a
principal, but an accessory always benefits from a statutory
reduction of punishment [Penal Code, arts. 60–62]. . . .
The Japanese cases have gone beyond the limits set by the
Penal Code, however, and have developed the concept of
a "conspiratorial coprincipal" [kyōbō kyōdō seihan]. Once a
conspiracy to commit a crime has been entered into, those
who actually carried out the acts constituting the crime as
well as those who did not are treated as principals.

This doctrine originated in 1922 with a decision of the old
Supreme Court and has been consistently expanded since then
to the point that today "the tendency in lower courts has been
to punish as conspiratorial coprincipals even those who merely
had the facts constituting the conspiracy confided to them."
Hirano, whose article was published in 1963, concludes that "it
is still undecided whether a conspiracy is an act or a state of
mind," but he adds, "A recent decision of the Supreme Court
seems to have ruled that it is necessary not only to prove the
existence of a state of mental agreement but also to produce
enough evidence to show the act of forming the conspiracy,
including the time and place of formation." [35] The case that he
had in mind was Suzuki v. Japan, Supreme Court, Grand Bench,
August 10, 1959—or, as it is more commonly known, the
Matsukawa case.

With eight suspects indicted and eight more in custody,
the procurators and police had to decide what to do about
several other names that had appeared in their confession documents. Ōta had provided the details of the August 13 conspiracy meeting at the NRWU offices, and from this they were
able to gain an understanding of the original NRWU meeting

35. Law in Japan, pp. 288–290. On the doctrine of coprincipals, see
also Ueda Seikichi and Gotō Shōjirō, Ayamatta saiban (Mistrials) (Tokyo,
1960), pp. 208–209.

on August 12 and to implicate the top leaders of the railroad workers' union. With this information in hand, on October 21, the police struck again, this time pulling in the "big shots" (ōmono) of the NRWU and one or two other key people, namely, Takeda, Saitō, Okada, Katō, and Honda Yoshihiro, chief of the Fukushima Bureau of the Communist party newspaper, Akahata.

The procurators now had twenty-one people in custody, but they were not entirely happy among themselves with the way things looked. They released Honda Yoshihiro without explanation, even though he was clearly named by Ōta as having attended the August 13 conspiracy meeting. They were also sufficiently worried about their case against Okada that in late November they released him and then rearrested and charged him just before the trial began on December 5. Satō Hajime was encouraged by this; on November 28 he wrote to his brother-in-law from prison: "The prosecution has lost much of its confidence about the case. This is seen clearly in the procurator's release of Honda and Okada. I read a recent news report that the procurators were split over this matter. Some are demanding a new investigation of the case." [36] There were all kinds of other little details that were bothering the procurators. Akama had said that Takahashi and a man identified only as Hirukawa had attended the August 15 conspiracy meeting—Akama had, in fact, sat between them—but Takahashi could prove that he was in Yonezawa at the time and Hirukawa also had an alibi. It was not an impossible problem; Akama readily changed his confession, saying that he did not know any of these people well. And Akama's confession was just too detailed and reinforced by

36. Matsukawa Bunshū Hensan Iinkai (Matsukawa Letter Anthology Compilation Committee), ed., Aijō wa kabe o tōshite, Matsukawa jiken no hikoku to kazoku no tegami (Love Penetrates the Walls, Letters Between the Matsukawa Defendants and Their Families) (Tokyo, 1954), p. 132.

other confessions for anyone to doubt that it was substantially correct. The important thing, therefore, was to keep Akama in a confessing mood.

Before the first of October the procurators moved Akama from Fukushima Central to Hobara police station, a rural office located about the same distance to the northeast of the city that Matsukawa is to the south. There Akama enjoyed unprecedented treatment. He was fed all he wanted, supplied with cigarettes, offered sake and taken to watch a local festival, and given free run of the police station to exercise and play table tennis with the men on duty. The police chief even took a bath with him one night (not as odd as this may seem, given Japan's ritual bathing culture; however, the chief did not have to wash his back!), and the fire chief dropped by to congratulate Akama for his contribution to the "extermination of reds" (aka taiji).[37] After having been returned to Fukushima Central police station on December 1, Akama sent a postcard to the chief of Hobara station saying: "I am much indebted to you for your care. . . . I want to finish my term in prison as soon as possible and return to the straight and narrow after my release."[38] This card was later cited by the judge in the verdict of the first trial as further evidence of Akama's self-admitted guilt.

The date of Akama's postcard, December 3, is significant, for it was only two days before the trial began. Ever since he had begun to confess in September Akama had vacillated wildly on whether he would sustain or denounce his confession when he got in court. It is impossible to know his true feelings, since his rights to counsel and to see counsel privately were repeatedly violated.[39] Part of the problem was that he did not know what

37. Satō Hajime, Hikoku (Defendants) (Tokyo, 1958), p. 61.
38. Fukushima Chihō Saibansho (Fukushima District Court), Matsukawa jiken dai-isshin hanketsu (Matsukawa Case First Trial Verdict) (Fukushima, January 12, 1951), p. 279.
39. See Ōtsuka Kazuo, "Matsukawa jiken ni okeru himitsu kōtsū

kind of lawyer he wanted. The League of Free Jurists (Jiyū Hōsō Dan), a famous old prewar association of liberal attorneys which became after the war virtually a Communist-front organization, came immediately to his aid, since its representatives were in Fukushima defending the workers who had been arrested in the Taira and Date cases. However, at each meeting he had with Ōtsuka Kazuo, one of the two Communist lawyers who led the defense in the Matsukawa case throughout its long history, the police chief was present and reported to the procurators anything Akama said that might conceivably indicate that he had admitted his guilt to his lawyer.[40]

The police wanted Akama to accept a lawyer assigned by the Fukushima Bar Association, and he did have several interviews with its representatives. These men indicated that they were willing to defend him whether he was guilty or not, and the interest of the police seems to have been more in shutting out the League of Free Jurists, which had often disrupted courtrooms in political cases, than in denying Akama adequate counsel. However, under pressure from his elder brother, who was a Communist, and influenced by a Christian minister who visited him in prison, Akama ultimately accepted the same lawyers who defended the rest of the suspects, namely, the League of Free Jurists. Also after being returned to Fukushima Central police station on December 1, he for the first time came in contact with

---

ken no shingai" (Infringement of the Right of Secret Communication in the Matsukawa Case), *Jiyū to seigi* (Freedom and Justice), January 1966, pp. 19–24. (*Jiyū to seigi* is the organ of the Nihon Bengoshi Rengōkai, The Federation of Japanese Attorneys.)

40. The chief attorneys in the Matsukawa case, who led the defense from the beginning to the end, were Okabayashi Tatsuo, one of the founders of the postwar League of Free Jurists, and Ōtsuka Kazuo, a dynamic young Communist who had been admitted to the bar only three months before the Matsukawa incident occurred and who was defending the Taira miners. Until the final verdict in 1963, Ōtsuka's career was associated entirely with the Matsukawa case. See *Asahi shimbun*, September 13, 1963.

the other defendants and became acquainted with their perspective on the case. Thus it was that, for whatever combination of conflicting pressures, Akama went into court on December 5 convinced that he had been tricked not by the Communists, as he had told the press in October, but by the police; and he was ready to recant his confession.

According to the slang that is used around Japanese courtrooms, the first trial of a case at a district court (of which there are forty-nine in Japan) has the qualities of being in a "fresh fish shop" (sakanaya), the second trial at a high court (of which there are eight) is more like savoring dried fish (karamono), and the third trial before the Supreme Court suggests nibbling on canned fish (kanzume). All this is a way of saying that the judicial process becomes more refined as one goes up in the hierarchy but that there is also a loss in pungency.[41] This was borne out in the Matsukawa case, both on the bench and in the performances of the prosecutors and defense attorneys. The presiding judge at the first trial, Nagao Makoto, was referred to in the press as "an old yoshin judge," that is a judge trained in prewar criminal justice and adept at conducting a yoshin, the pretrial investigation that formed the heart of the old inquisitorial procedure. He tended to side heavily with the procurators, who themselves usually merely said "meddling" (osekkai) whenever the defense challenged the facts of their case (e.g., on whether fishplates had been removed from the tracks in one or two places). One reporter who attended the first trial recalled judge Nagao as a type of elderly Japanese man who wore his hair close-cropped, what the Japanese call an igaguri-atama ("chestnut head"), and something like what we mean by the phrase "a tough old buzzard."[42]

However, a judge needed to be tough for this trial. During

41. Asahi shimbun, September 13, 1963 (round-table discussion).
42. Asahi shimbun, August 9, 1961 (round-table discussion).

1949, all of the trials involving Communists, particularly the People's Streetcar and Mitaka cases, had been disrupted by violent demonstrations in the courtroom and by singing and shouting from the defendants and audience. The first Matsukawa trial saw these practices come to a head and lead to demands for much stronger contempt-of-court rules than SCAP had thus far allowed. The defendants entered Fukushima District Courtroom at 9:41 A.M., December 5, 1949, singing the "Internationale" at the top of their voices; and a year later, on December 6, 1950, after ninety-seven days of public hearings and eleven days of on-site inspection, the trial ended with a courtroom riot as Nagao was attempting to read his verdict. During every court session the room had been packed with union members, families of the defendants, and students, who usually brought concealed red flags with them to be unfurled at proper moments, and a good deal of the court's time was taken up with arguments between Judge Nagao and chief defense attorney Okabayashi about the judge's refusal to allow more spectators into the courtroom than there were seats.

As for the defense strategy, most commentators on the case believe that the defendants' counsel made no attempt to present an adequate defense, either because the defense attorneys were themselves unskilled at using the new adversary procedures or because they actually were more interested in what political mileage they could get out of the case than in seeing the defendants acquitted. Okabayashi's standard gambits were that the whole case was nothing more than a frame-up engineered by "Yoshida fascists" and that the confessions had been obtained by torture, which was contrary to the new democratic constitution. Only in later years did he and other defense attorneys become much more careful in dealing with the facts of the case, perhaps after they had actually investigated it and found that they really did have a strong defense case.

The Communist party took a special interest in the trial:

Akahata covered it daily, and the party sent two of its leading central committee members, Takakura Teru and Hakamada Satomi, to Fukushima to serve as "special defense counsels" (*tokubetsu bengonin*). Some idea of Takakura's contribution can be gained from his first speech to the court: "Our first desire is to obtain true national independence for all Japanese. However, there are some in this country who do not want independence, and it is from their actions that we can discover the origins of this incident. In order to bring foreign capital into Japan they had to lower the wages of Japanese workers well below international levels. With this objective in mind they are trying to suppress the revolutionary workers and the Japanese Communist party, who are actually fighting to protect Japan's industries." [43]

Hakamada devoted himself almost entirely to the torture theme, haranguing the court with countless stories of prewar repression of the Communists by the Tokkō (Special Higher Police). One of his charges is interesting both because it is so bizarre and because it was still being repeated twenty years after the Matsukawa incident occurred. Both Kobayashi and Satō Hajime had testified that Inspector Tamagawa and NRP sergeant Anzai Inomatsu (no relation to senior procurator Anzai), in the course of interrogating them, had identified themselves as former members of the Tokkō. If they actually did so, they must have been merely trying to intimidate the suspects, since all members of the Tokkō had been purged and they would not have been holding their police jobs. [44] Anzai went on to say, so it is alleged, that he had served with the Tokkō in Manchuria where he had developed a taste for human flesh. "Sergeant Anzai said to me," asserted Satō, "that in Manchuria he had developed an

43. *Akahata*, December 17, 1949.

44. SCAPIN 115 of October 10, 1945, prohibited the reemployment in positions of responsibility of former members of the Tokkō. See Hironaka Toshio, *Sengo Nihon no keisatsu* (The Police of Postwar Japan) (Tokyo, 1968), pp. 30–34.

appetite for *sukiyaki* made from human flesh and that even now when he sees five or six men lined up he wants to cut them up." [45] Hakamada embellished these stories, and on December 19, 1949, in an interview at Japanese Communist party headquarters in Yoyogi, Tokyo, he charged that Anzai had threatened Kobayashi by saying, "I ate *sukiyaki* made of human flesh four or five times in Manchuria. . . . When you get the death penalty, my boy, we'll cut you up and preserve you in alcohol." Hakamada concluded, "Fukushima is different from Tokyo; it's in the countryside. The intrigues of the police and procurators there and their methods of framing people are beyond words." [46] Whether this propaganda was very crude or rather effective, given its audience, is impossible to know, but it began one strain of hyperbole on the defense side in the Matsukawa case that never declined so long as the case was before the courts. For example, the *Matsukawa nyūsu* (*Matsukawa News*) of October 20, 1969, was still ranting about the former Tokkō, Tamagawa, and the Manchurian flesh-eater, Anzai.

Just as police chief Arai had commissioned a classified study of the Matsukawa case from the police point of view, procurators Yamamoto Isamu and Suzuki Hisanori, who actually prosecuted the case, wrote one concerning the first trial for the edification of other public procurators. Entitled *A Study of the Courtroom Procedures Employed in the Matsukawa Case*, it was published in June 1952 by the Procuracy Research Institute and was classified "secret" (*hi*). [47] In this book Yamamoto and Suzuki dwell on the reforms needed in order to maintain order in court, and they accuse the defense counsels of slander. They speak of

45. *Akahata*, October 16, 1949. Satō repeated this story years later in his autobiography; see Nakasone Yasuhiro, et al., *Warera Taishōkko* (We, Children of the Taishō Era) (Tokyo, 1961), p. 280.

46. *Akahata*, December 20, 1949.

47. *Matsukawa jiken ni okeru kōhan tetsuzuki no un'yō ni kan suru kenkyū* (Tokyo: Kensatsu Kenkyū Sho, 1952), "The Procurator's Research Library Vol. 7." "Secret."

the special problems of the Communist party's packing the courtroom, of whether the defendants' right to counsel had been in-
fringed, and of the propriety of using as evidence statements
that the defendants made to each other or to their counsel and
which the police overhead (they see nothing wrong with the
latter practice). They contend that their investigation of the
case and presentation of it in court were as fair as they could be,
given the new procedures under which they had to work and the
highly political nature of the case. They also criticize the defense for not seriously attempting to establish the defendants'
alibis for the times of the alleged conspiracy meetings and the
actual perpetration of the crime. They felt that the defense did
not do so for fear that the procurators would then bring in
counterevidence on such contested points.

Very few items of evidence were actually explored during
the trial. Akama Mina testified that her grandson was home
shortly after 1:00 A.M. on August 17 and that she had not read
the document she signed at the police station in September. The
trial judge, however, ruled her evidence to be biased. Neither
Akama's parents nor his eleven-year-old cousin, whom he allegedly woke when he came in that night, were asked to testify
for either side. Other defendants' attempts to establish alibis
were based on the testimony of relatives or of union colleagues
and were in virtually every case ruled not reliable in the judge's
written verdict.

Possibly the most important piece of evidence in the first
and second trials was only mentioned at the very end of the first
trial. This was Takahashi Haruo's physical disability, something
he had not mentioned either in court or to his attorney, because
he was ashamed of it. Judge Nagao simply ignored it, saying
that Takahashi had been fully capable of walking during the on-
site inspection that the whole court had made during the middle
of the trial. Twelve years later, however, jurists and court reporters would be writing that if the government had really set

out to frame railroad workers for the Matsukawa wreck they could hardly have chosen two worse targets than Takahashi and Honda—one was a cripple and the other had been dead drunk on the night in question.

Some of the most important evidence cited against the defendants came about as a result of the on-site inspection or from the testimony of newspaper reporters. During the first part of April 1950 the entire court—judges, heavily guarded defendants, procurators, and defense attorneys—visited all the major sites of the case, from the Kuroiwa Buddha to the Tōshiba factory, allegedly in an effort to establish for the judges the credibility of the confessions. While on this outing and standing near the Morinaga bridge, police officer Satō Noboru, who was assigned to guard Honda, overheard Akama say to Honda, "Isn't it over there that we took a rest?" while pointing with his chin. The defense did not contest officer Satō's testimony when he repeated it later in court, and Judge Nagao wrote it into his verdict as a partial corroboration of Akama's confession.

Similarly, a reporter for the *Fukushima mimpō* interviewed Hamazaki on October 6, 1949, while he was in the custody of the police. Hamazaki, thinking that the reporter was friendly, said to him, "I've done a terrible thing, and I plan to tell the truth from now on." It has never been established whether Hamazaki was referring to his having committed the crime or to having confessed falsely to the police, but Judge Nagao took it as evidence of his guilt.[48]

Certainly the most highly contested point of law in the whole trial was the admissibility of Akama's confession. On the opening day of the trial Akama stood up and shouted, "I swear to God I'm innocent" (*Shimmei ni chikatte shiroi*), and he never afterward wavered from that. Having foreseen that some-

48. For Police Officer Satō's statement, see *Matsukawa jiken daiisshin hanketsu*, p. 304; for the *Fukushima mimpō* reporter's statement, ibid., pp. 308–309.

thing like this might occur, the procurators during the pretrial period had taken the precaution of having a judge of the Fukushima Regional Court, Judge Karamatsu Yutaka, hear Akama's confession *before Akama was indicted*. The procurators now proposed to introduce the affidavits of Akama's confession signed by Judge Karamatsu as the testimony of a hostile *witness* taken in advance of a trial by a judge as allowed under articles 223 and 227 of the Code of Criminal Procedure.[49] This evidence was to be used against both Akama and his fellow defendants, since Akama had been only a rape suspect at the time of questioning.

The defense naturally challenged these procedures as a violation of the new constitutional guarantees to protect the defendant, contending that since they all had been charged as coprincipals, one of them could not be singled out and his confession introduced as the evidence of a witness against the others. Judge Nagao ruled otherwise, saying that at the time Akama was interrogated he was a witness in the train wreck case, not a suspect or defendant, and that whatever comes about after testimony is taken down is immaterial: the deposition is a proper document before the court so long as it was not illegal at the time it was written. An immediate defense appeal of the ruling to the Su-

49. Article 223(1): "A public prosecutor, public prosecutor's assistant officer and judicial police official may ask any person other than the suspect to appear in their offices, question him or request him to formulate an opinion as an expert or act as an interpreter or translator, if it is necessary for pursuing the criminal investigation." Article 227(1): "When there is cause to believe that an individual who has voluntarily furnished information at the examination by a public prosecutor, public prosecutor's assistant officer or judicial police official in accordance with paragraph 1, article 223, may be subjected to pressures to withdraw or change such statements in testimony at the public trial, and when it appears that such testimony will be essential for proving the guilt of the accused, the public prosecutor may request a judge to interrogate the person as a witness, only before the first date fixed for the public trial of the case." As translated in Ministry of Justice of Japan, *Criminal Statutes* (Tokyo: n.d.), pp. 114–115.

preme Court was turned down. In later trials higher courts never challenged Judge Nagao on this, although they found fault with much else that he had done. Writing in the *Weekly Asahi* of November 29, 1953, Professor Hirano concluded that this ruling amounted to a restoration of the old *yoshin*, or preliminary hearing.

The climax of the first Matsukawa trial, as it is in all Japanese criminal trials under either the new or the old codes, was the procurator's *ronkoku*, or closing statement. As we have noted before, Japanese procurators belong to the Continental tradition and as such have considerably greater authority and discretion than has an American prosecuting attorney. The procuracy in Japan is somewhat analogous to a grand jury and a public prosecutor rolled into one. Nowhere is this facet of the procurator's powers made clearer than in his *ronkoku*. As Nagashima Atsushi of the Criminal Affairs Bureau, Ministry of Justice, explains:

> Not unrelated to discretionary prosecution is the traditional closing statement of the procurator at the trial. Article 293(1) of the Code of Criminal Procedure provides merely that "after the examination of evidence has been completed, the public procurator shall state his opinion in regard to the facts and the application of the law," but it has been a longstanding practice in Japan, as well as in some European countries, for the procurator at that time to express his opinion as to the appropriate penalty or other safety measures to be imposed upon the defendant. . . . The Court gives serious consideration to the recommended penalty— in part because the procurator can appeal the sentence if he feels that it is inadequate.[50]

In the first Matsukawa trial procurator Yamamoto rose to

50. "The Accused and Society: The Administration of Criminal Justice in Japan," in *Law in Japan*, p. 300.

the occasion with great skill. His *ronkoku*, some three hundred pages long, was undoubtedly the clearest presentation in the whole trial of the state's evidence against the defendants, and it was sufficiently admired by his superiors to have been printed by the (then) Attorney General's Office (today the Ministry of Justice) and distributed to other procurators to emulate.[51] The *benron*, the defense's answer to the *ronkoku*, was virtually nonexistent in the first trial, although that would change in later trials.

It took Yamamoto two full court days to read his *ronkoku*, ending on August 26, 1950. The very last item in the *ronkoku* is the *kyūkei*, the demand for punishment; and when he came to it Yamamoto went slowly over each defendant's part in the conspiracy and indicated whether or not the defendant had shown contrition. Finding that none had, he asked for ten death penalties: Suzuki, Abe, Sugiura, Honda, Satō Hajime, Takeda, Ninomiya, Akama, Takahashi, and Saitō. For the rest he asked for penalties ranging from life to one ten-year prison sentence (for Nikaidō Sonoko). They were indeed very stiff requests, and the journalists rushed out to file their stories for the evening Tokyo editions. The *Yomiuri* of August 27 carried the headlines: THE MOST SEVERE PUNISHMENTS IN COURT HISTORY. As it turned out, Judge Nagao did not accept all of Yamamoto's recommendations, but he still handed down the largest number of maximum penalties since the Great Treason Case of 1910 (in which an attempt on the life of the emperor was alleged).

From August until December court was adjourned while Judge Nagao and his two assistant judges retired to their offices to read all of the depositions and the transcript and to write their verdict (which itself runs to 414 densely printed pages). The

51. Hōmu-fu, Kenmu-kyoku (Attorney General's Office, Prosecution Bureau), *Matsukawa jiken ni okeru kenji no ronkoku* (The Public Procurator's Closing Address in the Matsukawa Case) (n.p., n.d.) "Procurator's Documents Vol. 13."

Fukushima District Court scheduled December 6 as the day to render judgment, and that morning everyone reassembled to hear Nagao read his verdict. He began by identifying each defendant by name, *honseki* (permanent registered domicile), and actual residence, and he then said, "Defendants Suzuki Makoto, Abe Ichiji, Honda Noboru, Sugiura Saburō, and Satō Hajime are condemned to death." The courtroom erupted. The spectators began to sing the "Internationale" and unfurl red flags, the defendants rose and shouted curses at the judge, and some of the three hundred policemen guarding the courtroom surged inside and started ordering people out. All of the defendants were returned to their cells, and Judge Nagao continued to read, until 3:45 that afternoon, to the small group of procurators, police, and newsmen that remained. He found that the nineteen men had acted as coprincipals (*kyōdō seihan*) but that Nikaidō Sonoko was only an accomplice. The punishments are listed in table 5.[52]

Press comment in the capital on these goings-on in Fukushima was restrained. All of the newspapers noted that it was legal for the judge to throw the defendants out while he was reading the verdict (Code of Criminal Procedure, art. 341) but that it was extremely unusual in Japanese legal history. Editorialists simply said that they understood the reasons why he had had to do it but they hoped that it would not happen very often. The *Asahi*'s "tensei jingo" ("vox populi vox dei") column asserted that Nagao had accepted completely the prosecution's *ronkoku* and that in doing so he looked more like a prewar judge than the type envisaged by the new code. All the papers also compared the Matsukawa verdicts with those in the Mitaka case,

52. Judge Nagao's sentences mirror perfectly Hirano's generalization: "Japanese criminal law is . . . subjective in that, if a criminal offense involves concert among several individuals, the person who committed the objectively harmful act may be considered morally less blameworthy, and hence be less severely punished, than those who psychologically or morally encouraged him." *Law in Japan*, p. 276.

where Akama's equivalent, Takeuchi, was alone found guilty and all the other alleged conspirators released. The papers agreed that the cases were different in that the actual perpetrators in the Matsukawa case had to be a group, not just one man. Nonethe-

TABLE 5

FIRST TRIAL VERDICT

December 6, 1950

Defendant	Prosecution request	Judgment
Suzuki Makoto	death	death
Abe Ichiji	death	death
Sugiura Saburō	death	death
Honda Noboru	death	death
Satō Hajime	death	death
Takeda Hisashi	death	life
Ninomiya Yutaka	death	life
Akama Katsumi	death	life
Takahashi Haruo	death	life
Ōta Shōji	life	life
Saitō Yuki	death	15 years
Hamazaki Futao	life	12 years
Okada Toramatsu	15 years	12 years
Katō Kenzō	15 years	12 years
Satō Shiroji	life	10 years
Nikaidō Takeo	15 years	10 years
Ōuchi Shōzō	13 years	7 years
Kobayashi Genzaburō	13 years	7 years
Kikuchi Takeshi	13 years	7 years
Nikaidō Sonoko	10 years	3 years, 6 months

less, the *Asahi* concluded, "Even judges are human beings, and in the Mitaka not-guilty verdict one suspects that they may have been influenced by adverse public opinion in Tokyo. This was not true in Fukushima." On December 7, 1950, a bitterly cold day, all twenty defendants were transferred to Miyagi Prison in Sendai, there to begin the movement to appeal their cases both to higher courts and to the world at large, and also to try to understand what had happened to them. It was also the beginning of what has been called variously "the greatest case of the century" or the "quagmire court" (*doronuma saiban*).[53]

53. *Sankei shimbun*, April 24, 1969, and *Tokyo shimbun*, eve. ed., October 17, 1960.

Chapter 5

The Two Zolas

*D*URING the late 1960s and early 1970s the United States began to experience a type of modern political event that had become quite well known in Japan during the previous two decades, namely, the protest demonstration or manufactured political happening. Such demonstrations are not the same thing as old-fashioned letter-writing campaigns or even picketing and political parades. For want of a better expression, the phrase *protest demonstration* is used here to refer to a fully orchestrated "movement," or *undō*, involving a campaign of coordinated mass rallies, petitions, long-distance marches, conferences, vigils, pleas by intellectuals and (in America) clergymen, propaganda films and dramatic productions, and generally the whipping up and organization of moral fervor behind some "cause." Examples include the anti-Security Treaty demonstrations in Japan during 1959 and 1960; the "ban-the-bomb" rallies in Japan, England, and various other countries during the 1950s and 1960s; the March on Washington movement for racial desegregation and civil rights in the United States; the antiwar "moratoria" and the demonstrations during the 1968 Democratic National Convention in Chicago; and in Japan during the 1950s and 1960s, the *Matsukawa undō*, or "Matsukawa movement," which is related to but distinct from the "Matsukawa case."

Seen from the inside—from the viewpoint of the people responsible for organizing and coordinating them—these movements are not spontaneous; but neither are they merely new examples of the familiar activities of Communist-front organizations or the staged rallies so common in the capital cities of dictatorships. Although they often originate with an organization such as a Communist party or one of its "united-front work" affiliates—as did the Matsukawa movement—the modern movement characteristically achieves a mass base and an autonomy that carries it beyond its original sponsor's ability to control or manipulate effectively. In a sense the modern political protest demonstration is nothing more than a typical "Save the Rosenbergs," "Germ Warfare in Korea," or "Free Morton Sobell" campaign that has become successful beyond the wildest dreams of its instigators. The Matsukawa campaign began very much like the Rosenbergs campaign in America, and in fact the two cases were widely compared in Communist writings of the time. In contrast to the campaign to save the Rosenbergs, however, the Matsukawa movement managed to overcome the initial liabilities of Communist sponsorship, became a mass movement, and accomplished something other than insuring that two potential martyrs were indeed martyred.

The essential strategy of the protest demonstration is to form a "united front"—to gain numerous adherents to a political party or program on the basis of tactical alliances between different, not necessarily hostile but in any case not previously cooperating, groups of citizens who unite to achieve a single overriding objective, such as nuclear disarmament, a civil rights law, or the freeing of the Matsukawa defendants. All such movements are subject to the strong temptation to subvert the strategy and to link the main objective of the movement with several other objectives. However, the leaders of the truly successful mass protest movements know that this is usually a prescription for failure and are therefore extremely cautious in allowing new objectives to be added. The art of managing a well-established movement includes knowing when to associate it with another movement—knowing, in other words, whether association will produce more adherents or destroy the moral basis of one or both movements.

In accordance with united-front doctrine, the instigators of protest demonstrations must be sensitive to the fact that many people will suspect Communist or other political parties of having ulterior motives in sponsoring such movements, and normally the instigators will attempt to disguise the ultimate sponsorship by delegating the movement's leadership to some offshoot committee or organization. The point of the movement is to gain adherents by championing a cause that arouses and concerns a broad spectrum of the population, and its leaders must beware of using symbols, such as red stars or pictures of foreign leaders, that may alienate the prospective audience. On the other hand, when the sponsor's identity is completely submerged and the cause is at the forefront of the movement, there is always a danger for the original sponsor that the movement will become too popular—that the cause itself will come to dominate the movement and result in the original leaders' being displaced. This is usually what happens in protest movements that really do effect some kind of political or social change. More commonly, such movements achieve little more than the recruitment of a few more adherents to the sponsoring political organization while the cause itself is allowed to be lost.

In the Matsukawa case, for example, the danger always existed that the Communist party would treat the defendants in the same way that the international Communist movement had treated the Rosenbergs: it would be so shrill in its propaganda that the defendants would surely become martyrs, thereby making good propaganda for the Communist party while allowing ten workers to go to the gallows. At a big rally in Tokyo on the evening of August 10, 1959, the day the first Supreme Court decision was handed down, Satō Hajime recalled a very high ranking Communist party leader's saying to the audience, "We thank you for your support in helping to save twenty Communist party members." Satō thought to himself that the Matsukawa struggle had not been waged to "save twenty Communist party members," and that it had actually become much more oriented toward improving the quality of Japanese justice. He believed that this leader's remark betrayed the insincerity of the party in its support of the Matsukawa defendants.[1]

When great protest movements begin to catch fire, and opinion leaders in the society who are not associated with the instigators begin to take up the cause, leadership difficulties arise. Even when these problems are reconciled for the sake of the uniting cause, part of the interest in such movements lies in the skill with which each party avoids having his reputation tarnished by his association with people who may have very different interests in the movement. In the Matsukawa movement, the major writer and intellectual who eventually became its leader, Hirotsu Kazuo, always managed to maintain what a group of Asahi reporters years later called a "nuance of difference" from the other leaders and their followers.[2] For example, except for his last book, he always avoided the term Matsukawa jiken ("Matsukawa case"), preferring to use the term Matsukawa saiban (the "Matsukawa trials"), since his stated interest was to see that the Japanese courts dealt out justice rather than political expediency. It was precisely this nuance of difference, as hard as it was on numerous occasions to maintain, that made Hirotsu's movement on

1. Nakasone Yasuhiro, et al., Warera Taishōkko, p. 296.
2. Asahi shimbun, August 9, 1961 (round-table discussion).

balance an asset rather than a liability for the development of Japanese democracy. It is also one of the reasons why the Matsukawa defendants are alive today.

Although a protest movement may secure a mass base and obtain a degree of legitimacy by sublimating any ulterior motives that some of its leaders may have for supporting the cause, it often has the net effect of maddening its opponents and a large part of the population. This is because its members claim to possess higher moral insight and dedication than other people in society—a claim that most men of good sense distrust and resent—and because it tends to use high-pressure tactics. Even when the methods of protest may not have directly influenced the outcome in a controversial issue—that is, when the protest only mobilized the attention of the public to the importance and significance of the question—a general suspicion arises that it was the pressure of the movement that produced the outcome. Thus, for example, in 1961, when the Sendai High Court handed down its not-guilty verdict in the Matsukawa case (on purely legal grounds and, as we shall see, using rather old-fashioned methods) the suspicion could not be allayed, even among people who agreed with the verdict, that the Matsukawa movement had influenced the court. Although a prosecution appeal was always possible when the "prestige of the procuracy" was at stake, many newspaper editorialists felt that the movement had made a prosecution appeal (the fourth appeal in the now twelve-year-old case) inevitable, and several prominent intellectuals demanded it. The case therefore continued before the courts for another nine years.

From its very beginning the modern political protest movement depends for its effectiveness on the availability of mass media of communications, and this in turn requires money. As a least common denominator, all protest movements are designed to mobilize the attentions of inattentive or less attentive citizens to the problem with which it is concerned. In order to do so a movement must communicate with them. Once it is in being it may be able to command attention by creating a news event— say, a march of a hundred thousand people through the heart of a city—which the press and television will feel obliged to report. However, until that stage is reached, money will be required to print books and pamphlets, purchase postage and stationery, and produce posters and movies. Even when the national press and other media do take up the movement, money will be required for salaries, transportation, supplies, and in legal cases, lawyers' fees. How to get enough money is always a problem; what the interests of its donors are, is another.

Between September 22, 1949, and December 31, 1963, the Matsukawa movement, according to its own accounting, took in ¥214,610,679 (ca. $596,141) and expended ¥220,572,300 (ca. $612,700). The largest source of income was trade union and other domestic donations, ¥85,753,763 (ca. $238,205); the second largest source was receipts from foreign and domestic film and play performances; and the third largest source, ¥21,048,968 (ca. $58,469), was "donations from abroad." [3] This latter source of funds, by far the greatest amount of it from Communist China, came entirely from Communist governments or organizations and was often cited by critics of the movement as evidence of foreign interference in the affairs of Japan. Moreover, these foreign funds were most important in the early years of the movement, before other sources had been developed. During 1951 and 1952 the revelation that Matsukawa money came from China tended to slow down the movement and caused many people to dismiss it as merely a Communist front. However, as we shall see, the movement's early leaders spent their money wisely, and after the campaign had passed the threshold from sectarian politics into a mass movement, the original foreign

3. Matsukawa Jiken Taisaku Kyōgikai (Matsukawa Case Countermeasures Council), *Matsukawa jūgo-nen* (Matsukawa Fifteen Years) (Tokyo, 1964), pp. 66–67.

donations were buried by the amounts of money flowing in from citizens' contributions. It was, however, a very long road to travel from the beginnings in Fukushima and Sendai after the first trial to the creation in 1958 of the Matsukawa Jiken Taisaku Kyōgikai (Matsukawa Case Countermeasures Council) with its thirty-two prefectural branches and its workers' associations in every industrial city. No one, least of all the defendants, knew how big the movement would become when Sugiura and his fellow prisoners started writing poems and letters in their freezing cells during the winter of 1950–51.

The origins of the Matsukawa movement actually go back to September 1949, immediately following the arrests of the first seven Communists (i.e., after Akama's arrest). The Japanese Communist party's central committee appointed a member of its central control commission, Wada Ichizō, to take charge of the Matsukawa case, and he activated two organizations, one a party-affiliated front and the other a fellow-traveling group, to come to the aid of the suspects.[4] The party affiliate was the Japanese branch of International Red Relief, originally founded by the Comintern in about 1923 and revived after the war with support from national parties and from Moscow. During 1949 this organization worked in Japan under the name Nihon Rōnō Kyūenkai (The Japan Labor-Farmer Relief Association), a name it used until November 1951, when its central committee, at a meeting in Sendai in connection with the Matsukawa case, changed it to Nihon Kokumin Kyūenkai (Japanese People's Relief Association). The fellow-traveling organization was the League of Free Jurists, mentioned in the last chapter, which provided the defense attorneys for the defendants.

4. Matsukawa Undō Shi Hensan Iinkai (The Committee to Compile the History of the Matsukawa Movement), ed., Matsukawa undō zenshi, taishū-teki saiban tōsō no jūgo-nen (Complete History of the Matsukawa Movement, Fifteen Years of Court Struggle by the Masses) (Tokyo, 1965), p. 89.

The relief association began by bringing together all the families of the defendants and, on November 16, 1949, setting up the Matsukawa Case Family Association. This group was then used to solicit funds, protest the "frame-up" against their relatives, and send letters to the local newspapers denouncing their allegedly biased reporting of the case. Another of the relief association's activities was to get out a pamphlet on the case, the first of several hundred such pamphlets that would ultimately be published. In April 1950 it produced *Tatakau hitobito* (*People Who Struggle*), containing essays by defendants Abe, Katō, Takeda, Kobayashi, Kikuchi, and Nikaidō Sonoko, and which is today a collector's item.[5] These early activities brought in a little money for the defendants' families and for the first trial, which was then under way, but they were not pursued vigorously, since there was no immediate need: *Akahata* was providing the publicity for the case, and funds were available from party coffers to pay for lawyers for both the Mitaka and the Matsukawa cases.

All of this was dealt a stunning blow during June 1950, while the first trial was still in progress. On May 31, a group of occupation soldiers in Tokyo was attacked and beaten up while observing an open-air Communist rally. It is still not clear to this day whether party leaders ordered the attack—which is highly doubtful—but SCAP reacted dramatically to this latest Communist affront to its programs and personnel. On June 6, 1950, the Supreme Commander directed the Japanese government to place all members of the Communist party's central committee under the ban of SCAPIN 550, that is, the purge ordinance. The result was that twenty-four Communist leaders were prohibited from engaging in any form of political activity and were obliged

5. On the family association, see ibid., pp. 101, 123; on *People Who Struggle* and its value today as a memento of the case, see Namba Hideo, *Kyūen undō monogatari* (The Story of the Relief Movement) (Tokyo, 1966), pp. 13–14.

to report periodically to the local police as if they were out of prison on parole. On the following day, June 7, seventeen more Communists, all of them editors of *Akahata*, were added to the list. Finally, on June 26, 1950, the day after the opening of the Korean War, SCAP proscribed *Akahata* altogether for having published North Korean propaganda. It did not reappear in Japan until May 1, 1952, two days after the San Francisco Peace Treaty took effect and ended the occupation.

These were serious blows to the Matsukawa movement, but it is important to understand that the Communist party itself did not disappear, nor was it outlawed in Japan. The purged leaders all went underground or into exile in China, but the party itself continued its united-front and magazine-publishing activities, although now under such innocuous titles as *Seinen jidai* (*Youth Age*), *Shin josei* (*New Girl*), *Jinmin bungaku* (*People's Literature*), and *Atarashii sekai* (*New World*). Up to the end of the occupation SCAP resisted efforts by the Yoshida government to have the party itself declared illegal, arguing that such a move would require Diet action, because SCAP did not wish to see the precedent of banning a political party established. The purge of individual Communist leaders satisfied General Headquarters and effectively prevented the party from engaging in propaganda against the United Nations forces in Korea.[6]

Meanwhile, the lawyers from the League of Free Jurists were turning the first Matsukawa trial into a political—and highly reportable—show trial, a process which culminated in the courtroom riot of December 6, 1950, the day the verdict was handed down. Throughout the trial the relief association also organized extra-courtroom activities. One such was on August 26, 1950, the day procurator Yamamoto finished his *ronkoku*; about forty people, relatives of the defendants, visited the homes of Judge

6. SCAP Monograph No. 11, "The Development of Political Parties," pp. 86, 149–150.

Nagao and procurator Yamamoto, where they sat down and chanted, "Don't kill them" (*hito o korosu na*).[7]

The full extent of these out-of-court pressures was not revealed until after the verdict. Numerous observers in court on December 6, 1950, noticed that Judge Nagao was shaking as he read his verdict and that he seemed to be suffering from nervous exhaustion. Those on the left interpreted these signs as evidence of a guilty conscience for having framed the defendants, but a more plausible explanation came to light less than a year later. Immediately after the first trial Nagao was transferred to the Nagoya High Court, and on April 14, 1951, he entered the psychiatric section of Nagoya Hospital suffering from depression. It seemed that he had received over three hundred extremely violent, threatening letters, including some from China, Bulgaria, Albania, and Switzerland. Several Communists in Nagoya were arrested for sending such letters, and during November 1951, the Committee on the Judiciary of the Diet's lower house discussed and condemned this foreign interference in Japan's affairs. However, the letters continued to come, and as late as 1953, Judge Nagao, who was then working in Fukui, was still receiving anonymous letters attacking his verdict.[8]

Letter writing, but not of the threatening anonymous kind, was always an important part of the movement, particularly letters written by the defendants themselves. After the first verdict and their transfer to Miyagi Prison in Sendai, the defendants organized themselves into a working association in order to carry out their appeal and to prepare for a long struggle. At first their relations with each other were strained: the temptation to blame Akama, Hamazaki, and the others who had confessed was overpowering. However, because virtually the entire leadership of two unions had been arrested, it was fairly easy to

7. *Yomiuri shimbun*, August 27, 1950.
8. *Asahi shimbun*, November 22, 1951; *Sangyō keizai shimbun*, November 22, 1951; *Shūkan asahi*, November 29, 1953.

establish a hierarchy among the defendants on the basis of union seniority and party discipline. Sugiura became the leader of the group because of his age and experience. After the verdict in the first trial the defendants pledged themselves to four principles: (1) to win in the second trial; (2) to fight to establish the truth to the end; (3) to maintain good physical fitness; and (4) to enlist and encourage their families in the appeal to public opinion.[9] Solidarity among the defendants was never publicly broken, although various of the more experienced union leaders in the group did write to their wives that Akama, Ōta, and others were "weak," and twenty years after the incident Sugiura was referring to Akama as "just a punk kid." [10]

During the period of the first trial, when all of the defendants were together in Fukushima city jail and in the courtroom, Sugiura took advantage of the relatively lax discipline to organize them so that they could work together under his orders. This became important because once they were moved to Miyagi Prison in Sendai regulation over them became much stricter. For example, they were no longer able to walk from the prison to the courtroom singing labor songs and shouting revolutionary slogans as they had done in Fukushima. Even in Sendai, however, the defendants bargained as a group with their jailers to obtain various rights, such as having adjacent cells and being allowed to mail the maximum number of letters (three per person per day). The prison authorities ultimately acquiesced to the prisoners' demands, even though it meant increasing the administrative staff, particularly the mail censors.

One of Sugiura's first initiatives was to put the entire group

9. Satō Hajime, Hikoku (Defendants) (Tokyo, 1958), pp. 14–15.
10. Matsukawa Jiken Bunshū Hensan Iinkai (Matsukawa Case Anthology Compilation Committee), ed., Aijō wa kabe o tōshite, Matsukawa jiken no hikoku to kazoku no tegami (Love Penetrates Walls, Letters Exchanged between the Matsukawa Defendants and Their Families) (Tokyo, 1954), p. 24; and interview with Sugiura Saburō, November 7, 1969.

of defendants to work writing letters to fellow Communists, to newspapers, to people they knew in their unions, to famous intellectuals, to people who might donate money—to anybody they could think of—and they did so at the rate of three hundred letters per person per month for a rough total of fifty thousand letters mailed from the Matsukawa defendants in Miyagi Prison by the end of 1951.[11] Many of these letters would later be collected and published, in turn calling forth, as we shall see, the single greatest asset the defendants ever obtained—namely, an intelligent, independently respected, non-Communist advocate for their cause.

Meanwhile, on the outside, the party, the lawyers, and the relief association shifted their activities into high gear following the first verdict. On December 7, 1950, the day after the sentencing in Fukushima, the Communist party issued an international appeal for support of the "Matsukawa victims," meaning, of course, not victims of the train wreck but the defendants, who were seen as victims of "fascist repression." According to the appeal: "In order to turn Japan into a colony and military base, foreign and home fascists have thrown thousands of patriots into prisons. Now they have engineered the so-called Matsukawa Incident and brutally sentenced twenty young patriots to death or to imprisonment for life or long terms. They [the defendants] are excellent fighters of the working class who fought heroically against the mass dismissals from the state-owned railways [and] in other enterprises carried out in the summer of 1949 in accordance with military colonial policy." [12]

Because of SCAP's watchful eye the Japanese Communist party could not identify the "foreign fascists" by name, but the Chinese—who were by now fighting the Americans in Korea—

11. *Matsukawa undō zenshi*, p. 236.

12. As released by the New China News Agency, January 9, 1951; and reprinted in U.S. Consulate General, Hong Kong, *Survey of the China Mainland Press*, No. 45, p. 10.

could and did. On January 9 and 10, 1951, the Peking *Kung-jen jih-pao* (*Workers' Daily*) ripped into "American imperialism" in Japan; and Li Chieh-po, chairman of the Chinese Railroad Workers' Union, pledged his support of the Matsukawa defendants. This was followed by a telegram protesting the sentences, addressed to the Japanese government and signed by Kuo Mo-jo, chairman of the Chinese People's Committee for the Defense of World Peace and Against Aggression. In August of that year the Chinese railroad union sent ¥640,000 to aid the Matsukawa "victims," in September the Chinese People's Relief Association—Sung Ch'ing-ling (Madame Sun Yat-sen), chairman—weighed in with better than three million yen, and in October the Chinese railroad workers came through with 17,000 Hong Kong dollars. There is no doubt that this Chinese largesse was due in part to the presence of the Japanese Communist party's secretary general, Tokuda Kyūichi, in exile in Peking, where he argued strongly for the support of the Matsukawa movement. In any case, the money reached Japan just when it was needed most. A small amount was paid out to support the defendants' families but the rest went for publishing and the attorneys' needs.

Appeals in Japanese criminal cases are complicated, and although the occupation's new Code of Criminal Procedure attempted to simplify matters, it had virtually no effect on the actual appeal procedures, either at the time of the first Matsukawa case appeal or twenty years later. There are three types of appeal in Japanese criminal law: *kōso* appeals, which are related to the actual matters in dispute and are normally made to a High Court; *jōkoku* appeals, which are confined to legal aspects of a case or to grievous error in a verdict or a sentence and are made directly to the Supreme Court; and *kōkoku* appeals, which are complaints and objections to orders or rulings of inferior courts and which are made to either a High Court or the Supreme Court. Both the prosecutor and the accused may appeal, the Supreme Court having ruled that it is constitutional—that is, not in violation of article 39 of the Constitution of 1947 forbidding double jeopardy—to give the procurator the right to appeal even against a judgment of acquittal (see Code, art. 351; and *Ishizaki v. Japan*, Supreme Court, Grand Bench, September 27, 1950). The Japanese see the stricture against double jeopardy as meaning that a citizen cannot be indicted twice for the same offense, not that—as in Anglo-American practice—he should not twice be judged by a jury of his peers, since Japan does not call juries. The judicial process through several courts is seen as a single proceeding, and a verdict of acquittal does not become final until the period has lapsed during which the procurators could appeal. In the Matsukawa case, the defense entered a *kōso* appeal to the Sendai High Court against the verdict in the first trial and a *jōkoku* appeal to the Supreme Court against the decision in the second trial, the Supreme Court ordered the case retried by the Sendai High Court, and the prosecution then made its own *jōkoku* appeal to the Supreme Court against the decision in the retrial. It all took fourteen years—article 37 of the constitution (the right to a "speedy trial") notwithstanding.

SCAP's Legal Section tried to shorten the Japanese appellate process, but its views were simply not compatible with the desires and expectations of Japanese citizens. In its official history of legal reform, SCAP wrote: "In the past, *kōso* appeal (second instance trial) was a repetition of the first instance trial, the case being tried over again from the beginning and a new judgment rendered by the appellate court. The new code amended this system and adopted the principle that the only consideration in *kōso* appeal was to judge whether the original judgment was reasonable. In case the original judgment was found unreasonable the appellate court was obligated to quash the decision and send the case back to the original court for rehearing." [13] This state-

13. SCAP Monograph No. 14, "Legal and Judicial Reform," p. 49.

ment turned out to be more hopeful than accurate. Several articles of the new code leave open loopholes whereby the appellate court can retry the case all over again if it wants to, particularly article 400: "When the original judgment is to be quashed on any ground other than the grounds mentioned in the two preceding articles [lack of jurisdiction or illegally dismissing the public action], the case shall be either sent back to the original court or transferred to another court in the same class as the original court by means of a judgment. However, if the court of *kōso* appeal recognizes that it may immediately render a judgment on the basis of the record of court proceeding and the evidences examined by the original court *and the court of kōso appeal* [italics added], it may render the judgment for the case." As a matter of fact most Japanese involved in serious criminal cases expect to receive at least two trials, and that is the way the system works. Needless to say, the accused has no guarantee that he will necessarily receive more favorable treatment on *kōso* appeal than he did in the trial court; quite the opposite. As Professor Nagashima notes, in 1958, of the total number of cases appealed, only 26.3 percent resulted in reversals of the original judgments, but of the cases appealed by public procurators, 69.1 percent resulted in reversals of the original judgments. It would seem, he concludes, "that appeals made by public procurators receive a higher rate of support by appellate courts than those of defendants." [14] As in the Continental procedure, Japanese criminal trials are extremely long and leisurely processes, and although press and judicial commentators regularly deplore their length, virtually nothing has been done to change the basic, multiple-trial pattern.

One further reason why Japanese trials are long is that defendants may participate directly in them, even when represented by defense counsel. The defendant in a Japanese trial may cross-

14. *Law in Japan*, pp. 300–301, n. 16.

examine witnesses, ask the judge to summon witnesses, make a brief statement at the opening of the trial about the facts charged against him, and use his right to speak last at the trial in order to make a prolonged statement—very commonly a political speech if the case has any political overtones. Also in appeals the defendant must prepare his own written appeal, in addition to an appeal brief filed by his attorney, and these appeal statements can be very long. In the kōso trial of the Matsukawa case the appeal documents, including defendants' statements and attorneys' briefs, add up to 2,117 pages, bound in three printed volumes. Of this total, 1,861 pages are statements written by the defendants, which range in length from Akama's 21 pages to Abe's 146 pages. Of course, the Matsukawa case documents are unusually voluminous partly because the case had twenty defendants and an extremely large number of defense attorneys: 174 during the kōso appeal alone, with the number becoming even larger for the Supreme Court sessions and the retrial.

Kōso appeals must be made by presenting a written application to the court of first instance within fourteen days after the verdict, and the supporting documents must then be filed on or before a date set by the appeal court—in this case the Sendai High Court. Chief defense attorney Okabayashi appealed the first verdict on the basis of every substantive ground allowed by law—prosecution illegally accepted, reasons for judgment contradictory, unjust punishments, and errors in the finding of facts (Code, arts. 378–382)—and filed his appeal documents on July 23, 1951. The Sendai High Court then set October 23, 1951, as the first day to hear the appeal in court, and a judicial conference met to select the judges who would sit.

The Sendai bench chose as president of the court Suzuki Teijirō, a fifty-year-old judge with twenty years of experience. He was from Iwate prefecture and thus was praised by the local press for having the admirable simplicity of a "northeasterner" (Tōhokujin). Even Okabayashi described him as an "honorable man"—before he heard Suzuki's verdict. Suzuki was a 1928 graduate of Tokyo Imperial University, where he had specialized in English law; and during World War II he had served as an army law officer in Southeast Asia, winding up in Saigon. Reporters covering the trial noted that he was much smoother than Judge Nagao and that the defendants were very pleased with him. When it was all over, the defendants were devastated by his verdict, and leftist reporters looking into Suzuki's background discovered that at the university he had been known as a *kugaku rikkō*, a "grind," or a self-made man who pulls himself up the social ladder by studying fiendishly hard. They concluded that he had been determined all along to mete out severe justice to the Communists who had caused the deaths of three men. As we shall see in the next chapter, they were not entirely wrong, since Judge Suzuki's appointment to preside over the Matsukawa appeal became linked to an alleged scandal involving a justice of the Supreme Court.[15]

Yamaguchi Kazuo of the Sendai High Procuracy led a group of three procurators in presenting the government's side of the case, while Okabayashi and Ōtsuka headed the large contingent of attorneys for the defense, usually about forty of them in court at any one time and all but one (of those who can be identified) a Communist or a Socialist. The one exception, Hakamada Shigeshi (no relation to Hakamada Satomi of the Japanese Communist party's central committee), was a young conservative, a member of Yoshida's Liberal party, and a self-selected defender because of his belief that the defendants had not received a fair trial. Hakamada, who belonged to the Sendai Bar Association, became extremely important to the defense side as a transmission belt because non-Communist outsiders wanting to aid the Matsu-

<hr>

15. See the column "Tengankyō" (The Magnifying Glass), in *Sandē mainichi*, November 29, 1953; plus *Shūkan asahi*, November 29, 1953; *Mainichi shimbun*, December 23, 1953 (interview with Suzuki); *Asahi shimbun*, August 9, 1961 (round-table discussion); and *Asahi shimbun*, September 13, 1963 (round-table discussion).

kawa movement would deal only with him, distrusting any contacts with the famous political lawyers of the League of Free
Jurists.

The first nineteen appeal-court sessions, ending on December 20, 1951, were taken up with legal arguments about *kōso*
procedures under the new Code of Criminal Procedure. The defense demanded a new trial, and though the prosecution did not
object, Judge Suzuki had to be convinced. Specifically, the defense attorneys wanted to reexamine on the stand the twenty
defendants, cross-examine witnesses on the finding of the crowbar
and wrench, introduce expert testimony on the capacity of a
physically handicapped person such as Takahashi to do what the
first verdict charged him with having done, reinvestigate on the
spot the routes and important places mentioned in Akama's confession, and call officers of the Fukushima and National Rural
Police to testify with regard to the voluntariness of Akama's confession. Judge Suzuki finally agreed and set late January 1952
as the time for questioning witnesses, scheduled an on-the-spot
investigation for March, and promised a verdict hopefully in
August. As it turned out a verdict was not forthcoming until two
years later, on December 22, 1953.

Outside the court during 1951 a great deal of activity took
place on behalf of the defendants, but none of it seemed to have
much effect. On the contrary, by the end of the year many
citizens had hardened their hearts to the Fukushima Communists, and the defendants observed that even the Tokyo leftists
seemed to be much more interested in the Mitaka case, which
had occurred in the capital, than in the Matsukawa case, which
was a "countryside affair." Nikaidō Sonoko was released on bail
on May 12, 1951, and she took charge of speech-making and
other activities in support of the defendants. During the same
month the relief association launched a major campaign to collect one million signatures on a petition to be sent to the Sendai
High Court demanding an acquittal judgment. Sonoko and the

relief association worked hard at the drive, but by the end of 1953 they had gathered only about 400,000 names. The Fukushima branch of the National Railroad Workers' Union, and the national congress of the railroad workers, were both coldly hostile to the whole case, and the Tōshiba workers at Matsukawa refused to have anything to do with the defendants. Although the national Tōshiba union was always a good source of funds for the movement, and the NRWU central organs eventually came around, the Fukushima workers remained suspicious of the case until the late 1950s, and even then unanimity of support was never obtained. The defendants rationalized this by saying that the Fukushima NRWU had fallen under Mindō-type leadership, but it is clear that lack of home support troubled them deeply.[16]

One reason why the public responded so lukewarmly was the clear Communist bias in the movement's propaganda and the widespread belief that the Communists were merely exploiting the case. The Communist propaganda campaign began at the end of 1950 with an open letter to Stalin and Mao Tse-tung, imploring their aid in the struggle for "freedom and truth" and signed by all members of the families of the accused, and it continued throughout 1951 with efforts to link the Matsukawa movement to the leftist struggle against the San Francisco Peace Treaty (signed September 8, 1951) and to the international campaign to "save the Rosenbergs" (arrested July 1950). Years later the relief association acknowledged that the letters to Stalin and Mao, which were published as a pamphlet in February 1951, would have been more effective had they been entitled "Letters to Japanese Workers" or "Letters to Citizens of Japan" rather

16. On the attitudes of Tokyo leftists toward the Mitaka and Matsukawa cases, see the letter from Sugiura Yoshiko, Sugiura's wife, dated June 25, 1951, at Yokohama, to Sugiura, in Aijō wa kabe o tōshite, p. 54; on the million signatures campaign, see Namba, Kyūen undō monogatari, p. 172; on the lack of support in the Fukushima area, see the letter from Suzuki Yaeko, Suzuki's wife, in Aijō, p. 27; and Matsukawa undō zenshi, pp. 223, 242, 278.

than addressed to the two famous Communist leaders.[17] Rising anti-Communist sentiment at this time also threatened to wreck the League of Free Jurists. Many prominent liberals vowed to resign unless the Communists were removed from positions of leadership, and in early 1951 Communists were purged from the executive committee (but not from the Matsukawa defense attorneys unit).[18]

However, since the Communists were the only group aiding the defendants during 1951, the party called the tune. The Communists systematically harnessed the Matsukawa movement to their international propaganda against the Korean war, the peace treaty, and American atomic weapons. In June Nikaidō Sonoko and Abe Eriko (sister of Abe Ichiji) were guests at the Soviet embassy to see a film entitled *The Liberation of China*; on August 6, 1951, Kobayashi wrote from prison for publication, "It is crystal clear that if we lose this trial we shall be involved in a war" (because the fascists would have been restored to power in Japan); and in Sendai the Matsukawa signature-gatherers joined forces with Rosenberg canvassers and added some ten thousand of their own names to the Rosenberg petitions for forwarding to President Truman.[19] Above all the movement attacked the peace treaty (which was between Japan and the United States and its allies, not the USSR or Communist China). As Satō Hajime recalled:

> During 1951, when the Japanese peace treaty was being signed in San Francisco, Kikuchi was busy writing an appeal statement to be submitted to the Sendai High Court. He reasoned that if the treaty were signed he could not expect

17. Namba Hideo, *Kyūen undō monogatari*, p. 172.

18. Jiyū Hōsō Dan (League of Free Jurists), ed., *Jiyū hōsō dan monogatari* (The Story of the League of Free Jurists) (Tokyo, 1966), pp. 200–202.

19. *Aijō wa kabe o tōshite*, pp. 95, 164; *Matsukawa undō zenshi*, p. 252.

to receive an acquittal. This was the prevailing feeling among all the defendants. The Dulles-Yoshida treaty would result in turning Japan into an American military base for a long time, and Japan would be limited in the exercise of her sovereignty by the domination of the United States. Because of this the defendants believed that their acquittal would be possible only with an overall peace treaty, and they adapted their movement for collecting a million signatures to the concurrent appeal for a Sino-Soviet peace treaty.[20]

This kind of propaganda had very little effect in Japan at the time, but the procurators did not object to it. In fact they welcomed it as grist for their mill.

In December 1951, the procurators called a press conference to denounce international interference in the Matsukawa case and made known for the first time the amounts of money the defense had received from Communist China. They quoted from the Peking *Jen-min jih-pao* (*People's Daily*) of November 12, where Saitō, Sugiura, and Satō Hajime had thanked the Chinese for their support, and from a violently anti-American letter published in the Chinese Communist party's organ and signed by Suzuki, Kikuchi, and Nikaidō Takeo. Although Chinese support continued without interruption, these revelations by the prosecution tended to alienate virtually all domestic editorial opinion from the defendants.[21]

During 1952 things began to change, first in the courtroom and then in terms of the public's response to the Matsukawa movement. The trial itself was extremely long—some 110 sessions—lasting from October 23, 1951, to July 23, 1953. The evidence produced in court did not establish the innocence of the defendants in any conclusive sense, but it did convince the

20. Satō Hajime, *Hikoku*, pp. 119–120.
21. *Mainichi shimbun*, December 24, 1951.

court and probably a majority of the public who were aware of the case that the first trial had been incredibly sloppy and crude in its handling of the evidence. Given the severity of the original sentences, the revelation of numerous errors committed during the first trial gave a strong impetus to the demand that the second trial be "fair." Out of the fourteen volumes of courtroom transcript produced by the second trial, six basic issues became salient: (1) the number of fishplates sabotaged, (2) Takahashi's physical condition, (3) Akama's gloves, (4) the origin of the wrench and crowbar, (5) the voluntariness of the confessions, and (6) the alibis for the August 13, 1949, conspiracy meeting. The defense attorneys themselves were not responsible for raising all of the points that appeared to favor the defendants, but their lapses turned out to be in the defendants' interests. Non-Communist observers were much more ready to believe that something had been wrong with the first trial when the prosecution or the bench uncovered a contradiction than when the defense did.

The biggest contradiction of all was introduced by the prosecution itself, apparently as a result of its reinvestigation of the case. The Sendai procurators, belonging to the High Procuracy, were more experienced than their Fukushima colleagues, and they had also had more time and a greater familiarity with the new Code of Criminal Procedure in preparing their case. The fact that they openly revealed a discrepancy in the original case shortly after the new trial of facts began has always tended to give the lie to charges that the procuracy framed the defendants. On February 16, 1952, chief procurator Yamaguchi put assistant procurator Shirai Tsunejirō of the Kōriyama branch, Fukushima Regional Procuracy, on the stand. Shirai explained that during the previous September he had discovered in the Fukushima procurators' warehouse two fishplates, four bolts, and one spike. They were collected at the scene of the Matsukawa wreck on August 18, 1949—the day following the initial investigation—

and were in addition to the two fishplates already introduced as material evidence. Procurator Yamaguchi also acknowledged that according to a railroad investigator's report not introduced at the first trial, the fishplates at the scene of the sabotaged tracks had been removed from the rails at two places (producing therefore four fishplates, one on either side of the track at two sites).

The procurators tried to downgrade this new evidence. Akama's confession said explicitly that fishplates had been removed at one spot, but Akama himself had not worked on the fishplates; he had pulled out spikes. It was perfectly possible that in the dark he had made a mistake about the extent of damage done by the other saboteurs, and this small discrepancy did not shake the veracity or the comprehensive quality of his confession as a whole. Furthermore, argued Yamaguchi, it was a bit like having a man confess to one murder and then discovering another body; four fishplates only made the saboteurs' crime that much worse.

However, the procurators were not allowed to get away with their revelation so easily. The press the next day was very unhappy. *Yomiuri* acknowledged that the Communist party's mobilizing activities and its "frantic efforts to charge a procurators' frame-up" were all propaganda, but the paper still wanted to know how such important items of evidence came to be "sleeping in the regional procurators' warehouse for three years." "In these days," the editor wrote, "we do not want to have to think back to the period of *kensatsu fassho* [fascism by the procuracy]." In response to these fears the procurator general in Tokyo launched an investigation of the whole Tōhoku procuracy, which did not, however, turn up anything amiss.

In later sessions of the court the procurators referred to their mistake ruefully as the *tsugime-ita jiken* ("the fishplate affair"), but they stuck to their story that it did not really affect the truthfulness of Akama's confession. Judge Suzuki agreed: the first trial had committed an error, but the error had not materially affected its judgment. The defense disagreed, saying that Akama's confession had been shaken to its roots. More important, the defense utilized the discrepancy as the basis for a line of questioning that really was damaging to the prosecution's case. The defense introduced a series of engineering professors from Yamagata University and experts from the Japanese National Railroads to testify about their experiments concerning the possibility of removing four fishplates, about eighty-five spikes, and about twenty-eight chocks in approximately a half hour, at night, and using only a standard railroad crowbar and a foot-long monkey wrench. According to one expert, pulling out one spike at night requires thirty-five to forty-five seconds, and one chock takes thirty to thirty-five seconds. At this rate eighty-five spikes and twenty-eight chocks would use up well over an hour (and it would have required more than five men using professional tools to have committed the sabotage in the time available between the passage of trains.)[22] However, the figures on the absolute numbers of spikes and chocks involved are ambiguous: some of the loose spikes recovered at the site might have been torn out by the wreck itself. In any case, of five experts who testified at the second trial, one thought the job was impossible, one could not decide, two called it "difficult," and one said it was possible.[23] Their testimony was obviously not conclusive, but it did point to the failure of the first trial to collect expert evidence. It also set off the vogue of amateur on-site inspections of the Fukushima –Matsukawa railroad tracks and impromptu demonstrations of rail sabotage on unused or specially laid track—a pastime that ultimately attracted some fifteen thousand unionists and Matsukawa-movement activists during their summer vacations.[24] During the second trial the prosecution wiggled out of the whole mess by calling a Japanese National Railroads track maintenance su-

22. *Nihon keizai shimbun*, October 27, 1958.
23. *Tokyo shimbun*, April 13, 1953.
24. *Matsukawa undō zenshi*, pp. 409–410.

pervisor to testify that the tracks at the site of the wreck had not been inspected for some time and that the nuts on the fishplates were probably loose.[25] Judge Suzuki agreed.

Takahashi's physical condition posed a problem almost as serious as the extra fishplates, but it too proved to be inconclusive. On virtually the last day of the first trial, that is, during its ninety-first session on September 9, 1950, Takahashi mentioned in his closing statement to the court that he could not have done what was alleged in Akama's confession because of a physical disability that he was forced to live with. It seems that in February 1944, when he was working at Niwazaka station on the Ōu Line, Takahashi had one day been caught between the station platform and a passing train and had suffered a broken pelvis and a damaged penis in the accident. He had spent many months convalescing in various hospitals, and in 1949 he remained unable to make very long walks at a rapid pace. Judge Nagao had dismissed this testimony in the verdict of the first trial, observing that Takahashi had not displayed the slightest difficulty in walking during the trial's on-site inspection.

During the second trial Takahashi complained of pain in his hip and was allowed to sit in court on a *zabuton* (a Japanese cushion) rather than on a chair. The defense explained that Takahashi had raised this matter so late in the first trial only because he was sure that they would all be exonerated and because he did not realize its full significance. He had also been reluctant to talk about the condition of his private parts in public. The defense further charged that Judge Nagao had had in his possession a statement of a medical inspection made at the time of Takahashi's arrest. Performed by a surgeon of Fukushima Hospital, this report allegedly stated that Takahashi was a partial cripple. Nagao, said the defense attorneys, had suppressed this report. In fact, the defense contended, Takahashi

25. From the procurators' *ronkoku*; see *Mainichi shimbun*, April 28, 1953, eve. ed.

was incapable of walking the distances alleged in Akama's confession in the time allowed; he had been able to make the on-site inspection only because it was a leisurely stroll spread over several days and with frequent pauses to rest.

In response to this challenge the prosecution produced the doctor from Fukushima Hospital, who testified that he had not examined Takahashi's pelvis at the time of his arrest. His report to Judge Nagao stated that Takahashi suffered from hemorrhoids and that he had recently undergone an operation to relieve that condition. It did state that while imprisoned Takahashi should not be out of bed and walking around—because of his recent operation.[26] From that point on, the Sendai High Court made independent inquiries, and both the prosecution and the defense called expert witnesses to testify on Takahashi's ability to walk between 14.5 and 16.5 miles (6 or 7 ri) at night in approximately five and a half hours.[27] The court discovered from records of the three hospitals in which Takahashi had convalesced during 1944 that he had been unable to walk when he was discharged. The prosecution countered, however, that his condition in 1944 had no bearing on his condition in 1949.

As for the experts, the defense's doctor, a professor at the medical school of Tōhoku University, testified that it was im-

26. For Takahashi's first mention of his physical disability, see Fukushima Chihō Saibansho (Fukushima District Court), Matsukawa jiken kōhan kiroku (Matsukawa Case Trial Record), XI, pp. 353 et seq.; for the testimony of the doctor who examined Takahashi, see Shakai taimusu, December 18, 1952.

27. According to a careful estimate made by a Matsukawa-movement inspection team, the round-trip distance from Takahashi's house to the site of the wreck and in accordance with Akama's confession is 28.684 kilometers (7 ri 11 chō, or 17¼ miles). It took the second trial's on-site-verification-of-evidence group five hours and twenty-eight minutes to complete the distance. According to Akama's confession and Takahashi's statements, Takahashi would have had to leave home sometime after 10:30 P.M., August 16, 1949, and to have returned home sometime between 4:30 and 5:00 A.M., August 17.

possible for Takahashi to have made the walk. The prosecution came in with three experts of its own, distinguished doctors from Tokyo (Tokyo University, Keiō University, and the Japan College of Medicine). These men all said that "depending on the defendant's spiritual power," it was possible for him to have made the walk. They also implied that their Tōhoku colleague was too young to know what he was talking about. Needless to say, the defense did not like these references to "spiritual power," charging that they were unscientific. But the prosecution argued to the court that this particular walk to commit a crime involved purpose and will, therefore the spiritual power of the defendant was relevant; and the doctors had said that he was physically capable of doing it if he were sufficiently motivated. Judge Suzuki did not necessarily accept this argument. He was more suspicious of the fact that Takahashi had mentioned his condition very late in the first trial; it looked to Suzuki like a desperate defense conjured up at the last minute. He decided that Takahashi's old injury had fully healed.

The dispute over Akama's glove was significant chiefly for what it revealed about the attitude toward confessions in Japanese courts. The postwar constitution and the new Code of Criminal Procedure both required that in order to convict a person who had confessed to a crime the procurators had to produce evidence to substantiate the confession. Akama's confession illustrates how this requirement was met. He had confessed to the crime of railroad sabotage and, among other things, had said that he had thrown the gloves he used in committing the crime into Nigori Creek. The police dragged the creek and found one glove, which was duly introduced into court as evidence corroborating the truthfulness of the confession. However, when the second trial raised doubts about whether the glove in evidence was actually Akama's, the questionable glove was withdrawn as evidence without seriously compromising the confession itself. This was because nobody really believed or distrusted Akama's confession on the basis of the glove or any other items of material evidence. The procurators and the judges were much more sensitive to internal and psychological factors, such as whether the confession and the confesser seemed to match in terms of Japanese social stereotypes, and to the fact that Akama, having prophesied the wreck, could not account for his whereabouts at the time it had occurred.

As for the glove matter itself, in his confession Akama had identified the gloves as *gunte* (army cotton gloves) and said that he had once had them repaired at a shoestore using hemp thread. This was confirmed by a police visit to the shoe repair shop. The court therefore appointed a professor at Yamagata University, who was a textile expert, to examine the glove, and he reported that it showed no sign of having ever been repaired with any distinctive kind of thread. The prosecution and the defense debated the issue, the procurators suggesting that Akama himself had pulled out the hemp threads and the defense charging that the whole confession was fraudulent. The court simply ignored the glove as "inconclusive corroborative evidence."

Questions about the origins of the crowbar and wrench found at the scene of the crime were similar to the glove issue and had the same effect on the court. The prosecution was unable to discover and produce in court the man who had found the wrench at the scene of the crime, and the tool supervisor of the Matsukawa track-maintenance crew testified that he thought the tools came from his unit but that he was unable to say so positively. The record books indicating how many tools of each type were stored in the shed were missing, and it was no longer possible to establish for certain that the Matsukawa crew had been robbed of anything. The defense also charged that the two tools found at the scene were not of a type commonly used on the Japanese National Railroads. The crowbar had a small blaze of olive drab or khaki colored paint on it, and it also had the roman letters X and Y stamped near one end of it.[28] The JNR, said the defense attorneys, did not mark their tools with army paint—the question of which army was left up in the air— and also did not use monkey wrenches. The prosecution in turn called railroad officials, who testified that the tools used by the railroad were not all standardized and that they really could not say whether these particular tools could have been found in a JNR shed. Again, the issue came down to "inconclusive corroborative evidence," this time concerning the confessions of the three young Tōshiba defendants on the tool theft.[29]

The issue of whether the confessions had been made voluntarily came much closer to the heart of the matter—although it was not *the* heart: that was whether the court believed the confessions were true, however they had been obtained. In the second trial the defense attorneys and each defendant who had confessed asserted repeatedly that the confessions had been extracted from them by the use of "coercion, torture, and threats." In response to these charges the prosecution did something unprecedented. It called five procurators (including Yamamoto, chief procurator in the first trial), four police officials (including Inspector Tamagawa and Sergeant Takeda), and Judge Karamatsu, in 1952 a judge of the Tokyo District Court, who in 1949 had taken down the pretrial depositions of the suspects as if they were witnesses. There was only one prior precedent in Japanese legal history of a judge being put on the stand and

28. The most thorough study of the crowbar and wrench and of their odd markings is contained in Matsukawa Jiken Bengodan Jōnin Sewa Kai (The Matsukawa Case Defense Attorneys' Standing Aid Association), ed., *Matsukawa jiken jōkoku-shin benron* (The Defense Arguments in the Appeal of the Matsukawa Case to the Supreme Court) (Tokyo, 1959), pp. 151–202.

29. For some of the anti-American suspicions raised by the inability to prove that the tools belonged to the JNR, see *Shakai taimusu,* February 24, 1953.

allowing himself to be cross-examined (that was in the "Teijin" or Teikoku Rayon Company case of 1934–1937, a corruption scandal involving three cabinet members, which ended with the defendants being acquitted after it was revealed that the police had extorted confessions from them). All of these official witnesses testified that the confessions were completely voluntary, and they maintained this position in the face of cross-examination. They also pointed out that they had been able to induce Akama to confess by telling him that Honda was putting the blame on him alone, a gambit that should not have influenced Akama if he were innocent, since he had not known Honda prior to the incident.

The sixth issue, alibis for the August 13 conspiracy meeting at the headquarters of the National Railroad Workers' Union, was of critical significance both to the court and to the observing public outside of court. An alibi is the best way to refute any criminal charge, even a charge of conspiracy in cases where the indictment has alleged specific times and places at which the conspiring occurred, and it has always been recognized in Japanese courts as an overpowering defense even when the defendant has previously confessed. During the second trial the defense produced as a surprise witness Mr. Hashimoto Takiji, chief of the cost accounting section of the Tōshiba Tsurumi factory, who on August 13, 1949, had been at the Matsukawa works as part of the management team taking part in the collective bargaining negotiations. The first verdict had contended that Ōta and Satō Hajime joined Takeda, Saitō, Ninomiya, Abe, Honda, Takahashi, Suzuki, and Katō on August 13, between 11:00 A.M. and 12:00 noon, at the railway workers' union offices in Fukushima to begin initial planning for derailing a train. Hashimoto now testified that the negotiations at Matsukawa on that day had lasted from about 10:00 A.M. until 12:30 P.M., and that he believed Satō was present either the whole time or, at least, at their conclusion.

Hashimoto's testimony was shaken by procurator Yama-

The scene of the crime.

(*Above*) The wreck, August 17, 1949.

(*Below*) A railroad fishplate.

(*Above*) The Tōshiba plant at Matsukawa.

C. Johnson

(*Below*) The Tōhoku Main Line at Matsukawa, with the Tōshiba plant on the right.

C. Johnson

(*Above*) Judge Nagao Makoto of the first trial.

(*Upper left*) The defendants during the first trial.
Left to right, front row, Ōta, Satō H., Takahashi, Akama, Honda, Abe, Ninomiya, Suzuki; *middle row,* Nikaidō S., Nakaidō T., Kikuchi, Kobayashi, Ōuchi, Satō S., Hamazaki, Sugiura; *back row,* Okada (obscured), Katō, Takeda, and Saitō.

(*Lower left*) Akama addressing the court during the first trial, Fukushima District Court.

Excerpt from the Suwa Memorandum.

Jiji Press

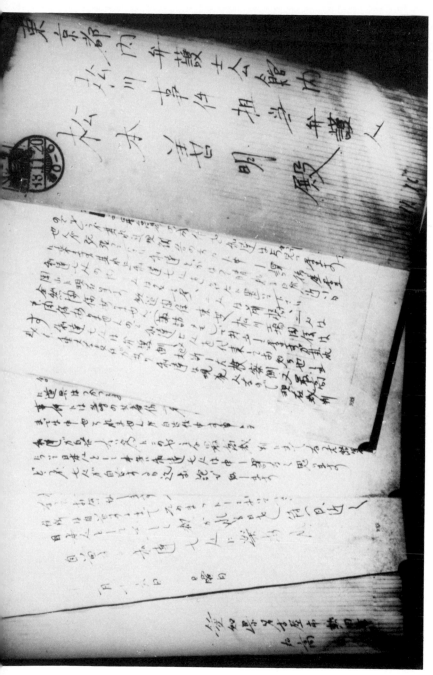

The anonymous letter of November 16, 1958.

Kyōdō

(*Above*) A Matsukawa Grand March column entering Tokyo.

(*Upper right*) Judge Monden Makoto of the Sendai retrial.

(*Lower right*) Sugiura Saburō in the hospital at the time of the final verdict.

Kyōdō

Taikō Sha

(*Above*) The Supreme Court Grand Bench courtroom on September 12, 1963, the day of the final verdict in the Matsukawa case.

(*Left*) Matsumoto Seichō.

(*Upper right*) Associate Justice Saitō Kitarō of the Supreme Court.

(*Lower right*) Hirotsu Kazuo outside the Supreme Court after the final verdict.

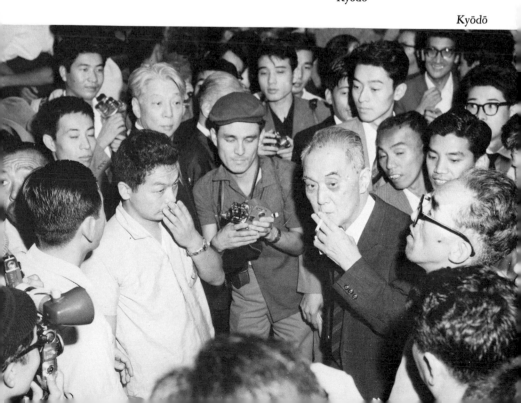

松　川　の　塔

　1949年8月17日午前3時9分、この西方200米の地点で、突如、旅客列車が脱線顛覆し、乗務員3名が殉職した事件が起った。何者かが人為的にひき起した事故であることが明瞭であった。

　どうしてかかる事件が起ったか。

　朝鮮戦争がはじめられようとしていたとき、この国はアメリカの占領下にあって吉田内閣は、二次に亘って合計9万7千名という国鉄労働者の大量馘首を強行した。かかる大量馘首に対して、国鉄労組は反対闘争に立上った。

　その機先を制するように、何者の陰謀か、下山事件、三鷹事件及びこの松川列車顛覆事件が相次いで起り、それらが皆労働組合の犯行であるかのように巧みに新聞、ラジオで宣伝されたため、労働者は出ばなを挫かれ、労働組合は終に遺憾ながら十分なる反対闘争を展開することが出来なかった。

　この列車顛覆の真犯人を、官憲は捜査しないのみか、国労福島支部の労組員10名、当時同じく馘首反対闘争中であった東芝松川工場の労組員10名、合せて20名の労働者を逮捕し、裁判にかけ、彼等を犯人にしたて、死刑無期を含む重刑を宣告した。この官憲の理不尽な暴圧に対して、俄然人民は怒りを勃発し、階層を超え、思想を越え、真実と正義のために結束し、全国津々浦々に至るまで、松川被告を救えという救援運動に立上ったのである。この人民結束の規模の大きさは、日本ばかりでなく世界の歴史に未曽有のことであった。救援は海外からも寄せられた。

　かくして14年の闘争と5回の裁判とを経て、終に1963年9月12日全員無罪の完全勝利をかちとったのである。

　人民が力を結集すると如何に強力になるかということの、これは人民勝利の記念塔である。

The inscription on the Matsukawa monument.

guchi's cross-examination. He could not be absolutely certain that Satō had been present—there were so many people, all strangers to him, in the room—and it was possible that Satō could have slipped out without his having noticed it. Nevertheless, he was sure he remembered Satō's calming down his fellow union members during a fairly heated exchange and that this had occurred toward the later part of the meeting. As we shall see, this testimony was of great importance to the court and is reflected in its verdict. Even more important, however, outside observers, quite willing to make *ad hominem* judgments about the individuals who testified during the trial, were tremendously impressed by the fact that a representative of management had come forward on behalf of one of the defendants. Most observers took statements made by fellow unionists or relatives at a discount. Outsiders like Hirotsu Kazuo concluded, however, that Hashimoto was a man "who would not make a mistake." [30]

While these issues were being debated in the courtroom, the Communist-directed Matsukawa movement continued on the outside to fulminate about a frame-up ordered and directed by the prime minister himself and to buttonhole every prospective Matsukawa-petition signer, but it seemed completely incapable of losing the stigma of a Communist-front operation. In February 1951, chief defense attorney Okabayashi published a pamphlet intimating that the true criminals in the case were certain famous ex-Communists, in particular the industrialist Tanaka Kiyoharu, which proved nothing more to the public than the old truth that the party reserves its greatest scorn for its former members. A year later the relief association brought out its first movie on the case, the first of at least five films that would ultimately be produced and shown to workers' gatherings all over Japan and at Chinese film festivals. Ōuchi, who together with

30. For Hirotsu's comment and the general reaction to Hashimoto's testimony, see *Yomiuri shimbun*, October 6, 1953; *Shakai taimusu*, October 28, 1953; and *Shūkan asahi*, November 29, 1953.

Kikuchi and Kobayashi had been released on bail at the end of 1952, made a visit to the Hokkaido coal mines to lecture the miners on the innocence of the Matsukawa defendants, but he was nearly shouted off the stage with cries of "Fool!" and "Why did you confess?" [31] The movement's only notable converts prior to 1953 were the daughter of first-trial procurator Yamamoto, who criticized in print her father's attitude toward the case, and the elder sister of locomotive fireman Itō, one of the men killed in the wreck. The movement tried repeatedly to obtain support for the defendants among the families of workers killed in the derailment, but with this one exception it never succeeded.

Within Miyagi Prison, strains appeared among the defendants, and despair over the case was growing. On February 18, 1953, Ōta Shōji wrote angrily to his wife Sumiko about Nikaidō Sonoko's marriage on January 29 to the former Mitaka defendant Yokoya Takeo: "She was supposed to have married in order to advance the struggle. It's intolerable that she's now thinking of settling down and refusing to move around while we carry on a stern life-and-death struggle." [32] Similarly, Honda Noboru called his younger brother a traitor and a sellout in answer to a letter from the brother berating Honda as "unfilial" for having gotten himself into prison and being unable to provide for the family's livelihood. [33] Years later Sugiura told of his difficulties in keeping the group from blaming Akama and also how he himself vacillated between being angry at the police for picking on a chimpira ("punk") like Hamazaki (who led them to Sugiura) and being angry at Hamazaki. All the prisoners read numerous Marxist and Communist books in prison, wrote poems about foods and weather they longed for, and continued to try to inform people on the outside about their case. Many of them thought that the second trial was going in their favor until they

31. Satō Hajime, Hikoku, pp. 134–135.
32. Aijō wa kabe o tōshite, p. 40.
33. Ibid., p. 76.

heard the procurator's *ronkoku* and read press reports predicting that the original verdict would be sustained. "At that point of despair," wrote Satō Hajime, "Mr. Hirotsu appeared, giving us endless power and courage." [34]

Hirotsu Kazuo (1891–1968) was an excellent example of what the Japanese call a Taishō liberal intellectual, meaning particularly those men of letters who as young men contributed greatly to the vivid, realistic school of Japanese literature that flourished around the time of the First World War and during Japan's "liberal" 1920s (i.e., during the Taishō period, 1912–1926). Their literary and artistic successes were genuine, and their influence on a country that has always respected its intelligentsia was immense. Some historians like to write about the subsequent "failure" of the Taishō intellectuals, because these literati allegedly did not restrain or prevent the movement toward nationalism and fascism during the 1930s—thereby assuming that they both wanted to and could; but the Japanese reading public tends to look on them as men of great humanity in an otherwise difficult and rapidly changing era. Hirotsu and his fellow writers of the twenties continued to have authority over Japanese public opinion after the war, the authority of their early liberalism perhaps even enhanced by the national experiences of war and defeat.

Hirotsu himself was born in Tokyo, the son of Hirotsu Ryūrō, a well-known Meiji novelist of the realist school. In 1913 he was graduated in literature from Waseda University and devoted himself to translating Anton Chekhov. His debut as a novelist came with his work *Shinkeibyō jidai* (*The Age of Neurosis*), and he went on to win literary prizes and to see his collected works published. Among his closest lifelong friends was the even better known novelist Uno Kōji (1891–1961), who had withdrawn from Waseda's literature department in

34. *Warera Taishōkko*, p. 289.

1911, before graduation. Uno, too, won several literary prizes, had his collected novels published, and developed a considerable reputation as a writer of children's stories. Hirotsu's critical work *Dōjidai no sakkatachi* (*Writers of the Same Period*) contains an admiring chapter on Uno's first major novel, *Kura no naka* (*Inside the Storeroom*).[35] Both of these men were members of the Japanese Academy of Arts and Letters.

During 1951 and 1952 Hirotsu and Uno saw each other frequently and talked about current trends and events, including the Matsukawa case. They were not Communists, at least not publicly, although years later an authority on the Japanese Communist movement responded to a question whether Hirotsu might have been a Communist: "I don't know, but I do know that the phrase 'fellow traveler' was invented to describe people like him." [36] Certainly at the time of the second trial all commentators assumed that Hirotsu was not a Communist, and his nonpolitical motives for interesting himself in the case were crucial to his gaining the support of other writer friends of his, such as Shiga Naoya, who were known not to like Communists. Hirotsu, Uno, Shiga, and other Taishō liberals had all at one time dabbled in proletarian literature, but they did not write political literature nor were they particularly interested in—or wise about —politics.

From 1949 until 1952 Hirotsu and Uno fully agreed with the investigating authorities' premise that the Matsukawa wreck

35. Hirotsu Kazuo, *Dōjidai no sakkatachi* (Tokyo: Shinchō Bunko ed., 1952), pp. 187–211.

36. There were secret members of the Japanese Communist party, particularly among the intelligentsia—for example, Saionji Kinkazu, who revealed his party membership only when he resigned from it. Saionji was residing in Peking during the Chinese Great Proletarian Cultural Revolution (1966–1969) and resigned from the Japanese Communist party when the Chinese split with and denounced the Japanese party. For Saionji's early career as a "liberal intellectual," see Chalmers Johnson, *An Instance of Treason: Ozaki Hotsumi and the Sorge Spy Ring* (Stanford, California, 1964).

had been caused by Communists in the railway workers' union. Uno later noted that a majority of the public, himself included, had accepted the first verdict without question. Three things caused them to look closer at the case and to begin to revise their earlier opinions. The first was a book of letters, essays, and poems written by the defendants which the firm of Getsuyō Shobō published on November 28, 1951. Entitled *Shinjitsu wa kabe o tōshite* (*Truth Penetrates Walls*), it is a curious work, including excerpts from Akama's *kōso* appeal petition (presumably because he could not write something original for this book); a long narrative with dialogue by Abe, which ends with the shouts "Long live the workers!" "Long live the Abe family!" and "Long live the Communist party!"; a seven-page poem by Sugiura; Katō's poetry on the theme of "mother" and Ninomiya's on "rain"; and an angry exposé of her arrest by Nikaidō Sonoko, which had been previously published in *New Girl* magazine. Members of the relief committee compiled the book, intending to send it to Judge Suzuki, and in their preface the compilers specifically compared the twenty defendants in Sendai with "the innocent Mr. and Mrs. Rosenberg in New York." To say that the work is sentimental in tone is without doubt the mildest comment one can make about it.

However, *Truth Penetrates Walls* impressed Hirotsu and Uno. They later wrote that as novelists they were good at telling when a person was sincere in what he wrote and that they detected the glow of innocence in these writings. As we shall see, editorialists and particularly other creative writers would later excoriate Hirotsu and Uno mercilessly for their "softheartedness" and "foolish opinions," but this did not shake the two novelists in their convictions. After the second trial Hirotsu became the most effective spokesman in the country (including the defense attorneys) for the position that it was *objectively* impossible for the defendants to have committed the crime they were charged with, but both Hirotsu and Uno always maintained that they gained their initial insight into the defendants' innocence subjectively and through their intuitions. With nothing more to go on in the way of evidence than a hunch, only writers of their known talents and reputation could have gotten a hearing in the press of the time.

Having been intrigued by *Truth Penetrates Walls*, the two novelists started to follow the Sendai appellate trial in the newspapers. Just like the court, they latched onto the testimony of Tōshiba accountant Hashimoto Takiji, which suggested a partial alibi for Satō Hajime on August 13. They were impressed by the fact that "a natural enemy" of trade unionists thought that something was wrong with the procurators' case. As they were mulling this over, the February 1953 issue of the magazine *Sekai* (*The World*) reached the newsstands.

Sekai is a monthly magazine published by Iwanami, the most intellectually distinguished publishing firm in Japan, and during the 1950s it represented and reflected the prevailing opinions of the leftish, Marxist-oriented professors, social critics, and publicists of Tokyo, notably of Tokyo University. During this period, writing for *Sekai* was synonymous with being labeled an "Iwanami intellectual," and both the magazine and the label meant to the rest of the country something like what "New York intellectual" means in the United States: a source of indispensable reading for anyone who claims to be well informed but having virtually no influence on the government or on broadly based public opinion. Until February 1953, with two or three minor exceptions, no non-Communist publication in Japan had printed an article favorable to the Matsukawa defendants. Then *Sekai* carried four pieces on the Matsukawa case. First was an article by Unno Shinkichi, the head of the Japanese Civil Liberties Union (Jiyū Minken Yōgokai), explaining how he had become interested in the case[37] and arguing that various

37. Unno had received a letter from an American missionary in Tokyo, who had written to him after one of the American's seminary

illegalities, particularly the reliance on confessions, had been allowed by the first trial. The second article was a factual synopsis of the case and of disputed points in the trial. The third article was by Inoue Hirasaburō, the seminarian who knew Satō and who had caused the case to be raised with the civil liberties union. The fourth article was a skillfully written appeal from prison by Satō Hajime himself and addressed to "all intellectuals, scientists, technicians, artists, and religious believers."

These *Sekai* articles were enough to convince Hirotsu and Uno that their intuition was sound, and it caused a good many other intellectuals to begin to wonder whether justice was being done in Sendai. Uno, in particular, said that Satō's appeal from prison impressed him, and on May 6, 1953, he and Hirotsu boarded the train for Sendai to see for themselves. There they met the conservative lawyer Hakamada, whom they liked and who assured them that the defendants were being framed, and they sat through a court session. After it was over they met Satō Hajime, Takeda, and Saitō. More than anything else, this interview with some of the defendants convinced the two novelists of the younger men's innocence, and it also led to some of Hirotsu's and Uno's most subjective (and later derided) commentary. Both older men observed that the defendants had "clear eyes, cheerful faces, and close haircuts." "They did not look like real culprits," wrote Uno, "their behavior was harmonious. They did not appear to be guilty at all." [38] Hirotsu and

---

students, a young Japanese who was a personal friend of Satō Hajime's, had said to his teacher that he was certain Satō was innocent.

38. Uno Kōji, *Yo ni mo fushigi na monogatari* (The Strangest Story in the World) (Tokyo, 1953), pp. 48–51. For similar comments by Hirotsu, see "Shinjitsu wa uttaeru" (Truth Brings Suit), reprinted in Matsukawa Jiken Bunshū Hensan Iinkai (Matsukawa Case Anthology Compilation Committee), ed., *Shinjitsu wa kabe o tōshite, Matsukawa jiken hikoku no shuki* (Truth Penetrates Walls, Writings of the Matsukawa Case Defendants) (Tokyo: Aoki Bunko ed., 1953), pp. 177–203, particularly p. 200.

Uno also noted that Judge Suzuki looked sleepy and had not appeared to be paying much attention to what attorney Okabayashi was saying. Two months later, on July 3, Hirotsu and Uno were back in Sendai for a second visit, and this time, on the return trip to Tokyo, they stopped at Matsukawa to inspect the scene of the crime. By now they were both completely hooked as Matsukawa buffs—and on the defense side.

During October 1953, three months before the second verdict, both men put their considerable literary talents to work in the two most famous magazines in Japan: *Chūō kōron* (*The Central Review*) and *Bungei shunjū* (*Literary Times*). Hirotsu wrote for the October *Chūō kōron* an article entitled "Shinjitsu wa uttaeru" ("Truth Brings Suit"), and Uno published in the October *Bungei shunjū* his novelette *Yo ni mo fushigi na monogatari* (*The Strangest Story in the World*). Hirotsu's piece has since become famous as the initial step in a literary involvement with the Matsukawa case that would last until the final verdict eleven years later. In this first article, Hirotsu gave a factual account of how he had become interested in the case, his reading of Hashimoto Takiji's testimony in the newspapers and of the February *Sekai*, and his two visits to Tōhoku; and he ends by demanding that the second trial be "fair." This article was reprinted subsequently in the Aoki Bunko paperback edition of *Truth Penetrates Walls*, Hirotsu's and Uno's interest in that book having made it a lively bestseller.[39]

Whereas Hirotsu's writing on the Matsukawa case was always in the form of high-class reportage, comparable to, say, Hannah Arendt's *Eichmann in Jerusalem*, Uno's *Strangest Story* was much more "literary." It included personal impressions,

39. On the importance of Hirotsu's first article concerning the Matsukawa case and for an appreciation of his career as a whole, see Mamiya Mosuke, *Hirotsu Kazuo, kono hito to no go jū-nen* (Hirotsu Kazuo, My Fifty Years With Him) (Tokyo, 1969), pp. 210–231 and passim.

harsh asides concerning other writers, speculation about who had actually committed the crime, and a good deal of anti-American innuendo. He told at great length an apocryphal story about how Yoshida Kenichi, the son of the prime minister and a distinguished scholar of English literature, had once jokingly suggested to an American friend of his, who was also an officer in SCAP's Civil Transportation Section, that if SCAP would only do him the favor of wrecking the last train at night to Kamakura (a wealthy and rather arty suburb south of Tokyo), he could be rid of all the major writers in Japan in one stroke and thereby promote his own literary career. It was not necessary for Uno to say more to suggest to his readers that another train wreck, that at Matsukawa, could also have been hatched by SCAP officers and Japanese government officials over a friendly cocktail in Tokyo.

Uno also told about a man who was supposed to have witnessed the Matsukawa wreck, and who then moved to Yokohama and died in an accident shortly thereafter. It was said that the dead man's family received an unusually large amount of money from an anonymous source. In a similar vein Uno reported on his recent inspection of the scene of the crime, where he had observed that the paths along the railroad tracks and the nearby roads were "wide enough for jeeps [!]." All of this was written in Uno's elliptical, highly literate style. He ended by noting that he had called his report *The Strangest Story in the World* but that the story no longer seemed incredible to him. Thus began a major stream of Matsukawa commentary that during the 1960s would blossom into a genre—namely, how SCAP, the CIC, G-2, the CIA, the Cannon Organization, or a group of Nisei terrorists had sabotaged the train at Matsukawa and blamed twenty innocent workers for it.

Hirotsu and Uno created a sensation in the Tokyo press and generated the kind of public interest in the case that had been lacking until then. The relief association moved at once to exploit these new developments. It formally established the Matsukawa Case Countermeasures Committee of the Japanese People's Relief Association (Nihon Kokumin Kyūenkai Matsukawa Jiken Taisaku Iinkai) as the central coordinating committee for all Matsukawa-movement activities, with offices in Fukushima, Sendai, and Tokyo. Five years later this committee would have grown so big and powerful that it reversed its child-parent relationship with the relief association and allowed the latter to affiliate with it under its new name, the Matsukawa Countermeasures Council (Matsukawa Taisaku Kyōgikai). Another reason for the change in 1958 was to free the council from the onus of having been created and sponsored by a Communist organization (the relief association) and to reflect the shift in the Matsukawa Committee's leadership: the original leaders of the committee in 1953 were Ozawa Michio (a member of the Akita prefectural committee of the Japanese Communist party) and Kuroda Shōji (a "red purgee" from the leadership of the communications workers' union in Miyagi prefecture), whereas the head of the council from its founding in 1958 until its demise after the defendants were released was Hirotsu Kazuo.

During the autumn of 1953, the Matsukawa Committee, now bolstered by the writings of Hirotsu and Uno, renewed its efforts to raise funds and to forge a mass movement. The four defendants who were out on bail and the case's defense lawyers crossed and recrossed the country lecturing to Communist and union organizations, and the letter-writing campaign reached a frenzy. The Asahi described mountains of letters and postcards arriving daily at the Sendai High Court, addressed to Judge Suzuki and demanding an acquittal verdict. During the three-day period of October 10–12, over twelve hundred letters arrived, all referring to the "made-in-Japan Rosenberg tragedy," and between the close of court and October 18 at least three thousand airmail letters came from Communist China alone. Each domestic letter to Judge Suzuki that was mailed by the committee cost it ¥10 in postage, and this was a major expense of the committee at the time. Altogether letters and donations were sent from some eighteen nations during the period of the second trial.

Union support and the mass letter-writing campaign helped create the impression of popular backing for the movement, but it was the involvement of famous Tokyo intellectuals that made the headlines and filled the columns of commentators. In the *Dokusho shimbun* (*Book Readers News*) one critic noted that both Hirotsu and Uno were politically neutral and writers of "good sense" but that neither of them had any direct evidence to support his contentions. He concluded that both men's work was closer to "politics" than to "literature." In the *Yomiuri* the prominent playwright and novelist Miyoshi Jūrō attacked both Hirotsu and Uno in an article entitled "Gusha no rakuen" ("Pleasure Garden of Fools"). Miyoshi argued in essence that even if the Matsukawa defendants wrote good prose and had honest faces, as Hirotsu and Uno contended, "Persons with such cheerful countenances and who write such honest sentences really should not go around committing such dreadful crimes." Hirotsu was stung to reply to this article, which he did in the October 6 issue of *Asahi*. He wrote that Japanese should find out whether their country's courts were fair; that Miyoshi, not he and Uno, lived in a "fool's paradise"; and that the cynicism of people like Miyoshi disturbed him greatly.[40] Thus the battle lines were drawn: conservative literati contended that Hirotsu and Uno were suckers for a united-front organization and had been taken in by the defendants' "cheerful countenances," while commentators on the left saw Hirotsu and Uno as heroes who were exposing the scandal that the administration of Japanese justice had become.

Later historians of the Matsukawa movement have judged

40. See *Dokusho shimbun*, September 28, 1953; and Hirotsu Kazuo, "Amasa to karasa" (Sweet and Salty), in *Asahi shimbun*, October 6, 1953. This article of Hirotsu's was reprinted along with "Truth Brings Suit" in the Aoki Bunko edition of *Truth Penetrates Walls*.

that the Tokyo press, particularly the *Asahi* and *Yomiuri* news-papers, were hostile to Hirotsu's and Uno's initial sallies into the case. Broadly speaking, this was true; however, it was an article in the *Yomiuri* that actually did the most to swell support for Hirotsu's next effort, an intellectuals' petition to Judge Suzuki. In the October 7 issue of *Yomiuri* an unsigned staff member wrote for the regular column "Editorial Notes" ("Henshū techō") an article entitled "Futari no Zora" ("The Two Zolas"). He retold the story of the famous French spy case of 1894 and how Emile Zola had come to the aid of Captain Alfred Dreyfus, who had been framed for the crime.[41] Hirotsu and Uno, he said, were Japanese Emile Zolas come to aid the Matsukawa defend-ants. That was enough; no writer could resist being cast in the role of the author of *J'Accuse!* Hirotsu's and Uno's influence soared. A month later a *Mainichi* writer, in a column entitled "The Political Consciousness of Literary Figures," demurred and said that the whole thing was crazy: Japanese writers live in a class by themselves, they are divorced from the working people and are visionaries, even if they happen to be poverty stricken they don't believe that poverty is unpleasant, and "without mean-ing to be too severe the writings of Hirotsu and Uno do not compare with those of Zola."[42] Such comments were, how-ever, increasingly rare. The *Dokusho shimbun* (*Book Readers News*) now reflected the prevailing line: "Yoshida Shigeru sank his claws into unionized workers for the sake of getting American military bases in Japan and to prevent the workers from taking the country in a progressive direction. That is what the Matsu-kawa case is all about. The whole thing is a frame-up."[43]

The two Zolas[44] approached six other very distinguished

41. For a recent study of the Dreyfus case, see Nicholas Halasz, *Captain Dreyfus, The Story of a Mass Hysteria* (New York, 1955).
42. *Mainichi shimbun*, November 4, 1953.
43. *Dokusho shimbun*, November 7, 1953.
44. Richard Storry entitled his classic study of Japanese ultranation-

literary figures and obtained their signatures on a petition which read:

> To Chief Judge Suzuki:
> At the time of the second trial in the Matsukawa case we place our honor and confidence in the belief that you have carried out an examination of all aspects of this case with caution and with attention to minute details. We who do not agree with the verdict of the original trial trust that in the second trial you will hand down a fair verdict to which all citizens of Japan can give assent. We believe that courtroom justice is the wellspring from which Japan is being reconstructed. We further believe that the most important consideration in furthering the peace of mind and aspirations of all of us living in this country is the impartiality of the courts. It is the undersigned who have presumed to send you this letter.

It was signed by Hirotsu, Uno, Kawabata Yasunari (winner of the 1968 Nobel Prize for literature), novelists Mushanokōji Saneatsu, Shiga Naoya, Ibuse Masuji, and Yoshikawa Eiji, and Kawamori Kōzō (French literary specialist and critic)—all of them preeminent in Japanese letters. The petition was written by Hirotsu in his own calligraphy on large-size Mino paper (an old paper manufactured in Gifu prefecture) and was delivered to Suzuki personally by attorney Hakamada. Just in case Judge Suzuki did not get the point or simply put the petition in his desk, a photograph of it was also published in the December

---

alism of the 1930s *The Double Patriots*, explaining, "Just as a double whiskey is presumed to have twice the strength of a single tot, so a 'double patriot' is credited with the possession of twice the normal inheritance of patriotic sentiment." It would seem that in postoccupation Japan, with the nationalists in retirement and the left wing in at least temporary ascendancy, the same configuration may have reappeared: everybody was "democratic," but the two Zolas (actually one and a half, since Uno rapidly lost interest in the case) were doubly so.

1953 issue of *Sekai,* exciting attention throughout the Japanese intellectual world.[45]

Numerous petitions followed. Another group of prominent writers, including Nakajima Kenzō, Toyoshima Yoshio, and Abe Tomoji, sent one to Suzuki, which raised the Rosenberg case in the United States but which also made this important point: "We request that you as chief judge and also as a fellow citizen seriously struggle to eradicate the wretched way of thinking which holds that even if the suspects in custody are not the true criminals, it still does not matter if we treat them as if they were the criminals." [46] This kind of thinking had appeared in the case up to that time and would reappear again, a cynical response to the procurators' crumbling case that "we know the wreck was caused by disgruntled workers; whether or not we have caught the true criminals, we have at least caught a representative bunch, and they should be punished as a lesson to others."

Petitions also came from musicians, poets, professors, technicians, and other opinion-leading groups. Universities held forums on literature and politics, prefectural labor union federations sponsored rallies, the case was debated in the Diet, parent-teacher associations took stands on the Sendai trial, and many prominent citizens were interviewed in the press for their opinions on the case—particularly in light of the two Zolas' stand. On October 28, Judge Suzuki announced that he was postponing his verdict from the then scheduled date of November 5 until December 22, presumably to let the furor cool down a little.

But things did not cool down. On November 2, some two thousand people met in Kyōbashi Public Hall in Tokyo to hear the bailed defendants, family members, and literary critics explain the case and to view the movie made by the relief association. This rally ended with the usual petition to the judge and

45. Also see *Sangyō keizai shimbun,* October 27, 1953.
46. *Shakai taimusu,* October 28, 1953.

also with "a strong protest about the delay in the verdict." The chairman of this rally closed the gathering by announcing that another protest meeting would be held in Sendai two days later. All the commentary was not on one side, however. On November 29, the mass circulation magazine *Weekly Asahi* (*Shūkan asahi*) devoted its entire issue to the Matsukawa case, and the leaders of the movement were deeply disappointed by its cool and investigative stance. *Asahi* reporters had been around to interview Japanese who had worked with Colonel Changnon in the Civil Transportation Section of SCAP, and they all derided Uno's hints that Changnon or any other officer in the section had ever had any other duty than to try to keep the railroads running. Also, a young man who had been involved with American clandestine operations in Japan at the time (a subject to which we shall return in a later chapter) categorically denied that Changnon was Colonel Cannon of the mysterious Cannon Organization, as Uno had suggested. People were suspicious of the procurators' case, but they were also suspicious of the Matsukawa movement and its leaders.

Two weeks later, on December 13, the *Weekly Asahi* published the answers to a questionnaire it had submitted to the editors in chief of Japan's leading magazines. They had been asked whether they were concerned about the case and how they had come to know anything about it. The chief editor of *Bungei shunjū* expressed great concern but acknowledged that the only thing he had read was Uno's novelette, which he had selected for the magazine. The editor of the Japanese-language *Reader's Digest* criticized legal specialists for not listening to public opinion; but the editor of the *Housewife's Friend* (*Shufu no tomo*) replied, "Seen from the point of view of the way the Communist party does things, I suspect that the prosecution's charges are true." The editor of the fast-rising weekly magazine *Heibon*, one of the most successful (even though of dubious taste) publishing ventures in postwar Japan, said that his readers couldn't care less about the case; and the editor of *Fujin gahō* (*Ladies' Pictorial*) responded that he was interested only because one of the defendants and one of the defense attorneys were women. The editor of *Chūō kōron* felt that the whole issue was whether Japan was going to be a country "ruled by law or ruled by political ideologies"; and Yoshino Gensaburō, chief editor of *Sekai*, wrote: "I do not regard this as a political case but as one involving fundamental human rights. . . . The legal order of a country governed by laws is maintained through the authority of the state, but when people lose confidence in the administration of justice, the legal order cannot be upheld. For law to be controlled by political beliefs is the first step toward fascism."

As the nation came to the eve of the verdict, rallies were held in many large cities. On December 21 trucks toured Sendai and distributed handbills calling for a not-guilty verdict, and at Ueno station in Tokyo many prominent intellectuals and Communist party leaders were observed boarding the Aoba (Green Leaves) Express for Sendai. From about 2:40 A.M. onward on December 22, a huge crowd carrying red flags began to gather in front of the Sendai courthouse, and a loudspeaker-equipped truck of the Countermeasures Committee led several choruses of the new Matsukawa song "For the Victory of Truth" ("Shinjitsu no shōri no tame ni"). Some five hundred policemen were on hand to control the crowd.

Inside the court building later that morning, Judge Suzuki got through only the briefest statement of his verdict before the courtroom was overwhelmed by the uproar. He annulled the original verdict, finding that the prosecution had been unable to prove the existence of the August 13 conspiracy meeting at the NRWU offices or of Okada's visit that same day to Tōshiba. With the collapse of the August 13 conspiracy, he argued, the alleged August 12 conspiracy could also not be confirmed. Therefore he declared Takeda, Saitō, and Okada not guilty and released them forthwith. The testimony of Hashimoto Takiji had been important in this judgment, plus the fact that the alibis of these three men seemed plausible even if not watertight. All the rest of the prosecution's case, however, including the crucial August 15 conspiracy meeting, Judge Suzuki found to have been proven. He therefore sentenced the remaining seventeen defendants as shown in table 6.

The headlines in the evening edition of the Tokyo *Asahi* for December 22 described the scene following the verdict as one

TABLE 6

SECOND TRIAL VERDICT

December 22, 1953

Defendant	First verdict	Second verdict
Suzuki Makoto	death	death
Abe Ichiji	death	life imprisonment
Sugiura Saburō	death	death
Honda Noboru	death	death
Satō Hajime	death	death
Takeda Hisashi	life imprisonment	not guilty
Ninomiya Yutaka	life imprisonment	life imprisonment
Akama Katsumi	life imprisonment	13 years
Takahashi Haruo	life imprisonment	15 years
Ōta Shōji	life imprisonment	15 years
Saitō Yuki	15 years	not guilty
Hamazaki Futao	12 years	10 years
Okada Toramatsu	12 years	not guilty
Katō Kenzō	12 years	10 years
Satō Shiroji	10 years	10 years
Nikaidō Takeo	10 years	7 years
Ōuchi Shōzō	7 years	7 years
Kobayashi Genzaburō	7 years	7 years
Kikuchi Takeshi	7 years	7 years
Yokoya Sonoko (née Nikaidō)	3 years, 6 months	3 years, 6 months (less 90 days already served)

of UTTER CONFUSION. Satō and Takahashi leaped from their seats and screamed, "Murderer!"; a mother in the spectators' gallery was heard to gasp, "My son!"; bailiffs dragged the prisoners away; and Judge Suzuki kept on reading. On the steps of the courthouse an impromptu rally took place, at which, according to a hostile account in the Yomiuri, the crowd listened to families of the defendants and workers' representatives "weep and blubber" (naki-jakuru). The crowd then moved en masse, accompanied by a brass band, to the front of the Sendai police station where speakers again protested the verdict. In Tokyo at six o'clock that same evening about two thousand workers and students gathered at Shiba Public Hall and demanded a jōkoku appeal to the Supreme Court, following which the students snake-danced through the Shimbashi district singing labor songs.

Postmortems began in the evening papers of December 22 and continued for weeks. Hirotsu declared that the court had been subjected to political pressures; a Japanese Communist party spokesman said that the independence of the Japanese courts had collapsed; procurator Anzai of the first trial (and in 1953 attached to the Osaka High Procuracy) expressed himself as satisfied with the verdict and criticized intellectuals and the press for trying to influence the decision through mass pressure; and in Kyoto, Ōyama Ikuo, a famous leftist politician and winner of the Stalin Prize in 1951, concluded that the Matsukawa case was the same thing as the Rosenberg case in America. In China the New China News Agency released a dispatch explaining that the verdict was part of an American plot to rearm Japan, but in the Mainichi that same day a writer of a letter to the editor compared the case with the political execution of Beria in the Soviet Union (which had only recently occurred): "For all of the Communists' pressure tactics, Beria did not have the right to appeal." [47] The

47. Mainichi shimbun, December 25, 1953. In addition to the New China News Agency dispatch, the Peking Ta kung pao (December 24,

Jiji shimbun entitled its December 23 editorial "Yo ni mo fushigi na monogatari" ("The Strangest Story in the World"), which was of course the title of Uno's novelette, but added the subtitle: "Red Demonstrators Surround Matsukawa Court." The paper denounced the Matsukawa movement and the propaganda that had accompanied the trial and said that the only issue was who had sabotaged the train.

Yomiuri was probably the most balanced in its editorial. It felt Akama's confession, which was unquestionably the most important (and now virtually the only) evidence left in the case, was too weak to form the basis for death sentences. At the same time the *Yomiuri* accused the intellectuals of having fallen victim to sentimentalism. Some of the more serious observers took their time before commenting. The distinguished psychologist Miyagi Otoya was also disturbed by the fact that the whole prosecution case, as well as the verdict, had come to rest on Akama's confession. He pointed out that Japanese confessions were often unreliable, and he strongly criticized the police for their careless, slipshod work. The *Asahi* editors concurred in this opinion but, after weighing the evidence pro and con, came down on Judge Suzuki's side. In his verdict the judge had written: "A person who commits a serious crime and then confesses to it does so because he hopes to have his punishment lessened. He often does not tell the literal truth and invents new details or implicates others. . . . However, the fact that these discrepancies exist does not necessarily mean that his entire confession is false." Given the Akama prophecy and his grandmother's initial inability to account for Akama's whereabouts on the night of the crime, Judge Suzuki concluded that parts of Akama's confession were true. On this same point—the importance of Akama's confession—Professor Kainō Michitaka, one of the most experienced

1953) and the *Jen-min jih-pao* (December 26, 1953) carried articles attacking the verdict.

observers of Japanese courts, concluded that Suzuki's verdict was not intentionally political and was, in fact, completely consistent with prewar criminal procedure—and that was what Kainō thought was wrong with it.[48]

The defense, of course, pledged to appeal to the Supreme Court, the prosecution having declined to do so despite the three acquittals. Normally, even a case as sensational as the Matsukawa case would have dropped from public attention while the complicated and time-consuming jōkoku appeal procedures were instituted. But in the Matsukawa case, at least one of the "two Zolas," Hirotsu Kazuo, was shocked and infuriated by the second verdict. His associate, Uno, more or less lost interest, but Hirotsu abandoned his former subjective stance and dove into a scrutiny of the first and second trial records with exceptional vigor and persistence. He revisited the scene of the crime and consulted often with the defendants. Four months after the second verdict, in the April 1954 issue of Chūō kōron, Hirotsu published the first of an unbroken series of articles on the Matsukawa trials that was to last until September 1958. Every month for four and a half years Hirotsu published in Chūō kōron an analytical article on some aspect of the case, for a total of fifty-six articles and well over two thousand pages of printed text. Gathered together they constitute his indispensable three-volume work on the case, Matsukawa saiban (The Matsukawa Trials). More than anything else Hirotsu's articles kept the Matsukawa movement alive and also fueled an entirely new movement called "criticism of the courts" (saiban hihan). They also established his identity with the case so closely that today the words Matsukawa and Hirotsu have become virtually synonymous. He never referred to himself as a "Zola," but the precedent established by Emile Zola was quite well known to him and may well have contributed to his special dedication.

48. Kainō, Hōritsu (Tokyo, 1957), p. 86.

Chapter 6

Criticism of the Courts

*E*VALUATION of the American occupation of Japan must of necessity be ambiguous. On the one hand, the occupation was enormously successful in terms of the number, range, and quality of the reform programs it developed and in terms of its ability to get the Japanese to pass the policies into law and actually to implement them. On the other hand, it was too easy—deceptively so. Every observer of the occupation has commented on the receptivity of the great majority of Japanese to the American-sponsored innovations and on their willingness to be "democratized." Expecting hostility and perhaps even fierce resistance, the Americans were always amazed (and deeply flattered) by the ease with which they set up shop in Tokyo and went to work as democratic mentors to the Japanese. Undoubtedly the Americans underestimated Japanese relief at discovering that the American occupation would not be harshly punitive, and they never fully appreciated how aware the Japanese were of the authoritarian steel that lay behind SCAP's "instructions." Playing the unaccustomed role of conqueror, the Americans did not really perceive that the harsh conditions of life in a defeated and occupied nation might make anyone docile and submissive, just in order to survive. Instead SCAP saw great progress being made as the Japanese agreed to one new law after another.[1]

Great progress was made, and it would be foolish to underestimate SCAP's accomplishments or to belittle the genuine iconoclasm that was churned up in Japanese society by the defeat, by the release from emperor worship, and by the American presence. But it was too easy. In contrast, for example, to the experiences that many Americans, Europeans, and United Nations officials were having in trying to assist or bring about economic, political, or social "development" in the Afro-Asian and Latin American worlds, the success of the occupation of Japan was anomalous: there was not enough arguing, backsliding, and contention to believe that anything was really happening. Japanese society did not seem to be giving off the heat that is inevitably generated by real social change. The naïve among the Americans attributed this tranquility to the enormous skill of the Americans as social engineers or to the irresistible attraction of the American example; the cynical believed that nothing at all was changing and that the Japanese were just lying low. Both were wrong.

The most experienced American observers knew that many of the occupation's innovations rested on brittle foundations. They did not expect the Japanese to argue with the Americans or to attempt seriously to resist the occupation. It would have been futile to do so, and the Americans obviously would not be there forever. But these same observers did expect that at some point the Japanese would start contending with each other over what

1. See, e.g., *Reports of General MacArthur: MacArthur in Japan*, Vol. I, Supplement (Washington, 1966), pp. 291–297. The title page of this book says that it was "prepared by his General Staff."

SCAP had done and, in the process, start shaping the occupation's reforms into social codes and norms that Japanese felt were truly theirs. Many of SCAP's changes had been long overdue in Japan and were welcomed by a majority of the population. The development of the labor movement and of political parties, the enfranchisement of women and the guarantees of basic political rights, the secularization of society and the opening up of access to channels of international communications, even land reform —all were indicated by Japan's development as an industrialized nation and by its dependence on world commerce, and they had been foreshadowed by prewar social trends. However, there were several concrete occupation reforms—for example, the no-war clause in the Constitution of 1947, the educational and police systems, and innovations in the legal and judicial systems—that were still a long way from being integrated into the Japanese social fabric. It was only natural to expect that at some point the other shoe of social change would have to drop—that the no longer quite so docile and receptive Japanese would have to decide among themselves what to accept, reject, or modify from the heritage of the occupation.

On September 8, 1951, the Japanese-American peace treaty was signed at San Francisco, and on April 28, 1952, it went into effect, ending the occupation. However, the American presence did not even begin to fade away for at least another two years. The Korean War was still in progress, and simultaneously with the signing of the peace treaty, the Americans and the Japanese concluded a Security Treaty that authorized the United States to station American military forces in Japan and committed the United States to the defense of Japan. More important for the years immediately following the end of the occupation, the Japanese economy was still deeply dependent on American expenditures. As was already discussed in chapter two, during 1949 the Americans had begun to reorient the Japanese economy more toward growth than toward democracy, and they had implemented policies of economic retrenchment in order to rationalize payrolls and to halt inflation. During 1950 these policies were accelerated with the curbing of union power under the cover of anti-Communist purges; and the economy in turn began to respond, being fueled by American procurements for the Korean War. As the representatives to a conference of Japanese Labor Relations Committees, held on April 13, 1951, in Aomori, observed, on the one hand, "there are frequent cases in which employers are using 'trumped-up' Communist charges as an excuse for firing certain employees, when the real cause may be personal dislike, dereliction of duty, or union activity"; on the other hand, "since the outbreak of hostilities in Korea there has been increased employment and fewer cases [of] nonpayment of wages." However, they also noted that "especially those industries favored by American procurement demands are prosperous, but this prosperity is not being reflected in wage increases." [2]

Indeed, the business revival in conjunction with the Korean War was not showing up in wage packets. Instead its profits were going into technical innovation, investment in new plant and equipment, and into the development of new products, all of which would begin to pay off only during the second half of the decade, when the Japanese economy embarked on its fantastic growth curve, which is not yet declining. During 1954 and 1955, Japan was still dependent on American offshore procurements in order to balance its international payments, but less so in 1955 than in 1954, when the end of the Korean War had produced a recession. Thus, truly postwar and postoccupation Japan began to come into view only in 1955, when unaided economic growth began, when the structure of party alignments that has been maintained more or less to this day was forged, and when the Japanese began seriously to discuss the occupation reforms. The

2. SCAP Archives, Tōhoku Civil Affairs Region, box 2571.

period from approximately 1955 to 1961 may therefore be called the first phase of genuine postwar social change in Japan, the period in which Japan came to grips with some of its new institutions and began to display some social conflict in the process.

Too often foreign observers speak of "the Japanese," seeming to forget that there are definite groups and parties within Japan and that they divide over numerous social and political issues. During the period of the great debates of the late 1950s, two major groups of allies emerged, which may be identified loosely, using their own terminology, as "progressives" and "conservatives." The progressives included the Socialists, Communists, most of the trade unionists, students, intellectuals, academicians, and many city dwellers. Their strong point was their vehement defense of the most liberal of SCAP's policies—an ironic turn of events in view of the fact that they were SCAP's bêtes noires during the occupation's final years. Their weak point was that they were admirers of Communist nations, particularly Russia and China, leading many Japanese citizens to suspect that underneath their protestations of love of democracy lay a deeper affinity for totalitarianism.

The conservatives included business leaders, the political party in power, and people knowledgeable about the United States and Western Europe. Their strong point was their leadership of economic recovery and growth, which was immensely popular with everyone in the country. Their weak points were their seeming subservience to United States foreign policy (particularly to aspects of it that had a great emotional impact in Japan, such as the testing of nuclear weapons) and a suspicion on the part of many people that the conservatives, given the chance, would try to reverse most of the democratic orientations laid down by SCAP. These two major groups were not at all homogeneous. Both of them were divided internally, with each including individuals with strong democratic commitments near the center as well as persons in the Communist camp on the progressive side and persons tending toward full reaction on the conservative side. Nevertheless, both sides characterized the other in terms of stereotypes: to the progressives, all conservatives wanted to turn back the clock to the 1930s and were typified by the former cabinet minister in the Tōjō cabinet who became the prime minister between February 25, 1957, and July 18, 1960—Kishi Nobusuke; whereas to the conservatives all progressives looked like the Socialist leader Asanuma Inejirō, who on March 9, 1959, in Peking, stated that "the United States is the common enemy of the Japanese and Chinese peoples," and who was himself assassinated by a right-wing youth on October 12, 1960.

The period 1955 to 1961 might well be called Japan's Wasshoi Era, *wasshoi* meaning something like "heave-ho" and being the chant of the thousands of students and union demonstrators who regularly snake-danced through downtown Tokyo. Wearing *hachimaki* (white towels around their heads) and black tennis shoes (*zukkugutsu*), and waving enormous banners and red flags, the demonstrators of the Wasshoi Era carried much of the political debate of the period into the streets. However, although the charges and countercharges, the propaganda, and the methods were usually shrill and frequently unfair, the debate was about substantive issues of social policy, and it contributed greatly to public education and to the development of contemporary Japan. The biggest issue of all was the debate over the renewal of the Japanese-American Security Treaty, which resulted in the forced cancellation of President Eisenhower's proposed trip to Japan and the ultimate resignation of Prime Minister Kishi.[3] But there were many other issues, including disputes over the power of the teachers' union, the role of the

3. The authoritative sources on the Security Treaty crisis are George R. Packard, III, *Protest in Tokyo* (Princeton, N.J., 1966); and Robert A. Scalapino and Masumi Junnosuke, *Parties and Politics in Contemporary Japan* (Berkeley and Los Angeles, Calif., 1962), chap. 5.

police, the constitutionality of the self-defense forces, atomic testing, and criminal justice.

Looking at underlying trends, and with the benefit of hindsight, several Japanese sociologists and social psychologists have concluded that, on balance, the conservative forces won the debate. Although the progressives made a lot of noise, and the national newspapers kept pouring more fuel on the controversies, the Japanese-American Security Treaty was renegotiated and the conservatives were always reelected. Professor Ishikawa has also observed that for all of the political turmoil of the period, the event which absorbed more Japanese than any other, including the Security Treaty struggle, was the marriage in 1959 of the crown prince to a commoner, the present Princess Michiko. Similarly, he believes that the most important change in this period was the consumer revolution, the emergence of a huge domestic demand for consumer products, brought about by economic growth and the decades of material hardship.[4] Mita Munesuke, a well-known authority on postwar society, studied trends in bestsellers to find out what the people were really interested in. He concludes that by 1958 the postwar fascination with topics such as modern history, politics, and sexual permissiveness (as in the "sun tribe," or taiyōzoku, books of Ishihara Shintarō) had virtually disappeared and that books such as Keieigaku nyūmon (Introduction to Business Administration), published in 1958, best typified the period. He goes further and says that by the end of 1960 even those who carried out the struggle against the Japanese-American Security Treaty had themselves been absorbed by and disappeared into the new consumer-oriented society that flourished during the 1960s.[5]

4. Ishikawa Hiroyoshi, Nihonjin no shakai shinri (The Social Psychology of Japanese) (Tokyo, 1965), pp. 116–119, 139–145. See also Ozaki Hotsuki and Yamada Munemutsu, Sengo seikatsu bunka shi (A History of the Postwar Culture of Daily Life) (Tokyo, 1966).

5. Mita Munesuke, Gendai Nihon no seishin kōzō (The Structure of Contemporary Japanese Values) (Tokyo, 1965), pp. 78–79.

These observations are unquestionably true—in the sense that the conservatives' strong point, the championing of economic growth, carried the day in postoccupation Japan, and that the progressives' weak point, their inclination toward the Communists in foreign policy, ultimately led to disaster for them at the polls and to seemingly irreparable fissures within their own ranks. However, at the same time it must be stressed that the progressives' defense of SCAP's democratic innovations against the encroachments of the conservatives was of great historical significance. The Japanese leftists did not even come close to winning a majority to their cause, but they did prevent conservative diehards from reestablishing an essentially authoritarian polity. Through their protests, the progressives put very definite limits on the type of conservative leader that the emerging Japanese consensus would tolerate—he had to be a man of "low posture" (tei-shisei), not high-handed or arrogant, as Kishi allegedly had been—and they reaffirmed Japan's desire not to be drawn so deeply into international politics as to endanger domestic prosperity or to be pulled into a war. Similarly, the progressive protest movement greatly strengthened the judicial system by continually calling attention to instances of backsliding, illegality, and lack of respect for a citizen's constitutional rights in the administration of justice. Although the Japanese Supreme Court has never yet dared to declare an act of the Diet unconstitutional, as it has the power to do, the progressives brought enough constitutional cases before it to breathe real life into the piece of paper that the Government Section of SCAP had, in 1946, sent over to the Diet for passage.

Of all of SCAP's reforms the one that in retrospect seems at least as important as any other was legalizing freedom of the press. Until 1945, the Censorship Section of the Police Bureau, a part of the Ministry of Home Affairs, carried on a continuous scrutiny of magazines and newspapers; and numerous prewar books were riddled with the maru-maru (printed circles) indicating the censor's deletions. Press freedom was not, however, an unmixed blessing, even to SCAP. Occupation authorities had to implement their own form of censorship in order to stop the press from attacking them, and they often charged that Japan's newspapers were more interested in competition for its own sake than in accurately reporting the news. For example, when in the case of Shimoyama's death the *Mainichi* adopted the suicide explanation, while the *Asahi* and *Yomiuri* held strongly to the murder theory, most people thought it was in order to be different; conversely, during the Security Treaty struggle, the *Mainichi* went the furthest in trumpeting the protesters' views, while the *Asahi* and *Yomiuri* at least tried occasionally to present both sides.[6] Despite these problems, SCAP itself acknowledged:

> Perhaps the most notable change in the Japanese press during the postsurrender period was the use of its new-found ability to criticize and expose injustice and corruption without fear of government reprisal. Gradually, almost gingerly at first, the press began to assert its democratic rights and to speak out boldly against public wrong. Civil servants in scores of public offices were jolted out of their traditional complacency by editorial attacks on bureaucratic red tape and inefficiency. Several graft or bribery cases which led to Diet investigations and which, in other times, might have been covered up by powerful political or financial groups, snowballed into national prominence through front-page revelations in the nation's newspapers.[7]

Nowhere was this more true than in the Matsukawa movement and in the criticism-of-the-courts debate. Until the second trial, only *Akahata* and other leftist organs had covered the case

6. SCAP Monograph No. 15, "Freedom of the Press," pp. 169–170; and Edward P. Whittemore, *The Press in Japan Today: A Case Study* (Columbia, S.C., 1961).

7. SCAP Monograph No. 15, "Freedom of the Press," p. 161.

regularly, but after the nation became interested in (and alarmed by) the Matsukawa trials, the national papers took it up and deprived *Akahata* of its monopoly. A *Mainichi* reporter made one of the key discoveries in the case (the Suwa Memorandum, to be discussed later in this chapter), and the demands on Hirotsu for statements and copy became so great that on August 14, 1959, two different articles by him appeared in the *Asahi* and the *Mainichi*. Although the press was far from being "responsible" and unquestionably contributed to some of the worst excesses in the struggles of the late 1950s, it is impossible to imagine the debates having occurred at all if a free press had not existed.

All the issues under debate by the progressives and conservatives tended to get mixed up together, and a victory by one "movement"—say, a good fight with the police over the Americans' attempt to expand the runways of their air base at Tachikawa into nearby Sunakawa village—would set off waves of jubilation and optimism in another movement—say, in the Matsukawa struggle before the Supreme Court. All of the various protest groups assisted each other, held joint rallies, exchanged leaders to give speeches, and borrowed propaganda themes in order to support a particular cause. There were differences between them, however, and occasionally one group would steer clear of another for fear of having the other's political commitments rub off on it. The Matsukawa movement came to fit into this complicated scene as the biggest segment of the larger campaign criticizing the courts for allegedly not defending the bill of rights clauses in the Constitution of 1947 and for handing down politically motivated decisions. The criticism-of-the-courts movement was itself, in turn, part of the even bigger progressive campaign to subvert the conservatives' foreign and domestic policies—most notably, the massive campaign to force abrogation of the Security Treaty. Although many critics of the courts would have been appalled to find themselves associated with Communists, the leaders of the Matsukawa movement regularly tried to tie their movement to anti-atomic-testing or Security Treaty struggles, usually to the disadvantage of all parties concerned. Part of the fascination in tracing the criticism-of-the-courts movement is in identifying how some figures, such as Hirotsu, managed to stay within the movement and also to be effective.

The debate over court performance under the new Code of Criminal Procedure was definitely two-sided. Although the initiative came from organizations such as the Matsukawa movement, the conservatives had their spokesmen. The most famous and most important of these was Tanaka Kōtarō, who between 1950 and 1961 was chief justice of the Supreme Court of Japan. Before the war Tanaka had been dean of the Faculty of Law of Tokyo Imperial University, and under the occupation he became, first, minister of education and then an elected member of the House of Councilors. In the eyes of the progressives, however, these achievements—including his prewar defense of academic freedom against the militarists—weighed less than the facts that Tanaka was also a member of the Catholic Church and a staunch anti-Communist. Back in 1951, when he was already chief justice, he had written an article for the journal Hōsō (Jurist), entitled "The Peace Treaty and the Judiciary," in which he denounced Communist countries for behaving like "international gangsters" and asserted that, in his personal opinion, judges who did not believe in the necessity of Japan's cooperating with the United States "and other free countries" were not fit to be judges. Similarly, in 1957, he published a book setting forth his political views, entitled Kyōsanshugi to sekaikan (Communism and a View of the World).[8] The Communists and leaders of the Matsukawa movement regularly tried to have him impeached for his views, and he was often smeared in the press, once by Hirotsu, who wrote that because he was a

8. Ienaga Saburō, Saiban hihan (Criticism of the Courts) (Tokyo, 1959), p. 36; and John M. Maki, Court and Constitution in Japan (Seattle, 1964), pp. 425–426.

Catholic, it was a foregone conclusion that he would wish to see the Matsukawa defendants hanged.[9] In 1961, Tanaka resigned from the Supreme Court to become the first Japanese judge appointed to the International Court of Justice, and he served in The Hague until 1970, when at the age of seventy-nine he retired.

It is a truism that it takes two to make a quarrel, and in the criticism-of-the-courts debate, the argument began with Chief Justice Tanaka's denouncing the out-of-court activities of intellectuals and attorneys on behalf of cases that were concurrently before the courts. On May 26, 1955, Tanaka sent an official instruction (which was his prerogative as the highest administrative official of the postwar independent judiciary) to all subordinate judges in the country calling the Matsukawa movement "indeed regrettable" (*makoto ni ikan de aru*) and admonishing them "not to listen to the noise of public opinion" (*seken no zatsuon ni mimi o kasu na*).[10] This instruction became immediately famous as Tanaka's "noise statement" and brought forth a vigorous rebuttal from the left. However, Tanaka never wavered. Four years later and only two months after the Supreme Court's first decision in the Matsukawa case, he wrote an article for the *Asahi Journal*, entitled "Criticism of Criticism of the Courts," in which he reasserted that his noise statement was an official instruction, not just his personal opinion, and that what had happened since he issued it had only confirmed the wisdom of his action. He also affirmed that when he originally made his comment, he had had in mind the goings-on surrounding both the Matsukawa and Yakai cases.[11]

9. *Mainichi shimbun*, August 14, 1959.

10. See "Twenty Years of the Supreme Court," in *Asahi shimbun*, December 14, 1967; and Yakai Case History Compilation Committee, ed., *Yakai jiken jūhachi-nen* (Eighteen Years of the Yakai Case) (Tokyo, 1969), p. 51.

11. Tanaka Kōtarō, "Saiban hihan o hihan suru," *Asahi jānaru*, I:33 (October 25, 1959), pp. 8–15.

During the 1950s, several famous cases—sometimes known as the eight great mistrials[12]—contributed to the rising criticism of the courts and caused many distinguished academic and judicial authorities to adhere to the Matsukawa movement. We shall review some of these cases in chapter nine, since they were all caused at least in part by the difficulties encountered in shifting from the old to the new criminal procedures; but one, the Yakai case, was almost as important as the Matsukawa case in launching the whole court-criticism movement. Differing from the Matsukawa case, it had no political overtones, and the leaders of the "Yakai movement" were very wary of linking their activities to those of the Matsukawa activists because of the latter's obvious political interests. In addition, the chief attorneys of the two cases did not particularly like each other. Masaki Hiroshi, chief attorney in the Yakai case, had been one of the members of the League of Free Jurists who, in 1949 and 1950, had called for the league's dissolution because it was infiltrated and dominated by Communists. Okabayashi Tatsuo, Matsukawa's chief counsel, was both a Communist and one of the league's postwar founders. He opposed Masaki's stand on the league, but he could not be too open in his criticism of him because Masaki was one of the most famous defenders in Japan.[13]

The Yakai case was another "confession case," but one having a different aspect from the Matsukawa case. On January 24, 1951, an intruder had brutally murdered and robbed an old farming couple while they slept in their farmhouse in Yakai village, Yamaguchi prefecture. The murderer, Yoshioka Akira, age twenty-two, was a locally known petty thief, who had com-

12. See, e.g., Ueda Seikichi and Gotō Shōjirō, *Ayamatta saiban, yattsu no keiji jiken* (Mistrials, The Eight Criminal Cases) (Tokyo, 1960).

13. Okabayashi Tatsuo and Nakata Naoto, "Matsukawa saiban tōsō no shomondai" (Problems of the Matsukawa Court Struggles), in *Matsukawa undō zenshi*, p. 805; and *Yakai jiken jūhachi-nen*, pp. 42–44. Also see Masaki Hiroshi, *Yakai saiban* (The Yakai Trials) (Tokyo, 1969).

mitted the crime in order to pay bills that he had run up drinking and for a prostitute. However, the police officials investigating the crime deduced that the double murder (one victim was axed and the other suffocated with a pillow) had been committed by several persons who must have been members of a conspiracy. They arrested Yoshioka, and after a day of denials he confessed that he alone had killed the old couple in order to get their money. The police did not believe him and forced him to name five other young men as his accomplices. They then arrested these youths (one of the five was subsequently released), beat them, and ultimately indicted five individuals (including Yoshioka) for the crime. The first and second trials found them all guilty; and it was not until October 25, 1968, that the Supreme Court, after having heard three separate *jōkoku* appeals, finally exonerated the four innocent men named by Yoshioka.

The case was brought into national prominence primarily by Masaki Hiroshi, who defended the four alleged accomplices against whom the only evidence was Yoshioka's confession. (The press has on occasion compared Akama to Yoshioka, because both men implicated others in their confessions and their unsavory reputations probably predisposed the police to believe them.)[14] In 1955, after being repeatedly frustrated in court, Masaki wrote a book, entitled *Saibankan* (*The Judges*), which was published in the extraordinarily successful series known as Kappa Books, put out by the firm of Kōbunsha (the source of more bestsellers than any other publishing house in postwar Japan). *Saibankan* is a very vivid account of the crime, of the police's torturing the four innocent suspects, and of the judges' sentencing them to the gallows; and it inspired one of Japan's leading motion picture directors, Imai Tadashi, to make his prize-winning film *Mahiru no ankoku* (*Darkness at Noon*), which is based on Masaki's version of the Yakai case. Both the

14. See the article by Aoyagi Fumio in *Yomiuri shimbun*, August 9, 1961.

book and the movie have acknowledged artistic merits, and they aroused extraordinary public interest in the case. However, the Supreme Court and the government were outraged by their appearance because the Yakai case was still before the courts. People still argue about whether Masaki used the only means remaining to him to force the Supreme Court to scrutinize the case (which all agree today was a gross miscarriage of justice), or whether by going out of channels he only succeeded in delaying settlement of the case until 1968.[15]

15. On June 18, 1966, I saw Imai's *Mahiru no ankoku* at the Tokyo Museum of Modern Art, where a print has been deposited as part of the Museum's permanent collection. The film has an enormous propaganda impact, particularly the scenes of the police beating the youths in the police station's *jūdō* room and the final shot showing the expression on one boy's face as he is locked up by the bailiffs after the second trial—a famous still of which is included in Yakai Case History Compilation Committee, ed., *Yakai jiken jūhachi-nen* (Eighteen Years of the Yakai Case) (Tokyo, 1969), p. 19. For a different evaluation of the film's artistic merits, note the comments by Joseph L. Anderson and Donald Richie:

> Much more socially conscious and much more of a protest film was Imai's *Darkness at Noon* (Mahiru no ankoku)—no relation to the Koestler novel—which won the 1956 *Kinema jumpō* "Best One" Award. Based on a case pending before the Japanese courts, it took a stand and even suggested a verdict while the case was still being heard. Five youths are accused of a brutal murder and the police "force" confessions from them. While the film did treat real problems—since the Japanese police apparently continue to be overzealous in obtaining confessions—it also unfortunately presented everything in terms of black and white. Like most Japanese films of protest . . . it refused to look beyond the immediate evils of a social condition and took a vehement stand without once asking why this condition was possible or how it could be corrected. Iwasaki Akira, the film critic, called the film "the Japanese Sacco-Vanzetti, Tom Mooney, and Rosenberg cases all rolled into one," and while this is an overstatement, the theme was explosive enough for Tōei to refuse to book the film, having allegedly received threats from high government sources. Eventually, however, Imai and Tōei got together and the director abandoned independent production for the security of a Tōei contract. For all of his faults, Imai in the

Hirotsu's continuing series of articles in *Chūō kōron* on the Matsukawa case, Masaki's book on the Yakai case, Imai's movie, and Tanaka's "noise statement" unleashed the criticism-of-the-courts movement, which itself had two aspects: (1) substantive criticisms of contemporary legal procedures; and (2) a debate over both the merits of laymen criticizing the courts and whether it was democratic for courts to be responsive to such criticisms. The substantive criticisms were numerous and wide-ranging. Participants without legal training, such as the historian Ienaga Saburō, were most concerned about what they believed was a tendency for the courts to operate exactly as they had in the prewar era, ignoring or twisting the provisions of the Constitution of 1947 and the Code of Criminal Procedure to fit their usual practices. Ienaga, for example, quoted Nakagome Noriyori, who had been a procurator in the famous obscenity case over the translation into Japanese of *Lady Chatterley's Lover*, as saying, "I advise young procurators that if they want to get ahead in their careers they should, on going through the door into the procurator's office, believe that the Imperial Constitution [i.e, the Meiji Constitution of 1889] still lives." [16] Ienaga thought that that was the way most procurators behaved without Nakagome's having to tell them to do so.

Professors of law or legal journalists dealt with the more strictly legal aspects of the courts' performance. Kainō Michitaka, for example, wrote an enormous series of articles drawing attention to the fact that the Supreme Court had not declared a single act of the Diet unconstitutional (and noting that American friends of his had written him to say they could not understand

---

past had frequently showed a well-rounded approach. In this film, however, he sacrificed technique in the heat of argument and was not above using tear-jerking of the most unabashed *haha-mono* variety to win sympathy for his characters. (*The Japanese Film: Art and Industry* [New York, 1960], pp. 283–284.)

16. *Saiban hihan*, p. 128.

why); that it was illegal in Anglo-American law to use the confession of one codefendant against another; that the 5:00 A.M. arrests of the defendants in the Matsukawa case contrasted markedly with the gingerly way in which the police treated Satō Eisaku (in 1954 the secretary-general of Yoshida's Liberal party and in the 1960s the prime minister) when he was arrested for his part in a big postoccupation shipbuilding scandal; and that it was perfectly logical for people to want to inquire into the backgrounds of Supreme Court justices—for example, into Chief Justice Tanaka's political opinions and his Catholicism. On the last point Kainō contrasted Japan with the United States, arguing that in America everyone with a minimum of political information knew something about the predilections and political backgrounds of Supreme Court justices, whereas in Japan people didn't even know their names.[17]

Two attorneys, Ueda Seikichi and Gotō Shōjirō, members of the Matsukawa defense team, wrote a book for the popular Iwanami New Library series, entitled *Ayamatta saiban* (*Mistrials*). In it they tell of a policeman who, because of his direct involvement in a sensational case (the Futamata case), exposed in court the fact that torture had been used to obtain a confession in the case. For his honesty the bureaucracy fired him from his job and indicted him for perjury. Needless to say, as members of the Matsukawa movement, these two attorneys argue that "truth prevails when the people intervene in court cases" and that it was only because of the mass movement that they were able to force the procurators to make available the evidence which would (allegedly, since it had not yet happened when they wrote their book) show that the Matsukawa defendants were innocent.

All of the criticism was not on just one side. Professor Aoyagi Fumio took on Hirotsu directly in the distinguished

17. *Hōritsu* (The Law) (Tokyo, 1957), pp. 24, 27, 83, 109.

legal journal *Jurisuto* (*Jurist*). (Incidentally, Aoyagi was not a disinterested party, since from 1955 to 1957 he had served as the Supreme Court's chief clerk in the Matsukawa case, preparing the case's legal documents for submission to the high bench.) He observed that in England newspapers were not allowed to comment on any aspect of a legal proceeding while it was before the courts, and he thought that the Matsukawa movement's pressure tactics were dangerously undemocratic. As for Hirotsu's own methods, he noted that if Hirotsu were correct that the defendants' truthfulness could be deduced from their prison writings, at least eight of them were also capable of writing lies, since they must then have made false confessions. Aoyagi acknowledged that Hirotsu had uncovered many questionable aspects to the first two trials, but he felt that these things had occurred because of the new American-inspired Code of Criminal Procedure. In Aoyagi's opinion, American adversary procedures make sense only when they take place in the presence of a jury. Since Japan did not call juries and had no intention of starting to do so, he advocated resurrection of the *yoshin*, or pretrial judicial investigation of a case, which had been a crucial part of the prewar procedures derived from the Continent.[18]

Numerous other books, articles, meetings, and speeches contributed to the mounting criticism of the courts. Even translations had an impact—for example, Judge Jerome Frank's *Not Guilty* (1957), a compilation by the famous American circuit court judge of cases in which the innocent had been wrongly accused and punished, which appeared in a Japanese translation shortly after its American publication. On the question of how democratic it was for the public to criticize the courts and for the courts to respond, opinion varied, depending on whether people agreed with the courts and on their personal involvement

18. " 'Hirotsu hyōketsu' no kentō" (An Examination of the "Hirotsu Verdict"), *Jurisuto*, special edition, September 1959, pp. 80–124.

with the legal system. The bar association's views are instructive. During 1960 some 259 attorneys were surveyed and were asked: Do you approve or disapprove of criticism of the courts, particularly criticism of the handling of cases that are still before the courts, such as Hirotsu Kazuo's criticism of the Matsukawa trials? Some 122 attorneys approved, but 137 did not. However, when the question was altered to ask whether they thought it was proper for attorneys in general (i.e., not laymen) to criticize courts on particular cases, 170 thought it was, and only 83 disapproved (six did not answer the second question).[19]

The climate of opinion created by these court protests, combined with the even bigger leftist movement against the Security Treaty, had a discernible effect on the lower courts. During this period, verdicts in political cases shifted farther to the left than most decisions handed down by Japanese courts in the earlier postwar years. For example, on April 1, 1958, the Fukushima District Court declared that the defendants in the Date station and Fukushima Railroad Superintendent's Office cases were not guilty, holding that the SCAP-inspired Law for the Fixed Number of Personnel in Administrative Organs (the Teiin Hō of 1949), under which the Japanese National Railroads had fired them, violated article 28 of the Constitution of 1947 (right of workers to organize and to bargain collectively) and was therefore unconstitutional. Similarly, on March 30, 1959, Judge Date Akio of the Tokyo District Court determined that the Security Treaty itself violated article 9 (the antiwar clause) of the constitution and that forcible protests against it were therefore no crime. Finally, in October 1959, the Tokyo District Court struck down as unconstitutional the Metropolitan Public Security Ordinance under which the police had intended to act during 1960 to control the anti–Security Treaty demonstrations. All of these rulings were ultimately quashed by a high court or by the

19. Ushiomi Toshitaka, *Hōritsuka* (Jurists) (Tokyo, 1970), pp. 211–212.

Supreme Court, but at the time they occurred they had a tremendous impact on the public and the government, and they contributed to both the development and the ferocity of the 1960 crisis. It was while this turmoil was going on that the Matsukawa case *jōkoku* appeal came before the Supreme Court, and the issues it raised—each issue being exaggerated by the Matsukawa movement, for maximum political effect—contributed as much to the criticism of the courts as any other case or issue.[20]

The Supreme Court of Japan is made up of a chief justice and fourteen associate justices; and it functions as a Grand Bench (all judges sitting, nine constituting a quorum) or as three petty benches, one for criminal cases, one for civil cases, and one for administrative cases. Membership of the petty benches is five justices each (three being a quorum); and when a case reaches the Supreme Court on appeal, it is first referred to the appropriate petty bench to see whether the smaller court can handle the appeal or whether it must be transferred to the Grand Bench. Only the Grand Bench can render decisions in cases involving the constitutionality of a law, and it must make a decision when a tie exists on a petty bench. Assignment of judges to each of the petty benches is made annually by judicial conference; the chief justice presides over sessions of the Grand Bench. Normally, criminal cases can come before the Supreme Court only on the grounds that they involve a violation of the constitution or that a lower court's verdict is inconsistent with one or more precedents established by the Supreme Court (Code of Criminal Procedure, art. 405). However, the Supreme Court may also accept "any cases which it deems involve an important problem of the construction of law or ordinance" (art. 406), and it may, if it chooses, quash an original judgment and render its own when

20. On the Date station verdict, see *Yomiuri shimbun*, August 26, 1959, eve. ed.; on the constitutionality of the Security Treaty, see Packard, *Protest in Tokyo*, pp. 132–133.

it discovers a gross error in the finding of facts (arts. 411 and 413).

On September 30, 1955, a year and a half after the second verdict, the Matsukawa defense lawyers filed their *jōkoku* appeal documents with the Supreme Court. These documents run to some 15,000 pages, including nine volumes (totaling some 8,869 pages) of appeal statements written by the defendants, and they detail forty-two different instances in which the defending attorneys contend that the second trial either violated the constitution or committed errors in the determination of facts. Among the items of constitutional law raised in the appeal, the defense claimed that the use of statements made by one codefendant against other codefendants violated article 31 (due process) and article 37 (no person shall be compelled to testify against himself) of the constitution; that the judges in the second trial showed malice and deception in their handling of the case, an alleged violation of article 76(3) of the constitution ("all judges shall be independent in the exercise of their conscience and shall be bound only by this Constitution and the laws"); and that the confessions used to convict the defendants were not made voluntarily, which violated article 38(2) ("confessions made under compulsion, torture, or threat, or after prolonged arrest or detention shall not be admitted in evidence"). The third petty bench (criminal) mulled over this mass of documentary material for some fourteen months and then, on December 26, 1956, decided that it could not handle the case, which was therefore transferred to the Grand Bench, which in turn took another two and a half years before handing down a decision.

Although the Supreme Court appeared to be taking its time —some people thought that it was stalling outrageously—the Matsukawa movement made sure that nobody forgot about the case during the long delay. The three defendants who were judged not guilty by the second court pledged to remain with their comrades in the struggle, and two days after the second verdict most of the defendants with lesser sentences were released on bail. This produced a defendants' organization outside of prison made up of Takeda, Okada, Saitō, Satō Shiroji, Katō, Kikuchi, Mrs. Yokoya, Kobayashi, Nikaidō, Ōuchi, and Hamazaki. All of them went to work trying to raise funds to keep the movement going after the drain of the second trial, and they attended the national conventions of Sōhyō and of the National Railroad Workers' Union, pleading for the support of organized labor. It was slow going, but they were buoyed by Hirotsu's continuing series of articles in Chūō kōron (the first collection of these articles, published by Chikuma Shobō, appeared on June 10, 1955). In an attempt to broaden their base of contributors, the movement's leaders named August 17 (the date of the wreck) and December 22 (the date of the second verdict) as International Matsukawa Days and sent letters appealing for support to leftist organizations around the world. Some Matsukawa movement representatives made a pitch at the convention of International Democratic Associations, held in Leipzig in June 1954. The following January, in Calcutta, chief defense attorney Okabayashi briefed the so-called Asian Lawyers' Conference on the case, in return for which the delegates obligingly passed a resolution to send a letter of protest to the Japanese Supreme Court. In addition to China and the Soviet Union, who were regular contributors, the big French Communist labor federation, the CGT (Confédération Générale du Travail), heeded the call and sent letters of protest and donations.

Things picked up considerably during 1956. The Matsukawa movement provided some organizational assistance to Sōhyō during its 1956 "spring offensive" (the annual struggle over contract negotiations), and Sōhyō therefore decided to put its Legal Affairs Section as well as its rank and file behind the movement. This was almost as big a break for the movement as having gained Hirotsu's support three years earlier; and it guaranteed that henceforth no Matsukawa demonstration, provided it was first cleared with the big labor federation, would ever fail for lack of participants. During the summer of 1956 the movement and Sōhyō together transported large numbers of workers and activists to Fukushima to participate in on-site inspections, picnics, and lecture meetings. These new Matsukawa recruits were divided into teams; the second 1956 team, for example, which numbered about a hundred participants and which made the excursion on August 12 and 13, included the chief of Sōhyō's Legal Affairs Section, a Tokyo University professor, a woman novelist, railroad men from Tokyo and Niigata, twenty teachers from Miyagi prefecture, a student delegation from Kyushu, a few Communist Diet members, and two assemblymen from the Minato Ward Council in Tokyo. Hirotsu came along, even though he was now beginning to suffer from rheumatism, and he delivered a lecture on the case to the team in a Fukushima public hall. These well-organized outings became very popular with the unions and could be seen in Fukushima and Matsukawa every summer for the next eight years.

Having finished writing their appeal briefs, the lawyers for the case, some two hundred strong, did not sit idle while waiting for the Supreme Court to read them and make a decision. Okabayashi has acknowledged that until their defeat in the second trial, the defense forces had not made much of an effort to find new evidence in the case, relying instead on the movement's protest and propaganda activities.[21] During 1956, however, the lawyers began to dig a little, and they turned up something that was to shake the whole nation's trust in the procuracy and in the system of criminal justice itself.

According to the prosecution's case in the first and second trials, Satō Hajime, the "outside agitator" from Tokyo who had been in Matsukawa on the day of the wreck to help the local union organize its resistance to Tōshiba's layoff plans, played a

21. *Matsukawa undō zenshi*, p. 803.

key role in the crime. He was allegedly present at both the August 13 and August 15 conspiracy meetings, and he was an actual saboteur. Following the second trial, in which evidence concerning the August 13 conspiracy meeting was rejected by the court (partly because Satō's presence at the collective bargaining table had been attested to by a management representative), Satō became even more central to the prosecution's case because he was the *sole* representative of the Matsukawa plant alleged to have attended the August 15 meeting of railroad workers in Fukushima. If it could be shown that he had not attended that meeting, then the whole question of what the courts called liaison conspiracy—that is, how the railroad workers of the JNR and the electrical workers of Tōshiba got together— would be reopened.

All sides agreed that on the morning of August 15 a collective bargaining session had been held at the Matsukawa plant and that Satō had put in an appearance at the negotiating table. During the first trial, Mr. Washimi Seizō, the factory's manager and chief company negotiator in the talks, had testified that Satō had been present and had spoken shortly after the meeting began at about 10:30 A.M. but that after this initial exchange of perhaps ten minutes duration he did not recall Satō's remaining in the room. All sides further agreed that later that same day, at about three in the afternoon, Satō Hajime had been present at the Matsukawa plant, working in the union office. The prosecution therefore contended that Satō left the collective bargaining meeting, caught the 11:15 A.M. train to Fukushima, attended the conspiracy meeting, and returned to Matsukawa in the early afternoon. Satō testified that he never left Matsukawa on August 15, and during the second trial some ten workers appeared as witnesses to that fact. The court, however, thought that Satō's fellow union members were merely trying to help him; and it put its trust in the testimony of Washimi. Satō, the court concluded, left the collective bargaining session shortly after it had started, walked for the two or three minutes it took to get to Matsukawa station, and spent the noon hour plotting train sabotage with Communist railroad workers in Fukushima city.[22]

Satō was no fool, and he had plenty of time in prison to try to recall what had happened on August 15. In May 1955 he was transferred to a hospital, where he had part of one lung removed because of tuberculosis, and he almost died from the operation. However, in the course of painfully writing his Supreme Court appeal statement before going to the hospital and in keeping up his end of the defendants' activities to further the movement, he thought he remembered that a record had been kept of the collective bargaining sessions.

Perhaps his memory was jogged (or his imagination stimulated) by a piece of information supplied by one of the movement's oldest activists. During 1954, Honda Yoshihiro, the chief of the Akahata bureau in Fukushima and himself at one time arrested and then released as a suspect in the Matsukawa case, was at the Matsukawa factory helping to make a movie for the movement. On that occasion he chatted with a Mr. Suwa Shin'ichirō, who in 1954 was chief of the General Management Section of the plant (now known as the Kitashiba Electric Company) and who in 1949 had been deputy chief, under the then Management Section head, Mr. Nishi Hajime. Suwa mentioned that he had not only attended the collective bargaining session on August 15, 1949, but he and Nishi had also taken notes on what was said for their boss, Mr. Washimi. "Where," asked Honda, "are those notes today?" "Why, the police have them," replied Suwa.

Honda passed on this information to the defense attorneys, and they in turn talked with Satō. In December 1956, defense

22. For the testimony of Washimi Seizō on February 10, 1950, see Fukushima Chihō Saibansho (Fukushima District Court), Matsukawa jiken dai-isshin hanketsu (Matsukawa Case First Trial Verdict) (Fukushima, January 12, 1951), pp. 323–324.

attorney Hakamada sent a letter to the Kitashiba Company in Matsukawa inquiring formally about the present whereabouts of the collective bargaining records, and on December 22, he received a written reply from Suwa saying that he had not seen them since September or October of 1949: he had turned them over to the police, and they had never returned them to him. Hakamada began to become suspicious, since these notes—now known among the defense attorneys as the Suwa Memorandum —had never once been mentioned in either the first or the second trials. If they had been of no value, why hadn't the prosecution returned them to the company? And if they did show that Satō had left the meeting, why hadn't the prosecution used them as evidence against him? Was there perhaps some suppression of evidence going on here?

Hakamada decided that it was worth putting a little pressure on the authorities—probably more to see if he could embarrass them than with any real hope that the Suwa Memorandum would establish Satō's alibi. He gave an interview to *Akahata*, published in the June 22, 1957, edition, saying that there was some new evidence that would show Satō Hajime had been framed and that the public procurators were suppressing this evidence. Of course, he had not at that time seen the Suwa Memorandum nor did he know whether it would help his case. The next day, June 23, *Asahi* picked up the story. It quoted the Matsukawa defense attorneys' charges that the state had suppressed a piece of evidence, and the newspaper article went on to wonder whether Satō Hajime, twice condemned to death, had received a fair trial. However, nobody on the procurators' side came forward to answer these allegations because, it seems, the procurators themselves could not remember the Suwa Memorandum and did not know where it was. It was therefore left to an enterprising reporter in Fukushima to discover it and make the biggest scoop of the case.

Kurajima Yasushi was chief of the *Mainichi shimbun's*

Fukushima Bureau. He had read the *Akahata* piece and started visiting the offices of the procuracy in the prefecture (which had been moved since the Matsukawa case, thoroughly disorganizing the procurators' files on old cases). He discovered the Suwa Memorandum in the office of Suzuki Hisanori, at that time chief of the Kōriyama Branch of the Fukushima Regional Procuracy and one of two procurators (the other was Yamamoto Isamu) who had prosecuted the case in court during 1949 and 1950. Suzuki would not give the Suwa documents to Kurajima; he merely said to the reporter that the notes were of no relevance to the case and that he just happened to have them along with a lot of other miscellaneous papers left over from the Matsukawa investigation. Kurajima reported all this in a headline story on the front page of the June 29 Fukushima edition of the *Mainichi*. This paper was read by the defense attorneys (pictures of the front page are reproduced in every Matsukawa history), but in Tokyo, neither the national editions of the *Mainichi* nor other papers picked it up, probably regarding it as some more of the enterprising local journalism that had flourished during and after the occupation and that had become something of a bore to the sophisticates of the capital. The whole case was still suspect as a Communist propaganda venture, and procurator Suzuki had said that the memo was of no importance. Presumably he could prove it. Therefore, nothing further was heard about the Suwa Memorandum for almost a year.

While these inquiries were being made in Tōhoku, the appeal itself had begun to stir within the old Supreme Court building located in Kasumigaseki—the Whitehall of Tokyo, the section of the capital where all the ministries and big government office buildings are situated. After the transfer of the case to the Grand Bench, the justices met frequently to discuss it. Justices Ikeda Katsu and Takahashi Kiyoshi, both of whom were prominent criminal law specialists and who would ultimately dissent from the court's verdict two years later, were put in charge of the case; and their initial review indicated that Akama was eligible for release on bail. He emerged from prison on January 12, 1957, with great headlines in *Akahata* saying that public pressure had brought about this decision. With Satō in the hospital, this left only seven defendants still in prison (Suzuki, Honda, Abe, Ninomiya, Takahashi, Sugiura, and Ōta), and the last of them would also have been bailed out by July 1, 1959, a month before the verdict.

In addition to these questions of bail, the Supreme Court had to decide what it was going to do about oral arguments. Normally, the Supreme Court—as a tribunal for ruling on matters of law rather than matters of fact—does not hear oral arguments. However, in criminal cases involving capital offenses, it may, at its own discretion, accept an oral presentation in order to help it decide whether a gross error of fact-finding may have occurred. In the Matsukawa case the defense attorneys asked the court for an unheard-of twenty days of oral argument, claiming among other things that they had new evidence to present. The longest period that all of the judges had come together in the past to listen to oral argument (which meant stopping work on all other cases) was two days—and that had been for the Yakai case.

On July 18, 1958, the Supreme Court, in a completely unprecedented ruling, allotted ten days to the Matsukawa case for oral argument. This was big news, and every evening paper carried it as a banner headline. It strongly suggested to court observers that the justices thought there was something wrong with the case and wanted to look into it closely. Since the court had already read the voluminous records of the previous trial, which supported the prosecution's case, it awarded nine and a half days to defense presentation and gave the procurators only two hours during which to reply. The Supreme Court set November 5 to 26, 1958, as the period for debate. Precisely why the court decided to devote so much of its time to this case has never been revealed, but a few observers thought that perhaps the criticism-of-the-courts movement was having its impact on the Supreme Court itself.

These developments were more than enough to arouse national concern over the case, but, in addition, a potential scandal within the Supreme Court itself brought public interest to a fever pitch. On June 1, 1958, Judge Ishizaka Shuichi became an associate justice of the Supreme Court, replacing a justice who had recently retired on reaching the age limit of seventy. Judge Ishizaka had enjoyed a distinguished career, including service as president of the Sendai High Court between October 1948 and September 1952, and moving on from there to become president of the Hiroshima High Court and of the Nagoya High Court before being elevated to the Supreme Court. Back in 1952, before leaving Sendai, he had participated in the judicial conference that had selected Judge Suzuki to preside over the Matsukawa kōso appeal trial. Although Ishizaka himself had left Sendai by the time Suzuki handed down his verdict, he followed the case from Hiroshima, and on the evening of December 22, 1953, the day of the second decision, he sat down and wrote a letter to his old colleague in Sendai.

A few days after the close of the second court, Ozawa Michio, then a cochairman of the Matsukawa Countermeasures Committee, had asked for and was granted permission to read the records of the trial at the High Court building. As he opened the boxes of transcripts and affidavits, he found sitting on top of them Judge Ishizaka's letter, which he purloined for possible use by the defense. Judge Suzuki had apparently put the letter from his old boss in with the court's records because it contained some highly flattering remarks about Suzuki's work. Although the movement has always paraphrased this letter to put it in the most damaging light possible, its actual text, which was published in full in the Akahata of September 17, 1958, does not really do more than raise some questions about Ishizaka's involvement in the case. Addressed to "Dear Suzuki," the letter thanks him for the decision handed down that day and expresses Ishizaka's confidence in Suzuki and his two associate judges. "Of course," wrote Ishizaka, "because I have not seen the evidence nor read any of the records, my qualifications to judge the accuracy of the verdict are limited. However," he continued, "in today's Japan, if we do not have faith in the sincerity, diligence, ability, and efforts of men like you and your colleagues, if one did not believe in the things that derive from these qualities, then there'd be nothing left to believe in. . . . By letting the public know that judges will not be intimidated by pressure and demonstrations, you and your colleagues have won our thanks and respect." Ishizaka went on to say that he would like to come back to Sendai on his next vacation and closed on a note of how well placed his trust in Suzuki had been. The letter was signed "Shuichi."

The Japanese language is not noted for its absolute precision of meaning, and some of the phrases in this letter are open to misinterpretation. According to the official history of the Matsukawa movement the letter to Judge Suzuki says, in effect, do not worry about the possibility that your verdict is not completely objective or persuasive, what counts is that you put away those Communists.[23] To the defense attorneys, the letter strongly implied that Ishizaka, in his role as president of the Sendai High Court, had specifically picked Suzuki from among all the available judges to hear the case because he knew that Suzuki would (or he even told him to) find the defendants guilty. On July 15, 1958, after Ishizaka had become a member of the Supreme Court (note that if the defense seriously believed its charges against Ishizaka, it nevertheless kept them private until he joined the Supreme Court), Ōtsuka Kazuo and other defense lawyers raised a storm in the press, demanding

23. *Matsukawa undō zenshi*, pp. 354–356. See also Kainō, *Hōritsu*, pp. 157–158.

that Ishizaka be disbarred because of his flagrant attempt to set up the Sendai court against the defendants. The chief justice answered, saying that the letter had been written after the second trial had ended and that it did not matter anyway, since the Supreme Court worked collegially and Ishizaka would not himself have a deciding influence on its decision. Nevertheless, Shiga Yoshio, a Communist member of the Diet and one of the three top leaders of the postwar Communist party, ripped into Ishizaka in the Judiciary Committee of the House of Representatives, calling him an old *yoshin* judge and accusing the Supreme Court itself of conniving at the frame-up of the Matsukawa defendants. On September 24, 1958, Ishizaka asked to be excused from hearing the Matsukawa case, and his withdrawal was accepted by his colleagues on the court. The incident continued to arouse controversy for several years, both because it illustrated how reckless criticism of the courts could be and because it warned many older members of the judiciary that in postwar Japan they should not expect their opinions and *obiter dicta* always to go unchallenged.

With ten sessions of oral argument scheduled before the Grand Bench, and with Judge Ishizaka out of the way, the defense lawyers and the movement turned their attention back to the Suwa Memorandum to see if they could crack it loose from procurator Suzuki in Kōriyama. On May 24, 1958, the Matsukawa attorneys had filed a petition with the Supreme Court charging the procuracy and investigating officials with suppressing evidence. The Supreme Procurator's Office flatly denied the charge, but the movement also activated its Communist Diet members to look into the matter. In sessions of the Diet throughout August and early September, 1958, Shiga Yoshio rose to interpellate the minister of justice or his representative on the whereabouts and contents of the Suwa Memorandum, usually to receive the embarrassed reply that the government did not know where it was (the Tokyo bureaucrats having not read reporter

Kurajima's article in the Fukushima edition of the *Mainichi*). When Shiga told the officials where they might find it, he finally got some results. On September 4, procurator Suzuki, under orders from Tokyo, asked Mr. Suwa to come to his office, and he personally returned to him his nine-year-old notes.

No one but Suzuki and Suwa had as yet read the memorandum; therefore the issue became one of persuading Suwa to reveal its contents. In late September defendant Satō Shiroji, out on bail, made the trip to Matsukawa, but he failed to see the memorandum because Suwa had locked it up in a safe deposit box in a bank. Okabayashi followed Satō north, and after a delay of several days, obtained Suwa's cooperation. On October 1, Suwa produced the memo and allowed Okabayashi to make a photocopy of it. For the rest of October the defense lawyers studied their photographs and then, on October 25, did two things: they released the memo to the press (on that same day *Akahata* published the photographed version), and they filed a formal request to have procurator Suzuki prosecuted on charges of having concealed evidence in a capital case. The Supreme Procuracy wired Suzuki to say nothing, since he might find himself a defendant in court. On November 1, the Supreme Court, which had been following all of these details in the daily press, stepped in and ordered Mr. Suwa to send the original of his memo directly to the court. It was now perfectly clear that the ten oral sessions scheduled for later that month were going to look closely at Mr. Suwa's notes.

The Suwa Memorandum itself consists of two cheap university notebooks made of very poor quality paper. They contain all kinds of penciled notes written in abbreviations or a hasty scrawl on things going on in the Matsukawa plant; and when they were released to the press, it was discovered that they included information about more than the August 15 collective bargaining session. The memo revealed that the plant's managers were in direct contact with the police and SCAP's CIC about the labor situation there and that Suwa and Nishi were jotting down in the record book items of information and gossip reported to them by the plant's guards for passing on to the police. Persons who knew the case well, such as Hirotsu, recognized in the Suwa Memorandum the origins of items, such as "Mrs. Ōta's prediction," that had helped to focus the attention of the initial investigators on the Matsukawa factory. The actual note said: "8/16. Mrs. Ōta is reported to have said in the dormitory that an amazing thing is going to occur today." Here was something that the defense lawyers might be asked to explain.

As for the notes concerning the August 15 collective bargaining session, they were very complex. Both Suwa and Nishi (who by 1958 had left Kitashiba and was working in Miyagi prefecture) had taken notes: first Suwa, then Nishi (while Suwa was out of the room meeting some police officials who had called), and then Suwa again. The memo concerns only the morning session, and it does not give a precise time for the ending of the meeting. In fact, the Suwa Memorandum, being nothing more than a hastily taken record and not by a professional stenographer, cannot be understood without interpolation. However, it does appear to contain cryptic signs throughout the record of the morning's talks indicating that Satō was present and speaking. Whether it established his alibi was for a court to decide.

On November 5, oral argument began at the Supreme Court with fourteen justices (i.e., without Ishizaka) in attendance. In Japan as elsewhere justices of the Supreme Court are likely to be elderly men, and this means that their health may be rather fragile. On the first day Justice Saitō Yūsuke said that he was feeling ill and asked to be excused. The court agreed to this because, with Ishizaka already out, it wanted to avoid the possibility of a seven to seven tie. However, during the fifth session,

Justice Kawamura Matasuke[24] suddenly entered the hospital suffering from heart trouble. That left only twelve judges—more than a quorum but very good news for the defense. The three justices who were forced to retire were all experienced in the criminal law, and every commentator on the case, including members of the Matsukawa lawyers team, has expressed the belief that had all three been present, the verdict might very well have been eight to seven against the defendants rather than the seven to five in their favor that actually resulted. The defense attorneys complimented themselves on having helped to bring about this windfall through their challenge of Ishizaka. There had been nothing wrong with his health, and it was after his resignation and partly to avoid an even number that the court had agreed to let Justice Saitō withdraw.[25]

Good health was not a prerequisite for membership in the Japanese judiciary, but it helped, given some of the pressures to which the courts were subjected. On March 9, 1958, the Matsukawa Countermeasures Council was formed in a convention held at Sōhyō Hall and attended by 150 delegates. This new organization of the Matsukawa movement elected Hirotsu Kazuo as its first chairman, and he led it through a full schedule of activities designed to attract public attention to the oral argument before the Supreme Court that fall. To the many novel ways that the movement had discovered to raise money, Hirotsu added sales, in Fukushima and on the Ginza, of the calligraphy of famous intellectuals, both Chinese and Japanese, such as Uno Kōji, Kawabata Yasunari, Kuo Mo-jo, and Hirotsu Kazuo. The leaders of the movement also used every device they could think of to

24. Note that Justice Kawamura Daisuke, who shares the same surname but is not related to Justice Kawamura Matasuke, did remain throughout the Matsukawa case hearings and voted with the majority in the court's decision.

25. *Yomiuri shimbun*, July 15, 1958, eve. ed.; *Akahata*, August 11, 1958, and September 17, 1958; *Yomiuri shimbun*, November 26, 1958; *Matsukawa undō zenshi*, p. 356.

arouse public sentiment on behalf of the defendants. For example, throughout the summer of 1958, any passenger going in or out of Yūrakuchō station in the heart of Tokyo's Ginza district was assailed by men with bullhorns shouting, "They're going to kill the innocent Matsukawa defendants." Probably the best of Hirotsu's publicity-attracting ideas was a "grand march" from Sendai to Tokyo (almost three hundred miles), scheduled to arrive on the front steps of the Supreme Court building on November 5, the day oral argument began.

The Matsukawa Grand March (Matsukawa Daikōshin) started off from Sendai on October 22 with 350 hikers. In each city they passed through, the marchers were greeted by a Matsukawa Action Day rally organized by the local Countermeasures Council. Finally, on November 4, they reached the outskirts of Tokyo, where they camped and prepared their signs, flags, and *hachimaki* for the triumphant entry the following day. At the same time that this march was going on (and being reported daily by newspapermen in helicopters), the council was preparing for a total of eighty-one rallies to be held in Tokyo alone during the period of oral argument. Police were mobilized to control the masses of demonstrators surrounding the Supreme Court; on November 5, the *Yomiuri's* headlines read: SUPREME COURT BARRICADED. Although no violence occurred, many commentators deplored this form of "pressure" on the courts, while a few hoped that its effects would be beneficial—that is, that it would force the public to take an interest in the courts and their procedures. Certainly no one in Japan could have failed to be aware that the Supreme Court was discussing the Matsukawa case.[26]

26. Letter-writing to the Supreme Court continued as it had during the first two Matsukawa trials. A month before it began hearing oral argument, the Supreme Court had received about four thousand letters, almost half of them threatening and using language like "dogs of authority" and "American dogs" to refer to the justices. Many letters were

During their nine and a half days, the defense attorneys presented a comprehensive review of the case. They argued that Suzuki, Honda, and Takahashi had alibis; attacked Ōta's confession as hopelessly inconsistent; claimed that Satō was present throughout the day on August 15 at the Matsukawa plant; and denounced the prosecution's attempt to offer the crowbar and wrench as corroborating material evidence, since it could not prove that these tools were adequate to commit the sabotage nor where they came from. This was all very interesting, and the judges listened closely. But the public was interested in whether the Supreme Court would accept new evidence—the Suwa Memorandum—and either decide the case then and there or send it back to the Sendai High Court for retrial. On November 15, Chief Justice Tanaka ruled on that issue. He decided that the Supreme Court was not the proper forum to pass on the guilt or innocence of the defendants, it being a court of law rather than a trial court. He added, however, that the Suwa Memorandum would become part of the materials contributing to the Supreme Court's decision, even though it had not been admitted as evidence. All observers interpreted this enigmatic ruling to mean that the defense had scored with its Suwa Memorandum gambit, since the court's decision to acknowledge the existence of the memo virtually foreclosed a straight rejection of the defendants' appeal, as the prosecution demanded. It looked as though the Supreme Court would have to refer the case back to a lower court for retrial, where the Suwa Memorandum could be read and debated properly.

The issue raised by Suwa's notes was not yet over, however. The problem with the Suwa Memorandum as evidence was that it did not prove unequivocally where Satō was on August 15, and to make any sense out of it at all required a good deal of de-

---

from abroad, with France being the leading source in this phase of the case. *Asahi shimbun*, October 5, 1958.

ciphering and interpretation. On November 24, during the ninth oral argument session, an extremely unusual exchange took place before the Supreme Court, one that every single newspaper reported verbatim the following day. After the defense speaker had finished his address, Justice Kotani said, "I'd like to ask a question about the Suwa Memorandum. Is the person listed in the memo as 'Satō Zenshō' a man from the Tōshiba company or from the labor union?" Okabayashi answered, "I think he's a labor union man." Kotani continued, "This 'Satō' and the letters 'tsuru' written in a circle, do they mean Satō Hajime of the Tsurumi factory?" Okabayashi replied, "Yes." The discussion went on like that for some time:

KOTANI: On page 12 of the memo it says "Satō speaking." Does this refer to "Satō Hajime" or "Satō Zenshō"?

OKABAYASHI: Satō Hajime.

KOTANI: What makes you think so?

ŌTSUKA (stepping in for Okabayashi): At this place it says, "As for the dispute here—agree." This means that after an argument over whether Satō Hajime as an outsider could participate in the collective bargaining session, the company agreed. Therefore this "Satō" must be "Satō Hajime."

KOTANI: On the back of page 13, there's a "Sa-chō" with a circle around it.

ŌTSUKA: That's Satō Hajime. Since Mr. Nishi didn't know the Chinese character for "Hajime" in Satō Hajime's name, he wrote it [in an abbreviated form] using the "chō" of his own name [the character "chō" being pronounced "Hajime" in Mr. Nishi's given name].

There was more, including a request by Kotani for an explanation of Mrs. Ōta's prediction. Ōtsuka explained that on the basis of internal evidence it appeared that Mrs. Ōta made the statement on August 18, not 16, and that it was written down later as "8/16" in error. Even Chief Justice Tanaka asked some questions. Concerning this whole exchange, the *Asahi* commented that although the chief justice had ruled that the Suwa Memorandum would not be admitted in evidence before the Supreme Court, what went on in court on November 24 strongly indicated that it was in fact in evidence, regardless of the ruling.

On November 25 the prosecution got its two hours to reply. The speakers were Murakami Tomoichi, chief of the Trial Department of the Supreme Procuracy, and three other procurators, including the chief of the Public Security Department. They were among the most skilled prosecutors in Japan, and they ripped fiercely into the defense's arguments. The Suwa Memorandum, they argued, indicated when the negotiations began but not when they ended, and it did not show Satō Hajime as being present for the afternoon session (both points are indisputably true). The prosecution had not used the Suwa Memorandum in earlier trials because it was inconclusive on any point. It was, they said, slanderous to suggest that the government had suppressed it. As for the case itself, the prosecution had offered eight confessions, voluntarily given, and they contained information that the police could not possibly have fabricated. The supreme procurators also added a new point with regard to Takahashi's alleged disability: Takahashi had not only participated in the on-site inspection during the first trial, he had also been a member of the so-called Democratic Investigation Team that the Fukushima National Railroad Workers' Union had sent to the scene of the wreck on August 17, immediately after it had occurred. There was, said procurator Murakami, no question of Takahashi's ability to walk whenever he wanted to.

All courtroom observers agreed that the prosecution had waged a brilliant counterattack. Murakami ended his presentation by saying that the whole case had been tried in the newspapers, and he demanded that the appeal be rejected. That concluded the oral argument—leaving most of the public about as confused as they were before it began. Despite all the publicity, the Suwa Memorandum only raised questions: How long a period of time did the memo cover? Was there time for Satō to have said the things he was recorded in the memo as saying and then slip out and catch the 11:15 train? If he didn't take that train, how did he get to Fukushima? After the oral argument had ended, a district court judge who had followed the case said to a *Yomiuri* reporter: "When I think of the defendants as being guilty, I can see the evidence proving their guilt; if I think of them as being innocent, then the evidence shows their innocence." [27]

The Supreme Court closed its doors and went into conference, promising a decision on August 10, 1959. In the interim the movement kept up the pressure. During February it sponsored a play entitled *The Matsukawa Case* in a downtown Tokyo theater; the play was so one-sided that a television network which had scheduled a telecast of it for February 15 canceled out at the last moment. The *Mainichi's* theater critic panned the play, commenting that this kind of "criticism of the courts" was going too far and that despite Judge Tanaka's warning about "noise" four years earlier, he had heard nothing but noise from the Matsukawa movement. He also noted that the Communist party had packed the audience and turned it into a cheering section. [28]

On February 15, 1959, the defense attorneys tried again to make their charges of the suppression of evidence stick. They asked both the Sendai and Fukushima procurators for indictments against procurator Suzuki, and they now added procurator Yamamoto and one of his associates to the list. They also sought

27. *Yomiuri shimbun*, August 9, 1961.
28. *Mainichi shimbun*, February 18, 1959. For a favorable review, see Kanagawa Ken Matsukawa Tōsō Shi Hensan Iinkai (Kanagawa Prefecture History of the Matsukawa Struggle Compilation Committee) and Kanagawa Ken Matsukawa Jiken Taisaku Kyōgikai (Kanagawa Prefecture Matsukawa Case Countermeasures Council), eds., *Kanagawa ken Matsukawa tōsō shi* (History of the Matsukawa Struggle in Kanagawa Prefecture) (Yokohama, 1964), p. 128.

to press perjury charges against all the procurators and against police inspector Tamagawa. The defense attorneys charged that the procurators knew that the Suwa Memorandum proved Satō's innocence and that they therefore suppressed it in order to frame him. Tamagawa, they said, had lied during the second trial when he testified that he had not frightened Akama or forced him to confess. Not surprisingly, both the Sendai and Fukushima procurators' examining boards turned down these requests to indict their fellow officials. The defense, however, was satisfied; it had found one more forum in which to make political accusations and have them reported in the press. Nor was that the end of its attempts to charge various officials with frame-ups; during 1961 some more hitherto unknown evidence turned up and once again made people wonder why the procurators had kept it hidden so long!

In Miyagi Prison the defendants who had not been released on bail were beginning to show signs of seriously deteriorating health. They had been there for more than nine years, throughout the hardest days of Japan's reconstruction, and they had not seen the prosperity that had come to Tōhoku or the rebuilt cities of the rest of the country. Satō had tuberculosis, Sugiura palsy, Honda heart trouble, and Ōta some undetermined mental affliction. With a recent precedent in mind in which the Supreme Court had ordered bail for a prisoner under a death sentence (one of the defendants in the Yakai case), the Supreme Court's Third Petty Bench set bail of up to ¥100,000 for the remaining defendants, and they were all released. One of the more joyous reunions was that of Takahashi and his wife and daughter; the daughter, who was then nine, had been only five months old when Takahashi had been arrested.

As the day of decision approached, the Matsukawa Countermeasures Council repeated its Grand March tactic of the previous autumn, only this time it organized four nationwide marches to converge on the Supreme Court building on the morning of August 10. The marchers set out about a week before the scheduled day even though it was typhoon weather and extremely hot and muggy. In Tokyo, as August 10 dawned, the crowd that had gathered outside the Supreme Court building to wait for the verdict was already large, many people having spent the night in hopes of getting into the courtroom in the morning. Police were everywhere in Kasumigaseki, and a big crowd of office workers and supporters stood on the steps of the Nōrinshō (the Agriculture and Forestry Ministry) across the street from the Supreme Court, waiting for the news. Shiga Yoshio of the Japanese Communist party showed up with a sound truck and led the crowd in yells while a police helicopter buzzed overhead.

Inside the Grand Bench room all was quiet and serene. The spectators' gallery included some of the defendants and their families, Hirotsu, Nosaka Sanzō (secretary general of the Communist party), and many other famous intellectual and political leaders. Hirotsu later wrote that as he sat there looking up at the big portrait of Prince Shōtoku, the seventh-century giver of laws, the only sound he could hear was the faint whirring outside of the helicopter. The scene was in marked contrast to what had happened at the first and second trials.

Chief Justice Tanaka took only thirty minutes. He stated that the verdict of the second trial was quashed and that the case was remanded to the Sendai High Court for retrial. The Supreme Court itself, he continued, was split over this decision seven to five, and both the majority opinion and five different dissenting opinions from each of the justices in the minority, including himself, were available. He read only a brief extract from the majority opinion. Voting with the majority were Justices Kotani, Shima, Fujita, Irie, Kawamura, Okuno, and Takagi, while the minority was made up of Justices Ikeda, Tarumi, Takahashi, Shimoiizaka, and Chief Justice Tanaka. The court then adjourned. Immediately after the verdict the supreme procurator adopted what the press called a "high posture": he stated that he would move at once to strengthen the Sendai High Procuracy with the toughest prosecutors he could find for the retrial, particularly those with experience in convicting Communists.

Outside, after the verdict, Hirotsu could be seen standing on the steps of the South Entrance, cane in one hand, bullhorn in the other, leading the crowd in one "Banzai!" after another. "We intend to fight to the finish for our friends the defendants," he said. On the southern approaches to the city, just as the decision was being read and a little behind schedule, the Grand March column from the Kyushu, Shikoku, and Kansai areas was crossing the Rokugō bridge. Former defendant Okada Toramatsu was leading a column of about 350 Sōhyō and Countermeasures Council members, one of whom heard the decision over a transistor radio he was carrying. The column broke up and took over the bridge, waving red flags, dancing, and throwing both arms in the air to shouts of "Banzai! Banzai! Banzai!" [29]

The decision itself was intensely controversial, and no commentator in Japan has recorded it as one of the Supreme Court's more valuable efforts. In essence, the majority made proof of conspiracy the chief issue in the case. Clearly influenced by the Suwa Memorandum, it argued that the prosecution had failed to show the times and places at which the "liaison conspiracy" meetings had occurred and that without conclusive evidence of these joint plotting sessions the whole case became highly dubious. Regardless of whether they agreed with the decision, many outside observers and all five dissenters on the court ridiculed the reasoning behind this judgment.

The dissenting opinions of Justices Tarumi and Shimoiizaka, both former presidents of the tough Osaka and Tokyo High Courts and both famed criminal law specialists, typified what the minority thought was wrong with the decision. Tarumi

29. On Hirotsu, *Mainichi shimbun*, August 11, 1959; on the Rokugō bridge demonstration, *Yomiuri shimbun*, August 10, 1959, eve. ed.

pointed out that in no law known to him was it necessary for the prosecution to prove the time and place at which a conspiratorial agreement took place in order to establish the existence of a conspiracy.[30] Instead the prosecution must infer the existence of a conspiracy on the basis of the conduct of the conspirators that it can observe. Conspiracy is normally proved through circumstantial evidence, the testimony of a conspirator who has turned state's evidence, or the evidence of the out-of-court declarations or acts of the conspirators. The majority opinion, wrote Tarumi, changes the law of conspiracy in a highly unrealistic way. So long as the majority refused to declare that the individuals charged with actually committing the sabotage (three

30. Tarumi refers to the American law of conspiracy in support of his opinion (see *Jurisuto*, special issue, September 1959, p. 140, s.v. par. 3), and it may therefore be useful to cite a recent authority on that subject, in addition to those quoted by Tarumi. The *Harvard Law Review*, in one of its "Developments in the Law" articles, asserts:

Today . . . it is established that conspiracy is a continuing crime, extending beyond the initial communication of agreement. It seems, therefore, that the criminal act of the modern crime is not the communication of agreement, but the act of agreement itself, that is, the continuous and conscious union of wills upon a common undertaking. . . .

Conspiracy is by nature a clandestine offense. It is improbable that the parties will enter into their illegal agreement openly; it is not necessary, in fact, that all the parties ever have direct contact with one another, or know one another's identity, or even communicate verbally their intention to agree. [The parties must know of each other's existence, not necessarily their identity: they might be masked, and they might conspire by gestures.] It is therefore unlikely that the prosecution will be able to prove the formation of the agreement by direct evidence, and the jury [in Japan, the judges] must usually infer its existence from the clear cooperation among the parties. But in their zeal to emphasize that the agreement need not be proved directly, the courts sometimes neglect to say that it need not be proved at all.

"Developments in the Law: Criminal Conspiracy," *Harvard Law Review*, vol. 72 (1959), pp. 926, 933.

of them from the NRWU and two from Tōshiba) were innocent, there is no problem in inferring from their overt behavior
the existence of a conspiratorial agreement. The only issue, he
thought, was the validity and legal acceptability of the confessions, which tied the instigators and conspirators to the actual
saboteurs.

Shimoiizaka took up that issue (along with many others)
in an extremely long dissent. He went over every detail of
Akama's arrest and interrogation, quoting extensively from the
confession documents, and concluded that Akama had not only
made a legal confession but had also made numerous statements
to the police, to his attorneys, and to his guards during the first
trial that indicated he had not lied and had confessed voluntarily.
In short, all five dissenting justices contended that the Suwa
Memorandum was irrelevant to the case regardless of what it
contained. It was not absolutely necessary for the prosecution to
prove that Satō was at the NRWU offices at noon on August 15
in order to sustain its charges of conspiracy and sabotage. The
confessions, eight of them, were more than adequate evidence to
convict the defendants, and it was up to a judge's freely formed
opinion to decide whether they were true.

Generally speaking, most informed opinion out of court supported the minority view.[31] In a lead article in *Jurisuto* entitled
"The Matsukawa Decision and the Question of Conspiracy,"
Professor Hiraba of Kyoto University observed that the current
decision seemed to break with an earlier precedent of the Supreme Court, that of only a year earlier in the Nerima case
(Justice Tarumi also made this point in his dissent). In that
decision, which was also a "Communist case," the court had held
that strict evidence had to be introduced to prove the existence
of a conspiracy but that the process by which the conspiracy was

31. Statement of former judge Date Akio of the Tokyo District
Court and subsequently a professor at Hōsei University, in *Mainichi
shimbun*, August 9, 1961.

formed did not have to be proved. It also held that it was up to
the free discretion of a judge whether to admit the confession of
a codefendant as evidence against his partner or partners. The
Nerima decision (May 28, 1958) had been widely denounced by
court critics at the time it was handed down, and members of
the Matsukawa movement had taken it as a setback for their
cause. However, the first Matsukawa *jōkoku* appeal seemed to
alter the Japanese law of conspiracy and make it necessary for
the prosecution to prove both the formation as well as the
existence of a so-called antisocial combination.

The press in general seemed bewildered and irked by the
decision. The *Nihon keizai* thought that there had been a great
many retrials ordered lately, citing the Yakai and other cases,
and said that the Supreme Court was insufficiently sensitive to
the plight of both the victims and the defendants in criminal
cases. As a matter of fact, the Supreme Court's decision to have
the case retried was rare. During its first twenty years, the Supreme Court has overturned only about one percent of the lower
court decisions in criminal cases that have come before it; and
some court reporters have nicknamed it the *Kikyaku-in*, or Dismissal Court, because of its penchant for handing down the verdict of "appeal dismissed." [32]

Several editors and Hirotsu said that they wished the Supreme Court had issued its own not-guilty verdict, if that was
what it intended, rather than send the case back to Sendai to be
retried. There was general dismay over how long the case had
dragged on; the *Yomiuri* editors wrote that after the court had
sat on the case for five years it was an outrage for it to decide
to have it "done all over again."

The court-criticism movement also came in for comment.
Most editorial writers felt that it was permissible and desirable
in a democracy for people to protest laws that they did not like,

32. *Asahi shimbun*, December 14, 1967.

but they argued that it was illogical and absurd for people to carry on demonstrations over questions of fact. The size and strength of the Matsukawa movement had also scared a good many individuals. The novelist Osaragi Jirō wrote that "a kind of civil war situation had been expected" around the Supreme Court building when the multiple Grand Marches arrived, and in the September special Matsukawa issue of *Jurisuto*, the editor noted ominously that "if the Court had upheld the original verdict, the consequences would have been terrible." It was also noted by the press that members of right-wing organizations had appeared on the streets on August 10 passing out "save our courts" handbills and denouncing the demonstrations.[33]

The year 1959 was not ripe, however, for a reaction to the movement. That would not appear until 1961, after the Security Treaty struggle had ended. During 1959 the Japanese left was riding the crest of a wave, and the Matsukawa movement both profited from and reflected this strength. Early in the year, for example, former defendant Okada and defense attorney Ōtsuka had taken time out from the case for a brief trip to China and North Korea at the invitation of the Chinese People's Relief Association, and the Chinese had held rallies in Peking to support both the movement's activities and the Supreme Court's decision. In Tokyo during the autumn of 1959, when the Security Treaty struggle came to a head, Okabayashi was active in a campaign to unseat Chief Justice Tanaka. Okabayashi declared that Tanaka was unfit to hold his office because of the dissenting opinion he had written in the Matsukawa case. Tanaka had once again become a target because the Sunakawa case, which concerned the enlargement of the American air base at Tachikawa and in which the Tokyo District Court had held the Security Treaty to be unconstitutional, was then before the Supreme Court. Judge Tanaka did not resign nor was he impeached, and

33. Osaragi: *Asahi shimbun*, August 11, 1959; right-wing groups: *Tokyo shimbun*, August 11, 1959.

on December 16, 1959, he presided when the Grand Bench quashed the Sunakawa decision. Nevertheless, he recalled years later that he had been placed under a great deal of public pressure.[34]

Some observers were pleased with the Supreme Court's Matsukawa decision, particularly older, more experienced jurists and retired Supreme Court justices.[35] They saw in it a recognition that there was something badly wrong with the case, but they also felt that the court had acted responsibly in not itself deciding on the issues, which it was neither competent nor equipped to do. One Kyoto university philosopher reminded his fellow citizens that it was just as important not to punish the innocent as it was to punish the guilty.[36] Everyone agreed that the new Code of Criminal Procedure was partly to blame for the length of time that the case had taken and for the numerous mistakes the prosecution had made with it. This was because domestic jurists had not known at once how to make the new code work. However, these same commentators expressed optimism that through cases such as Matsukawa the legal profession would both learn the new procedures and alter the code to suit Japanese social needs. They all looked to Sendai to see how the case would be retried now that a decade had elapsed. As it turned out, the Sendai retrial would prove to be a vindication less of the new Code of Criminal Procedure than of the old *yoshin* tradition of a smart, independent judge making an investigation of the case for himself.

At 7:30 on the morning of August 28, 1959, an *Asahi* reporter stood on a street corner in Kasumigaseki watching a load-

34. *Mainichi shimbun*, September 3, 1959; *Asahi shimbun*, February 5, 1960, and September 11, 1963.

35. See the article by former Supreme Court justice Mano Tsuyoshi in *Tokyo shimbun*, August 11, 1959; and the collection of articles in the *Asahi shimbun*, August 9, 1961.

36. Tanaka Michitarō, reported in *Asahi shimbun*, August 9, 1961.

ing operation at the Supreme Court building. A truck was pulled up to a side door, and court clerks and workmen were stacking in it pieces of rail, some fishplates, boxes of spikes and tools, and some seventy-two cardboard cartons containing 135 volumes of court documents. Included in one of the boxes was the original of the Suwa Memorandum, the most famous piece of evidence in the biggest criminal case in Japan's modern history. After the truck was loaded it took off, escorted by a police car with its siren blaring, for Ueno Station. Across town the *Asahi* man watched the truck being unloaded into a special baggage car attached to the rear of the 9:00 A.M. express for Sendai. As he fully understood and reported in his paper that evening, the Matsukawa case documents were going home to Tōhoku.

Chapter 7

Once More from
the Beginning

THE MATSUKAWA train wreck took place in a quiet, evergreen valley known to local residents as the Matsukawa–Kanayagawa Gap. No houses are situated in the valley itself, which is planted in rice and surrounded by rolling, wooded hills; but there are farmhouses at both the north and south entrances to the gap. The soil in this part of Fukushima has a rich, rust-colored hue, flecked with some kind of gold or mica-like particles, and the entire setting is one of rural peace and tranquility. None of these features of the valley has changed since 1949, but the visitor to the scene of the crime today does not see it as it was when the wreck occurred. During the early 1960s, the Japanese National Railroads modernized the Tōhoku Main Line, electrifying and doubletracking its entire length. This means that now two rail lines run through the Matsukawa valley, the old one on which the wreck occurred on the west side, and the new one on the east side. Each is located perhaps ten to fifteen feet up the sides of the valley, curving slightly to follow its contours and leaving the floor free to be flooded for rice growing. Today the old tracks are used for *kudari* trains—those going away from Tokyo, or northbound—and the new ones for *nobori*, or "toward Tokyo" trains (*kudari* and *nobori* are the Japanese equivalents of "up train" and "down train" but are always oriented with reference to the capital, regardless of compass directions). There is also one other new feature in the valley—a tall, concrete obelisk erected next to the *nobori* tracks, which overlooks the whole valley and faces west toward the spot where the wreck occurred.

On the front of the obelisk there is a black marble slab carved with the words *Matsukawa Monument* and the following inscription, written by Hirotsu Kazuo (see photo section):

> At 3:09 A.M. on August 17, 1949, at a point two hundred meters west from here, a passenger train unexpectedly derailed and overturned, killing three members of its operating crew at their stations. Some human agency caused this accident to occur.
>
> Why did it occur?
>
> The Korean War was about to begin, and this country was occupied by the United States. The Yoshida cabinet had just completed its forcible firing of ninety-seven thousand railroad workers, and the National Railroad Workers' Union was rising up in opposition to these massive layoffs.
>
> The Shimoyama and Mitaka incidents, also caused by unknown conspirators, immediately preceded the Matsukawa train wreck; and because all the newspapers and the radio accused trade unionists of being the criminals responsible for these incidents, the workers were crushed before they could react. Unfortunately their labor unions were divided and unable to develop any kind of effective resistance.

The authorities did not even try to discover the true criminals who had caused this wreck, but instead arrested twenty workers, including ten members of the Fukushima Branch of the National Railroad Workers' Union and ten workers at the Tōshiba Matsukawa factory, who were engaged at that time in a struggle against the firing of workers. The courts found them all guilty and handed down sentences including the death penalty and life imprisonment. Reacting against the outrageous ruthlessness of the authorities, the people suddenly erupted in anger; and without regard for class or ideology, they banded together in the cause of justice and truth. Throughout every corner of this land people started relief activities in behalf of the Matsukawa defendants. The size and scope of this movement of popular solidarity has no precedent in either Japanese or world history. They gathered relief funds even from abroad.

In this way, after fourteen years of struggle and five courtroom trials, on September 12, 1963, the people finally grasped total victory—the judgment of not guilty.

When the people unite, their strength is limitless. This monument commemorates the people's triumph.

On its back the obelisk bears the simple inscription: "Erected September 12, 1964, to prevent any more Matsukawas."

Between August 10, 1959, when the Supreme Court ordered the Matsukawa case to be retried, and September 12, 1963, when the Supreme Court upheld the Sendai High Court's retrial verdict of not guilty (and thereby made the erection of the monument a year later appropriate), Japan's preoccupation with the Matsukawa case reached levels not witnessed during any of the three courtroom hearings of the 1950s nor, for that matter, in connection with any other criminal case in recent Japanese history. During these years Matsukawa activists marched back and forth between Sendai and Tokyo, judges tried their hands at railroad sabotage, thousands of people toured the countryside south of Fukushima in accordance with the "Akama route," procurators and prosecution witnesses faced charges of manufacturing evidence and of perjury, and day after day the newspapers devoted whole editions to the events in Sendai and in the Supreme Court building in Kasumigaseki. During this period the Matsukawa case became, as the editors of the *Sankei shimbun* wrote on April 24, 1969, the "greatest case of the century."

Feelings ran high on both sides of the case following the first decision of the Supreme Court, and it is remarkable that anything like a fair trial could have been held in accordance with the Supreme Court's order. Conservatives were outraged by the pressure tactics of the Countermeasures Council, while Hirotsu, the defendants, and their lawyers remained extremely suspicious of what they believed were government efforts to railroad the defendants. Each side hurled charges at the other. For example, on August 14, 1959, only four days after the Supreme Court's decision, Hirotsu defended in the newspapers the mass movement he was leading. He contended that it was the government that had begun the practice of trying the case in the public media, referring to the chief cabinet secretary's initial characterization of the Matsukawa incident as a "left-wing ideological crime" and to the echoing of this theme by the press and radio. He said that the Countermeasures Council, as its name implied, was only trying to bring some countervailing political pressure to bear in the face of long-standing conservative pressure.

Controversy continued, focusing on the Sendai High Court's procedures for selecting a panel of judges to hear the retrial. Even before a judicial conference could be convened, the defense attorneys fired off a declaration to the president and each judge on the High Court demanding that Judge Suzuki, who had presided over the second trial, and an associate judge in the first trial who had been elevated to the High Court both be barred from either hearing the case or participating in the conference.

The defense alleged that they were biased. Thus it was that on September 1, 1959, only eighteen judges of the Sendai High Court—minus the two allegedly offensive judges—met to choose three of their numbers to sit for this difficult case. As president they selected Judge Monden Makoto, age fifty-five and chief of the Criminal Affairs Section of the Sendai High Court; and to assist him they named two other less experienced judges. Immediately after the announcement of Monden's appointment, the Miyagi prefectural Countermeasures Council complained that he was known to favor the minority opinion in the recent Supreme Court's Matsukawa decision and that he personally had a reputation for giving a lot of guilty verdicts. The council doubted that the retrial could possibly be fair. It did have one piece of evidence to support these charges. Only five days earlier, on August 25, 1959, Judge Monden had found Saitō, Takeda, Okada, and Akama guilty in the Date station case, upholding the prosecution's appeal and reversing the Fukushima District Court's verdict, which had freed them on the grounds that SCAP's law fixing the maximum number of governmental personnel was unconstitutional. However, as we shall see, the appointment of Judge Monden, old-fashioned though he unquestionably was, would prove to be one of the luckiest breaks for the Matsukawa defendants since Hirotsu had taken an interest in their case.

No doubt one reason for the defense's extreme sensitivity to every detail of the retrial procedure was Chief Justice Tanaka Kōtarō's dissent from the Supreme Court's August decision. The defense lawyers knew that Tanaka's opinion carried a great deal of weight with lesser judges in Japan, and also that the five dissenting justices included both the Supreme Court's leading criminal law specialists and the two justices who had been assigned to work directly on the Matsukawa case materials. During September 1959 Chūō kōron published a special Matsukawa issue in which Hirotsu attacked Tanaka's dissent as ideologically

motivated, and defendant Sugiura contributed an article accusing
Tanaka of seeking through his minority statement to murder
Communist workers.[1] During early 1960 some sixty defense
attorneys followed up these attempts to smear Tanaka by bringing impeachment charges against him before the Judicial Impeachment Committee of the Diet. The petitioners' stated complaints were patently frivolous—for example, that in writing in
his dissenting opinion that his colleagues in the majority suffered
from hallucinations, Tanaka had insulted the authority of the
judiciary—and the Diet dismissed them out of hand. However,
all of this maneuvering had at least one intended effect: it kept
the case on the front pages.[2]

Meanwhile, the prosecution was not sitting idly by. The
Supreme Procurator's Office chose Takahashi Shōhachi of the
Public Security Section, Tokyo High Procuracy, who was well
known as a veteran of the May Day, Sunakawa, and numerous
other sensational "Communist cases," to lead the prosecution
in the retrial. He had a reputation for being tough and thorough,
and he immediately organized a Matsukawa Case Special Trial
Department within the Sendai High Procuracy to gather all
available evidence and witnesses who might still be around
eleven years after the crime had been committed. By mid-
December 1959, three months before the trial was set to begin,
he had already lined up forty-one witnesses. However, as in the
case of Judge Monden and despite the defense attorneys' continuous screams of outrage, the defendants were lucky to have
drawn procurator Takahashi: he was keen to win but he was
also honest.

On March 21, 1960, with a mild spring rain falling over

1. See "Matsukawa jiken tokushū gō" (Matsukawa Case Special
Issue), Chūō kōron ("kinkyū zōkan," or, "Emergency Issue"), No. 860
(September 1959), pp. 29, 52.
2. On the attempt to impeach Tanaka, see Yomiuri shimbun, April
29, 1960.

Sendai, the Matsukawa case retrial got under way in a specially outfitted criminal courtroom in the hall normally used by the Sendai Summary Court. There were seats for some seventy spectators, all of them continuously filled by members of the Countermeasures Council or special guests of the movement from Tokyo (such as, on opening day, the movie director whom Hirotsu had commissioned to make a feature film about the Matsukawa case). As the defendants entered the court, their local supporters serenaded them with the latest Matsukawa song—"Tatakai no retsu o katameyō" ("Harden the Fighting Ranks")—and reporters who had witnessed earlier Matsukawa trials felt right at home.

The first four sessions of the retrial were taken up by furious argument over the nature of the retrial itself. The prosecution insisted that the court was to conduct a second kōso inquiry into all aspects of the case, but the defense argued that the Supreme Court had already declared the prosecution's case doubtful and that the only thing the retrial court had to do was quickly read the Suwa Memorandum and declare the defendants not guilty. On April 13, 1960, Judge Monden decided the issue entirely in favor of the prosecution: there would be no limits on the retrial, and all relevant evidence on all aspects of the case would be completely reexamined. The howls from the defense lawyers were deafening. In a press conference Okabayashi said that he was considering a special appeal (tokubetsu kōkoku) to the Supreme Court, claiming violations of articles 31 (due process) and 37 (right to a speedy trial) of the Constitution. He did not do it, but he continued to object every time the prosecution requested that a new piece of evidence be admitted or a witness be called; and after each day's proceeding he complained to reporters of the court's unfairness.

Hirotsu Kazuo did not go along with the defense attorneys or the Matsukawa Countermeasures Council in these protests. He wanted the whole case reopened, and as things turned out, he was considerably more perceptive in understanding what was at stake than the lawyers themselves. Had Monden ruled in favor of the defense and restricted the retrial solely to proof of the existence of the August 15 "liaison conspiracy" meeting, the court might very well have found that the first two verdicts were valid. However, the effect of Monden's ruling was to order the prosecution to prove every aspect of the original indictment, from the alleged August 12 telephone call to the Tōshiba factory down to the actual commission of the sabotage. Among other things, Monden reopened the issue of the August 12 and August 13 conspiracy meetings, which the second trial had rejected as unproved, and he allowed the prosecution to call as witnesses and use the affidavits of the three defendants who had been judged not guilty at the second trial (they could not, of course, be retried because of the constitutional prohibition against double jeopardy). He also encouraged the prosecution to offer what came to be known as new evidence—namely, the preindictment and pretrial depositions, records, and documents that the police and procurators had amassed during the course of their investigation.

This is not the kind of evidence normally allowed in court under Anglo-American procedures (and hence in Japan under the postwar Code of Criminal Procedure), but it is exactly the kind of evidence that formed the heart of a case under the Continental and the prewar Japanese systems. Before the retrial had ended, the prosecution had turned over to the court some 1,687 affidavits, most of them never before seen by a judge or the defense, constituting virtually (but not quite) all of the police records of the 1949 investigation. These records proved to be sensational: they offered for the first time a glimpse into how the police had broken the case, and they laid the foundations for a not-guilty verdict. Had it not been for Monden's old-fashioned stance as an investigating judge, a stance which he assumed throughout the trial, these documents would probably never have seen the light of day. The defense attorneys did not realize what a favor he was doing them when he asked to see all the records and when he pointedly told the procurator that article 299(1) of the Code of Criminal Procedure applied: "Where documentary or real evidence is going to be produced for examination, the opponent party must be afforded, in advance, an opportunity to inspect it." As we shall see, Monden himself read these massive "new evidence" documents more closely than either the prosecution or the defense, as he gleefully pointed out to both parties in his verdict. The only other person in Japan who was as interested as Monden in these old records was Hirotsu Kazuo.

That, however, is to get ahead of the story. The revelations of the "new evidence" were not actually disclosed in all of their detail until Monden handed down his verdict. Prior to the close of court, which was when Monden and his associate judges finally got a chance to sit down privately in their libraries to read and to reconstruct the case, the prosecution and the defense engaged in a highly spirited—if not ultimately very edifying— "courtroom battle" of the sort that is supposed to typify American-style adversary procedures. Throughout this period the procurator kept introducing items of "new evidence," but he did not actually turn over everything he found in the procuracy files until the time of his closing address (ronkoku). The courtroom contest included surprise witnesses and dramatic presentations of evidence, but in the long run it served less to bring out "the facts" than to heighten Judge Monden's old inquisitorial suspicions. There were altogether seven major issues before the court between March 21, 1960, and April 27, 1961, the period when it held open hearings and conducted an on-site inspection.

The first was Akama's prophecy. It will be recalled that Sergeant Takeda of the Fukushima Municipal Police initially heard Akama's name in the course of his questioning two juvenile delinquents, Iijima Yoshio and Andō Sadao, concerning their whereabouts on the evening of August 16, 1949. They told him that they had met Akama at the Kuroiwa festival and that he had said to them, "There's a good chance there's going to be a train wreck tonight." Akama later acknowledged in his confessions that he had said something of the sort to these two acquaintances of his. During the earlier trials, the courts had always accepted the validity of this prophecy because Akama himself had confessed to making it.

In the retrial, however, the prosecution was obliged to introduce the original records of Sergeant Takeda's interrogation of the two hearers of the prophecy, and these documents raised some serious questions. In Sergeant Takeda's affidavit of September 6, 1949—three days before Akama was arrested—Andō quotes Akama as having said that a train "was derailed" (dassen shita), but in the sergeant's report of September 9, Iijima is quoted as thinking that Akama said "may be derailed" (dassen ga aru'n ja nai ka). Throughout both youths' depositions the key tenses of Akama's "prophecy" change continuously from past to future, suggesting that possibly the pair had not heard Akama on the evening of August 16 but on August 17 and that Akama's statement was not a prophecy but a comment about something that had happened the previous evening. The police affidavits easily give rise to the thought that Akama did not prophesy anything but that Takeda allowed the two delinquents to say that he did so in order to free themselves from involvement in the rape case for which he was holding them.

During the retrial, procurator Takahashi put both Iijima and Andō on the stand to testify that it was certainly at the Kuroiwa festival that they heard Akama talk about train wrecks. In addition, the prosecution produced two brand-new witnesses who claimed that they too had heard Akama's prophecy. These two witnesses—Kikuchi Toni, a thirty-five-year-old employee of the Fukushima rice cooperative, and Tanji Shintarō, a thirty-one-year-old farmer—both swore in court that they had been with

Andō at the Kuroiwa festival and that Akama had made remarks in their presence about a train wreck. At the time they had thought that this was just "crazy talk" by a wild kid, but in light of the wreck that had occurred later that very night they had remembered the incident all these years. Tanji, in particular, resisted the defense's efforts to shake him in cross-examination, and on the evening of September 15, 1960, the *Yomiuri* carried headlines calling him the prosecution's "trump witness" (*kiri-fuda shōnin*). The defense attorneys, of course, tore into this testimony, suggesting that it was perjured, and they brought out the fact that prosecution officials had apparently taken Kikuchi on a vacation to a hot spring early in 1960. Kikuchi explained that he had merely been the guest of a police official who was teaching him *jūdō* at a gymnasium in Fukushima and that his friendly relations with policemen had been misunderstood by the defense attorneys and various reporters. Even the judges asked the two men a few questions about why they had not reported something so unusual as a prediction concerning a train wreck at the time it had occurred, and the judges expressed some wonderment at the extraordinary feats of memory they had just witnessed in court. Although during the year after the verdict the defense tried unsuccessfully to have Kikuchi indicted for perjury, none of his testimony or the cross-examination had as much effect on the court's belief in the prophecy as the revelation in the "new evidence" affidavits that the tenses of Akama's remarks were inconsistent with making a prophecy.

Because of the furor that had surrounded the Suwa Memorandum before the Supreme Court, the memorandum itself and the question whether Satō Hajime had an alibi for August 15, 1949, were two of the most thoroughly debated issues in the retrial. The prosecution was ready in advance to tackle this problem, having discovered a new and different record of the August 15 collective bargaining session at the Tōshiba plant; it called this new transcript the *dankō* memo ("negotiations memorandum"), which was subsequently renamed on Judge Monden's orders the Tanaka Memorandum, after the name of its author, Tanaka Hidetaka, a former member of the executive committee of the Tōshiba factory union. The Tanaka memo was the union's equivalent of the Suwa memo, and the prosecution now wished to introduce it—even though it too showed Satō present and speaking at the bargaining table—because its author, Mr. Tanaka, was prepared to testify that the sessions had begun at 9:30 A.M., not 10:30 as alleged by Suwa. If this were true, it would have given Satō enough time to have attended the meeting and still have caught the 11:15 train for his conspiracy appointment in Fukushima. The former factory manager, Mr. Washimi, also appeared as a prosecution witness and testified that he thought the negotiations had begun at 9:30 A.M.

Part of the problem was that the Americans had introduced "daylight saving time" into Japan, and nobody could be sure when the talks had begun. During his day on the stand, Tanaka identified the old record he had kept for his union—it was written on *warabanshi* (cheap straw paper), now encased by the prosecution in celluloid—and said that he believed the sessions had commenced at 9:30 A.M. Satō was indeed recorded in the Tanaka memo, which was much more complete than Suwa's, as talking throughout the meeting. However, the defense called both Suwa and Nishi to Sendai to testify, and Suwa maintained in the face of hard prosecution challenges that the meeting had started at 10:30—he remembered looking at his watch, which he identified as an Elgin—and that it had ended at noon. If that were the case, Satō could never have made it by train to Fukushima in time.

The prosecution did not regard the Tanaka memo as anything more than a ploy to try to dampen the impact of the now nationally famous Suwa Memorandum. It also took the line, suggested by one of the Supreme Court's minority opinions, that the state did not have to prove when and how Satō got to

Fukushima, only that a conspiracy had existed, of which he was a part. The procurator speculated that Satō could have taken the bus or been driven in a truck, and he even called into court the president of the Fukushima Bus Company to testify about bus schedules during August 1949. Unfortunately for the procurator's hypothesis, this gentleman revealed that the only available bus left Matsukawa at 12:30 P.M., too late for the conspiracy meeting. Of course, the defense attacked this entire line of argument, explaining that it was the prosecution who had charged Satō with being at a given place at a given time— whether or not the law of conspiracy demanded that the state do so—and the defense had merely refuted those charges.[3] The court ultimately agreed, holding that the Tanaka memo reinforced the Suwa memo and that whether or not a conspiracy had existed to derail a train, Satō probably had not attended any noon meeting in Fukushima on August 15.[4]

The arguments in court over the crowbar and wrench found at the scene of the crime probably took up more time and contributed less to the retrial than any other single issue. The point of it all was the prosecution's ultimately futile efforts to prove that these tools had been stolen from the Matsukawa track-

3. On this point, see Hirotsu Kazuo, *Matsukawa jiken to saiban* (The Matsukawa Case and Trials) (Tokyo, 1964), p. 433.

4. A month before Monden delivered his verdict, including his assessment of the meaning of the Suwa Memorandum, another judge came to a quite different conclusion. In 1959, the Matsukawa defense attorneys had initiated a court action (a "demand for indictment," or *kiso seikyū*) intended to force the procuracy to indict procurators Suzuki, Yamamoto, and Tajima on charges of suppression of evidence. On June 30, 1961, a judge of the Fukushima District Court, who heard the attorneys' complaint, dismissed their petition on the grounds that charges of suppression of evidence depend upon that evidence's being of some worth or value. He rejected the charge of suppression because, in his view, the Suwa Memorandum was not important evidence and to have suppressed it would have been meaningless. See *Asahi shimbun*, July 15, 1961, and July 24, 1961.

maintenance crew's shed. Both parties debated two questions: (1) Did the Matsukawa crew own any wrenches like the one found at the scene? (2) If the crew did possess wrenches of the proper kind, how many, and was one missing on the morning of August 17? An endless series of witnesses contributed their thoughts on these two questions, but one—produced by the prosecution—made headlines and also strained even conservative observers' faith that the procurators were being completely honest in their finding of evidence eleven years after the crime had occurred.

On the morning of July 29, 1960, procurator Takahashi came into court with a police officer who was carrying a wrench virtually identical to the one found in the rice paddy. This policeman testified to the judges that on August 19, 1949, two days after the alleged theft, a Mr. Shibugawa Katsunari, in charge of track maintenance throughout the Japanese National Railroad's Fukushima Subdivision, had removed this particular wrench from the Matsukawa shed because it was just like the one discovered at the scene of the wreck and he wished to insure that the two wrenches would not be confused with each other. At some undetermined time later on Shibugawa had turned the wrench over to the police, and still later an unknown official had delivered this second wrench to the police box in front of Kanayagawa station with a tag attached (the label was still tied to the wrench that morning in 1960) that said, "For Mr. Shibugawa, Matsukawa Inventory and Track Section." According to the witness, the police were supposed to return the wrench to Shibugawa but instead put it on a shelf in the Kanayagawa police kiosk and forgot about it for eleven years, until the prosecution rediscovered it during its preparations for the retrial. The sole importance of this find, so far as the prosecution was concerned, lay in its proof of the fact that the Matsukawa crew had possessed nonstandard, foot-long monkey wrenches.

The defense, however, was simply outraged by these revelations. It was too much, said the defense attorneys. First the prosecution digs up two new hearers of Akama's prophecy; then it presents another new witness (to be mentioned below); and now it finds a wrench that has been conveniently sitting in a policeman's billet for better than a decade. Nor was that the end of the matter. The prosecution introduced old photographs of the inside of the track-maintenance shed, which appeared to indicate places in a tool rack for *three* such wrenches. During October Shibugawa himself took the stand and produced records of an inventory made a few months after the wreck, which indicated that two monkey wrenches had been visually confirmed as part of the Matsukawa crew's equipment. This number was consistent with the photo showing places for three, and one of them had been stolen back in August. But in that case what was to be made of the newly found wrench (unless Shibugawa had made his removal after the inventory, the exact date of which could not be determined precisely)? If there had been three wrenches and one of them had been stolen, why did Shibugawa take only one of the remaining two and how did the maintenance crew end up still having two wrenches? It was at this point that a *Tokyo shimbun* reporter characterized the Matsukawa retrial as a "quagmire." In his *ronkoku*, procurator Takahashi tried to repair some of the damage done by this highly confusing testimony. He argued that the Matsukawa crew had in fact possessed only two wrenches; one had been stolen and the other had been removed after the wreck by Shibugawa. Monden was not convinced. Noting that the procurator had said that the Matsukawa crew owned two wrenches and that an inventory taken after the wreck disclosed two wrenches, he concluded that the wrench found in the rice paddy probably had not come from the toolshed at Matsukawa station and that (on the basis of similar if less sensational testimony) it was equally impossible to tell whether or not the crowbar had come from there.[5]

The other new prosecution witness who so enraged the defense was a Mr. Kunijima, a plant guard at the Tōshiba factory. He took the stand to testify that he recalled Ōta, not Sugiura, on August 12, 1949, receiving a telephone call within the Tōshiba plant's guardhouse from the National Railroad Workers' Union offices in Fukushima. The prosecution introduced this statement because it now believed that Abe had called Ōta rather than Sugiura and had told him to tell Sugiura to send a representative to the conspiracy meeting the following day. On the evening after this testimony the defense called a press conference at its ryokan (or Japanese-style inn) in Sendai and denounced Kunijima as a perjurer. Its only evidence of perjury, however, was its contention that nobody could possibly remember a detail such as a telephone call to another person for eleven years.

Contrary to the defense's allegations, Kunijima may have been correct. The post office's call-record book (the postal and telephone services are administered by the same ministry in Japan) indicated that on August 12 two calls had been made to the Tōshiba plant from the NRWU's number. The defense countered this evidence with the Tōshiba factory's guard station log book, which showed that Ōta had left the factory shortly after nine o'clock on the morning in question. Kunijima discounted this, replying that the times entered in the log book were inexact and that a record of Ōta's departure did not prove that he had not received one or both calls. Ultimately Monden

5. See *Tokyo shimbun*, July 14, 1960; *Yomiuri shimbun*, July 15, 1960; *Yomiuri shimbun*, eve. ed., July 29, 1960; *Asahi shimbun*, eve. ed., September 13, 1960; *Yomiuri shimbun*, eve. ed., October 11, 1960; *Yomiuri shimbun*, October 12, 1960; *Mainichi shimbun*, October 12, 1960; *Nihon keizai shimbun*, eve. ed., October 13, 1960; *Mainichi shimbun*, eve. ed., October 15, 1960; *Tokyo shimbun*, eve. ed., October 17, 1960; and *Asahi shimbun*, eve. ed., February 14, 1961.

acknowledged that telephone calls had been made by the railroad workers' union to the Tōshiba factory union on August 12, but he concluded that they had had nothing to do with the case, and the defense tried without success to have Kunijima indicted for perjury.

On August 13, 1960, after four months of intensive examination of evidence, the court interrupted formal deliberations for the rest of the month in order to get a little fresh air, and also to give Monden and his colleagues a chance to do some practical investigating. Monden ordered the most complete on-site inspection yet undertaken by any of the Matsukawa courts. Among many other details, he directed that a tent and a 60-watt bulb be rigged at the southern end of the Nagaigawa Signal Station, just as there had been on the night of August 16, 1949, and that a light be hung on the house of Honda Kiyomatsu, in front of which the three NRWU conspirators had allegedly passed and been seen eleven years earlier. He also directed that all the judges, procurators, defense attorneys, and court clerks accompany him on an all-night walk to and from the scene of the crime and that they be prepared to try to pull up spikes and remove bolts, using only a crowbar and a monkey wrench, from a section of railroad track that he had had specially laid. After all the reporters joined in, the expedition involved between 150 and 200 people; and it proved to be one of the high points of the trial. Its purpose, of course, was to test the veracity of Akama's confession against the actual terrain through which he had allegedly walked.

During the day on August 13 the court and everyone connected with it traveled by train from Sendai to Fukushima and gathered at about 7:40 that evening in front of Fukushima station. Dressed in an open white shirt and duck shoes and carrying a cane, Judge Monden led the party through the NRWU offices and around the Fukushima railroad yard. Shortly after 9:00 P.M. they reached the Suzuki lumberyard, from where Monden, flanked on either side by chief procurator Takahashi and chief defense attorney Okabayashi, guided the party to the Nagaigawa foot-crossing over the Tōhoku Main Line tracks. As the judicial inspection party approached this now famous spot, with reporters' flashbulbs going off all around them, one of the more revealing episodes of the evening took place. From at least 250 yards away Okabayashi began to exclaim that he could see the tent and the light-bulb, but procurator Takahashi, looking fixedly at the ground over which he was walking, insisted over and over again that he could see nothing. Takahashi virtually walked into the tent before he acknowledged its existence (as, of course, Akama had completely failed to do in his confession). It was therefore up to Monden to decide whether someone passing that spot at night would have observed the tent and its light, and he concluded that such a person would have done so.

At 1:30 in the morning the inspection team reached the Matsukawa–Kanayagawa Gap and set to work dismantling the tracks. The next evening all the newspapers in the country carried big pictures of Judge Monden struggling with a monkey wrench over a fishplate nut while one of his colleagues, Judge Sugimoto, put his weight on one end of a crowbar, trying to loosen a spike. According to the Asahi account, Monden gave up on the wrench and shifted to the crowbar but was unable to budge a single spike with it until the procurator prompted him with a few tips. Watching this procuratorial advice, Okabayashi was overheard to utter, "Fake, fake" (ayashii zo). Monden, however, claimed to have been satisfied. The whole party got back to Fukushima at 8:30 A.M. on August 14, and the fifty-five-year-old chief judge ordered everyone to take off the remainder of that day and August 15 for a rest.

On August 16 the court was back at work. Suwa Shin'ichirō, author of the famous Suwa Memorandum, served as a guide to the Tōshiba Matsukawa factory (in 1960 known as the Kitashiba factory), including stops at the police box, trade union office,

Yasaka dormitory, and factory manager's office (where the labor negotiations of August 1949, which Suwa had recorded, had been held). At the end of the day Monden gave an interview to reporters. He asserted that he had been most impressed by the tent at the Nagaigawa crossing and that he did not see how a person passing it could have failed to observe it.

On the day after the court finished its explorations in Fukushima—that is, on August 17, 1960, the anniversary of the wreck—the Countermeasures Council itself sponsored a massive on-site inspection made up of some two thousand people from all parts of the country. This one was carried out during daylight, and Hirotsu Kazuo personally guided it. At the Nagaigawa crossing, in the lovely countryside of northern Fukushima, he stood on a temporary platform and delivered a lecture to the assembled flag-bearing activists on the significance of the tent that had stood at that spot some eleven years earlier. According to the press, residents of the area had by now grown accustomed to numerous Tokyoites dressed in business suits marching through their property and exclaiming excitedly over such prosaic landmarks as a railroad crossing, an old wooden bridge, and a stream that the locals had aptly named the Muddy.

The court had one more stop on its itinerary before returning to Sendai and resuming the hearing of testimony. On August 26, 1960, Monden led his associates to the Metallurgy Department of Tokyo University's School of Engineering, where he had arranged for a professor to conduct some tests on monkey wrenches. Although the newspaper photos show Monden and his academic expert seemingly pleasurably absorbed in a test of the strength of a foot-long wrench, the tests themselves proved to be inconclusive: a monkey wrench of that size was somewhat too weak to move a fishplate nut every time it was tried, but occasionally it might.

Back in Sendai it was the defense's turn to come into court with some surprise witnesses, causing the prosecution to mutter darkly about the manufacturing of evidence.[6] On September 8, 1960, chief defense attorney Okabayashi requested subpoenas for Hirama Takashi, age thirty-nine, a traveling salesman of Matsukawa, and Murakami Yoshio, alias Murata Giichi, age forty-three, a factory worker of Nihonmatsu. Okabayashi introduced them to the court as persons having important evidence concerning the true criminals in the case. (This was the defense lawyers' sole effort in the entire history of the case to show who might have committed the crime, assuming that the defendants were innocent.) He also charged that the police had tampered with his witnesses and had tried to get them to change their stories. Judge Monden set September 16 and 17 for the pair to appear in court.

They had a strange story to tell. Both men had been petty thieves and burglars who had become acquainted with each other in the Fukushima city jail in early 1949. On the night of August 15, 1949—that is, the night before the wreck occurred—they had been out together, trying to break into a warehouse located on the Rikuu Highway near where it crosses the Tōhoku Main Line tracks. They had failed to gain entry, and so on the following night, August 16, they had set out again, looking for a burglary target and thinking perhaps of trying the warehouse a second time. However, it was a poor night, for it was raining, and at around 1:30 A.M. they gave up and parted company near Kanayagawa. Murakami walked south, toward Matsukawa, and Hirama took a hill path in the direction of Fukushima. After Murakami had gone only a short distance he allegedly met three "tall" men

6. The fabrication of evidence was not unknown in Japanese criminal trials of this period. During March 1965, the procuracy arrested a group of defense lawyers and supporters of Hirasawa Sadamichi, the artist who had been sentenced to death in the 1948 Imperial Bank poisoning case, for inventing evidence purporting to explain how Hirasawa had come by some ¥150,000 which he had possessed and which he could not account for at the time of his arrest. See *Asahi Evening News*, March 18, 1965.

(*se wa takakatta*), and then six more after that. They were carrying something heavy, and they spoke Japanese in a dialect different from that of Tōhoku. Murakami was scared, having no way to escape, and while pretending to hold a dagger in one hand, he said, "Good evening," which the strangers returned. Shortly afterward, as Murakami sat resting and having a smoke just north of the Matsukawa plant, he heard the unforgettable sound of the train wreck, and he hurried quickly from the area.

Hirama related a similar experience. From his hill path he too had seen seven to nine tall figures passing through the night. He thought that they might have been a village police unit and had avoided them. It should be noted that references to "tall" Japanese in 1949 Japan meant Nisei Americans (that is, Americans of Japanese ancestry, who were members of their families' second generation as United States citizens), and this testimony unmistakably implied that the railroad saboteurs had been special operatives of SCAP.

Monden was skeptical. He asked how they remembered on what night they had had this encounter and how they knew the exact time when it had occurred. Both men answered that the previous night's burglary attempt dated it for them and that they had been wearing wristwatches. Procurator Takahashi on cross-examination elicited from them that in May of 1959 they had visited a hot spring at the defense's expense and that both of them had also recently made a trip to Tokyo on defense business. He also asserted that the police had checked their stories years before and had established that the men were actually elsewhere than they had claimed to be on the night of August 16, 1949. In return, Okabayashi brought out that in the police investigation of the two burglars' stories, the first question police officers had asked them was, "When did you join the Communist party?" Also, during their first interrogation, the police were evidently convinced that the burglars must have seen Akama and company, and tried repeatedly to get them to change the

numbers of men they claimed to have met from seven or nine
to three. The defense did not make any further use of this
testimony and only briefly mentioned it in its closing address.
The press had a field day with the implications of this story,
but most observers concluded that the two burglars had only
served to make the defense's methods look as questionable as
some of the prosecution's. We shall return to the problem of
the "nine tall men" in the next chapter.[7]

Another subject of debate before the court seemed to have
been won by the prosecution, but it also illustrated how enormously difficult it was for the state to prove its detailed conspiracy charges. According to the first and second trials, Katō
Kenzō had spent most of the day on August 16, 1949, at the
Matsukawa plant, where that evening he had informed the
Tōshiba plotters of the cancellation of kudari freight number
159. In accordance with that vital piece of information, he
supposedly directed them to wreck nobori number 412, since
its schedule afforded them the greatest amount of time between
trains in order to carry out the sabotage of the tracks. In the
Supreme Court's majority decision, the justices expressed doubt
that Katō, who had left Fukushima on the 11:38 A.M. train
intending to devote the day to assisting his fellow workers at
Matsukawa, could have obtained the information concerning
the cancellation of train number 159, or that the decision to
cancel it had even been made before he left the railroad yard.
During the retrial the defense naturally followed up this point
and introduced a railroad worker who testified that the cancellation order had not reached the Fukushima superintendent's
office of the JNR until around 5:00 P.M. on August 16. It

7. See, inter alia, Matsukawa Jiken Taisaku Kyōgikai (The Matsu-
kawa Case Countermeasures Council), Yami ni kieta ku-nin (The Nine
Men Who Disappeared into the Dark) (Tokyo, 1961). "Matsukawa
Shiriizu No. 7."

seemed, therefore, that Katō could not have known about it and could not have informed the Tōshiba conspirators.

The prosecution had to prove that Katō did know about the train's cancellation—and this it could not do. But the state did establish that he could have known about it. Procurator Takahashi put on the stand the chief dispatcher at Utsunomiya station, the central point for controlling traffic up and down the Tōhoku Main Line, and he testified, on the basis of his daily records, that the decision to cancel number 159 had been communicated to Fukushima by 10:00 A.M. on the day in question. Had Katō used his knowledge of dispatching and his contacts in the superintendent's office (he had, of course, been laid off by the JNR) to obtain this information? No one could prove that he had.

None of the issues so far mentioned prefigured Monden's verdict, although each of them was reflected in it. However, the last major issue—Akama's alibi and confession—came very close to what Monden would subsequently treat as the heart of the case. After his arrest, Akama had explained to the police that on the night of the Kuroiwa festival he had returned home at around 1:00 A.M. and that his grandmother, Akama Mina, could verify that fact. When the police instead showed him an affidavit signed by her stating that he had come in closer to 4:00 A.M., he was overcome by despair and confessed. The question raised during the retrial was at what time, according to Akama Mina, had Akama actually returned home—1:00 A.M. or 4:00 A.M?

A decade earlier, during the first trial, the following exchange had taken place in court between chief defense attorney Okabayashi and Akama Mina, age seventy-four:

OKABAYASHI: On that night [August 16, 1949] about what time did Katsumi return home?

MINA: It was between twelve and one. I know because I had one of my grandchildren staying with me [Akama's cousin,

Onodera Itsuko, age eleven], and when I woke her to go to the toilet at about midnight, Katsumi wasn't home yet.

OKABAYASHI: Therefore, he came home between twelve and one, did he?

MINA: Yes.

OKABAYASHI: Was it well before one?

MINA: No. I think it was just about one. . . .

OKABAYASHI: Grandmother, have you ever been called in by the police and questioned about Katsumi?

MINA: I have.

OKABAYASHI: Was it about something similar to what I have asked here?

MINA: Yes, they wanted to know what time Katsumi came home.

OKABAYASHI: Well, did you answer the same way then?

MINA: Yes, I told them that he got home between twelve and one.

OKABAYASHI: When you were questioned, were you asked just to state the time of his return, such as "When did he come home?" or did the man tell you to answer a particular time?

MINA: When I answered "between twelve and one," the policeman said, "He returned home about three or four, didn't he?"

OKABAYASHI: And how did you respond to that?

MINA: I said that he came home between twelve and one and that I was sure of it because he was in bed when I got up at about 2:30 to go to the bathroom again. [All three people— Akama, Mina, and Akama's cousin—slept in the same room.]

The first court had rejected this testimony, which it heard on March 20, 1950, citing in support of its ruling an affidavit dated September 26, 1949, in which procurator Yamamoto questioned Mina about these matters. According to this very short affidavit, Mina had said that she had not actually observed Akama's return but had asked him the following morning and had been told it was at about 1:00 A.M. The court therefore dismissed her testimony as hearsay.

The old lady herself had died on February 20, 1954, and was not around for the retrial. However, there was the matter of the "new evidence," and it contained the first affidavit she had signed for the police, dated September 17, 1949, while Akama was being questioned but before he had been charged or had confessed to the Matsukawa sabotage. Through this statement she spoke from the grave; a *Yomiuri* reporter later wrote that her "testimony" was the high point of the retrial.

The September 17 affidavit does not record Mina as saying that her grandson returned home at 4:00 A.M.; in it she says that it was at one. She does say that she was having trouble keeping straight the three nights of the Bon festival, but she contends that Akama was home by one o'clock or earlier every night, because he was out on bail and did not want to have any further trouble with the police. At no point does she say that he returned home at four. Her first affidavit to the police is, in fact, virtually identical to the testimony she gave in court the following March. When Sergeant Takeda told Akama that his grandmother had turned against him, he must either have allowed Akama to read a doctored affidavit or, more probably, only showed him the name on the genuine affidavit. In any case, Akama swore that, according to Takeda, his grandmother had placed his time of returning home at 4:00 A.M. Takeda had therefore demanded to know where he had been all night and had invited him to confess to sabotaging the tracks at Matsukawa. The revelation that Akama Mina had never said that Akama was gone until 4:00 A.M. did not, of course, establish his alibi beyond all doubt; however, it did cause Judge Monden to scrutinize with the greatest possible care the statements of the other alleged saboteurs concerning their whereabouts on the night of the wreck.[8]

8. For Akama Mina's testimony of March 20, 1950, see Fukushima

As the public hearings of the retrial drew to a close, it became apparent once again that the only real evidence linking the defendants with the crime was the confessions of the youngest and least mature among them. Throughout the various Matsukawa trials these confessions—as in so many other Japanese criminal cases—had seemed conclusive both in terms of their numbers (eight confessions) and their relative internal consistency. Equally important, they had appeared to have been corroborated by various unwitting, out-of-court remarks made by the defendants. During the first trial's on-site inspection, for example, Akama had allegedly pointed to the Morinaga bridge and said to Honda, "There's where we rested." Similarly, Hamazaki had appeared to confide to a journalist that his confession was truthful. During the retrial, one of the two chief defense attorneys, Ōtsuka Kazuo, himself took the stand to testify about these matters. After complaining bitterly about how the police had violated his right to confer privately with his clients before the first trial, he asserted that on October 5, 1949, during his first genuine interview with Akama at Hobara police station, Akama had said to him, "I had no connection with the case. However, I want you to act like you don't know that or it'll go hard for me with the police." It was not until after Akama's return to Fukushima jail, according to Ōtsuka, that Akama felt sufficiently free from police intimidation to tell the truth publicly.

Chihō Saibansho (Fukushima District Court), *Matsukawa jiken kōhan kiroku* (Matsukawa Case Trial Record), V, 68–69. For her affidavit of September 26, 1949, see ibid., XII, 23. For Judge Nagao's ruling on her testimony, see Fukushima Chihō Saibansho, *Matsukawa jiken dai-isshin hanketsu* (Matsukawa Case First Trial Verdict) (Fukushima, January 12, 1951), pp. 391–392. For her affidavit of September 17, 1949, see Sendai Kōtō Saibansho Dai Ichi Keijibu (Sendai High Court, First Criminal Affairs Division), *Matsukawa jiken sashimodoshi-shin kōhan shiryō* (Matsukawa Case Retrial Documentary Materials), II, 155–156. This latter volume is marked "Matsukawa jiken sashimodoshi-shin made kensatsukan ga intoku seru mono" ("Items concealed by the procurators until the Matsukawa case retrial").

Ōtsuka also argued that virtually all of the allegedly incriminating admissions of the defendants—which the police had overheard and reported—were ambiguous. Affirmative answers to questions like "Have you told the truth?" could only be taken as admissions of guilt if one assumed, as the police consistently did, that the original question referred to the defendants' confessions. Ōtsuka discounted Akama's remark made during the first on-site inspection, alleging that it was not entirely certain that Akama had made it at all and that, in any case, Akama was only alluding to a statement contained in his confession. According to Ōtsuka, Akama said, or implied, "There's where we are supposed to have rested, according to my confession document."

Monden himself questioned the defense attorney about these issues. He referred to a police report of eavesdropping on an interview between Ōtsuka and Ōuchi on October 23, 1949. According to this document, "When attorney Ōtsuka asked defendant Ōuchi, 'Have you told the truth?' Ōuchi replied in a weak voice, 'I, Kikuchi, and Kobayashi stole the crowbar.' " [9] Monden now asked Ōtsuka, "What about that?" Ōuchi had said no such thing, asserted Ōtsuka. He had merely affirmed to his attorney that he was now telling the truth, and the police read a meaning into his reply that was consistent with their own theory of the case. Monden made no further comment on this highly unusual testimony, only taking a few notes.

In the eyes of the press the prosecution had appeared during much of the retrial to have been on the defensive about its case. However, as in most other criminal trials, when the procurator began his ronkoku, this impression began to fade. Spread over three days, beginning on February 14, 1961, procurator Takahashi and his associates delivered to the court a six hundred thou-

9. *Matsukawa jiken sashimodoshi-shin kōhan kiroku* (Matsukawa Case Retrial Court Record), X, p. 414; and *Asahi shimbun*, eve. ed., December 10, 1960.

sand-word summary of the state's evidence against the defendants.[10] Procurator Takahashi took special pains to refute the charges that the government had been biased against the trade unions and that frame-ups had become the virtual stock-in-trade of the prosecuting attorneys. He said that he was turning over to the court every scrap of evidence that he had uncovered, including some 1,687 signed depositions, regardless of whether any of it served the prosecution's case, in order to lay to rest the insinuations that the government's case was based on anti-Communist preconceptions. Unfortunately for the procurator, neither he nor his staff had read the mass of documents that he was now so scrupulously turning over to the court.

In the course of his summary, the chief procurator argued that Akama had not seen the tent at the Nagaigawa crossing because it had been raining and that, despite some confusion among his witnesses eleven years after the fact, there had been only two monkey wrenches in the Matsukawa track crew's tool shed and that one of these had been stolen by the conspirators. Finally, on February 16, he asked the court for the same penalties that had been handed down by the second trial. As he demanded, in the name of the state, that Suzuki, Honda, Sugiura, and Satō be sent to the gallows, some defendants interrupted the court with shouts of "Lie! Not guilty!" but Monden gaveled them down with the admonition to save it for the *benron*—the defense's summary—which was soon to begin. In his *ronkoku*, procurator Takahashi had made only passing reference to the question of the alleged alibis of the saboteurs, and very little was said about it in the extensive press commentaries that fol-

10. Sendai Kōtō Kensatsuchō (Sendai High Public Procurators Office), *Kensatsukan iken yōshi* (Procurators' Brief), Sendai High Court, February 14–16, 1961; printed in Hōmushō Keijikyoku (Justice Ministry, Criminal Affairs Bureau), *Matsukawa jiken sashimodoshi-shin ronkoku* (The Procurators' Closing Address in the Matsukawa Case Retrial), "Kensatsu Shiryō No. 113" (May 1961), 671 pages.

lowed the procurator's address. This would prove to be a serious oversight.

The defense's benron did not begin until more than a month later, on March 28, 1961, having been delayed in order to allow the defense attorneys to read the "new evidence" deposited with the court by the prosecution. Fifteen court days were allotted to the benron, and it lasted until the court closed on April 27. As every commentator at the time noted, the defense's summary was one of the most vigorous ever offered in a Japanese court; many thought that its force boded well for the vitality of the postwar Code of Criminal Procedure, in contrast to the lack of skill the defense attorneys had displayed in earlier Matsukawa trials. Nevertheless, from the point of view of the Matsukawa movement, the benron began on an inauspicious note. In Tokyo the day before the defense's presentation began, the Tokyo High Court handed down its verdict in the Sunakawa case. This was the big case concerning American bases in Japan that had helped to precipitate the Security Treaty struggle and that the Supreme Court had ordered retried after overturning the Tokyo District Court's earlier decision that the Security Treaty was unconstitutional. Times had changed. The Security Treaty had by now been renegotiated, Ikeda had replaced Kishi as prime minister, and the country was absorbed in the "income doubling" scheme for economic growth. The Tokyo High Court found all seven Sunakawa defendants guilty and fined them ¥2,000 each. This was certainly a minimal punishment (¥2,000 is less than $10), but the Matsukawa movement still took it as a defeat for the "progressive forces."

In Sendai, however, the progressives were not defeated. Chief defense attorney Okabayashi began the benron by characterizing the state's case as a "fabrication" (netsuzō), and he and his colleagues continued like that for day after day. Attorney Ishijima, for example, opened his address to the court with the remark that the confessions were "based on a plot theory concocted by the investigating authorities." The defense's arguments were comprehensive, including detailed assertions of each defendant's alibi and statements by the defendants themselves, exercising their right to speak last. Satō Hajime, for example, reminded the court, "I was sent as a labor organizer from Tokyo to Matsukawa on August 11, 1949, only five days before the wreck occurred. I fail to understand how so many witnesses can claim to know me well." In all of this massive argumentation and documentation, one speech to the court stood out above all others. This was the presentation of attorney Ishijima Yasushi, the defense attorneys' specialist on the course of the investigation of the Matsukawa case prior to the first trial. His main point was ultimately accepted by Monden and was reflected in the judge's verdict, but even Monden drew away from the implication of frame-up that for the first time in the case seemed to have found some solid basis in evidence.

Mr. Ishijima had spent the previous month closely reading the official documents that the procurator had opened for the court's inspection. On March 29, 1961, the second day of the benron, he presented to the court a police report written by the now rather notorious Sergeant Takeda Tatsuo, dated September 19, 1949, and addressed to his immediate superior, the chief of the Fukushima Municipal Police. Concerned with Akama's very first confession, which had been made on that same day, Takeda's report contains the sentence: "Hamazaki and Satō Hajime of the Tōshiba Matsukawa factory have been identified as suspects." That was odd. In Akama's first confession he had only said that there had been two saboteurs from Tōshiba, whom he did not know by name, in addition to the three from the National Railroad Workers' Union, including himself, whom he did know by name. It was not until September 21, after having been shown photographs of Tōshiba workers, that he identified Hamazaki and Satō. Prior to Akama's second confession of September 21, their names had never once been mentioned in the course of the investigation; yet here they showed up in an official police report with a serial number and an earlier date of receipt stamped on its cover. Was it Akama who had identified the Tōshiba saboteurs—or was it perhaps the police who had singled them out?

Procurator Takahashi rose and demanded the right to study the Takeda report and to reply. His request was granted, and the date of April 27, 1961, the last day of the benron and of the court, was set for this purpose. When the time came Takahashi argued that Sergeant Takeda's report had not been written on September 19 but sometime after September 21 and that the stamped date of receipt on it was an error. As evidence for this assertion, Takahashi pointed out that the serial number on Takeda's report was 6150 and that the next lowest serial number for a report concerned with the Matsukawa case was 6115, bearing the date stamp of September 26, 1949. Therefore, said Takahashi, the actual date of receipt of Sergeant Takeda's report had to be sometime after September 26.

Monden entered the argument at that point. He, too, had been casting a highly experienced eye on these police reports. He noted that Satō Hajime's age, as reported in the Takeda document of September 19, was different from the age given on Satō's arrest sheet dated September 22. Monden went on to suggest that if Takeda had actually written report 6150 after Satō had been arrested, he would have consulted the arrest record and gotten Satō's age right. He also observed that the serial numbers of police reports were not chronological, citing a Takeda report of an interrogation of Ōta dated October 20 but carrying the serial number 5980. Monden asked the procurator to explain this, but Takahashi, growing noticeably weary, merely reaffirmed his belief that the dates and serial numbers of police reports were correlated and that it was obviously impossible that the date of September 19 could be correct. In effect, he left the issue for Monden to decide.

The last day of court ended with the defense attorneys charging once again that the only evidence in the case against the defendants was their confessions and that these had been manufactured by the police in order to frame trade unionists and members of the Communist party. Judge Monden closed the court and told reporters that he intended to have a verdict by August 8, 1961. Press opinion praised him for what by Japanese standards had been a speedy trial, and legal authorities expressed astonishment at the role of the "new evidence" in the case and at the unusually strong defense presented by the defendants' attorneys.

While the nation waited for Monden's verdict, the Matsukawa movement put on its by now highly professional entr'acte. Beginning in 1959, Hirotsu and the directors of the Counter-measures Council had started to amass the funds and talent to make a feature-length movie about the Matsukawa movement; and on January 27, 1961, they released for nationwide distribution some thirty-six prints of the 35-millimeter version and sixty-seven prints of the 16-millimeter version. Entitled simply *The Matsukawa Case*, this large-scale cinematic undertaking had been financed by ¥9.44 million from Communist China, ¥1 million from North Korea, ¥2 million from the Central Council of Soviet Labor Unions, and ¥38.52 million raised domestically.[11] Although a special committee headed by Hirotsu and Ōta Kaoru, the chairman of Sōhyō, had been formed in February of 1960 to make plans for the film, its members argued among themselves for some seven months about the contents of the scenario, delaying the film's completion until 1961. The filming, once it actually got under way, took only eighty days; conveniently, many of the crowd scenes for the second trial were shot on loca-

11. Matsukawa Undō Shi Hensan Iinkai, ed., *Matsukawa undō zenshi* (Complete History of the Matsukawa Movement) (Tokyo, 1965), pp. 556–559.

tion in front of the Sendai High Court while the fourth trial was in progress.

The movement claimed that during the first ninety days following the film's release some 3.7 million people saw it (including a large captive audience of workers attending union meetings). The Countermeasures Council sent a print to China, where the regime released a Chinese-language version, which was seen by, among many other Chinese viewers, the noted Communist novelist Pa Chin. In its evening edition of May 26, 1962, the *Yomiuri* carried an article entitled "Pa Chin Deeply Moved by Movie 'The Matsukawa Case,' " which told of Pa Chin's recent articles in various Shanghai magazines praising the film's "completely faithful record of this heroic struggle for truth." In Japan, the film did not make a stir comparable to that of Imai's *Darkness at Noon*, but it did receive some comment in various movie magazines.[12] The scenario was built around Akama's confession and the first and second trials, and it made considerable use of documentary techniques, such as photos of the wreck and of newspaper headlines in its titles and throughout its length. Needless to say, the film's dramatic credibility was compromised by its ideological slant and by its portrayal of Akama as an unusually handsome and articulate victim of evil policemen and corrupt procurators.

12. See, e.g., *Eiga hyōron* (Film Review), XVIII:3 (March 1961), pp. 16–20. My comments about the film are based on Matsukawa Geki Eiga Seisaku Iinkai (Matsukawa Film Drama Production Committee), ed., *Matsukawa jiken* (The Matsukawa Case), the eighty-page, mimeographed, final scenario for the film. For the scenario of an earlier, documentary film made by the Council, see "Shinario, 'Matsukawa jiken,' fuirumu ni yoru shōgen" (Scenario, "The Matsukawa Case," Testimony through Film), *Eiga hyōron*, XVI:1 (January 1959), pp. 116–134. Some extremely lurid advertising posters for the 1961 film, as well as an account of its production, are contained in *Matsukawa undō zenshi*, pp. 549–567.

Other activities of the Countermeasures Council during this period were of a more customary kind. In March 1961, one of the defense attorneys attended a meeting of the World Federation of Trade Unions (Communist) in Prague and solicited letters of support from the delegates; in addition to the movement's usual foreign supporters, he signed up two new groups for the letter-writing campaign—the East German Railroad Workers' Union and the International Longshoremen's and Warehousemen's Union of the United States.[13] During early July, 1961, a national convention of Matsukawa activists met to plan activities for the period August 1–8 leading up to the verdict. The convention decided on the format of rallies and marches that had been used in the past and determined that they should be even bigger. It planned two marches, one leaving from Tokyo and the other from Aomori, both scheduled to arrive in Sendai on August 8. At the end of July some four thousand people rallied in the outdoor amphitheatre in Hibiya Park, Tokyo, to send off the Tokyo contingent with cheers and a speech by Hirotsu; and at ten o'clock on the morning of July 27, some two thousand people wearing safari hats or hachimaki to protect their heads from the sun actually began the thirteen-day trek northward. The Tokyo marchers soon divided into two columns, one following the Tōhoku Main Line, led by Abe, Akama, and Kikuchi; and the other paralleling the Jōban rail line, led by Hamazaki, Ōuchi, and Okada. The Aomori march started out with only a modest contingent of sixty Tōhoku activists. However, both marches picked up adherents as they advanced, and on the morning of August 8, the *Asahi* quoted the Sendai police as expecting a contingent of six thousand people from the south and five thousand from the north to converge on the courthouse at around 8:30 A.M. The police requested assistance from all of the Tōhoku prefectures.

13. *Matsukawa undō zenshi*, p. 586.

The movement had employed these so-called big marches during the Supreme Court hearings, but this time public reaction to them was much less tolerant. On the afternoon of August 2, 1961, the Japanese Bar Association (Nihon Bengoshi Rengōkai) met in emergency session and sent extremely strong telegrams to the Supreme Court, the Supreme Procurator's Office, and the Sendai High Court denouncing the "Matsukawa mass march" and other high-pressure activities of the Countermeasures Council. Hirotsu was stung to reply in the *Mainichi* of August 4 that far from causing damage to the legal system, "Our actions are for the purpose of defending the courts from unfair authoritarian influence." The *Asahi* did not agree; its editors supported the demand that the courts be entirely free from any outside pressures. Although Hirotsu did not know it yet, the movement had gone too far, and instead of helping the defendants, it was now actually stimulating strong public support for a prosecution appeal of the forthcoming verdict of the Sendai High Court.

On August 5 the Tōhoku Main Line column of the Tokyo mass march passed through Matsukawa and paused at the site of the wreck. Even though it was raining, Abe made a speech in memory of the railroad workers killed there, and his group placed summer wild flowers on the spot where the train had crashed. The marchers then followed the "Akama route" into Fukushima. The next day the Chinese Communists held a rally in Peking to demand a not-guilty verdict in the Matsukawa case. As August 8 itself finally dawned in Sendai, the plaza in front of the courthouse was a sea of people, flags, emergency telephone lines, and news-service tents. Inside the courtroom some seventy members of the Countermeasures Council filled all of the visitors' seats, having stood in line since 7:30 A.M on August 4 to get them. The *Yomiuri* noted that this was the first time in Japanese court history that people had lined up so early to get into a courtroom. Other newspapers covered the scene with their usual thoroughness, including a long *Asahi* dispatch—surely embellished—on how each of the three judges had spent the fateful night of August 7–8. All was thus in readiness for one of Japan's most important and also most dramatic criminal verdicts.

That evening the headlines all over Japan proclaimed the startling news: Zen'in Muzai ("All not Guilty"). Monden's verdict had not been leaked in advance (as it might well have been, given its length), and although some observers had expected it, many had not. Commentary on the verdict and its meaning went on for days. The lawyer Masaki Hiroshi (of the Yakai case) remarked, "This wonderful result was obtained because of the court-criticism movement and public opinion." Contrary to his view and an opinion that was soon to lead to a major cause célèbre in its own right was the statement of the famous woman novelist Hirabayashi Taiko: "To me this was an unexpected decision. . . . I believe that some of them are guilty. . . . I question whether this verdict was based on the principle of 'no punishment in case of doubt'; it seems rather to have been a result of the pressure on the judges' psyches of the mass march outside." [14] Before very long Matsukawa movement activists would reply to Miss Hirabayashi with a vengeance.

Spokesmen of each political party in the country issued statements on the verdict, ranging from the conservatives' reference to "ideological struggle in the courtrooms" through the democratic socialists' praise for the court's having given the benefit of the doubt to the defendants, to the socialists' applauding the "victory of the masses" and the Communists' contention that it was a "triumph of fairness and truth." The director of the National Police Agency blamed the new Code of Criminal Procedure for having hampered the original investigation, but he seemed willing to write the whole case off as an unfortunate snarl that dated from the era of foreign occupation. Similarly, the Nihon keizai wrote editorially that it hoped the prosecution would

14. Yomiuri shimbun, eve. ed., August 8, 1961.

not appeal; and the *Mainichi* rather optimistically urged the procurators now to bend their efforts to catching the "true criminals." Hirotsu, lapsing somewhat from his usual position that a not-guilty verdict was objectively unavoidable, thanked Judge Monden personally for his courageous action.[15]

There was, however, a great deal of dissent from the verdict. Arai Yutaka, the former chief of the Fukushima National Rural Police and by 1961 a high official of the National Police Agency, angrily called for a prosecution appeal. Similarly, a former attorney general, Satō Tōsuke, felt that the verdict had raised serious doubts about "the health of the Japanese judicial system." Clearly believing that the defendants were guilty, he blamed the not-guilty verdict on the fact that Japan had lost the war. In Satō's opinion the occupation-sponsored Code of Criminal Procedure had weakened Japan's own traditions of judicial investigation and relieved judges of responsibility for determining the facts. He was opposed not so much to Monden's findings as to the fact that the "new evidence" revealed that the first two trials had been hopelessly bungled. He also castigated in no uncertain terms Hirotsu's movement and called for a new "criticism of the courts" movement to reform the American-derived procedures under which the Matsukawa case had been tried.[16] In Fukushima itself, people had spent all of August 8 either watching the Sendai High Court building on television or listening for the news on their transistor radios. A quick series of interviews by the *Asahi* revealed that most citizens of the province where the wreck had occurred found the verdict "unconvincing" (*warikirenai*).[17]

Judge Monden announced his findings at 11:28 A.M., August

15. *Mainichi shimbun*, eve. ed., August 15, 1961. Also see the article "If Mr. Hirotsu Had Not Existed," in *Sankei shimbun*, eve. ed., August 10, 1961.
16. *Tokyo shimbun*, August 9, 1961.
17. *Asahi shimbun*, eve. ed., August 8, 1961.

8, 1961. He then spent the rest of the day reading his extremely long and complex analysis to the reporters and observers who remained in the courtroom. Three generalizations were offered by trained observers who studied the case's fourth decision. First, whereas the Supreme Court had been concerned primarily with the question of the "liaison conspiracies" and had ordered the case retried because it suspected that Satō Hajime had an alibi for at least one of them, Judge Monden concentrated on the actual commission of the sabotage. On the basis of the "new evidence," he concluded that Honda had an alibi and that Takahashi's and Akama's alibis were highly probable. These issues had hardly been raised by either the prosecution or the defense in the course of the retrial.

Second, Monden agreed that Sergeant Takeda's report of September 19, 1949, posed a challenge to the government's assertion that its investigation had been honest, but he refused to write into his verdict the conclusion that the police had framed the defendants. Instead he criticized Takeda's report as the product of a "hypothetical investigation" and the result of "occupational overconfidence." Third, Monden took as his working rule that if doubts were raised about the actual commission of the sabotage, then the issue of conspiracy faded into insignificance; and he decided the case in accordance with the legal principle that "in dubious cases the more liberal constructions are always to be preferred." Most trained observers reading his opinion disagreed on this latter point and concluded that the verdict was based simply on the prosecution's having presented "insufficient evidence" to sustain the charges of either sabotage or conspiracy.

Monden's verdict, which takes up some 244 densely printed pages and one entire issue of Hanrei jihō (Review of Leading Cases), differs from most Japanese verdicts in that it is written in a comparatively easy, accessible style. In fact, the judge was later severely criticized by a Supreme Court justice for having produced a "high posture" (i.e., arrogant) verdict and for having been much too candid in what he had to say in it. Monden began by drawing attention to the importance of the 1,600-plus items of new evidence and explained that he and his colleagues had checked each of these documents against the "old evidence" —that is, the evidence that had been introduced during the first and second trials. The result of this analysis, he said, was that the "present court noted many vital points of disagreement overlooked by both the prosecution and the defense." [18]

His first chapter is entitled, "Concerning Honda's Alibi." Honda had claimed that on the night of August 16, 1949, he had gotten drunk at Takeda's house and had left at about ten-thirty, escorted by Takeda's sister, for the NRWU offices at Fukushima station, where he had slept all night on a cot. According to hitherto unrevealed affidavits, a large number of workers had testified to the truthfulness of Honda's assertions, but the prosecution in the first trial had rejected their evidence in favor of the testimony of one Kimura Yasushi, a night worker on duty at the office, who held that Honda had been there on the night of August 15, not August 16. A careful reading of all of Kimura's statements indicates that the night he saw Honda asleep was, in fact, August 16 and that he changed his story several times, possibly having been induced to do so by the police. The new evidence also revealed that on the morning of August 17 railroad union officials from all over the prefecture had telephoned the NRWU offices in Fukushima, trying to confer with Honda about the wreck, and that they had eventually forced someone to wake him and make him come to the telephone. These revelations were unquestionably the most sensational aspect of the whole verdict, causing the Asahi to write

18. "Matsukawa jiken hanketsu zembun, sashimodoshi ato no dai-ni-shin hanketsu" (Complete Text of the Matsukawa Case Verdict, The Decision of the Second Trial Following the Return of the Case), Hanrei jihō (Review of Leading Cases), No. 275 (November 11, 1961), p. 15.

editorially that if Honda indeed had a solid alibi for the night he was supposed to have led the sabotage party, then Akama's confession was surely worthless.

Monden proceeded in his next two chapters to study the alibis of Takahashi and Akama and concluded that these too held up well. He accepted the veracity of the two statements by Takahashi's wife and Akama's grandmother that both men were in their respective beds while the tracks were being torn up. He also observed that Takahashi's conversation with his landlady on the morning of August 17 about the wreck (which allegedly revealed his criminal knowledge) was probably to be explained by his having listened to the 7:00 A.M. radio news, as he had claimed, rather than by his having been a saboteur: even according to Akama's confession, the saboteurs had not stayed at the scene of the crime to watch the wreck.

With reference to Sergeant Takeda's suspiciously dated report on Akama's confession, Monden concluded that the date stamped on it was correct. Before the police send reports upward to their superiors or to the procurators they habitually list the details of a suspect's age and address as these are given on the arrest record. If Takeda had made the report after Satō's arrest (on September 22), he would have consulted the arrest record and would not have given Satō's age as twenty-one instead of what it actually was, twenty-eight. Monden further noted that, according to Takeda's report, the police had singled out Satō for scrutiny because he was an "outside agitator" and that they were suspicious of Hamazaki because he was "known to be an active member of the Communist Youth League." These police presumptions as to motive were enough evidence for Monden that the police had, in fact, conducted an "investigation based on a hypothesis." He concluded that Takeda's report reflected the "overconfidence" and "bias" of the police and that it virtually destroyed the credibility of Akama's confession.

Concerning Akama's prophecy, Monden merely observed

that "prophecies" are not couched in the past tense. He criticized the defense for failing to investigate Akama's alibi and for neglecting to call as witnesses all of the inhabitants of Akama Mina's house on the night of August 16–17, 1949. Monden made a close textual analysis of all of Akama's confession documents and concluded that Akama had contributed many of the seemingly conclusive details in his confessions only after he had read about them in the newspapers. For example, Akama described the glove that he had allegedly dropped into Nigori Creek only after the police had retrieved the glove from the creek. In making this study of how Akama had remembered new details about the crime several weeks after he had begun to confess, Monden used a special volume of newspaper articles from Fukushima dating from the months following the wreck which the defense had compiled for the retrial in order to demonstrate how government press releases had been biased against the defendants. Monden had not been particularly interested in the old newspaper articles concerning the Yoshida government's comments in Tokyo, but he had been fascinated by the local reporting on the progress of the investigation. He made the defense's volume of newspaper clippings a part of the official record of the trial. With the thoroughness of a person now more fully acquainted with the Matsukawa case than anyone else in the country—including Hirotsu—Monden produced a book-length verdict that touched on every aspect of the case in detail and that provided the foundation for Hirotsu's last and most significant book, *Matsukawa jiken to saiban* (*The Matsukawa Case and Trials*), published by Iwanami in 1964.

Whether Monden's verdict seems persuasive when read a decade later and several thousand miles removed from Japan, it was not read with an open mind by Japanese citizens in 1961. This was for the simple reason that the Matsukawa movement had generated the most intense fears that left-wing coercive tactics, and not the "new evidence," had dictated the verdict. As

soon as the immediate excitement over the decision had sub-
sided, editorialists and opinion leaders began to consider the
pros and cons of a prosecution appeal. One incident above all
others led most newspapers to conclude that the prosecution
should appeal. That was the Hirabayashi Taiko case. Miss
Hirabayashi (b. 1905) was quite well known as a female pioneer
in the genre of proletarian literature and had become by 1961
something of a Japanese Dos Passos. In her youth she had
worked as a telephone operator and as a waitress, and she had
then gone off to Manchuria to lead a Bohemian life. Upon
returning to Tokyo from the Continent, she married the writer
Kobori Jinji and made her literary debut with a short story concerning conditions in a charity hospital, which she published
in *Bungei sensen* (*Literary Front*), a journal of left-wing letters.
Later she went on to win a prize for her work from the *Asahi
shimbun*, and in 1938 she was imprisoned as a member of the
so-called Labor-Farmer Group, a radical faction of the prewar
Communist movement. Following the end of the occupation,
she became considerably more moderate in her political views
than she had been before the war, but she could still claim a
large reading public and considerable political influence.

In the *Asahi* of August 10, 1961, two days after Monden
had delivered his verdict, Hirabayashi contributed an article, sub-
titled "The Freedom of Dissent," in which she expressed her view
that the "intransigent court-criticism movement" had made a fair
verdict impossible. She claimed to have watched television
throughout the day on August 8, and although she did not conclude that Monden had been subverted by the demonstrations,
she thought that an appeal was indicated in order to relieve suspicions that he might have been. On August 12, the editor in
chief of the Tokyo *Asahi* commented that he had hoped that the
Sendai verdict had ended the Matsukawa case once and for all
but that he recognized that Miss Hirabayashi was not alone
among their countrymen in wanting to know what impact the

Countermeasures Council had had on the case. Coming on the heels of the Bar Association's criticism of the big march, these two articles foreshadowed the reaction that had been building up to the movement's tactics.

It was the movement's reaction to Hirabayashi's expressions of doubt that caused all of its efforts to boomerang; the attacks on her virtually guaranteed that every segment of the press would demand a prosecution *jōkoku*. Following publication of her article, Hirabayashi received threatening telephone calls throughout the nighttime hours and numerous poison-pen letters in the mail; and on August 19, her house in Tokyo was attacked with rocks and its walls were defaced. Hirotsu came quickly to her defense, calling the attacks "outrageous," but this did not cause them to stop. In the August 31 issue of *Shin shūkan* (*The New Weekly*), a popular magazine controlled by the big labor federation, Sōhyō, and actually on the newsstands a week before August 31, the editor published a short story that savaged Miss Hirabayashi. The story deals with an oppressed girl hospital-worker who, by an odd coincidence, has the same name as Hirabayashi Taiko. The girl's husband has been unjustly sentenced to death for a waterfront murder he did not commit, and his wife carries on an arduous struggle to have him freed by the courts. She is bolstered in her sacrifices by reading the early works of her namesake, Hirabayashi Taiko, from whom she draws inspiration and whom she worships from afar. The story ends with the girl's suicide by hanging herself on a hill behind the hospital. On the same day that she receives word from the Supreme Court that her husband's appeal has been denied she also reads in the newspapers about how the famous proletarian novelist, Hirabayashi Taiko, wants the prosecution to appeal the Matsukawa case verdict. The author of the short story ends by asking rhetorically, What caused the poor waif's suicide—the hopelessness of her husband's position or the treachery of her idol? We shall never know.

The furor aroused by this story and by the direct attacks on Hirabayashi was tremendous. For example, the president of Rikkyō University damned Sōhyō in the newspapers as "undemocratic"; and the editor of *Shin shūkan* answered in defense that Miss Hirabayashi had to be stopped, as she alone had enough influence to cause the prosecution to appeal. The editor was particularly outraged by a statement Hirabayashi had made that she, as a writer, could tell instinctively that the confessions in the Matsukawa case were at least partly truthful and that some of the defendants were therefore guilty. It did not seem to cross the editor's mind that it was precisely on the basis of such alleged insight possessed by novelists that Hirotsu himself had originally claimed to have divined the defendants' innocence. It is not clear whether Hirabayashi in making her claim was merely needling Hirotsu or whether all Japanese creative writers presume that they can tell whether or not someone else's writing is "sincere."

On September 1, 1961, the Japan P.E.N. Club, whose then current president was the future Nobel laureate Kawabata Yasunari, himself a signer of Hirotsu's 1953 petition in the Matsukawa case, met in emergency session to consider the threat to free speech posed by the attacks on Hirabayashi. Although the writers passed a resolution criticizing the Matsukawa movement and *Shin shūkan* for its activities, events had already bypassed them. On August 22, the prosecution had filed its request with the Supreme Court for a *jōkoku* review of Judge Monden's verdict.[19]

19. An embarrassing episode in my investigation of the Matsukawa case occurred on the evening of June 19, 1968, in Tokyo. I had been invited by the Japanese intellectuals' organization known as the Bunka Fōramu (Japan Cultural Forum) to address it on a subject unrelated to the case. In the course of a small dinner meeting beforehand, I mentioned that I was reading the Matsukawa case records and inquired among the distinguished intellectuals present what they thought of Mr. Hirotsu Kazuo's works and activities on behalf of the defendants. All heads

After the verdict on August 8, the prosecution had until August 22, 1961, in which to make an appeal or to let the decision stand. Throughout this two-week period the Matsukawa movement sponsored "appeal-smashing rallies" in various cities around the country, and delegations of intellectuals called on the minister of justice and the supreme procurator to plead with them not to appeal. It was not these pressures, however, that caused the procurators to delay. Despite the fact that a good deal of public sentiment had built up for an appeal, the prosecution still had to find some basis in law for one, and it finally came up with an approach that was distinctly odd. Rather than appealing primarily on the basis of article 411 of the Code of Criminal Procedure (gross error in fact finding), the prosecution noted that Monden had utilized the mass of documentary evidence that the prosecution had turned over to the court for purposes of determining the facts in the case. The procurators claimed that they had made these documents available solely in order to refute the charges that they had framed the defendants, but that Judge Monden, in his verdict, had admitted these documents as evidence in the case itself using the provisions of article 328, a famous loophole in the new code that allows a court to read *otherwise inadmissible* documentary evidence in order to test the credibility of admissible statements made by the accused or witnesses before the trial or in open court. Assuming a stance closer to the traditions of Anglo-American law than to those of Japanese law, the prosecution now took the "liberal" tack that

turned to the end of the table, and someone with a twinkle in his eye suggested that perhaps Miss Hirabayashi would care to answer that question. Looking at me as if I were a benighted fool, Miss Hirabayashi said softly that Hirotsu was a minor writer whose reputation rested almost entirely on his Matsukawa journalism. I did not realize until at least a year later, when I had read much further into the case materials, what a gaffe my question had been in view of Miss Hirabayashi's presence. For an account of this meeting of the Bunka Fōramu, see *Bunka fōramu nyusu*, No. 118 (July 1968).

in reaching his conclusions Monden had erred in using police documents rather than the direct evidence produced in court, and that it was contrary to the precedents of the Supreme Court and to the law for evidence read under article 328 to be used to determine the facts in a case.

This approach was assuredly more clever than intelligent on the part of the prosecution. Most judicial authorities in Japan had been appalled by the revelations of the "new evidence" in the Matsukawa case, but they did not think that the new evidence should be ruled out of court or that Monden should have ignored it in writing his verdict. Expert commentators on Monden's verdict were most concerned about the fact that the American-inspired Code of Criminal Procedure had caused a twelve-year delay in bringing these materials to light.[20] They were more likely to listen to arguments in favor of modifying the code in a direction away from purely adversary procedures (in order to avoid a repetition of any more "new evidence" scandals) than to support an appeal which contended that under adversary procedures it was not fair for the judges to have based their decision on police records unfavorable to the prosecution. That was precisely the view of the matter that the Supreme Court ultimately took. However, another two years were required in order to have that point established, and even then the Supreme Court was not unanimous.

On October 26, 1961, the Supreme Court set the machinery in motion for a second *jōkoku* hearing of the Matsukawa case. The court's First Petty Bench named Justice Saitō Kitarō to preside over the appeal and assigned Justices Irie, Takagi, and Shimoiizaka to hear it with him. These four jurists then set April 30, 1962, as the date by which the prosecution had to file its brief in support of its appeal. That procuratorial document turned out to be four volumes in length, and because of its size,

20. See, e.g., the comments by Professor Aoyagi Fumio in *Yomiuri shimbun*, August 9, 1961.

the court had to give the defense until November 28, 1962, to deliver its tōbensho, the defense's formal reply to the prosecution's appeal. After both sets of documents had been received, the court scheduled three days for oral argument—February 14–16, 1963—and promised a decision for the fall of 1963. Whatever the reasons for the prosecution's appeal—to defend its own integrity, because it genuinely thought Monden had erred, or because public opinion demanded it—the appeal caused the case to drag on for another two years, almost to the point where the statute of limitations, fifteen years in this case, came into effect.

Undaunted by the appeal and sensing the possibility that the prosecution, by continuing the case, had handed the movement a golden opportunity to humiliate the government once and for all, the Matsukawa Countermeasures Council kept up the pace of its activities throughout the period of appeal. The council itself had continued to grow beyond its prefectural and municipal assemblies set up in 1958 and had organized "Matsukawa defense circles" within numerous enterprises and businesses. For example, the Mamoru Kai (Defense Circle) within the Iwanami Publishing Company became a kind of employees' club, holding regular monthly meetings and fund-raising campaigns throughout this period.[21] Needless to say, the council and Sōhyō continued to sponsor the ever popular on-site inspection trips to Fukushima; and a group of defense attorneys attended the Afro-Asian Lawyers Conference held on October 15, 1962, in Conakry, Guinea, to report on the Matsukawa case.

At its national convention in 1962 the Socialist party for the first time passed a resolution backing the Matsukawa movement, and the Countermeasures Council began to establish cooperative ties with many other Japanese and international leftist groups. The council had become part of the left-wing establishment in Japan, and it now issued declarations opposing the Japanese–South Korean diplomatic negotiations that were getting

21. *Matsukawa undō zenshi*, p. 642.

under way and lent its forces to unrelated labor struggles or local election campaigns. A majority of the defendants, all of whom were out on bail, went to work as staff employees of the council at its offices in the 'Heiwa to Rōdō' Kaikan (Peace and Labor Hall), a building in Shimbashi, Tokyo, that houses numerous ban-the-bomb, trade union, and anti-American front organizations. Even the "sit-ins" that were taking place in the United States during these years had an impact on the movement: some activists proposed that the movement hold sit-ins in Tokyo just before the Supreme Court came in with its verdict, but the council's leaders vetoed this idea as "inappropriate." [22]

With the beginning of oral argument in February 1963 the case once again took over the front pages. The First Petty Bench had to move the hearings to the Grand Bench courtroom within the Supreme Court because of the crowds in attendance. In its tireless search for interviews and other ways to satisfy the reading public's interest in the case, the *Asahi* discovered that Judge Monden was now working as president of the Fukuoka Family Court—a transfer which, although the paper could not prove it, raised suspicions that Monden's bureaucratic superiors had demoted him because of his Matsukawa verdict. Monden gave the *Asahi* an interview, but he was completely circumspect in his answers, saying that he was confident that the Supreme Court would sustain his verdict and that, after Sendai, he was enjoying the flowers and the warmth of the southern island of Kyushu. Still, it seems odd that an experienced criminal court judge should wind up presiding over a family court, handling domestic and juvenile cases. He might, however, have wanted a change and sought the transfer; in Japan one does not ask directly about such things.[23]

The oral argument went over material that was by now completely familiar to thousands of Matsukawa buffs in Japan,

22. Ibid., pp. 685–686.
23. *Asahi shimbun*, eve. ed., February 14, 1963.

but no one, least of all Supreme Court justices, seemed to tire of having the Suwa Memorandum, the tool theft, Akama's prophecy, and all of the other famous details of the case, reexplained to them. At the end of February, after the oral presentations had ended, intellectuals began sending a series of petitions to Justice Saitō's office. One, calling for a "judgment the people can support," was the standard Hirotsu effort and was signed by himself, Shiga Naoya, Satomi Ton, Satō Haruo, Niwa Fumio, and Kawabata Yasunari. But another, saying that "innocent men have been punished long enough," raised eyebrows among Tokyo's cognoscenti. It was signed by some 130 leading figures, including Tanizaki Jun'ichirō, a novelist every bit as famous as Kawabata but one whose dislike of Hirotsu was well known and reciprocated.[24] Other signers of this petition included the prominent novelist Ibuse Masuji, Tokyo University's postwar president Nambara Shigeru, and the prize-winning humorist Tokugawa Musei. This non-council petition implied that members of the "establishment" also wished to see the Matsukawa case ended and that they would no longer be restrained in making their views known because Hirotsu and the leftists had preempted the field.

"Big marches" and noisy demonstrations prepared the way as usual for the fifth verdict, but most people were so accustomed to them by now that they received comparatively little comment in the press. Sugiura gave an interview to the *Asahi* from his hospital bed in Yokohama, where he had lain for five months suffering from palsy and the paralysis of half his body (he later improved greatly). He vowed that he would attend the Supreme Court's delivery of its verdict on September 12, 1963, even if his doctors had to carry him there.

On September 12 itself the First Petty Bench again had to

24. See *Tokyo shimbun*, March 1, 1963; and Itō Sei, "Hirotsu Kazuo no yuki-kata" (Hirotsu Kazuo's Manner of Doing Things), *Gunzō*, December 1968, pp. 178–181, particularly p. 180.

use the Grand Bench room because of the interest in the case. Only Justices Saitō, Irie, and Shimoiizaka attended, Takagi having voted with the majority but retired from the court because of age before the verdict was read. The decision—by a vote of three to one—was "appeal dismissed." This meant that Judge Monden's decision, if not his reasoning for it, had been sustained and that the Matsukawa defendants were finally free men and women. Legalistically speaking, this decision was more interesting than the first Supreme Court verdict because it pitted two of the court's most prominent criminal law specialists in a friendly competition with each other. They were the presiding justice, Saitō, who voted with Irie and Takagi to form the majority, and Shimoiizaka, who dissented.

The majority decision takes up only ten pages of a special Matsukawa issue of *Jurisuto*, to which Saitō added two pages explaining his vote and Shimoiizaka contributed a ninety-four page defense of his dissent. In its formal verdict, the court rejected all the prosecution's various legal bases for its appeal and then reexamined the question whether Monden had made errors in fact finding. The members of the majority wrote that they did not "completely affirm the Sendai High Court's reasoning in finding a verdict of not guilty," but they sustained its decision in the case because they too found that Akama's confession was not trustworthy. They then dissected Akama's confession in detail and found many statements contrary to fact in it, especially Akama's insistence that only two fishplates had been removed. This was a detail the justices thought no actual saboteur would have gotten wrong—fishplates are not easily removed from rails at any time—and they further concluded that an error in the confession about the amount of sabotage accomplished tended to undermine the credibility of statements concerning the time it required, the tools used, and the number of saboteurs who had participated.

In his two-page supplementary opinion, Justice Saitō completely concurred in these findings but said that he wanted to comment on the distressing fact that so many criminal cases had appeared in Japanese courts in which the sole evidence against the accused was his confession. Saitō, who had served before and during the war as the deputy chief of the Judicial Department of the government of Manchukuo, has also written two books on criminal investigation, the most important of them being On the Finding of Facts (Jijitsu nintei ron). In opposition to much legal practice in Japan, he declared that he heartily disliked the confession as a form of evidence and demanded greater attention in the future to investigative processes. Implying that he was not entirely convinced of the defendants' innocence, Saitō wrote that, nonetheless, since the doubtful points contained in the key confession (e.g., the persons attending the "liaison conspiracies," the wrong number of fishplates, the unseen tent, and so forth) could not be explained, there was no alternative but to acquit the defendants. He called for better police work and for procurators to stop leaving it up to judges to resolve obvious inconsistencies in confessions.

Shimoiizaka stood on the opposite side from his colleague. He had voted with the minority in the 1959 Supreme Court decision and his rereading of the evidence had not caused him to change his mind. He held that the confessions concerning the stealing of the tools and the actual tearing up of the tracks were valid and that they had been corroborated by such items as the sighting of five men by the engineer of the train that had passed the scene just before 2:00 A.M., by the tools found at the site, and by the out-of-court remarks of the defendants. He also felt that the crime itself established the existence of a conspiracy, although he acknowledged that the charge of conspiracy against those defendants who did not also participate in the theft or the sabotage had not been proved. He believed that the Supreme Court should have ordered the case retried a second time—indicating both that he thought the defendants could be found guilty and that his real grievance was against Judge Monden's verdict.

The majority decision itself contained some criticism of Monden's use of "exaggerated phraseology" and "improper expressions" in his verdict, and it suggested that the verdict's wording was one reason why the prosecution had appealed. Shimoiizaka, however, went beyond this mild rebuke and castigated Monden in some of the strongest language ever used in a Supreme Court decision. "I find the thought insufferable," he wrote, "that things like the Sendai High Court's verdict can pass through the Supreme Court with a clean bill of health." One of the things that most bothered him was the hint in Monden's verdict that the defendants had been framed. He pointedly observed that the majority decision from which he was dissenting dismissed the appeal on the grounds of "insufficient evidence," and not on what he implied were Monden's grounds of "not guilty by reason of having been framed." In short, Shimoiizaka, who said that he agreed with Saitō's strictures against the overreliance on confessions, admitted that the prosecution had not proved its case. However, he believed that it could have proven it if it had worked harder, and he was infuriated by what he considered Monden's levity and the insinuations in his verdict. The *Asahi* commented that Shimoiizaka's blast at the lower court judge was unprecedented; a group of reporters thought that one reason for the attack might have been Monden's humiliation of the prosecution, something that older judges in Japan are likely to view as a form of lese majesty.[25] In Fukuoka, Monden got the point and seemed quite chastened in his meeting with reporters; he said simply that he would not presume to differ with the conclusion of a justice of the Supreme Court.[26]

The final verdict naturally brought jubilation to the Matsu-

25. *Asahi shimbun*, September 13, 1963. Also see *Asahi shimbun*, eve. ed., September 12, 1963.
26. *Asahi shimbun*, eve. ed., September 12, 1963.

kawa movement. The *Asahi* estimated that some twenty thousand people attended the September 12 "final victory" rally in Hibiya Park, Tokyo, following which youthful members of the movement snake-danced through the district around Shimbashi station. Although the exoneration of all the defendants would seem to have called for an end to the Countermeasures Council, it continued in existence for another year and was then succeeded by a smaller "liaison committee" which functioned for the rest of the decade. Among the tasks remaining to the council were its suit against the government for damages (a task that involved trying to prove that the defendants had been framed and which we shall discuss in the next chapter), the writing of a 938-page history of the Matsukawa movement, and the erection of a monument to the case and the movement at the site of the wreck.

On August 18, 1964, the national delegates convention of the Matsukawa Countermeasures Council decided to disband the organization one month later. In addition to noting that its mission had been accomplished, the council leaders observed that its manpower was now needed for the newly emerging struggles against normalization of relations between Japan and South Korea and against the visits to Japan of United States nuclear submarines. The council sponsored a final rally in Fukushima later that month, at which Sōhyō chairman Ōta Kaoru acknowledged that back in 1949 he too had thought that the defendants were guilty but that Hirotsu's writings had enlightened him. On September 12, 1964, the Matsukawa monument was ceremoniously unveiled in the valley where the wreck had occurred.

Hirotsu remained prominently identified with the Matsukawa case and with popular criticism of the courts until his death on September 21, 1968, at the age of seventy-seven. Whenever he traveled around the country or appeared on speakers' platforms, total strangers would approach him and ask for legal advice or beg him to write an article about their particular lawsuit.

After the Countermeasures Council disbanded and his own sixth and final book on the case had been published, Hirotsu donated his collection of Matsukawa materials and court records to the Library of Modern Japanese Literature (Nihon Kindai Bungaku-kan), where it can be consulted today.

Although Hirotsu suffered from arthritis and spent most of his remaining years living in the seaside resort of Atami, he tried after the close of the case to become interested in other legal battles. For a while he did some reading on the Yakai and Ōme cases (the latter was another Communist train-wrecking incident), but his heart was not in it. Following his death the prominent intellectuals' magazine Gunzō (*Image of the Masses*) devoted part of a special issue to Hirotsu and his accomplishments. Among the writers who paid tribute to him was Matsumoto Seichō, the most widely read author in postwar Japan—a kind of left-wing Erle Stanley Gardner and a figure whom we shall encounter again in the next chapter. With more candor than the other eulogizers, Matsumoto wrote that Hirotsu had been more of a critic than a creative writer. Hirotsu had once told Matsumoto that he found the Matsukawa case intensely interesting because it was "like solving a crossword puzzle," and Matsumoto concluded that Hirotsu's great contribution to the case had been his utterly objective dissections of the first and second trials that had appeared in the mid-1950s. "It may be in bad taste to say so," Matsumoto added, "but Mr. Hirotsu seemed to have been deprived of a great source of pleasure when the trials came to an end." [27]

The trials, however, had not yet come to an end. On August 17, 1964, the statute of limitations on the Matsukawa case foreclosed further prosecution of suspects, but the case could not be closed. The defendants were suing the government in an effort to prove that they had been framed and were therefore entitled

27. Matsumoto Seichō, "Matsukawa saiban no 'tanoshimi'" (The "Enjoyment" of the Matsukawa Trials), Gunzō, December 1968, p. 207.

to several million yen in damages. As part of this suit the plaintiffs charged that the government had known all along who were the "true criminals in the Matsukawa case"—charges that reawakened the interest of the public as well as of post-Hirotsu writers such as Matsumoto Seichō. In addition to these legal maneuvers, however, the case did not die for the simple reason that the Supreme Court's not-guilty verdict had naturally prompted the question, "Well, then, who did do it?"

Chapter 8

The Black Mist

PERHAPS the most common Japanese political metaphor is that of "currents" or "streams." The leading faction of a political party is called the "mainstream faction," while its opponents are said to belong to the "antimainstream" of the party. Similarly, general social trends are thought of as "currents," and movements or opinions that run counter to this "main current" are portrayed as "undercurrents." Another often used metaphor is that of "booms" (*būmu*), or fads. This has been used to describe the tendency in Japan, following the appearance of a mass political culture and the explosive development of mass media of communications, to make public fads out of suddenly popular individuals, or ideas, or behavioral styles—for example, the Beatles, books about sexual permissiveness, the crown princess, "scientific management," Mishima Yukio's rediscovery of patriotism, or the use of tranquilizers. A boom is marked by a flood of publications about the current topic, always including numerous inexpensive books and hundreds of articles in the highly competitive weekly magazines. Often a boom occurs within the "undercurrent" or "antimainstream" and thus has little or no lasting influence as such, but its very appearance as a reaction to or forerunner of the mainstream of social change serves to point the direction in which the main current is moving.

During the early 1960s, the mainstream of social and political policy in Japan was devoted to extremely rapid economic growth; the government was embarked on a program to "double income" (shotoku-baizō) and the public responded with a "consumer revolution" (shōhi-kakumei). Occurring in the midst of this mainstream movement was a phenomenon identified by a group of Japanese scholars interested in popular culture as the "black boom" (kuroi būmu).[1] This countercurrent was revealed by the sudden appearance of a large number of articles and stories purporting to explain various odd crimes and incidents that had occurred during the occupation but that had stopped with the end of the America occupation and of the Korean War. These stories were immensely popular—collections of them constituted the best-selling books in postwar Japan—and they were invariably anti-American. Perhaps their function was to give vent to the ambivalence of many Japanese toward their relations with Americans since the United States had changed almost overnight from being Japan's enemy and occupier to becoming Japan's political tutor and number one trading partner. Possibly they reflected a growing fear that the new prosperity could be lost as a result of Japan's being drawn into the Cold War by its American ally. The popularity of these stories also revealed increased national self-confidence and a desire to pass judgment on the occupation and its achievements.

One man above all others was responsible for the "black boom," the very name of which comes from the word, kuroi

1. Ozaki Hotsuki and Yamada Munemutsu, Sengo seikatsu bunka shi (A History of the Postwar Culture of Daily Life) (Tokyo, 1966), pp. 103–104.

(black), that he used in the title of each of his works published during this period. This man was Matsumoto Seichō (b. 1909). To give merely one indication of Matsumoto's influence, George Packard considers his articles to be part of the cause for the public outcry that erupted during 1960 when it was revealed that U-2 aircraft (called the "black jets") had been operating from bases in Japan. Packard writes:

> [One] reason for the shock in Japan was the then current rash of "exposés" of U.S. intelligence activities in the popular journals. *Bungei shunjū*, for example, was running a serialized version of Matsumoto Seichō's *Dark [Black] Mist Over Japan [Nihon no kuroi kiri]* in twelve monthly installments during 1960 [in addition about fifty-five thousand copies of the book were sold between May and October 1960]. Matsumoto, a popular detective story writer, "solved" a number of mysteries of the occupation era: the murder of President Shimomura [sic; it should, of course, be Shimoyama] of the National Railways Corporation, looting of diamonds confiscated during the war in Japan, derailment of a train at Mitaka, overturning of a locomotive at Matsukawa, and the testing of a deadly poison on Japanese employees of the Imperial Bank to perfect germ warfare techniques. The writer linked all of these crimes and others to a secret U.S. intelligence plot which had as its ultimate purpose the launching of war in Korea. Matsumoto's book was at the top of the best-seller list in May 1960 and he had a wide circle of ardent admirers. It is impossible to understand Japanese reactions to the U-2 without an awareness of these popular suspicions about U.S. intelligence; for many, the U-2 was the only evidence needed to prove all the other tales of horror.[2]

2. George R. Packard, III, *Protest in Tokyo* (Princeton, N.J., 1966), pp. 231–232.

Needless to add, the revelation of the presence of U-2s in Japan and of their activities contributed directly to the Japanese-American Security Treaty crisis of 1960.

Matsumoto has made some very interesting (and profitable) conjectures concerning the Matsukawa case, but before we consider these, it is necessary to know something about their author. He is indeed a writer of "detective stories," but it would be an error to suppose that he is merely a teller of detective stories or that his *kuroi kiri* ("black mist") tales fit easily into that often underestimated genre. Matsumoto's background and political commitments predispose him to write mysteries about particular types of events, and more to the point, he holds to a definite theory of the proper purpose and locale of the detective novel.

Born in the city of Fukuoka in northern Kyushu—the setting for many of his tales—Matsumoto Seichō endured a miserable childhood, marked by family poverty, his father's infidelity to his mother, and an eye ailment that almost blinded him. He received only an elementary education, but he read with the passion of the autodidact while holding down various odd jobs in and around Fukuoka. Today, as one of the wealthiest writers in Japan, he delights in recalling how other writers used to look down on him because of his lack of formal education. He contends that his varied experiences in factories and offices and his lack of ties to the establishment were ideal preparation for his future vocation.

During 1929 Matsumoto was arrested in the roundup of leftists known as the April 16 Incident; he had been identified as a member of a proletarian literary group associated with the Yawata Steel Plant. Prior to his arrest and imprisonment, his favorite reading had been the journals *Bungei sensen* (*Literary Front*) and *Senki* (*Battle Flag*), but the proletarian literary movement seems to have had little influence on him other than arousing his interest in stories about common people. He never wrote "proletarian literature" as such. After his release from prison Matsumoto discovered that his family had decided to protect both themselves and him by destroying his private library; this was at a time when rightists were directing their activities against all forms of "dangerous thoughts." He managed to find part-time work in the advertising department of the Western Main Office of the *Asahi shimbun*, where he was employed steadily as a designer of advertising posters until 1950, except for three months in 1942 and 1943 which he spent in the army, having been drafted and then released because of poor eyesight.

Throughout these years Matsumoto read detective stories, which he had loved since his childhood, particularly those of Edogawa Rampo, who had virtually created the genre in Japan.[3] Matsumoto believes that Rampo's early stories, such as *Nisen dōka* (*The Two-sen Copper Coin*), *Shinri shiken* (*A Psychological Experiment*), and *Imomushi* (*The Green Caterpillar*), were brilliant pieces of social observation, but he senses that the master declined into ero-guro ("the erotic and grotesque"), as prewar mysteries were often called, after he became popular. Matsumoto notes that virtually every writer who followed Rampo copied this later style, whereas he, Matsumoto, had by the post-war period become dissatisfied with stories divorced from the lives of real people or with what he calls "puzzle novels designed for narrow-minded mystery maniacs."[4] Matsumoto therefore took up the pen to write the kind of novels that really intrigued him, and also to try to win one of the several literary prizes that his newspaper offered and that he advertised. By 1950 he was in need of extra money, having by then a wife, four children, and

---

3. Edogawa Rampo's name is, of course, a pun on the names of a ward in Tokyo and of Edgar Allan Poe. His real name is Hirai Tarō. For some of his stories in English translation, see Edogawa Rampo, *Japanese Tales of Mystery and Imagination*, James B. Harris, trans. (Tokyo, 1956).

4. As quoted in Fukuoka Takashi, *Ningen Matsumoto Seichō* (*The Man Matsumoto Seichō*) (Tokyo, 1968), p. 206.

his parents to support, during some of the harshest days of the postwar period.

Matsumoto entered and would have won the 1950 *Shūkan asahi* (*Weekly Asahi*) prize novel contest, except for the fact that he was disqualified as an *Asahi* employee. Nonetheless, the noted detective story writer Kigi Takatarō (the nom de plume of Hayashi Takashi, in real life a famous neurophysiologist and specialist on Pavlovian psychology at Keiō University) praised Matsumoto's work and saw to it that it was published. And in 1952 Matsumoto's second novel, *Aru "Kokura nikki" den* (*Commentary on a "Kokura Diary"*) won what is perhaps the most coveted literary prize in Japan, the Akutagawa Prize. At the age of forty-two Matsumoto had made his debut, and it was a resounding success; he quit his job with the *Asahi* and embarked on one of Japan's most financially rewarding literary careers.

The striking thing about Matsumoto's stories is their realism and penetrating sociological insight, often closer in form to narrative nonfiction than to the novel. Instead of wanting to thrill a reader or make his hair stand on end, Matsumoto has written that he aims "to intrigue him with the forebodings that we all experience in our daily lives." [5] Particularly noteworthy is Matsumoto's knowledge of Japanese bureaucratic organization and style, including the bureaucracy's occasional corruption, and political appointees' exploitation of almost feudally loyal lower officials. He has even published a long series of purportedly nonfiction articles, similar to his *kuroi kiri* stories, under the general title *Gendai kanryō ron* (*On Contemporary Bureaucracy*). One of his great best sellers, *Ten to sen* (*Points and Lines*), which has sold over a million and a quarter copies since its publication in 1957, concerns the murder of a bureaucrat and an innocent waitress—faked by an industrialist, his wife, and their bureaucratic

5. Ibid., p. 207.

allies to make it look like a "love suicide." It immediately caught the imagination of thousands of Tokyoites who were working in precisely the kinds of ministries that Matsumoto described.[6]

As a highly successful popular writer, Matsumoto is not in the least modest about his achievements. In a 1970 interview he compared himself to G. K. Chesterton, H. G. Wells, and Dostoyevsky, and stated that he had written the first Japanese detectives stories to qualify as literature.[7] He is also a political activist. Matsumoto has long been associated with leftist causes in Japan, including support for the election of Communist and Socialist candidates (notably Mr. Minobe, who during the late 1960s became the Socialist governor of Tokyo), and he has made two well-publicized trips to Havana and Hanoi. These activities have inevitably led to charges that he belongs to the Communist party, but he denies them, saying that he respects the Communist party for its incorruptibility, not its doctrines. It is doubtful that Matsumoto holds his political convictions very strongly. He seems more to reflect the shifting opinions of the Tokyo white-collar office workers, whom he understands so well and whose fantasies he chronicles, rather than to be trying to propagandize them. He has written for *Akahata* (the Japanese Communist party organ), *Shakai shimpō* (the Socialist party organ), and *Ushio* (backed by the powerful Buddhist organization Sōka Gakkai), but he has written chiefly for the big mass circulation magazines that pay so well.

In an afterword to his *Nihon no kuroi kiri* (*The Black Mist over Japan*), Matsumoto asserts that he did not write his sensational book because of a preconceived anti-American bias. Instead he claims that he merely sought to understand the numerous mysterious incidents which had occurred during the

6. *Ten to sen* has been translated into English as *Points and Lines* by Makiko Yamamoto and Paul C. Blum (Tokyo and Palo Alto, Calif., 1970).

7. *Japan Times*, November 2, 1970.

occupation, and that he concluded solely on the basis of his investigations that they had all been caused by Americans. In the single-volume edition of the *kuroi kiri* tales, Matsumoto takes up six of these incidents, three of them of some concern to us in this book, namely, the Imperial Bank incident, the Shimoyama case, and the Matsukawa case.

With regard to the fatal poisoning during January 1948 of the employees of a Tokyo branch of the Imperial Bank—a crime for which Hirasawa Sadamichi was convicted and imprisoned—Matsumoto believes that these murders were actually committed by an experimental bacteriological warfare unit of the United States Army attached to SCAP-GHQ. He charges that during the occupation the Americans had set up a secret research installation in Yokohama, where they employed several former officers of the Imperial Japanese Army in order to obtain from them and to perfect the results of wartime Japanese research on chemical and bacteriological weapons. He also says that the weapons developed at this center were later used by the Americans during the Korean War. In his view the bank poisoning was merely a test that was run by the Americans and their Japanese collaborators to see how their latest poison worked. Although Matsumoto is unable to offer even a scrap of evidence for these charges, the importance of this particular article lies in his drawing attention to alleged cooperation between SCAP and former Japanese militarists. In postwar Japan the public had vivid memories of the old and feared Kempeitai (the military police, who played a role in wartime Japan somewhat comparable to that of the Gestapo in Germany or the NKVD in Russia), and many people were prepared to believe the most lurid stories about the military adventurers of the Kwantung Army (who had allegedly been engaged in research on bacteriological warfare). Matsumoto and other writers have repeatedly suggested that many former Kempei members as well as operatives of the Imperial Army's Tokumu Kikan (Special Operations Units, i.e., espionage and clandestine services organizations) were recruited after the war by the Americans to work for the occupation's Counter-Intelligence Corps (CIC) or later for the CIA.

Matsumoto could speculate somewhat more easily on the Shimoyama case, since it has never been fully explained and no one has ever been charged with the crime, if indeed it was a crime and not a suicide. In his study of this case, Matsumoto presents an insightful and more or less accurate analysis of the bureaucratic rivalries that existed within SCAP headquarters, particularly between the Government Section and General Willoughby's G-2, which controlled the occupation's CIC.[8] According to Matsumoto, the Government Section, as the main policy-making body for the democratization of Japan, was oriented toward eliminating rightist tendencies in Japan and was therefore willing to tolerate a strong Communist movement toward this end, whereas G-2 was alarmed by the growing Communist dominance over the trade unions.

Matsumoto asserts that Lieutenant Colonel Donald R. Changnon, director of the Rail Transportation Division of the Civil Transportation Section, SCAP-GHQ, was allied with and backed by G-2 and the CIC in a plot to break the hold of the Communists over the National Railroad Workers' Union, regardless of the violence this would do to policies championed by the Government Section. According to Matsumoto, Shimoyama was too independent for Changnon's liking, and the colonel and the CIC therefore came up with a scheme to replace Shimoyama and at the same time turn public sympathy away from the Communists: they would murder the president of the Japanese National Railroads and blame Communist workers for it. In a later study, Matsumoto offers a detailed reconstruction

8. *Nihon no kuroi kiri* (Tokyo, 1962), pp. 58–72. On factions within SCAP headquarters, cf. Frank Kluckhohn, "Heidelberg to Madrid —The Story of General Willoughby," *The Reporter*, August 19, 1952, pp. 25–30.

of the crime, including the kidnapping of Shimoyama from the Mitsukoshi department store, his death (allegedly by having the blood drained from his body with a large hypodermic syringe injected into his right armpit, which would account for his bloodless corpse), the removal of his body from the Tabata marshaling yard aboard an occupation train, and the final placing of his body on some tracks in northern Tokyo by CIC agents.[9] Matsumoto does not argue that this action was either ordered or approved by senior occupation officials but that it was, instead, plotted and carried out by lowel-level zealots—a kind of military behavior that had occurred often during the 1930s in Japan and that he thought was likely to characterize other armies.

The lower-level officer acting independently of his superiors also provides Matsumoto with an explanation of the Matsukawa case. He believes that it was devised and executed by the CIC detachment in Fukushima, possibly in conjunction with local Japanese officials and perhaps with some CIC operatives brought in from outside the prefecture. The actual saboteurs, according to Matsumoto, were Nisei American soldiers, who traveled from Fukushima to the site down the Rikuu highway in four radio-controlled jeeps. The tools they used, two of which were discarded at the scene, belonged to the United States Army, hence the blaze of khaki colored paint on the crowbar; and the train they chose to sabotage was selected after CIC had been notified of the cancellation of freight number 159, information of this sort being routinely passed on to CIC offices. Matsumoto argues that the CIC officers' motive was to stop the burgeoning growth of the Communists in Fukushima prefecture by discrediting them as terrorists, which was precisely the effect that the Matsukawa case had on local and national opinion.

Surprising as it may seem, distinguished Japanese historians

9. Matsumoto Seichō, "Saisetsu: Shimoyama kokutetsu sōsai bōsatsu ron" (Reexamination: The Murder Theory [of the Death] of JNR President Shimoyama), Gendai, August 1969, pp. 96–116.

have praised these conjectures of Matsumoto's as genuine contributions to an understanding of the occupation period. Ienaga Saburō, for example, wrote in the *Rekishi hyōron* (*History Review*) of September 1961, "It is disgraceful that historians have not produced a contemporary history comparable to *Black Mist over Japan*." Similarly, Hirotsu once encouraged Matsumoto to pursue aspects of the Matsukawa case that he, Hirotsu, was unable to go into because of his commitment to criticism of the trials themselves; and during the 1960s Matsumoto was named a member of the intellectually respectable Association to Study the Shimoyama Case, which included several prominent academics.[10] Matsumoto seems to enjoy being regarded as a "historian," and he is always willing to be interviewed as an expert on the Matsukawa case (such exposure has certainly not hurt sales of his books).[11] When one of his goggle-eyed admirers asked him whether he had been afraid of being assassinated by the CIA after he published his version of the Shimoyama incident, Matsumoto answered (with a "grim smile"), "Well, I may be murdered, but I cannot allow such considerations to distort my conclusions." [12] Nevertheless, Matsumoto has never claimed that his *kuroi kiri* tales were based on anything other than his own *suiri*, or "deductions" (from which comes the phrase *suiri shōsetsu*, or "detective story"),[13] even though he does maintain that sooner or later evidence will turn up to confirm at least his *suiri* concerning the Matsukawa case.

Matsumoto's "black mist" articles are ultimately more sig-

10. Matsumoto Seichō, "Matsukawa saiban no 'tanoshimi' " (The "Enjoyment" of the Matsukawa Trials), *Gunzō*, December 1968, p. 204; and Shimoyama Jiken Kenkyū Kai (Association to Study the Shimoyama Case), ed., *Shiryō Shimoyama jiken* (Documents of the Shimoyama Case) (Tokyo, 1969), p. 620.

11. See, e.g., *Shūkan yomiuri*, August 28, 1970, p. 21.

12. Fukuoka Takashi, op. cit. (n. 4 above), p. 21.

13. Interview with Matsumoto, *Mainichi shimbun*, August 9, 1961.

nificant as part of the popular protest movement on behalf of the Matsukawa defendants than as serious explanations of who actually committed the crime. They did, however, stimulate a great many amateur sleuths to look into the case from his point of view, and they reminded several experts on the case that there has long existed some evidence, probably apocryphal but conceivably genuine, which tends to support Matsumoto's reconstruction of the case. Matsumoto Seichō was certainly not the first person to suggest that a group of Americans had sabotaged the train at Matsukawa; he merely repeated many old rumors in a more polished way and published them at an opportune time.

Uno Kōji, in his *The Strangest Story in the World*, published in 1953 (see chapter five), was the first novelist to report widely on some of this evidence, even though he himself made numerous errors with it and caused some *Asahi* journalists to ridicule him as a result. In his book Uno cited two unusual pieces of information: (1) an anonymous letter, postmarked June 11, 1952, and mailed from Kyōbashi post office in Tokyo to various leftist attorneys, trade union offices, and publications in the city; and (2) some gossip concerning Lieutenant Colonel Changnon. The items are indirectly related.

The anonymous letter has always intrigued specialists on the Matsukawa case because part of its contents can be verified and because, as we shall see later, a similar letter led directly to the breaking of the Kaji Wataru spy case, the most sensational incident involving United States clandestine agents in postwar Japan. The Matsukawa letter of June 1952 was entitled "Murder Will Out," and it was written in faltering *English*, obviously by a Japanese who was not a native speaker of English. Consisting of three poorly typewritten pages, the letter has been published both in its original form and in Japanese translation, together with much commentary and analysis, in numerous works on the Matsukawa case.[14] Here is what it says (except where noted, quotations from the letter are from the English original):

There was a witness [words indistinct; from the Japanese: "who happened to pass"] the scene of the derailment and saw about a dozen of [sic] American soldiers making off rails from the sleepers. When the witness saw it, he wondered what they were doing, but not very much. So he would merely explain away his suspicion by [thinking] that they were inspecting or repairing rails.

Moreover, one Japanese who was in the gang, followed him to his home and when he was just entering the door, called him back in Japanese.

This stranger told him not to tell others what he had seen that night. "You will be tried by the American military court if you do," the stranger warned him. Naturally he could not manage to understand what all this was about. He just said, "I won't."

The next morning he knew. He could not help feeling uneasy about the derailment case, particularly when he read in the newspapers that trade union leaders were made suspects.

Five days later, a stranger called on him and gave him

14. See Shūkan asahi, November 29, 1953; "Matsukawa jiken no 'kuroi kiri' " (The "Black Mist" over the Matsukawa Case), Shūkan asahi, September 27, 1963; Akaiwa Sakae, " 'Kaibunsho' no imi suru mono" (The Significance of the "Mysterious Letters") and text of the Matsukawa letter, Ushio, Vol. II, No. 2 (February 1953), pp. 67–72; Kira Shunri, "Matsukawa jiken: kumei no shin hannin" (The Matsukawa Case: Nine True Criminals), Bungei shunjū, June 1966, pp. 276–287; Matsukawa Jiken Taisaku Kyōgikai (The Matsukawa Case Countermeasures Council), Shin hannin wa dare ka (Who Are the True Criminals?) (Tokyo, n.d., ca. 1959); Uno Kōji, Yo ni mo fushigi na monogatari (The Strangest Story in the World) (Tokyo, 1953), pp. 75–76; and Yoshihara Kōichirō, Matsukawa jiken no shin hannin (The True Criminals of the Matsukawa Case) (Tokyo, 1962), pp. 125–136.

a plan showing the location of the CIC in Fukushima City, telling him, "Come here tomorrow. Someone there wants to talk to you."

This witness was Kinsaku Saito [Saitō Kinsaku] by name, who lived in Shibukawa Mura [a village about a half hour's walk south of Matsukawa station]. His fear increased so that he instinctively felt that he might be jailed. So, he ran away from home and came here to his younger brother in Yokohama, who was a tricycle [i.e., a pedicab] driver. He became a tricycle driver, too.

However, on January 12, 1950, two months after he became a tricycle driver, he became missing. Five days after his disappearance, a policeman [from this point on the photographs of the English text cannot be read easily; the remainder of the letter is, therefore, a retranslation by the author into English from the Japanese translation] discovered his pedicab and, reading the address on its registration certificate, notified Kinsaku's younger brother, Hiroshi. In March, forty days after his elder brother disappeared, Hiroshi received the news that his brother's body had floated to the surface in a canal. Hiroshi and other members of Kinsaku's family went to identify the body, but it had already been cremated. They asked the authorities about the autopsy to determine the cause of death. They were told, "He had no wounds. He was not wearing the glove on his right hand but it was in a pocket in his overcoat. There was alcohol in his stomach. He was wearing a wristwatch, but he had no money on him." It did not appear that he had been attacked by a thief or had been in a serious fight. The police said to them, "Perhaps he was so drunk he fell in the canal and died of a heart attack."

The place where the body was found was very far from the place where the pedicab was found. The autopsy results also seemed too complete in view of the fact that the body was supposed to have been in the water for forty days.

A few days later an unknown man called on Hiroshi and without telling him his name gave him ¥100,000. This man said to him, "You'd better not say anything to others about your elder brother's death."

Hiroshi was a worried man. Someone was pursuing him so he moved from Mori-machi, Isogu Ward, Yokohama, to Nakamura-machi, Minami Ward, in the same city; and later he fled to the country district where he was born [i.e., Shibukawa village, Fukushima]. At present he's still there having disturbed and terrifying dreams every night [end of letter].[15]

There are many unexplained things about this letter, including the fact that it was written in English. However, this much can be confirmed: Saitō Kinsaku was a real person and he did die in Yokohama. His family resided in Shibukawa village, Fukushima prefecture, during 1949 and 1950; and Saitō left a widow and three children living there. Saitō himself was born in 1910 in Fukushima, but before the war he accompanied his parents to Manchuria, where during the 1930s he worked for the South Manchurian Railroad and for the Shōwa steel works at Anshan. After the outbreak of war with China, he ran a laundry in Kirin until he was called up by the army. At the end of the war he was interned by the Soviets in the Voroshilov prisoner-of-war camp until his repatriation in September 1948. It was said by his family that he had become "Communist to the core" while in Russian custody.

Saitō Kinsaku's younger brother, Saitō Hiroshi, had similarly been interned in Siberia, and after his return to Japan, he had worked for a short period of time as a day laborer in

15. The English text and the translation are based on the version of the letter printed in *Shūkan asahi*, November 29, 1953.

Fukushima city. During 1953, Hiroshi gave an interview to the
Asahi in which he stated that his brother had been an enthusiastic Communist and party member. At the time of the Matsukawa wreck his brother had taken a strong interest in the case,
declaring those arrested to be innocent, but both Hiroshi and
Kinsaku's widow were certain that Kinsaku had not observed
either the sabotage or the crash itself. Kinsaku and Hiroshi had
indeed both left Fukushima for Yokohama, where they ran a
pedicab service, but this had occurred on November 17, 1950,
more than a year after the date indicated in the anonymous
letter. Hiroshi last saw Kinsaku on January 12, 1951, when he
rode away in his pedicab carrying a Negro American soldier.
Five or six days later Hiroshi reported his brother missing, and
two weeks after his disappearance his pedicab was found. A
month and a half after that Kinsaku's body, severely decom-
posed, appeared in a canal.

The Asahi also checked with the Yokohama medical ex-
aminer, and he confirmed the details that Hiroshi had reported.
In the doctor's opinion Kinsaku had probably fallen into the
canal while urinating, perhaps while he was drunk, and had
suffered a heart attack from the shock of the cold winter water.
He had not been murdered. Furthermore, his body had not
been cremated before the family identified it, and Saitō Hiroshi
laughed at the suggestion that someone had given him ￥100,000.
Hiroshi had returned to Fukushima after his pedicab business
had failed, but he did not complain of horrible nightmares. In
short, the letter contains several factual errors despite its circumstantial accuracy. Its main point that Kinsaku witnessed Americans sabotaging the tracks at Matsukawa has, of course, never
been confirmed, nor has any person or party ever come forward
and claimed authorship of the letter.

Uno Kōji reported the contents of this anonymous letter
in his influential book on the Matsukawa case, at the same time
saying that it might well be a fabrication by a crank. Uno was,

however, less circumspect in relating various other rumors that he had collected in the course of investigating the case. He told of Lieutenant Colonel Changnon's responsibilities as head of SCAP's Rail Transportation Division and of that officer's alleged difficulties in obtaining the full cooperation of Japanese National Railroads president Shimoyama in carrying out the authorized reduction in railroad personnel. However, Uno went beyond these bits of gossip, which may or may not have been true, and said that Changnon was in fact Colonel Cannon, a man whose name had become notorious in Japan during 1952 and 1953 as the head of an American espionage organization known to Japanese as the Cannon Organization (Kyanon Kikan).[16] This was a sensational charge. If Changnon were in fact Colonel Cannon, he might quite conceivably have masterminded both the Shimoyama and Matsukawa incidents, or at least so Uno implied and many Japanese believed.

As the Asahi established beyond a shadow of a doubt in 1953, Colonel Changnon was assuredly not Cannon, and Uno and all subsequent writers on the case who have perpetuated Uno's speculations have slandered Changnon in suggesting that he was.[17] Mr. Kanematsu Manabu, in 1953 chief of one of the JNR's bureaus and a man who had worked with Changnon during the occupation, flatly repudiated Uno's story, identifying the Changnon-Cannon of Uno's book as Colonel Donald R. Changnon, a pleasant-tempered man who, to the best of his knowledge, had no duties other than trying to get the Japanese railroads back into economically viable operation. The Asahi also asked one of the genuine Colonel Cannon's former agents, Yamada Zenjirō, to look at a picture of Changnon. "He's not Cannon," said Yamada.

Who, then, was Cannon and what relation does he have to the Matsukawa case? Without access to classified American

16. Yo ni mo fushigi na monogatari, p. 78.
17. Shūkan asahi, November 29, 1953.

archives, it is impossible to answer either question definitively, but on the basis of public records it seems highly probable that he was nothing more than the chief of the Kanagawa prefectural CIC unit (an important post because Kanagawa prefecture includes the major city of Yokohama, its capital) and that he had no connection whatsoever with the Matsukawa case. However, he was named during 1952 as the American responsible for the kidnapping and year-long confinement of the famous novelist Kaji Wataru, and as a result of that involvement it has been suggested that he was also responsible for virtually every other incident that occurred during the same period. As late as 1970 a Nisei American, resident in Japan, confessed that he had been a member of a clandestine group led by Cannon that had participated in the Matsukawa sabotage operation.

The Kaji case, in which Colonel Cannon's name figured, has no relationship to the Matsukawa case, but an understanding of it is necessary to an evaluation of the charges that the Americans were also responsible for the Matsukawa case. The kidnapping and subsequent release of Kaji Wataru constitutes the only concrete, verified example available to left-wing writers that American secret operatives were at work in Japan. The very existence of the group that seized Kaji, regardless of the explanations later offered and the eventual outcome of the case, was sufficient to convince many Japanese that Uno Kōji's innuendoes and Matsumoto Seichō's later "deductions" were probably accurate.

Kaji Wataru (b. 1901), whose real name is Seguchi Mitsugi, has twice in his life come to the attention of his fellow countrymen because of his involvement with foreigners: once during the Sino-Japanese War (1937–1945) and once during the Korean War (1950–1953). Kaji, a 1927 graduate of Tokyo University's Literature Department, is a writer and literary critic; his best-known books deal with twentieth-century Chinese culture, notably A Critical Biography of Lu Hsün. In early 1934 he was arrested for violation of the Peace Preservation Law because of his leftist literary pursuits, but he was not brought to trial until November 1935, when he received a two-year prison sentence, suspended for five years. In January 1936, fearing further harassment because of his political views, he went to Shanghai, intending to study Chinese literature. He did not return to Japan until May 1947.

During World War II Kaji became famous as a Japanese who sided with the Chinese Nationalists. Associating himself with such figures of the Chinese revolution as Lu Hsün, Rewi Alley, and Kuo Mo-jo, Kaji retreated in the face of the Japanese invasion to Chungking, where from 1939 until 1944 he headed the Japanese Anti-War League and broadcast Allied propaganda to the Japanese troops. The Kuomintang's right wing, led by Ch'en Li-fu, suspected him of Communist sympathies and curtailed certain of his activities, but he was still working as a "psychological adviser" to the Nationalists as late as November 1944. Because of his wartime resistance to Japanese aggression, he became as celebrated upon his return to Tokyo as Nosaka Sanzō (since 1955 secretary general of the Japanese Communist party), who under the nom de guerre Okano Susumu had spent the war years in Yenan working with Mao Tse-tung.[18]

Between 1947 and 1951, Kaji Wataru lived in Tokyo, freelancing as a political commentator and writing fiction. During late 1951 he dropped out of sight, but no one paid much attention to his then current whereabouts until September 1952. During that month copies of an anonymous, typewritten letter in imperfect English arrived by mail at various newspaper offices (Shūkan asahi published it on November 30, 1952, and again on January 30, 1953) stating that on November 25, 1951, Kaji Wataru had been kidnapped by a colonel of American intelligence and that he was being held even at that moment in American custody. This was a serious charge because, the oc-

18. See the section entitled "Wataru Kaji," in Andrew Roth, Dilemma in Japan (Boston, 1945), pp. 234–242.

cupation having ended on April 28, 1952, the Americans no longer had any right to arrest and detain Japanese in Japan. The letter ended by asking whether Kaji would be released, or would he perhaps meet the same destiny that had befallen JNR president Shimoyama? [19]

This letter was taken seriously because it coincided on several points with a postcard that Kaji's family had received from him in January 1952. Kaji said in his card that he had been seized by a group of foreigners and was being held at a foreign residence in Japan. Shortly after the circulation of the anonymous letter a former Japanese employee of the Yokohama CIC came forward and revealed that he had met Kaji the previous April while Kaji was being held by the United States Army. Finally, on December 7, 1952, the Asahi gave the entire story prominent coverage under a headline which asked: Is THE AMERICAN ARMY HOLDING MR. KAJI UNDER HOUSE ARREST?

After that events moved rapidly. The following day, December 8, the Left-Socialist Diet member Inomata Kōzō rose to interpellate the government spokesman in the Judiciary Committee of the lower house on the whereabouts of Kaji and to ask whether the Asahi's story was true. The government did not know the answer to either question. However, Inomata, an old leftist attorney affiliated with the League of Free Jurists, answered his own questions. On December 7, he said, Kaji Wataru had reappeared at his own home in Tokyo and had asked to be put in contact with Inomata in order to tell his story to a person whom he thought he could trust. Kaji claimed that the United States Army had released him on the evening of December 7, having let him out of a jeep near Meiji Shrine in Tokyo.[20]

19. See text of letter in Japanese translation in Ushio, February 1953, p. 71. Also see the analysis of the letter by Professor Inui Takashi of Hōsei University, pp. 62–66.

20. Inomata gained a great deal of prominence because of his involvement with Kaji. See Inomata Kōzō, Teikō no keifu (A Heritage of

On December 9, Inomata read a statement by Kaji to the Diet, and on December 11 Kaji himself testified before the Judiciary Committee. Kaji's story, in essence, was that on the night of November 25, 1951, more than a year earlier, while he was walking in the fashionable Fujisawa beach resort area of Kanagawa prefecture, a United States Army sedan had pulled up beside him, six men had jumped out and slugged him, and he had then been thrown into the car and driven off. Inside the automobile a Nisei American interpreted for an American officer, variously identified as Major, Lieutenant Colonel, or Colonel J. Y. Canon, or J. Y. Cannon. Cannon's interrogation of him there and later at a CIC villa allegedly concerned whether Kaji was a Communist and a Russian spy. His abductors threatened him, says Kaji, and decided to hold him until he agreed to cooperate. In February of the following year (1952), Kaji told the Diet, Cannon said that he personally was finished with Kaji but that he was turning him over to two colonels, never accurately identified, who wished to discuss another matter with him. According to Kaji, these two new officers tried to sign him up as a double agent working against the Soviet Union; and when he would not agree, they flew him to Okinawa, where he was interned in a mountaintop house. On December 7, Kaji claims, a cable arrived at the Okinawan retreat, and he was quickly loaded aboard a B-17 bomber, flown to Tokyo, and released later that night.[21]

On the day following this sensational Diet testimony, the United States Army's Far East Command (FEC) issued a statement saying that it had arrested and held Kaji briefly in late 1951 because he was a "spy for a foreign power in Japan" but

---

Resistance) (Tokyo, 1964), pp. 61–94 (on Kaji, the Cannon Organization, and the CIA), and pp. 95–144 (on the Shimoyama and Matsukawa cases).

21. *Nippon Times*, December 7–11, 1952. The full text of Kaji's statement before the Diet is printed in the issue of December 11, 1952.

that it had not detained him after the end of the occupation. And at Camp Gordon, Georgia, Lieutenant Colonel J. Y. Cannon, who had until shortly before been attached to FEC Headquarters in Tokyo, flatly denied Kaji's charges in a statement to the press. However, it was not long before some enterprising American journalists began to tumble to what had probably happened. On December 13, 1952, Rutherford Poats, the manager of the United Press agency in Japan, filed a story based on "inside sources" who claimed that Kaji was indeed a Soviet spy, that he had been arrested in 1951 by the CIC with the full knowledge of the Japanese National Rural Police, that several other Communist spies were soon to be arrested on the basis of information that Kaji had revealed, and that Kaji had been turned over to officials of the U.S. Central Intelligence Agency for possible use as a double agent. This CIA involvement in the case had already been revealed by the New York Times on December 11, 1952.[22]

Headlines in the Tokyo dailies of December 14 read: BIG SPY HUNT REPORTED ON IN TOKYO AREA. On that same day the National Rural Police arrested at thirty-nine-year-old man named Mitsuhashi Masao and charged him with violation of the law prohibiting unlicensed radio broadcasts. Two days later Mitsuhashi confessed. He was a repatriated prisoner of war from Siberia and had been trained by the Soviets in radio espionage. He admitted that he had served as a courier and a sender of coded radio messages for a number of Soviet spies operating in Japan, including Kaji Wataru. He had made his transmissions from the Fujisawa beach area of Kanagawa prefecture, and he had narrowly escaped being caught at the time that the Americans arrested Kaji, who had just completed a contact with Mitsuhashi.

This whole episode concerning Kaji Wataru became some-

22. New York Times, December 11, 1952, p. 4; Nippon Times, December 12–13, 1952; I. F. Stone's Weekly, Vol. II, No. 44 (December 6, 1954), pp. 2–3.

what murkier on December 18, 1952, when the U.S. embassy in Tokyo sent an official note, the contents of which have never been made public, to the Japanese government. According to leaks from this three-page communication, Mitsuhashi had been repatriated from the USSR in 1947, landing at Maizuru. There he had been closely interrogated by CIC agents, and he had revealed then that he had been trained to spy for the USSR. The CIC therefore had set him up as a double agent and had released him. About three times a month he had transmitted messages to the Soviet Union and to North Korea, but only after clearing them with the CIC. The Americans' investigation of Kaji, who had been introduced to Mitsuhashi by another Soviet agent, began in April of 1950; and the CIC had hoped to wrap up the Kaji case before the end of the occupation but had been unable to do so. It had, therefore, turned Kaji over to its successor, the CIA. It was embarrassing to the American government, so the embassy's note allegedly says, that neither it nor the Japanese government knew anything about these goings-on. However, according to the embassy, the CIC had obtained considerable information from Kaji, all of which it had passed to the Japanese police; and relations between the American and Japanese counterintelligence services were and remained cordial and cooperative. Finally, the leaks from the American explanatory note also hinted that Kaji had been kept in custody at his own request in order to avoid reprisals from other Soviet agents. In any case, said the Americans, Kaji had lied in his testimony under oath before the Diet.[23]

During 1953 the Japanese government indicted both Kaji and Mitsuhashi for violations during 1951 of the Radiowaves

23. *Nippon Times*, December 14, 16, 17, 18, 19, 20, 21, 24, 1952; and Kyōto Daigaku Bungaku-bu Kokushi Kenkyū-shitsu (National History Research Center, Department of Literature, Kyoto University), *Nihon kindai-shi jiten* (Dictionary of the Modern History of Japan) (Tokyo, 1958), p. 83, s.v. "Kaji Wataru jiken."

Control Law. Both were found guilty, and Mitsuhashi was sentenced to four months in prison. Kaji appealed his case, and after interminable delays (partially caused by Kaji's tuberculosis), on November 25, 1961, the Tokyo District Court found him guilty and sentenced him to two months at hard labor with the sentence suspended for one year. Both Kaji and the prosecution appealed this verdict (the prosecution because of the light sentence), and on June 26, 1969, the Tokyo High Court acquitted him. Kaji always denied his involvement in any spy case. He maintained that the case had been fabricated by United States intelligence authorities to cover up their earlier demands that he act as a spy against the USSR, which he had declined. The High Court, however, reversed his earlier conviction solely on the grounds that the state had not produced sufficient evidence. Whatever the ultimate truth, Kaji Wataru is today a free man.[24]

When it first occurred, the political issue raised by the Kaji case was whether American agents were operating independently in Japan after the peace treaty had come into effect. Over the years since 1952, however, the issue has instead become merely the fact that there were groups such as that one led by Colonel Cannon operating in Japan during the occupation and that an anonymous letter concerning one of their cases proved to be accurate. If Kaji had been taken out of circulation by the CIC working clandestinely, could not the CIC also have engineered the Matsukawa case?

That question weighed most especially on the minds of the Matsukawa defense attorneys now that their own clients had been declared innocent. Not only did the lawyers have a certain interest in seeing that the public regarded their clients as genuinely innocent rather than as the mere beneficiaries of a bungled prosecution and various legal technicalities, but the former defendants and their families stood to make an enormous amount

24. *Japan Times*, June 27, 1969.

of money from the Japanese government as a result of the not-guilty verdict. However, in order to sue the government for sizable damages, the plaintiffs had to prove in civil court that government officials had willfully and maliciously framed them. And in order to do that, it would obviously be of considerable help to be able to demonstrate who had really committed the crime and that the government had known it all along.

On September 12, 1963, the very day that the Supreme Court upheld the Sendai High Court's verdict of not guilty in the Matsukawa case, the defense lawyers launched their own efforts to identify the "true culprits." They had to move fast because only a year remained before the fifteen-year statute of limitations on the crime of train sabotage would prohibit further arrests and because the police expressed not the slightest interest in pursuing the case further. The chief of the Public Safety Department of the Supreme Procuracy said to the press, "The fact that the defendants were declared not guilty does not cause us to go looking for other criminals unless we have some evidence that they exist. We do not have such evidence." But the defense lawyers thought that they, themselves, did—and they made it public. On the evening of September 12, chief defense attorney Okabayashi held a press conference at which time he released still another, hitherto unknown, anonymous letter, which the defense lawyers had been investigating and holding in their files for some five years.

This letter, in Japanese handwriting, was dated November 16, 1958, and was postmarked at the Shōwa post office in Nagoya on November 20, 1958. It was addressed to Matsumoto Yoshiaki, one of the Matsukawa defense lawyers although certainly not one of the better-known ones. Precisely why the letter was sent to him remains a mystery (but one that some sleuths have tried to unravel, as we shall see). The letter was written during the period of the first oral argument of the Matsukawa case before the Supreme Court, and the writer of the letter refers to the testimony given during the third day of oral argument, which had taken place the day before he wrote. There is one other unusual fact about this letter: it carries a return address on the envelope in which it was sent. This address is given as "Aichi prefecture, Nagoya city, Atsuta ward, at Marutaka" (*Aichi-ken Nagoya-shi Atsuta-ku Marutaka de*). Aside from the fact that anonymous letters do not usually carry return addresses, there are two other noteworthy features: (1) Nagoya being one of Japan's largest and best-known cities, residents of Nagoya almost never write the prefecture in which their city is located on return addresses (suggesting that the writer of the letter had not lived in Japan or Nagoya for very long); and (2) there is no district or street called Marutaka in Atsuta ward. This latter fact led to a great deal of investigating by the defense lawyers and later by journalists, with the result that a Marutaka Inn (Marutaka Ryokan) was discovered in Atsuta ward and is presumed to have been the temporary residence of the letter writer.

The key paragraph of the letter itself reads: "The culprits in the Matsukawa case were nine men, the seven of us and two who were from a section in charge of Communists [note that this identification of seven to nine saboteurs came before the testimony of the two former burglars, Hirama and Murakami, during the Sendai retrial in 1960]. The defendants who have been accused were not the criminals, and the fact that they've had to spend ten years in prison for a crime they didn't commit is too bad, particularly since they're Japanese. As a result of consultations among the seven of us and depending on the outcome of the hearings before the Supreme Court, we intend to surrender to the police." [25] Presumably "they" did not do so because the outcome of the Supreme Court and subsequent court sessions was favorable to the defendants.

This letter has been investigated and reinvestigated in-

25. *Asahi shimbun*, September 13, 1963.

numerable times, including interviews with the staff of the Marutaka Inn, tests of the paper on which it was written, analyses of the handwriting and language contained in it, and attempts to correlate its information with other clues to the actual perpetrators of the sabotage. One of the most intriguing items about the letter is the phrase "a section in charge of Communists" (kyōsan-gakari) used in its first sentence. This is an unusual term in standard Japanese, and the Asahi was frankly puzzled by its exact meaning until the newspaper discovered that it was a phrase employed during the occupation by SCAP's CIC to mean "concerned with the Communist party." [26]

The linguistic analysts were divided. One team, made up of an expert from the Scientific Investigation Section of the National Police Agency and a professor of Tokyo Foreign Languages University concluded on the basis of the letter's style and various errors made in writing Japanese characters that the author was a person who had received only a basic education, before or during the war, and was from eastern Japan, but not from Tōhoku. On the other hand the chief of the Regional Dialects Research Office of the National Language Research Institute observed that despite many linguistic oddities in the letter, it contains words that are commonly used in the district around Nihonmatsu city, Fukushima prefecture. The prominent detective story writer (and the Japanese translator of Mrs. Shelley's Frankenstein) Takagi Akimitsu contributed an interesting theory. He believes that the letter was written by the true criminals and that, because of the author's several references to himself and to the Matsukawa defendants as "being Japanese," the letter writer was probably a rightist and a demobilized serv-

26. Ibid.; Shūkan asahi, September 27, 1963; and Kira Shunri, in Bungei shunjū, June 1966, p. 287. A former employee of SCAP's CIC has informed me that the phrase kyōsan-gakari was used during the occupation to mean "officer or section in charge of Communists," just as rōso-gakari meant "officer or section in charge of trade unions."

iceman, perhaps one of the late returnees from the Siberian prisoner-of-war camps. He thought that the wreck was probably engineered by a group of former soldiers.[27] As we shall see, Takagi may very well have come closer to the mark than any other investigator or analyst.

At the time of the publication of this letter, the prosecution dismissed it out of hand as pure publicity-seeking by the defense lawyers. However, the defense attorneys persisted in their investigation and issued reports on March 7 and on August 1, 1964, concerning the letter and on their research conducted after its publication. The report of August 1, the most comprehensive one issued, contains two theories about the identity of the true criminals, both theories perhaps being related.[28] One theory is that the wreck was plotted and executed by the United States Army's CIC detachment in Fukushima city; the other is that the actual saboteurs were male members of the Japan Girls' Opera Troupe (Nihon Shōjo Kageki Dan), that had performed at the small, rundown theater called the Shōgaku-za near Matsukawa station on the night of August 16, 1949. The defense attorneys implied in their report that either or both parties could have been the real criminals and that the police had never thoroughly investigated either, particularly the revue troupe, because the authorities suspected that such an investigation would destroy their case against the Communist workers.[29]

In the section of the report dealing with possible American involvement in the case, the defense lawyers submit some new

27. Shūkan Asahi, September 27, 1963.
28. Matsukawa Undō Shi Hensan Iinkai (The Committee to Compile the History of the Matsukawa Movement), ed., Matsukawa undō zenshi (Complete History of the Matsukawa Movement) (Tokyo, 1965), pp. 745, 750–752.
29. Matsukawa Jiken Bengodan Jōnin Sewa Kai (The Matsukawa Case Defense Attorneys' Standing Aid Association), Shin hannin tsuikyū no tame ni (In Order to Catch the True Criminals) (n.p., n.d. [August 1, 1964]), mimeo.

evidence. They reprint a statement given to them shortly before the Sendai High Court's verdict in 1961, by a Mr. Nagazawa Shigemi, who was at the time of the Matsukawa incident the editor in chief of the important Fukushima newspaper, *Fukushima mimpō* (*Fukushima Citizens' News*), and who during 1963 was editor of the *Shin Ibaraki taimusu* (*New Ibaraki Prefecture Times*). Nagazawa had participated in one of the 1961 on-site inspections organized by the Countermeasures Council, and comments he had made at that time brought him to the attention of the defense lawyers.

According to his written statement (known as the Nagazawa Report), he had been in a good position as editor of the *Fukushima mimpō* to know and communicate with the police, the CIC, and the political and economic establishment of Fukushima at the time of the wreck. He had, for example, been acquainted with the Japanese translators who worked for the United States Army's military government team and for CIC in Fukushima city. Nagazawa heard enough to convince himself that American officers and local conservatives, who knew each other well and spent a good deal of time together at the local hot springs for which Fukushima is famous, plotted the Matsukawa incident in order to break the hold of the Communist party on the economy of the prefecture. Among the local conservatives named by Nagazawa was the owner of the *Fukushima mimpō*, who was also chairman of the Fukushima Public Safety Commission—that is, the police commission set up in accordance with SCAP's police reform measures. He also lists various police and procuracy officials and the JNR prefectural superintendent as part of this Japanese-American conspiracy of civic leaders. Nagazawa thinks that the Americans themselves did not carry out the sabotage but knew of and acquiesced in the local leaders' arranging to have it done.

Whom the plotters got to cause an incident that could be blamed on the Communists leads to the second half of the defense attorneys' report, namely, the part concerning the Girls' Opera Troupe. Information about the presence and performance of this theatrical company in Matsukawa on the evening of the wreck appears in the very earliest press reports on the case, but almost no hard information on its members and their backgrounds has ever been published. The police claimed to have investigated the troupe, as they did virtually every other person in the area, but silence about the results of that investigation has reigned ever since. Matsukawa is an odd place for a one-night stand by any kind of outside theatrical group, and during 1949 the only explanation for its presence was that the troupe expected a fair audience because of the Bon festival. Who, precisely, made up this band of performers and where had they disappeared to on August 17, 1949?

Not much is known. It seems as though this song-and-dance company had performed widely during World War II in Korea and Manchuria and that its owners had developed close contacts with former officers of the Japanese army and, after the war, probably based on these old associations, with the CIC. Nagazawa and another writer on the case, Kira Shunri, have offered highly circumstantial evidence connecting the impressario of the revue troupe to the president of the Tōhoku Dock Company and characterizing that man as a regular user of the Marutaka Inn on his visits to Nagoya.[30] The *Asahi* discovered the coincidental fact that the Marutaka was occasionally used by the Nagoya police for banquets and celebrations of major police achievements.

A rough hypothetical reconstruction of the case based on the defense's information would run as follows: The Americans in Fukushima and the local conservative establishment, some of whom were former military officers, plotted an incident in the summer of 1949 in order to discredit the Communist party.

30. Ibid., and Kira, *Bungei shunjū*, June 1966, pp. 276–287.

In one way or another these men arranged for seven to nine other, nonlocal men, probably demobilized soldiers belonging to the Japan Girls' Opera Troupe, to carry out the sabotage, possibly with the assistance of one or two Nisei American soldiers attached to the Fukushima CIC detachment. After committing the crime the troupe hastily left Matsukawa and dispersed. The police, who were in on the plot all along, did not investigate the opera troupe but instead framed twenty innocent Communist party workers, including the trade union leaders who had been creating trouble in Fukushima with their demonstrations and strikes at Taira and other places. The actual saboteurs were seen in the vicinity of the wreck site by two burglars, who had accurately counted nine of them; and the letter from the Marutaka Inn, which also mentions nine saboteurs, was from the true criminals. Presumably the authors of the 1958 letter were feeling pangs of guilt about letting a group of innocent men go to the gallows almost ten years after the crime, but they abandoned their idea of confessing when the court's decision went in favor of the defendants. They sent their letter to attorney Matsumoto only because he had been prominently featured in the *Chū-nichi shimbun* of Nagoya, not because of any earlier involvement of his with the CIC, as one other writer has alleged.[31] The true criminals' choice of meeting (or reunion) place at the Marutaka, their use of CIC terms such as *kyōsan-gakari*, and their chauvinistic remarks about Japanese were all consistent with their army backgrounds and the influence of their sponsors during 1949.

There is not one shred of hard evidence to support this theory, although during the late 1960s it was the one that the Matsukawa defense attorneys and individuals directly connected with the old Matsukawa Countermeasures Council most commonly advanced. Even editor Nagazawa's charges against his

31. Kira Shunri, op. cit., pp. 280, 283–286.

former employer and associates in Fukushima are backed only by stories of how the *Fukushima mimpō* seemed to have an inside track to the police department and the procuracy in reporting the first Matsukawa trial and other criminal cases—none of which is very surprising in view of the fact that the newspaper's publisher was also chairman of the police commission. The only strength of this hypothesis lies in its relatively consistent allegation of motive to those whom it accuses—namely, a desire to cripple the Communists by involving them in a criminal case; but this motive does not seem as strong as the one attributed to the Communists themselves, namely, a desire to retaliate against the Dodge line. Moreover, the Communists had already been involved in enough violent disturbances so that anti-Communist forces might have been expected to wait for the Communists to leave themselves open to arrest rather than fabricate a case against them. Nevertheless, the Matsukawa case remains unsolved, and the circumstantial evidence and anonymous letters which surround it will continue to recommend the defense's reconstruction to many Japanese.

As we noted earlier, the attempt to find the "true culprits" also figures importantly in the defense's attempts to sue the government for damages on behalf of the now-cleared Matsukawa defendants. During the occupation the Americans had completely renovated Japan's laws concerning the liability of the state in cases of official error or illegal acts committed by public officials. The old Meiji Constitution provided for state redress in case of official error, but the principle that the state could be held liable for illegal acts by its agents did not exist. Even when redress for error was in order, the old Criminal Indemnity Law (Law Number 60 of 1931) only allowed a person acquitted after arrest or detention to petition, not sue, the government; and it did not state when indemnity should be paid. The American drafters of the Japanese Constitution of 1947 separated these two contingencies—possible error by the state and possible damages suffered because of illegal acts by officials—and wrote articles into the constitution to cover each of them.

Article 40 of the 1947 constitution deals with error: "Any person, in case he is acquitted after he has been arrested or detained, may sue the State for redress as provided by law." In order to implement this provision (in addition to completely rewriting the Civil Code), the Diet passed the Criminal Indemnity Law (Law Number 1 of 1950, also known in some texts as the Criminal Compensation Law). This law provided that "indemnity could be denied, in whole or in part, where the court in its discretion found that the person caused himself to be subject to criminal procedure, as by making a false confession, or if the person was guilty of part of the offenses with which he was charged." [32] However, the state has rarely contested cases in which false arrest and confinement have occurred, thus assuming an absolute liability, and it pays compensation at the rate of so many yen per day, as fixed by a court, for each day of wrongful detention. In the Matsukawa case the Sendai High Court heard the plaintiffs' requests for compensation under this particular law immediately following the Supreme Court's September 12, 1963, decision. On December 23, the court set the rate of ¥400 per day and ordered almost ¥16 million paid to the remaining seventeen former defendants (the three defendants released by the second court had already received their compensation some seven years earlier).

In addition to providing for criminal indemnity, where the question of intention or negligence on the part of the state is never the issue, the Constitution of 1947 also makes the state liable for "illegal acts" committed by officials. Article 17 of the constitution reads: "Every person may sue for redress as provided by law from the State or a public entity, in case he has

32. SCAP Monograph No. 14, "Legal and Judicial Reform," p. 59. Italics added.

suffered damage through illegal act of any public official." To implement this article, the Diet enacted the State Redress Law (Law Number 125 of 1947, also known in some texts as the National Compensation Law). Because under this law the right of recovery is based specifically on the illegal act of a public official (or, alternatively, on such things as defects in the construction of public installations), both the Criminal Indemnity Law and the State Redress Law provide that filing a claim under one does not preclude filing under the other. Needless to say, however, the state does not recognize any absolute liability under the latter law, and the plaintiff must prove the existence of "bad faith or grievous error" (*koi mata wa jūdai na kashitsu*) (State Redress Law, article 1, clause 2) in civil court.

On May 19, 1964, some thirty-seven former defendants and members of their immediate families filed suit in Tokyo District Court charging that they had been arrested as a result of a political plot, that the authorities had suppressed evidence in their cases, and that they had been tortured in the course of the investigation. For the mental and physical damages that had been caused them, they asked the state for a whopping ¥209,184,703 and a formal apology signed by the minister of justice to be published in newspapers throughout the country. It was one of the largest suits ever brought against the Japanese government, and its eventual settlement at about one third of the original request was the first "public safety case" ("public safety" is a euphemism in Japanese legal circles for a case concerning political activities or rights) in which the courts recognized the obligation of the state to pay compensation. Litigation over this suit did not come to an end until August 1, 1970.

The Matsukawa compensation suit outraged the government. The Litigation Bureau (Shōmu-kyoku) of the Ministry of Justice took the position that the plaintiffs had been "investigated and indicted as criminal suspects. The fact that they were ultimately judged not guilty does not mean that the investigating authorities had acted illegally." It also expressed the strongest opposition to having police and procurators brought into a civil courtroom as witnesses, particularly in view of the fact that several of the public officials involved in the case in 1949 were, by 1964, very prominent figures indeed.

On January 27, 1965, the litigants came together for the first time in the courtroom of Judge Shiraishi Kenzō and two other assistant judges of Department 33 (civil) of the Tokyo District Court. The thirty-seven plaintiffs were represented by some eleven attorneys (different from the criminal law specialists who had defended them until then); and five officials, headed by the vice-chief of the Litigation Bureau, represented the minister of justice. This was a preparatory session in which the court was trying to decide what, precisely, were the contested issues and how they were to be investigated. The government fought a losing battle against allowing the plaintiffs to raise the question of frame-up. Preparatory meetings were also held on March 26, May 14, and June 7, resulting in a decision by Judge Shiraishi and his associates to reconstitute themselves as a "special tribunal" that would conduct a trial, beginning on July 9, 1965, to determine the truth of the plaintiffs' charges. The court divided the case into four elements for purposes of conducting this inquiry—the nature of the official investigation of the crime, the indictments and trials, the voluntariness of the confessions, and the political background at the time of the incident—and it ordered some 141 policemen, procurators, and other witnesses to appear before it, including Mr. Arai Yutaka, who had headed the Fukushima police in 1949 and who by 1965 was head of the National Police Agency.

The taking of testimony got under way during July 1965, but only a month later, during August, possibly because of Tokyo's notorious summer heat, Judge Shiraishi took the whole court on the last official on-site inspection of the Matsukawa case. The three judges plus a staff of six court clerks, three

former defendants (Akama, Suzuki, and Hamazaki), some thirteen lawyers for the plaintiffs, and six attorneys for the government made the trip to Fukushima. There they visited the
Fukushima District Court, the procuracy, and the Fukushima
and Hobara police stations. The Communist party newspaper
Akahata, with its characteristic prejudgment of the findings in
any court case, on August 17, 1965, ran headlines describing these
visits as A LOOK AT PLACES WHERE EVIDENCE WAS SUPPRESSED.

Perhaps inspired by the example of Judge Monden, Judge
Shiraishi also decided to inspect the scene of the wreck at night.
Thus from 9:30 P.M. on August 16 until 6:00 A.M., August 17,
a total of about sixty people, guided by the former defendants in
accordance with the "Akama confession," made the twenty-nine-
kilometer walk to and from Matsukawa. The *Asahi* of the following day carried a picture taken at 1:40 A.M. of Judge Shiraishi,
wearing glasses and white cotton gloves, using a crowbar to pull
up a railroad spike. The judge commented to the press that because of the electrification of the Tōhoku Main Line, it was
getting much harder to carry out a faithful Matsukawa on-site
inspection than it had been during earlier years. On August 20,
the court moved on to Sendai to view Miyagi Prison and then
returned to Tokyo. During April 1966, Judge Shiraishi again took
his special tribunal to Fukushima, where he heard testimony from
local railroad workers on social conditions at the time of the
wreck.[33]

During September 1965, in Tokyo, National Police Agency
chief Arai testified for the first time. He put all responsibility
(as well as blame) for the conduct of the investigation onto
Fukushima Criminal Affairs Bureau head Honda. However, he
was called again during December to explain why, if he had not
been primarily responsible for the investigation, he had taken

33. *Asahi shimbun*, August 17, 1965; *Akahata*, August 17, 1965;
Asahi shimbun, April 22, 1966, eve. ed.

credit for breaking the case in the National Rural Police booklet
A Study of the Matsukawa Case, published in 1953 (see chapter
four). This line of questioning proved most embarrassing to the
then head of the National Police Agency, but Arai continued
to disclaim any credit even though he had written the preface to
the official, classified police report describing how the investigators had solved the crime. The defense played up this pamphlet
as "a government manual for framing Communists," and the
government itself would clearly have been much happier had the
defense never obtained a copy of this study.[34]

During the course of the long compensation trial, the government sustained major damage to its position on two fronts.
First was the testimony of Satō Tadao, former chief of the
Fukushima Municipal Police. He told the court that the plans
for the first series of arrests (Suzuki and six others) were formulated at a meeting of the investigation's leaders, held on
September 20, 1949, at the Fukushima police station. They based
their decision to proceed with arrests on Sergeant Takeda's report of September 19, which described Akama's initial confession
and identified the Tōshiba saboteurs as Satō Hajime and Hamazaki. Takeda himself later contradicted Police Chief Satō's testimony, but the impression had been strongly communicated to
the court that Takeda's report, containing the names of Satō and
Hamazaki even before Akama had ever uttered them, had been
dated September 19. That had, of course, been the defense's
contention in its final argument before the Sendai High Court a
few years earlier.

The second blow to the state's insistence that it had conducted a strictly legal investigation and indictment was even more
damaging than the testimony that Sergeant Takeda had indeed

34. *Nihon keizai shimbun*, September 6, 1965, eve. ed.; *Nihon
keizai shimbun*, September 7, 1965; *Akahata*, September 8, 1965; *Akahata*,
December 15, 1965; *Matsukawa tsūshin*, No. 146 (September 18, 1968),
p. 4.

embellished Akama's confession. Saitō Yuki, a former member of the executive committee of the NRWU branch and one of the defendants freed by the second court when the judges rejected the state's theory of an August 13, 1949, conspiracy meeting, charged that the procurators had known from the moment they began to investigate him that he possessed an airtight alibi for August 13. Saitō had spent the entire day at the Kōriyama police station, trying to obtain the release of the executive committee's vice-chairman, who had been arrested on August 12. He had been accompanied on his trip to Kōriyama by a fellow railroad worker, Shishido Kinichi; and the chief procurator in the first trial, Mr. Yamamoto, had personally taken a deposition from Shishido that sustained Saitō's alibi. More important, Saitō further charged that the visitors' log book of the Kōriyama police station would show that he had made four visits to the police station on the day in question. During the second trial both the chief of the Kōriyama police and procurator Yamamoto had denied that Saitō had been in Kōriyama on August 13, but they were unable to produce the police station's visitors' log because it had mysteriously disappeared. The second trial threw out the charges of an August 13 conspiracy not because Saitō had established his alibi but because a representative of Tōshiba had testified that Satō Hajime had been in Matsukawa all day.

During the retrial of 1960 and 1961, in the course of trying to find out whether the Suwa Memorandum had been intentionally suppressed, the defense attorneys heard about a group of documents, known as the keisatsu bunsho ("police documents"), that had been impounded by the procurators but that had not been included in the mass of materials turned over to the court by chief procurator Takahashi. During the compensation trial, the defense asked the court to subpoena these documents, and they turned out to include the long-missing Kōriyama Police Station Visitors' Log. Presumably procurator Takahashi had not delivered it to the court in 1961 because Saitō had long since been acquitted by the second court, and the issue in which the log figured had become moot. The log was, however, quite relevant to the issues being contested in the compensation trial. The Kōriyama visitors' log did indeed record Saitō as a caller at the police station on August 13, and it therefore became the last of a long series of items of evidence, including the extra fish-plates, the Suwa memo, and Sergeant Takeda's September 19 report, that the police and procurators appeared inexplicably to have mislaid or suppressed.[35]

On April 23, 1969, Judge Shiraishi and his colleagues delivered their decision, which was quite complicated and full of legal hair-splitting. Shiraishi explained that in the final Supreme Court decision of 1963, presiding justice Saitō had upheld the not-guilty verdict because "the evidence was insufficient" (shōmei fujūbun ni yoru muzai); he had not found that the Matsukawa case was "a case that should never have been prosecuted" (kiso-subekarazarishi jiken). However, that latter question was intrinsic to the plaintiffs' civil suit; therefore Shiraishi and his associates had completely reinvestigated that aspect of the case. Their conclusion was that the prosecution had committed "grave errors" amounting to an illegality within the sense of the State Redress Law, but the judges refrained from finding the state guilty of "bad faith." Specifically, Shiraishi concluded that Akama's confession was a false and fictitious document, that the prosecution should have seen to it that the Suwa Memorandum and the Kōriyama visitors' log were admitted into evidence, and that on various occasions during the second trial the "procurators deceived the court." For these delicts he ordered the state to pay the plaintiffs ¥76,259,833 (ca. $211,555), but he rejected the

35. Matsukawa tsūshin, No. 146 (September 18, 1968); Matsu-kawa tsūshin, No. 147 (April 15, 1969); and Matsukawa Jiken Zenkoku Renraku Kaigi (Matsukawa Case National Liaison Council), Matsukawa jiken kokka baishō saiban (The Matsukawa Case State Compensation Trial) (Tokyo, n.d., ca. 1967), pp. 16–17.

plaintiffs' demand that the state publish an official apology, saying that the case and their acquittal had already been sufficiently publicized.[36]

Although there were no precedents for a settlement of this size, the newspapers generally applauded it as fair. Still the case did not end. The prosecution decided to appeal Shiraishi's decision to the Tokyo High Court. Virtually no public spokesman supported this action, particularly in view of the fact that three of the plaintiffs had died during the course of the long compensation trial (one former defendant, Ōta Shōji, in 1967 in a factory fire in Fukushima, and relatives of Kikuchi and of Katō), but the prosecution went ahead anyway. Finally, on August 1, 1970, Judge Nakanishi Hikojirō of the Tokyo High Court upheld the district court's decision with only minor modifications (he reduced one claim by ¥1,938, or slightly more than $5).[37]

The reexamination of the whole case in civil court thus resulted in a decision closer to Judge Monden's in the retrial than to that of the Supreme Court in the case's final criminal verdict. Although the state was not explicitly found to have knowingly constructed a false case against innocent citizens, the compensation trials strongly implied that the original investigators had been blindly biased against the individuals they arrested. In an editorial the Asahi pointed out that this conclusion had some public significance: government officials, through their "grievous errors," had allowed the true criminals responsible for a train derailment to go unpunished.[38]

36. Matsukawa Jiken Zenkoku Renraku Kaigi, Matsukawa jiken kokka baishō saiban hanketsubun (Text of the Decision in the Matsukawa Case State Compensation Trial) (n.p., n.d. [1969]); Mainichi shimbun, April 24, 1969; Japan Times, April 24, 1969; Sankei shimbun, April 24, 1969; Asahi shimbun, April 24, 1969; Asahi shimbun, editorial, April 25, 1969.

37. Matsukawa nyūsu, No. 4 (October 20, 1969), mimeo; Japan Times, August 2, 1970; Asahi shimbun, August 2, 1970 (brief of decision).

38. Asahi shimbun, April 25, 1969.

It is conceivable that Matsumoto Seichō (and his predecessors and copiers) have correctly identified the true culprits, although neither he nor like-minded analysts have ever produced a plausible motive for the Americans' engineering or executing the crime. Only by positing insubordinate American officers who clearly exceeded their authority and their orders are Matsumoto and company able to lay blame where their politics dictate. However, there is one element of believability in the fanciful left-wing explanations of the case, namely, their conclusion that the Matsukawa incident was a skirmish in the Cold War. In one sense the Matsukawa case was obviously an outgrowth of the Cold War: the Dodge line and the decision to promote Japan's rapid economic recovery were both dictated in part by the United States' perceptions of the Chinese revolution and of the Soviet Union's international ambitions. If the Matsukawa incident was a Communist-inspired backlash against these American policies, as the police who investigated the case assumed, then it can certainly be considered an indirect outgrowth of the Cold War era of world politics.

However, Matsumoto Seichō believes that the Matsukawa case was part of the Cold War in the direct sense—that is, in the sense that its perpetrators were actual representatives of one of the two Great Power protagonists of the Cold War. If one accepts, as the courts have held, that domestic Japanese workers acting primarily from economic motives did not commit the crime, then Matsumoto's hypothesis of foreign inspiration becomes at least worth considering, given the social and political environment in which the incident took place. There is, however, one line of speculation that Matsumoto and other left-wing writers have always ignored, namely, the possibility that the true criminals were agents of the *other* main Cold War protagonist, the Soviet Union.

At this late stage in this study of the Matsukawa case, I trust that I might be allowed to contribute my own *suiri* (reasoning, or deduction) concerning the true criminals, one that I acknowledge has no greater basis in fact than Matsumoto Seichō's. If one assumes that the twenty individuals charged with the crime were literally innocent—that the police did not frame the guilty parties (a possibility that neither I nor many other observers would rule out entirely)—then it is conceivable that either American or Soviet agents committed the crime. The case against the Americans has already been presented. The case against the Russians would run somewhat as follows.

By 1949 Stalin had turned the entire international Communist movement against the United States and its allies and had set it to work consolidating or further expanding the Soviet empire that had emerged from World War II. Parts of the international movement were independent of his control, particularly the Chinese and Yugoslav movements, but the evidence for this independence in the Chinese case was not believed at the time because Chinese and Soviet interests were then running along parallel lines. One exception to this general global picture in 1949 was the Japanese Communist party. Because of the special political environment in which it had to operate—a country under American military occupation—Moscow allowed the Japanese party to pursue policies considerably less militant than it ordered for its other clients. However, by 1949 Stalin was beginning to conclude that more could be gained, internationally, by using the Japanese Communist party to disrupt American policies in Japan than by allowing it to continue its efforts to win a parliamentary majority through legitimate political processes. During January 1950 Stalin altered his position on the Japanese party and ordered Communists in Japan to launch militant attacks against the United States.

During 1949, immediately prior to Stalin's decision to put the Japanese Communist party itself to work on sabotage and other violent activities (even though it meant liquidating the party's hard-earned postwar reputation for incorruptibility and vigorous trade union leadership), it seems likely that he might have ordered disruptive operations carried out in Japan by other agents under Moscow's control. Stalin's motive would have been to make the Americans' effort to turn around their basic policy for the occupation as difficult and as protracted as possible and perhaps so to inflame the inevitable popular displeasure with economic retrenchment as to produce insurrections. What agents did he have at his disposal?

Other than the Communist party, there was only one significant group: the prisoners of war that the Soviets had captured in their 1945 invasion of Manchuria and North Korea, many of whom were still being held in Siberian internment camps. Mitsuhashi Masao, who had allegedly sent messages illegally to the USSR for Kaji Wataru, was one of them already back in Japan; Saitō Kinsaku, the pedicab driver who allegedly witnessed the sabotage at Matsukawa, was another. All Japanese prisoners of the Soviet Union were subjected to the most vigorous Communist indoctrination, and those who were allowed to return to Japan the soonest were the ones who had shown the strongest "progressive tendencies" in the camps.[39] A very considerable number of them joined the Japanese Communist party. It will be recalled (chapter two) that on June 27, 1949, one of the largest contingents of Soviet prisoners, some two thousand strong, arrived at Maizuru, every one of them "saturated in red doctrine," as the press at the time put it. If the Soviets had taken the trouble two years earlier to train Mitsuhashi in radio espionage, it does not seem unlikely that they had also trained in sabotage operations some of those who came home during the summer of 1949. Many Japanese prisoners in Siberia were from Tōhoku, and

39. The most complete study of the repatriation of Soviet prisoners-of-war and of the problems that they posed for the occupation is U.S. Department of the Army, *Reports of General MacArthur, MacArthur in Japan, The Occupation: Military Phase* (Washington, 1966), pp. 179–193, particularly "Soviet Indoctrination of PW's," pp. 187–191.

the Communist party regularly included in its appeals to the citizens of the northeast reminders that support for the party was one way to bring their men home sooner. Some of these returnees might have been responsible, six weeks after their arrival in Japan, for carrying out the Matsukawa sabotage. This is, of course, pure speculation. It is derived from considerations of motive, timing, and examples of the known activities of some Siberian returnees. It has one other distinguishing feature, and that is that none of the leftist writers in Japan who have made careers out of speculating about the Matsukawa case has ever speculated along these lines.

The "black mist" surrounding the Matsukawa case seems also to have had its effect on certain mentally unstable or highly suggestible individuals in Japan. Almost every year, on the August anniversary of the Matsukawa case, someone comes forward to confess that he is a former CIA agent who was responsible for one or another bizarre crime, or that he actually participated in the sabotage at Matsukawa. During 1969 it was a Mr. Matsumoto Masaki, who claimed that he had started on his nefarious work as one of Cannon's agents in Yokohama. The press reported what he had to say, but it also added that after the police had investigated his story, Mr. Tsuchida Kuniyasu, director of the criminal affairs bureau of the Metropolitan Police Department, advanced him ¥30,000 because he was broke and recommended that he receive treatment at a mental hospital.[40]

Similarly, during 1970, a man named Nakajima Tatsujirō published an article in which he told of being trained before the war in Harbin as a secret agent for the Kwantung Army. After the surrender he allegedly went to Taiwan, where he was recruited by the U.S. Office of Strategic Services. He reports that on August 14, 1949, he arrived by ship at Sasebo from Taiwan. He then journeyed to Tokyo by train accompanied by a Nisei

40. *Japan Times*, August 15–16, 1969.

agent of the CIC, and on August 16, together with four Japanese and two Nisei, he boarded an airplane at Tachikawa. The seven of them flew to Sendai, gathered at the Sendai CIC office, drove to Matsukawa, and sabotaged the tracks of the Tōhoku Main Line until about 3:00 A.M. on August 17. In response to this published confession, Takahashi Shōhachi (the procurator in the retrial), Sugiura Saburō (head of the former defendants' association), and Matsumoto Seichō all denounced it as a probable phoney. Matsumoto particularly derided Nakajima's claims that his associates were from the Cannon Organization. By 1970 Matsumoto had concluded that the Cannon Organization worked only in the Yokohama–Tokyo area and would not, in any case, have been involved in a Fukushima operation. Matsumoto and the others concluded that Nakajima had been too deeply influenced by Matsumoto's *Black Mist over Japan*. No one in an official position took the slightest interest in the confession.[41]

Although there is no continuing governmental effort to solve the Matsukawa case, the statute of limitations having long been in effect, the families of the three men killed, as well as the Japanese man-in-the-street who lived through the postwar era, would still like to know who did it. Many different individuals have tried their hands at solving the case, but none of the offered solutions, some more satisfying than others, is backed up by genuine evidence. It seems likely that the only persons who really know who committed the Matsukawa crime are the ones who actually carried it out. It is even possible that one or more among that group are reading this book in English, in the United States, at this very moment—no doubt with smiles on their faces.

Until he or they—Japanese, American, or Russian—should choose to tell us about it, Matsumoto Seichō has made the

41. *Tokyo shimbun*, August 12, 1970; *Asahi geinō*, August 20, 1970; "Nakajima Tatsujirō to iu otoko no shōtai" (The True Character of the Man Named Nakajima Tatsujirō), *Shūkan yomiuri*, August 28, 1970.

greatest contribution to their true identity merely by his invention of the phrase *kuroi kiri*. For indeed the "black mist" continues to hang over the otherwise sunny, green valley north of Matsukawa station in Fukushima prefecture.

Chapter 9

Plus Ça Change

SOCIAL and political change in postwar Japan—or, more narrowly, the degree to which the "democratizing" objectives of the American occupation have been attained—are intensely controversial subjects, both within the country as matters of public policy and among independent observers who seek a factual understanding of Japanese society. No one doubts that during the twenty-five years since World War II Japan's economy has been transformed. During the late 1940s Japan was a smashed and beaten country; during 1970 foreign commentators were writing books about the "emerging Japanese superstate" and predicting that by the end of the century Japan would have become the richest nation in the world.[1] Even with regard to the economy, however, many thoughtful Japanese are concerned about the alliance between big government and big

1. See, e.g., Herman Kahn, *The Emerging Japanese Superstate* (Englewood Cliffs, N.J., 1970); and Robert Guillain, *The Japanese Challenge* (Philadelphia and New York, 1970).

business that has brought about this growth, and they wonder whether the nation's great assets are or will continue to be used for democratically determined goals. Thus, while no one questions that changes of a revolutionary magnitude have occurred, a controversy exists concerning the nature, depth, and rate of these changes. The Matsukawa case, which was before the courts throughout Japan's postwar transformation (1949–1970), offers a platform from which to explore some important aspects of this controversy.

At first glance the Matsukawa case seems to provide evidence for the view that nothing very much, other than per capita productivity, has changed. Take, for example, the National Railroads, still Japan's largest single enterprise. During 1949 SCAP and the Yoshida government faced the problem of making the railroads economically viable and ordered the firing of a hundred thousand employees in order to ease conditions of featherbedding. In some localities the workers resorted to sabotage in retaliation against these layoffs, reflecting in part the primitive collective bargaining situation that existed at the time, the newness of the railroad workers' union, the dispersal of the industry (making picketing ineffective), the lack of labor solidarity, and the political motives of some trade union leaders. During 1970 all of these problems, with the exception of sabotage, were still quite familiar to Japanese newspaper readers. The Japanese National Railroads (JNR) were still in the red, management was still talking about firing some thirty thousand excess workers, and the unions were still plotting the formation of "people's councils" in order to defend their jobs.[2]

However, the similarity between the two situations is only superficial. In 1949 Japanese referred to their railroad system as a kōtsū jigoku ("transportation hell"): trains were dangerously

2. See Japan Times, February 18, 1970; July 5, 1970 (editorial); September 11, 1970 (editorial); and New York Times, June 21, 1970, p. 78.

overcrowded, their equipment was antiquated, and union troubles made them proverbially unreliable. Twenty years later Japan was operating one of the finest rail systems in the world, including the 120-mile-an-hour Tōkaidō Express linking Tokyo with Osaka, with plans well under way for a 150-mile-an-hour train which would connect Fukuoka in the southwest with Hokkaido in the northeast. Moreover, these state-of-the-art trains were an economic success: in the six years between 1964, when the Tōkaidō Express went into service, and 1970, the streamliners carried some 250 million passengers and accounted for 30 percent of the passenger revenue on the JNR system. The problem in 1970 was not technical ability or consumer demand but the fact that the original network of rail lines, laid out before 1931, had been designed to meet the political objective of opening up rural areas rather than the economic objective of optimal efficiency. By 1970 many of these rural lines could no longer be justified on either political or economic grounds, but political opposition to shutting them down was intense. The unions also faced the ubiquitous problem of new equipment—a universal fear of all organized labor—but they no longer had to resort to machine-breaking or sabotage: unionism and the ability to bring effective collective pressure to bear on management were a well-established part of the Japanese economy. SCAP's reforms of 1949 had helped to make the JNR a going concern, but an entirely different kind of reform was required in 1970 in order to keep it going.

Similarly, in the legal field, cases were occurring twenty years after the Matsukawa case that might cause some individuals to think that reform of criminal procedure had been superficial. There was, for example, the so-called ¥300 million theft case of 1968–1969. On December 10, 1968, a lone robber held up a bank's armored van that was being used to deliver almost ¥300 million in workers' year-end bonuses to a factory in western Tokyo. A year later the police still had no clue to the culprit, and the press, particularly the *Asahi*, was needling the Metropolitan Police Board mercilessly for having spent on the fruitless investigation almost as much as had been stolen. The robbery was the largest in Japan's criminal annals, and no doubt the police overreacted to the pressure put on them by the press. On December 12, 1969, detectives arrested a twenty-six-year-old man, a chauffeur for the Tokyo office of the Canadian Wheat Board, on the sole evidence that he lived in the vicinity of the spot where the robbery had taken place, could not establish his alibi for Friday, December 10, 1968, and had allegedly said to friends of his that he wanted to do "something big to make an impact on the world." Characteristically, the police did not initially charge him with the robbery but arrested him for the crime of "intimidation" (several months before the robbery he had allegedly threatened his landlady with an iron pipe during the course of an argument). The police then proceeded to question him, hoping to obtain a confession concerning the robbery.

When this arrest was first announced, the press was jubilant. Helicopters hovered over the arrested man's house in Fuchū, Tokyo, taking pictures; reporters hounded his neighbors, asking about his criminal tendencies; and the police released to the newspapers some of the most absurd circumstantial evidence ever recorded (e.g., the fact that he was a subscriber to the *Asahi shimbun*, one of the nation's largest newspapers, when there was some evidence that the robber also read it). In the midst of all this, the suspect suddenly recalled where he had been on that Friday in question, more than a year earlier. He had been in downtown Tokyo taking an English test in connection with a new driving job. Unfortunately he had not passed the test, nor could he remember either the name or the location of the company. The police, disinclined to believe this alibi, continued to question him, until the personnel manager of the company that had considered hiring him came forward and established the alibi beyond all doubt. The press of December 14 carried big pictures showing the police inspector in charge of the case releasing the suspect and apologizing with a downcast face; and the *Asahi*, not reflecting for several weeks that it had helped to bring about this sorry affair, excoriated the police for resorting to their old methods of arrest on one charge followed by a prolonged interrogation in order to obtain a confession to a more serious crime. No doubt people like Akama Katsumi also thought that the incident had a familiar ring.[3]

What does the ¥300 million robbery case indicate about the reform of police procedure and the protection of civil rights in postwar Japan? Superficially it suggests that nothing had changed; the police in 1969 were still conducting investigations in ways that the reformers had tried to eliminate twenty years earlier. However, such a conclusion ignores the complexities of social change, which is more a process that goes on within people's minds than a condition that can be perceived merely by comparing similar cases at different points in time. In 1949 people still expected the police to seek confessions from suspects without alibis, and the new Code of Criminal Procedure had only barely come into effect in an effort to bring about a change in police and judicial methods. In 1969, under intense public pressure for quick results, the police clearly reverted to older practices, as they themselves later acknowledged and as the press and the public loudly deplored. No one in the country thought that police and criminal procedures had not changed at all under the influence of the Constitution of 1947 and the revised Code of Criminal Procedure, but opinion was divided over what this relapse by the police meant and how well the postwar criminal-law system was working.

Generally speaking, American legal reformers during the occupation and American legal specialists twenty years later have expressed themselves as quite satisfied with the reforms under-

3. *Asahi shimbun*, December 10, 1969 (editorial); December 14, 1969 (editorial); *Japan Times*, December 11, 13, 14, 16, 19, 1969.

taken and the way they have worked in practice. During the summer of 1949, in the same month that the Matsukawa incident occurred, Alfred Oppler, chief of SCAP's Legal Section, wrote, "Judges, public procurators, and lawyers are daily faced with problems of law for the solution of which no precedent exists. Nevertheless, the impression prevails that their adjustment to the changes will be smoother and more rapid than anticipated by those who expected an almost chaotic confusion."[4] Twenty years later American commentators on the Japanese Constitution and the legislation derived from it were saying the same thing and criticizing Japan's court critics for failing to see the great strengths of the new system despite its manifest conservatism.[5] Of course, these observers are aware that the Matsukawa case and several other mistrials like it constitute anomalies in their picture of otherwise successful reform, but they overcome this problem simply by making no mention whatsoever of them.

On the other hand, many Japanese legal observers on both the left and right are dissatisfied. Some believe that SCAP went too far in its reforms while others think that SCAP did not go far enough. For example, Professor Aoyagi Fumio of Sophia University blames the state's bungling of the Matsukawa case almost entirely on the new Code of Criminal Procedure and argues that the reformers made a mistake in completely abolishing the old pretrial judicial investigation.[6] On the other hand, Professor

---

4. "The Reform of Japan's Legal and Judicial System under Allied Occupation," *Washington Law Review*, XXIV:3 (August 1949), 323.

5. See, e.g., John M. Maki, *Court and Constitution in Japan* (Seattle, 1964); and Dan Fenno Henderson, ed., *The Constitution of Japan, Its First Twenty Years, 1947–1967* (Seattle, 1968).

6. " 'Hirotsu hyōketsu' no kentō" (Examination of the "Hirotsu Verdict"), *Jurisuto*, Special Issue, September 1959, pp. 80–124; and "Matsukawa jiken zakkan" (Miscellaneous Impressions of the Matsukawa Case), *Jurisuto*, No. 284 (October 15, 1963), pp. 20–22. Also see *Yomiuri shimbun*, August 9, 1961.

Ushiomi Toshitaka of Tokyo University applauds SCAP's efforts to democratize the prewar judicial system but concludes that the reforms were undercut by the failure to purge prewar judges. Referring to the demythification of the emperor, Ushiomi writes, "Although the Emperor declared publicly that he was only an ordinary mortal, the judges made no such change at all." [7] Even the Supreme Court wrote thirteen years after the Code of Criminal Procedure had come into effect that it had "not met our expectation." [8]

In my opinion and in light of the Matsukawa case, neither the uncritically sanguine nor the highly critical position can stand unchallenged. On several points the American reforms were hopelessly out of tune with Japanese preferences and social requirements, and attempts to implement them contributed to some of the mistrials, such as the Matsukawa case, that occurred under the new code. On several other points, however, the new code worked better than the old one in obtaining justice for Japanese citizens. After all, it must be remembered that the Matsukawa case had three victims, not twenty-three, as might have been true had the police and the procuracy had their way. In order to understand what has changed in Japanese criminal procedure since SCAP undertook its reform, let us look briefly at four specific problems: reliance on confessions, length of trials, procuratorial prejudgment, and the "rebureaucratization" of the judiciary. The pattern of development in each of these areas suggests that more desired change has occurred than most Japanese observers are willing to believe and less than most American commentators believe, and that some change has taken an unintended and unanticipated direction.

The single greatest problem of postwar criminal procedure in Japan is that of confession. Regardless of article 38(3) of

7. *Hōritsuka* (The Jurists) (Tokyo, 1970), p. 58.
8. Supreme Court of Japan, *Outline of Criminal Justice in Japan* (Tokyo, 1963), p. 45.

the constitution ("No person shall be convicted or punished in cases where the only proof against him is his own confession"), the confession issue runs like a litany through the overwhelming majority of criminal cases that have come before the courts, and it invariably has been the focus of dispute in those sensational cases where the defendants have recanted their confessions. The Matsukawa case is merely the best-known example. False confessions elicited by the police also formed the central problem of the Yakai case (see chapter six), where the police and procurators apparently realized early in their investigation that all but one of the confessions they had obtained were false but where they preferred to sacrifice four innocent men rather than admit their mistake. Bound by the bureaucratic "principle of unity among procurators" (*kensatsukan ittai no gensoku*), no investigator dared to reveal what they all knew, thereby driving the case through seven trials (including three *jōkoku* hearings before the Supreme Court) and eighteen years (1951–1968) of litigation.[9] Similarly, one could simply list the most important criminal cases of postwar Japan: the Hachijōtō case, the Nihō case, the Sachiura case, the Mitaka case, and the Futamata case. Each one involved a false, coerced, or contested confession, and each required between eight and fifteen years to reach a settlement.[10]

The tendency of Japanese police and procurators to rely on confessions derives from many sources, including Continental procedures, Japanese values, and the bureaucratization of the prewar state. The best justification for SCAP's decision to alter the formal basis of Japanese criminal procedure from the Continental to the Anglo-American tradition was the need to make

9. Masaki Hiroshi, *Yakai saiban* (The Yakai Trials) (Tokyo, 1969), pp. 33, 169.

10. Ueda Seikichi and Gotō Shōjirō, *Ayamatta saiban* (Mistrials) (Tokyo, 1960); *Asahi shimbun*, September 13, 1963; December 14, 1967; July 31, 1970 (eve. ed.); August 1, 1970 (editorial); and *Japan Times*, August 1, 1970.

the practice of obtaining confessions more difficult and to prevent its misuse. Even so, it must be said that here is an area in which American reforms probably did not go far enough. The Americans seem not to have appreciated how deeply rooted the practice was in Japan nor to have understood that basic values of a people could not be changed merely by writing a prohibition into a constitution.

For example, it is apparent that Mr. Oppler and his associates did not anticipate the ease with which certain older Supreme Court justices would try to get around the constitutional prohibitions against coerced confessions. In a dissenting opinion to a 1951 murder case Supreme Court Justices Sawada and Iwamatsu blandly wrote: "[I]n cases like the present one the [trial] court must, of course, follow up the allegation that the confession of the accused at the police station was given under compulsion or torture, but it is not required that the results of such inquiry be set forth. In other words, when [the trial court] pronounces a judgment of guilty in circumstances like these, if it has decided that the confession was made under compulsion or torture, then it does not use the confession as material for its finding of fact." [11] Professor Maki prefaces this decision in his collection of Supreme Court cases with a notable understatement: "This decision is of interest because of the light it sheds on certain police methods and because of the minority opinions, which reveal the thinking of some of the justices on the nature of evidence and on the function of the courts." [12] We shall return to this question of the thinking of some Supreme Court justices and how it has changed over time.

Another problem that has come up repeatedly in Japan and that the SCAP reforms did not anticipate is some clear understanding of what constitutes a coerced confession. Japanese com-

11. In Maki, *Court and Constitution in Japan: Selected Supreme Court Decisions, 1948–1960*, p. 202.
12. Ibid., p. 191.

mentators have sometimes referred for guidance to the United States Supreme Court's decision in the Ashcraft case (1943), in which Justice Jackson, joined by Roberts and Frankfurter, dissented to a verdict which held that interrogating a suspect for thirty-six hours was "inherently coercive." [13] Jackson wrote: "It probably is the normal instinct to deny and conceal any shameful or guilty act. Even a 'voluntary confession' is not likely to be the product of the same motives with which one may volunteer information that does not incriminate or concern him. . . . 'Voluntary confessions' in criminal law are the product of calculations of a different order, and usually proceed from a belief that further denial is useless and perhaps prejudicial. To speak of any confessions of crime made after arrest as being 'voluntary' or 'uncoerced' is somewhat inaccurate, although traditional." [14] In Japan, where the police and procurators can hold a man for up to twenty-three days without charging him, it is unclear precisely what ought to be their policy with regard to interrogations, and the American precedents, either the decisions or the dissents, only indicate the size of the problem, not how to solve it.

Although confessions still predominate in all Japanese criminal trials, the situation has improved with the passage of time. For example, on July 24, 1970, the Tokyo District Court acquitted a man charged with murder in a case in which the sole evidence offered by the prosecution was his confession. The defense demonstrated that the accused had the I.Q. of an eight-year-old child and that his confession was so well written that it had clearly been elicited from him by the police and written by someone else. In the early 1950s, when the new Code of Criminal Procedure had only recently come into being, such a case might easily have gone on for a decade before an acquittal was obtained.

13. See, e.g., Kainō Michitaka, Hōritsu (The Law) (Tokyo, 1957), p. 83.

14. E. E. Ashcraft v. State of Tennessee, 322 U.S. 143 (1943), 160–161.

Certainly no trial court of the first instance would have over-ruled the procurators' indictment.[15]

It is extremely unlikely that mistrials such as the Matsukawa and Yakai cases could occur in Japan today, more than two decades after the promulgation of the new code. There now exists a number of legal precedents as well as a great deal of judicial experience in dealing with such "confession cases." How-ever, the occurrence of several bungled prosecutions and mistrials such as Matsukawa may have been extremely useful. Although the Americans in SCAP's Legal Section hoped that the transition to the new procedures would go smoothly, nothing has a greater educative effect on the public and through it on the judiciary than an unfair trial. As Thurmond Arnold has observed:

> [T]he cultural value of the ideal of a fair trial is advanced as much by its failure as it is by its success. Any violation of the symbol of a ceremonial trial rouses persons who would be left unmoved by an ordinary nonceremonial injustice [vide the two Zolas]. . . . [For example,] harmless an-archists may be shot by the police in a strike. Liberals will be sorry and forget. But let them be unfairly treated by a court, as happened in the Mooney case [a 1916 anarchist bombing in San Francisco in which the accused was con-victed on the basis of perjured testimony], and, before the dissatisfaction has died away, the prejudice or phobia which created the unfair atmosphere of the trial will receive a public analysis and examination which otherwise it would not get.[16]

How much more true this is when the ideal of a fair trial itself is being implanted within a society in accordance with a

15. Japan Times, July 25, 1970.
16. "The Criminal Trial," in Herbert Jacob, ed., Law, Politics, and the Federal Courts (Boston, 1967), p. 34.

highly publicized program of reform. The Matsukawa case, through the activities of Hirotsu and the Matsukawa movement on behalf of the defendants, probably caused more Japanese to think about the administration of justice in their country than a thousand successful prosecutions would have. The result is that in contemporary Japan, while confessions are still more honored in the criminal courts than they are in either England or the United States, it is increasingly rare for a false or coerced confession to lead to an individual's conviction.

The Japanese judiciary took fourteen years to produce a definitive decision on the criminal charges arising from the Matsukawa case and another seven years to decide whether the former defendants deserved compensation from the state. Article 37(1) of the Constitution of 1947 guarantees that "in all criminal cases the accused shall enjoy the right to a speedy and public trial by an impartial tribunal," but in fact Japanese trials—all of them—are anything but "speedy." The Matsukawa case does not even come close to being Japan's longest trial; and considering that it involved five hearings, two of them before the Supreme Court, Matsukawa was actually a comparatively rapidly settled case.

The longest trial in Japan, the May Day Riot case of 1952, took seventeen years and nine months for just the first instance hearing before the Tokyo District Court. One judge, Hamaguchi Seirokurō, spent virtually his entire postwar career presiding over the eighteen hundred courtroom sessions that this one trial required. Of course, the case had some 214 defendants, and they were charged with the crime of riot (Penal Code, art. 106), a notoriously difficult prosecution requiring that the state prove the existence of "a common will among the rioters" and that there was "disturbance of the peace." A similar 1952 riot case in Nagoya was before the first instance court for sixteen years before it returned a verdict of guilty. Since the first verdicts in both of these riot cases were handed down only during 1969 and 1970, if either side chooses to appeal, the cases may well continue until all the defendants have died.[17]

The extraordinary length of most Japanese trials is relevant to the question of change because it indicates just how little prepared the Japanese judiciary actually was to put SCAP's new laws and codes into practice, the optimism of the Legal Section and article 37(1) of the constitution notwithstanding. Among the various reasons for excessive trial length, former Chief Justice Tanaka has listed the following:

> a general lack of familiarity with the new system of law and its administration; a general unfamiliarity with the basic concept of the rule of law; a still underdeveloped sense of proper procedure in the courtroom; a certain inexpertness in the preparation of cases by attorneys, especially the older ones who began their careers under the prewar system; a tendency on the part of some judges in the lower courts not to make clear decisions in cases that they assume will end in appeal to the Supreme Court; and an obvious willingness on the part of the defense attorneys to discover and to take full advantage of any possible constitutional pretext as the basis of an appeal.[18]

Long trials are not a good thing, and SCAP's attempt to guarantee speed was entirely justified. Most of the defendants in the May Day Riot case, for example, were unable either to find work or to marry during the seventeen years that their case was before the court even though they were out on bail. In fact, as the Matsukawa case illustrates, it is entirely possible for the state through the prolonged trial to punish with prison terms those individuals whom it indicts even though they may ultimately be

17. *Japan Times*, November 12, 1969; January 22, 1970; *New York Times*, January 29, 1970.
18. Maki, *Court and Constitution*, p. xxx.

acquitted. Nevertheless, SCAP did not seriously consider the likelihood that its sweeping reforms would produce such long trials, and it made no effort to spell out what constituted a "speedy" conclusion. Article 37(1) came into conflict with the numerous other safeguards for the rights of the accused written into the constitution, and therefore it usually gave way.

Twenty years after promulgation of the Code of Criminal Procedure, trials have become shorter for the simple reason that procurators, judges, and attorneys have gained a much greater familiarity with the law. For example, in the Tokyo University Auditorium case of January 1969, in which the police arrested hundreds of riotous students, the procurators brought charges of "obstructing performance of official duty" (Penal Code, art. 95) and of "trespassing" (Penal Code, art. 130) rather than of "riot" because they had learned that it was much easier to obtain evidence for the former offenses. Within a year after the incident most of the accused had been found guilty and had been sentenced. Similarly, from among the thousands of radical students arrested in the Shinjuku Incident of 1968, the procurators indicted only twenty-one ringleaders and charged them with instigating a riot, which carries a potential punishment of up to ten years imprisonment at forced labor. This was much more effective than holding a mass trial for several hundred defendants, as had been attempted in 1952.

Postwar Japanese trials have never been speedy by American or English standards. Partly this reflects the persistence of the Continental ethos; as Sybille Bedford remarks, "This unrestricted waiting—a very bad thing every way you look at it—does not seem to be caused to any extent by the moderate pace of the trial courts, it is inherent rather in the mechanism and spirit of the criminal prosecution in even a vestigial inquisitorial system, as that system with its predilection for packaged guilt must rely on a lengthy, cautious preliminary investigation conducted by a semi-administrative judiciary, without any possible regard for the passage of time." [19] In Japan, as in Europe, justice is expected to proceed at a slow pace. Nevertheless, trials during the 1950s were extremely long even by Japanese standards, and their excessive length was an unintended consequence of SCAP's root-and-branch reforms, an effect that might have been mitigated by a somewhat less radical modification of the old system.

SCAP's key reforms in the field of criminal law were the safeguards for the rights of the accused contained in the Constitution of 1947, its setting up of the judiciary as an administrative body entirely separate from the Ministry of Justice, and its rewriting of the Code of Criminal Procedure. In all of this change, however, SCAP seems to have slighted the problem of procuratorial discretion and the numerous difficulties that flow from it.

According to Japanese law, all criminal cases except juvenile offenses are entrusted to the procuracy, which determines whether the accused shall be indicted. Courts cannot try cases that have not been indicted by a procurator, and the procurators make the decision to prosecute or not to prosecute entirely on their own discretion. This is not an insignificant power. During 1964, for example, the procurators decided not to prosecute some 41.1 percent of the cases brought to them by the police. The actual number of these cases was 309,094. Of the 58.9 percent (443,791 cases) that they did indict, three-quarters (333,014 cases) were handled by a summary court (one judge empowered to impose prison sentences for up to three years). Thus only 110,777 cases actually went to a public trial, and of these 80 percent were "confession cases." What this means is that only about 3 percent of the total number of cases considered by the procurators were actually contested in a court and decided by a panel of judges. And during 1961 to 1963 the procurators' conviction rate for those cases it did bring to trial varied between

19. *The Faces of Justice* (New York, 1961), p. 159.

99.1 and 99.3 percent. As Professor Ushiomi concludes, "The fate of a criminal suspect is actually determined not by trial but by a procurator who decided whether or not he will be indicted." [20]

This prejudgment of a case by a procurator is not necessarily a bad thing (it can, for instance, spare an innocent man a trial) nor is it an unknown feature of other legal systems. It is not, however, what was intended by the various occupation reforms, and the controls over procurators to prevent its abuse have not proven very effective. Moreover, the real danger of procuratorial discretion becomes apparent when the power of prejudgment is put alongside the bureaucratic structure of the procuracy itself.

The procuracy (Kensatsu-chō) is a rigidly hierarchical official organization which is divided into five strata. During 1967 these were one procurator general (kenji sōchō); one assistant procurator general (jichō kenji); eight senior procurators (kenjichō); 1,072 procurators (kenji), and 762 assistant procurators (fuku-kenji). They worked in public procurator's offices spread around the country and distinguished as: the Supreme Procuracy (1), the High Procuracy (8), branches (shibu) of the High Procuracy (6), the Regional Procuracy (49), first-class branches of the Regional Procuracy (81), second-class branches of the Regional Procuracy (159), and District Procurator's offices (570). Between procurators and assistant procurators there is a clear bureaucratic separation, the latter usually being appointed after many years of service as a police officer or as a secretary in a procurator's office. Assistant procurators do not compete with procurators for choice positions. However, within the stratum of procurators, status gradings and steps of promotion are rigidly fixed, making for intense competition for the only desirable attainments that vary at all, namely, locality within which to

20. Hōritsuka, p. 147.

work and functional assignment (e.g., "public safety" cases versus pollution cases). Among procurators there is what Ushiomi calls an "abnormal enthusiasm" to be assigned to the offices in Tokyo, Osaka, Kobe, Yokohama, Kyoto, Nagoya, Fukuoka, or the prefectures in the Kantō plain because they contain so many branches that an ambitious man has a chance to advance to branch chief.[21] It is virtually the only way that one can get ahead in this work through one's own initiative. Needless to say, Japanese procurators are civil servants, not elected officials, and one does not build the basis for a political career by becoming known as a "fighting D.A.," as in the United States.

The occupants of the top of the pyramid, the procurator general, his assistant, and the eight senior procurators, control assignments to locality and post, thereby exerting tremendous influence over their subordinates. Because of this rigid bureaucratization and the near-fatal dangers to a career caused by an error, procurators do not exercise their discretion over indictments singly; and once a collective decision to indict has been made, they stick to it through thick and thin, no matter what is brought out in court. The Matsukawa and Yakai cases illustrate this rule perfectly.

Perhaps the most famous instance of procuratorial obstinacy in the face of error is what some Japanese cynics have labeled the King of the Jail case, referring to a homicide case that began in 1913 and was settled only after fifty years, twenty-one of which the wrongly accused defendant spent in jail. On August 13, 1913, a silk-cocoon dealer in Nagoya was murdered, and two men, the actual murderers, were arrested. Under police torture they confessed and implicated a third man, Yoshida Ishimatsu, whom the procurators then indicted as the mastermind behind the murder and who, in April 1914, was sentenced by the Nagoya District Court to be hanged. His two "accomplices" were sentenced to

21. Ibid., p. 167.

life imprisonment. On appeal Yoshida had his sentence reduced to life, and he remained in jail until 1935, when he was released as a result of an amnesty.

Yoshida then set out to prove his innocence. With the help of two reporters he located the two accomplices and obtained from one of them a statement that they had falsely implicated him. However, all of Yoshida's attempts to obtain a retrial were rebuffed on grounds that his release had made the case moot. After the war he persisted, but when he finally did obtain the assistance of a procurator in bringing the case into court, the procurator himself was banished to the provinces. The procurator had violated the unwritten rule among his colleagues that a procurator must never find a defendant innocent after his fellows have concluded he was guilty. Because of this procurator's banishment and the activities of a journalist, the Supreme Court heard Yoshida's appeal directly; and in April 1961, it ordered the case retried under article 435 of the Code of Criminal Procedure (retrial after a conclusive finding of guilty because of, *inter alia*, an offense committed by a procurator). That retrial began in December 1962 in the Nagoya High Court, and on February 28, 1963, at the age of eighty-three, Yoshida Ishimatsu was declared not guilty. His girl friend, who some fifty years earlier had provided him with a valid alibi, was also in court to see him exonerated.[22] Although this case is one of the most extreme ever recorded of the procuracy's refusing to acknowledge that it had made a mistake and of chastising its own members who failed to maintain the united front, the phenomenon itself is not at all unusual—as the Matsukawa case illustrates.

SCAP's reformers were not unaware that the strengths of the system in which the procuracy monopolizes prosecutions— namely, the placing of the public's interest in a prosecution, as determined by an impartial bureaucracy, above any spirit of re-

22. *Mainichi Daily News* (Osaka), March 1, 1963.

taliation or an individual citizen's complaint—are also its weaknesses. Therefore SCAP wrote various laws and provisions in order to create safety valves. One is a greatly attenuated form of grand jury created by the Inquest of Prosecution Law (Law Number 147 of 1948). It establishes eleven-man citizens' committees which "examine into the propriety of decisions by public prosecutors not to institute prosecution, and submit proposals and give advice concerning improvements in the management of the system of public prosecutors." [23] When such a committee receives a request for an investigation from an injured party, it conducts an inquest and sends the results to the chief of the district procurator's office. Although inquest verdicts are not binding on the district's chief procurator, they do provide a check over his subordinates and bring to his attention cases in which he may decide to overrule an earlier decision and to order a prosecution instituted.

SCAP's other main innovation was to provide in the Code of Criminal Procedure (art. 262) that a person who is dissatisfied by a procurator's decision not to prosecute may appeal directly to a court. If the court decides that the "application is well-founded" (art. 266), it may institute the prosecution itself and "designate from among practicing attorneys" (art. 268) a lawyer who shall replace the regular procurator and shall act as the court's own prosecutor for the case. For all intents and purposes, the only cases that are treated in this manner are those in which a citizen charges an official, usually a procurator or a policeman, with "abuse of authority" (Penal Code, articles 193 and 194) and a procurator has refused to indict his fellow official.

Both of these checks on procuratorial discretion have only rarely been used and are so little known to the general public as to constitute almost no check at all. Between the time that the Code of Criminal Procedure came into effect and 1970, for

23. Dandō, Shigemitsu, *Japanese Criminal Procedure*, trans. B. J. George, Jr. (South Hackensack, N.J., 1965), p. 342.

example, there have been only seven cases in which a request for a trial of a civil servant for having abused his authority was even heard by a court. Once was in connection with the Matsukawa case, when the defense attorneys attempted unsuccessfully to have the procurators in the first and second trials indicted for suppressing the Suwa Memorandum (see chapter seven). Another occurred during 1970, when the Fukuoka District Court turned down a trial request by the Socialist party, which wanted to institute indictment proceedings against a group of Fukuoka policemen who had roughed up some Tokyo students. The students had passed through Fukuoka on their way to the port of Sasebo, where they were going to protest a visit by an American aircraft carrier. In both of these cases the press spent as much time trying to explain the law being invoked as it did on the contested issues.[24]

Procuratorial discretion is a well-established part of both Continental and Japanese law, and the Japanese, except for leftist critics of the courts such as Professor Ushiomi Toshitaka, seem quite satisfied with it. It may be that SCAP's escape clauses from the general principle provide sufficient pressure on the procurators to keep them self-policed, and the small number of cases in which the escape clauses have actually been invoked may testify to the clauses' general effectiveness. Nevertheless, Ushiomi's charges that procuratorial discretion amounts to procuratorial judgment seem irrefutable. Moreover, as the Matsukawa case clearly illustrates, in political cases or instances of a mistake by the procuracy, the bureaucratic interests of procurators are likely to override their commitment to serve the public's interests.

One effective remedy for procuratorial error or bias would appear to be judicial vigilance and verdicts that compel procurators to support confessions with witnesses and other forms of

24. *Japan Times*, September 4, 1970.

material and circumstantial evidence. That was precisely the view of SCAP. Reflecting American theory and practice of government, SCAP reformers decided that one of the best ways to counteract the danger of bureaucratic self-interest was to vest power in several different organizations and to put them in competition with each other. SCAP diagnosed the problem as follows: "While the modern administration of justice in Japan, developed during the Meiji era, drew heavily from continental European practice, the Japanese judges did not enjoy the independence of their French and German counterparts. By virtue of their education and social background they were primarily legal technicians and servants of the State rather than guardians of justice." [25]

SCAP therefore separated the judiciary from any connection with the Ministry of Justice or the procuracy and left it only tenuously joined to the cabinet. SCAP vested the entire authority for judicial administration, including such functions as assignment and transfer of judges to specific courts, appointment and removal of court personnel other than judges, and financial affairs of courts, with the Supreme Court. The cabinet, which was itself made responsible to the Diet under the Constitution of 1947, only selects Supreme Court justices (except for the chief justice, who is appointed by the emperor after nomination by the cabinet and who therefore holds a rank equivalent to that of the prime minister); it appoints inferior judges from a list of persons nominated by the Supreme Court.

This new structure greatly strengthened judicial independence, and it made judges immune to the pressures that had been applied to them by the minister of justice under the old system. Why then, one might ask, has it taken Japanese judges so long to start throwing out of court criminal cases in which the only evidence against the accused is his own confession (e.g., the

25. SCAP Monograph No. 14, "Legal and Judicial Reform," p. 97.

first and second Matsukawa trials) or for the Supreme Court to begin to use its constitutionally sanctioned power of judicial review to declare some Diet legislation null and void? Ushiomi Toshitaka, writing in 1970, has two explanations, one derived from the other: first, SCAP did not purge prewar judges at the same time that it made them independent; and, second, these older judges have rebureaucratized the judiciary under the administration of the Supreme Court.

Ushiomi advances these explanations in the form of four hypotheses that he believes accurately characterize the postwar judiciary twenty years after its inception. First, judicial decisions affecting popular sovereignty, peace, and basic civil rights diverge farther from the principles of the constitution as one goes up the judicial hierarchy, district court decisions being closest to the constitution and Supreme Court decisions being the farthest removed. Second, the greatest shortcoming of judges in general is their subservience to administrative authority (gyōsei kenryoku) and to faits accomplis. Third, judges have become divided into two classes—those in active service and those directly concerned with the administration of the judiciary—and as the latter have become more powerful than the former the judiciary has been rebureaucratized, and the justice it distributes has come under a subtly conservative influence. Fourth, judges trained when the old Meiji Constitution was in force do not share the same values as judges trained under the postwar constitution.[26]

In my opinion, Ushiomi overstates each of these tendencies and is more alarmist about their consequences for Japanese democracy than is warranted by the record. Nevertheless, his hypotheses do help to explain some aspects of the Matsukawa case and similar cases, and they offer insights into the state of SCAP's reforms two decades after the occupation finished its work. The judiciary may not have changed as much as Pro-

26. Ushiomi Toshitaka, Hōritsuka, pp. 1–2.

fessor Ushiomi would like, but it has changed and is continuing to change in a democratic direction more than he appreciates.

Newly appointed judges in postwar Japan have tended to be extremely cautious in using their powers, possibly reflecting the influence on them of a conservative Supreme Court, and prewar judges who were carried over into the postwar system do not appear to have been profoundly affected by the reforms. Judges Nagao and Suzuki, for example, who presided over the first and second Matsukawa trials, were trained under the old system, and so, far from questioning the procurators' case put before them, they tended rather to assume its validity. However, the timidity of lower-court judges and the numbers of prewar judges have both tended to decline over time. By the decade of the sixties many new judges had come into the system at the lower levels, producing the phenomenon identified by Ushiomi in which lower court decisions appear to be more iconoclastic than high court or Supreme Court decisions. For example, the *Asahi* in 1968 reported that among the 507 trainees entering the Judicial Training Institute—which prepares *all* new judges who have passed the examination in order to become a judge—some 90 percent considered the Japanese Self-Defense Forces to be in violation of article 9 of the constitution and therefore unconstitutional.[27] This view was in marked contrast to several Supreme Court decisions upholding the constitutionality of defensive armed forces in postwar Japan.

The growing disparity of social outlook between prewar and postwar judges is also reflected in a rising tide of intrajudicial controversy. The Matsukawa case affords several instances of this: for example, Supreme Court Justice Ishizaka's alleged influence on Judge Suzuki during the second trial, the arguments provoked by Chief Justice Tanaka's directive cautioning judges not to listen to the "noise" of public opinion, Supreme

27. *Asahi shimbun*, October 2, 1968, quoting *Hōgaku seminā*, October 1968.

Court Justice Shimoiizaka's criticism of Judge Monden for allowing the implication of a police frame-up to appear in his verdict, and Monden's unusual transfer to the Fukuoka family court after he had found the Matsukawa defendants not guilty.

During 1970 another such controversy illuminated the judicial generation gap. The then current chief justice, Ishida Kazuto, publicly denounced a subordinate judge, Fukushima Shigeo, who was attached to the Sapporo District Court in Hokkaido and who was also a member of the Association of Young Jurists (Seihōkyō), an organization known for its leftist traits and anti-government activities. Judge Fukushima's possible conflict of interest came to the chief justice's attention when Fukushima was designated to hear a suit concerning the constitutionality of the government's building a missile base in Hokkaido and when the government's attorney challenged his impartiality in judging the case because of his affiliations. Chief Justice Ishida demanded that judges be politically neutral and, echoing Chief Justice Tanaka some twenty years earlier, went so far as to declare that extreme militarists, Communists, extreme nationalists, and anarchists were unfit to be judges.

Two months after the chief justice made this statement some twenty-nine professors and novelists filed a petition with the Diet's Judicial Impeachment Committee to have Ishida removed. The petition stated, among other things, that under the influence of older judges the functions of the courts in Japan had shifted from the defense of civil liberties to the "control of demonstrators." Not surprisingly, the Diet decided not to impeach Ishida; of some approximately twenty-four hundred impeachment petitions that have been lodged with the Judicial Impeachment Committee since SCAP set it up (including three against former Chief Justice Tanaka), only two judges have actually been removed from office, one for professional negligence and the other for bribery. The 1970 case continued into the autumn with Judge Fukushima first resigning and then withdrawing his resignation after he was formally reprimanded by the president of the Sapporo High Court because of his political affiliations.[28]

Naturally enough, supporters of the chief justice in this affair saw his action as a defense of the constitution against leftists who were scrupulous only in defending the rights of their fellow believers, whereas supporters of Judge Fukushima contended that judicial independence had been destroyed by conservative politicians in the Diet and their friends in the Supreme Court secretariat. Actually, the incident seemed to be merely one more instance of the continuing controversy over the impartiality of the judiciary in Japan, a controversy that, although occasionally undignified, has contributed immensely to political education in Japan and that is itself testimony to the lively health of Japanese democracy. Despite its outcome, the Ishida-Fukushima incident did not indicate that one group was able effectively to silence the other, although it did demonstrate which group is currently in the ascendancy.

One of the ways the conservatives have continued to dominate the judiciary is through bureaucratic influence. When, in 1948, the courts were separated from the Ministry of Justice, judicial administration passed to the Administrative Secretariat of the Supreme Court (Saikō-saibansho Jimu-sōkyoku). Professor Ushiomi, in order to demonstrate that judges attached to or at one time affiliated with the secretariat dominate the Japanese judiciary, studied the careers of some 1,219 judges at all levels of the hierarchy. He found that while judges who have at one time or another worked in the secretariat formed only 11.7 percent of his sample, they occupied some 86 percent of the key posts in the judicial system, including the staff of the secretariat itself, the investigators of the Supreme Court who

28. *Japan Times*, June 30, 1970; July 4, 1970; July 16, 1970; October 29, 1970; October 31, 1970; and *Asahi shimbun*, October 28, 1970 (eve. ed.), article by Matsumoto Seichō.

check on the performance of subordinate judges, the instructors in the Judicial Training Institute, and the personnel of the Tokyo High, District, and Family courts, which commonly set precedents for the rest of the country in judicial decision-making. Ushiomi's conclusion is that the prewar Ministry of Justice has been replaced in the postwar world by the Administrative Secretariat of the Supreme Court and that the new agency performs exactly the same function as the old, namely, keeping judges in line through bureaucratic pressure and in accordance with the dictates of political authorities in Tokyo.[29]

This view is partly accurate, but it is overstated and does not give sufficient weight to the fact that much high-court conservatism has been in response to radical decisions by lower courts or decisions in which lower courts appeared to have succumbed to political pressures. Far from forming a reactionary cabal, the administrators of the court system have been more concerned to develop a heritage of trust in the courts among the people and to see to it that the more powerful postwar judges do not try to advance their own political opinions against those of the popularly elected Diet. It is unquestionably true that the postwar Supreme Court has been made up of conservative justices, but the fact remains that in the Matsukawa case the judges of the Supreme Court upheld the rights of the accused after the lower courts had failed to do so. More important, they did this as a matter of law rather than because of political pressure. Ushiomi is correct in pointing to the disparity in 1970 between the social outlooks of older and younger judges; but in his enthusiastic applause for the postwar breed, he seems to ignore the contributions of the Supreme Court of the 1950s to the institutionalization of the system itself and to its just resolution of difficult cases such as Yakai and Matsukawa. If, in fact, Japan's "independent judiciary" has rebureaucratized itself, one can only

29. *Hōritsuka*, pp. 65, 105–107.

hope that when the new class of the Judicial Training Institute ultimately takes over the Administrative Secretariat, it will contribute as much to the rule of law in Japan as have its early postwar predecessors.

In retrospect the Matsukawa case affords grounds for criticizing some of the occupation's schemes for legal reform and invites a mild mockery of Hirotsu and his occasionally mindless demonstrators. However, both the occupation reformers of the 1940s and the court critics of the 1950s addressed themselves to authentic problems of social organization. If they did not solve them to everyone's satisfaction they nonetheless gave important impetus to the evolution of a more just and humane criminal law in Japan. It is dissatisfying to conclude a study of the Matsukawa case without knowing who were the true criminals, but the outcome of the case was actually a victory for Japanese society and for Japanese justice. How much more dissatisfying it would have been to conclude with the knowledge that the measures designed by both conqueror and citizen to make the government more responsive to the people had instead sent to prison or the gallows twenty possibly innocent citizens. That did not happen, and the Matsukawa case goes into the archives as a significant instance in which men were well enough served by the institutions they had created.

Glossary of Japanese Names

A. Defendants

Readings are based on *furigana* given in Matsukawa Case Countermeasures Council, *Matsukawa jūgo nen* (Fifteen Years of Matsukawa) (Tokyo, 1964), p. 43 et seq.

Abe Ichiji   阿　部　市　次
    Clerk of the National Railroad Workers' Union in Fukushima
Akama Katsumi   赤　間　勝　美
    Confessed saboteur and former railroad track maintenance worker
Hamazaki Futao   浜　崎　二　雄
    Alleged saboteur from Tōshiba's Matsukawa factory
Honda Noboru   本　田　昇
    NRWU official charged with having led the sabotage party
Katō Kenzō   加　藤　謙　三
    Former railroad dispatcher who allegedly informed Tōshiba conspirators of train schedules
Kikuchi Takeshi   菊　地　武
    One of the alleged tool thieves from Tōshiba

424 · CONSPIRACY AT MATSUKAWA

Kobayashi Genzaburō   小 林 源 三 郎
    Charged with conspiracy and tool theft
Nikaidō Sonoko   二 階 堂 園 子
    The sole female defendant, from the Tōshiba factory
    a. k. a. Sasaki   佐 々 木
    Nikaidō Sonoko's family name at birth
    a. k. a. Yokoya   横 谷
    Nikaidō Sonoko's married name
Nikaidō Takeo   二 階 堂 武 雄
    Member of the Tōshiba-Matsukawa factory union
Ninomiya Yutaka   二 宮 豊
    Executive-committeeman of the NRWU in Fukushima prefecture
Okada Toramatsu   岡 田 十 良 松
    Chief secretary of the Fukushima Trade Union Congress
Ōta Shōji   太 田 省 次
    Vice-chairman of the Matsukawa plant union
Ōuchi Shōzō   大 内 昭 三
    One of the Tōshiba employees charged with tool theft
Saitō Yuki   斉 藤 千
    An alleged conspirator from the NRWU executive committee
Satō Hajime   佐 藤 一
    The "outside agitator," a representative of the national federation
    of Tōshiba unions
Satō Shiroji   佐 藤 代 治
    A member of the Tōshiba factory union's executive committee
Sugiura Saburō   杉 浦 三 郎
    Head of the union at Tōshiba's Matsukawa factory
Suzuki Makoto   鈴 木 信
    Former railroad employee and chairman of the Communist
    party's Fukushima committee
Takahashi Haruo   高 橋 晴 雄
    The slightly lame former railroad worker who was charged with
    having been a member of the sabotage party
Takeda Hisashi   武 田 久
    Chairman of the NRWU's Fukushima prefectural branch

B. Other Names

Andō Sadao 安 藤 貞 男
One of the youths who claimed to have heard "Akama's prophecy"

Anzai Mitsuo 安 西 光 雄
Chief of the Fukushima procuracy at the time of the sabotage

Arai Yutaka 新 井 裕
Chief of the National Rural Police in Fukushima prefecture

Date 伊 達
A railroad station north of Fukushima, scene of the "Date case"

Hakamada Shigeshi 袴 田 重 司
One of the leading defense attorneys, from Sendai

Hirabayashi Taiko 平 林 た い 子
The woman novelist who doubted the validity of the 1961 not-guilty verdict.

Hirama Takashi 平 間 高 司
One of the burglars who, on August 17, 1949, was in the vicinity of the crime

Hirotsu Kazuo 広 津 和 郎
Novelist and head of the Matsukawa Countermeasures Council

Hobara 保 原
The police station north of Fukushima where Akama was detained

Honda Izumi 本 田 泉
Chief of the Criminal Affairs Bureau, Fukushima National Rural Police

Honda Yoshihiro 本 田 嘉 博
Chief of Akahata's Fukushima Bureau

Iijima Yoshio 飯 島 義 雄
One of the juveniles who reported "Akama's prophecy"

Ishizaka Shuichi 石 坂 修 一
The justice of the Supreme Court whom the defense charged with interference in the case

Jōkoku 上 告
In Japanese law, an appeal to the Supreme Court

Kaji Wataru 鹿 地 亘
    The spy suspect whom the Americans detained during 1951–52

Kanayagawa 金 谷 川
    The railroad station immediately north of Matsukawa

Kōso 控 訴
    In Japanese law, an appeal to a High Court

Masaki Hiroshi 正 木 ひ ろ し
    The chief defense attorney in the Yakai case

Masuda Kaneshichi 増 田 甲 子 七
    Chief Cabinet Secretary at the time of the Matsukawa incident

Matsukawa 松 川
    A village in northern Fukushima prefecture

Matsumoto Seichō 松 本 清 張
    Detective novelist, author of *The Black Mist over Japan*

Mitaka jiken 三 鷹 事 件
    The Mitaka railroad sabotage case of the summer of 1949

Monden Makoto 門 田 実
    Presiding judge in the Sendai retrial of the Matsukawa case

Murakami Yoshio 村 上 義 雄
    One of the burglars who claimed to have seen the saboteurs

Nagaigawa 永 井 川
    A railroad signal station between Fukushima and Kanayagawa

Nagao Makoto 長 尾 信
    Presiding judge in the first trial of the Matsukawa case

Nishi Hajime 西 肇
    A Tōshiba executive who helped write the Suwa Memorandum

Okabayashi Tatsuo 岡 林 辰 雄
    Chief defense attorney for the Matsukawa defendants

Ōtsuka Kazuo 大 塚 一 男
    Second-in-command of the Matsukawa defense lawyers team

Ōu Honsen 奥 羽 本 線
    The main line railroad that connects Fukushima with Aomori via Akita

Saitō Kinsaku 斉 藤 金 作
    The mysterious eyewitness who was named in the first anonymous letter

Saitō Kitarō   斉 藤 朔 郎
  The justice of the Supreme Court who presided at the final appeal
Shimoiizaka Masuo   下 飯 坂 潤 夫
  One of the justices of the Supreme Court who dissented from the court's decisions in the Matsukawa case
Shimoyama Sadanori   下 山 定 則
  President of the Japanese National Railroads who died mysteriously in 1949
Shiraishi Kenzō   白 石 健 三
  Presiding judge in the Matsukawa state compensation suit
Suwa Shin'ichirō   諏 訪 親 一 郎
  A Tōshiba executive, author of the Suwa Memorandum
Suzuki Hisanori   鈴 木 久 学
  A procurator in the first trial, later charged with having suppressed the Suwa Memorandum
Suzuki Teijirō   鈴 木 禎 次 郎
  Judge of the Sendai High Court who presided at the second trial
Taira jiken   平 事 件
  Labor disturbances in 1949 in the city of Taira
Takahashi Shōhachi   高 橋 正 八
  Chief procurator in the Sendai retrial of the Matsukawa case
Takeda Tatsuo   武 田 辰 雄
  Fukushima police sergeant who obtained Akama's confession
Takeuchi Keisuke   竹 内 景 助
  The sole convicted culprit in the Mitaka case
Tamagawa Tadashi   玉 川 正
  The police inspector in charge of the Matsukawa investigation
Tanaka Hidetaka   田 中 秀 教
  Author of the Tanaka Memorandum, the union's equivalent of the Suwa Memorandum
Tanaka Kōtarō   田 中 耕 太 郎
  Chief Justice of the Supreme Court during the 1950s
Tōhoku Honsen   東 北 本 線
  The Northeast Main Line of the Japanese National Railroads
Tōshiba Denki   東 芝 電 気
  The Tokyo-Shibaura Electric Company

Uno Kōji   宇 野 浩 二
  One of the "two Zolas," author of *The Strangest Story in the World*

Washimi Seizō   鷲 見 誠 三
  Factory manager of Tōshiba's Matsukawa plant

Yakai jiken   八 海 事 件
  The Yakai murder case, helped fuel the "criticism of the courts" movement

Yamaguchi Kazuo   山 口 一 夫
  Chief procurator in the Matsukawa case's second trial

Yamamoto Isamu   山 本 諫
  Chief procurator in the first Matsukawa trial

Bibliography

THIS bibliography provides information on the particular editions of materials relating to the Matsukawa case that I consulted in writing this book. A copy of each item is in my personal library or the East Asiatic Library, University of California, Berkeley. For a different bibliography on the case, see Matsukawa Undō Shi Hensan Iinkai (History of the Matsukawa Movement Compilation Committee), ed., *Matsukawa undō zenshi* (Complete History of the Matsukawa Movement) (Tokyo, 1965), pp. 908–927. Bibliographical information is supplied below under the following headings:

    I. Court Documents (listed in chronological order)
   II. Works on the Matsukawa Case
      A. Books and Pamphlets (listed alphabetically by author or issuing agency)
      B. Periodicals (listed alphabetically by title of periodical)
  III. Works on the Era of the Matsukawa Case
      A. Books
      B. Periodicals

IV. Special Collections
V. Works in English

I. COURT DOCUMENTS

Fukushima Chihō Saibansho (Fukushima District Court). *Matsukawa jiken kōhan kiroku* (Matsukawa Case Trial Record) [Fukushima, December 1949–December 1950]. Mimeo. Fifteen volumes.

Hōmu-fu Kenmu-kyoku (Attorney General's Office, Prosecution Bureau). *Matsukawa jiken ni okeru kenji no ronkoku* (The Procurators' Closing Address in the Matsukawa Case) [Fukushima, August 25–26, 1950]. "Kensatsu Shiryō 13."

Fukushima Chihō Saibansho. *Matsukawa jiken dai-isshin hanketsu* (Matsukawa Case First Trial Verdict) [Fukushima, January 12, 1951].

Suzuki Makoto, et al. *Matsukawa jiken kōso shuisho* (Matsukawa Case Kōso Appeal Documents) [July 1951]. Three volumes.

Sendai Kōtō Saibansho (Sendai High Court). *Matsukawa jiken kōhan kiroku dai-ni-shin* (Matsukawa Case Trial Record, The Second Trial) [Sendai, October 1951–December 1953]. Mimeo. Fourteen volumes plus supplement.

Sendai Kōtō Kensatsuchō (Sendai High Procuracy). *Kensatsukan iken yōshi, Matsukawa jiken kōsoshin no jijitsu torishirabe ni taisuru* (Procurators' Brief, With Regard to the Investigation of Facts in the Matsukawa Case Kōso Appeal Trial) [Sendai, April 28, 1953]. Handwritten. Mimeo.

Matsukawa Jiken Taisaku Iinkai (Matsukawa Case Countermeasures Committee), ed. *Matsukawa jiken shiryōshū* (Collected Materials on the Matsukawa Case), No. 1 (Tokyo, January 30, 1954). Excerpts from the verdicts of the first and second trials.

Matsukawa Jiken Shiryō Kankō Kai (Committee to Publish the Materials of the Matsukawa Case), ed. "Akama hikoku no jihaku" (Defendant Akama's Confession), *Matsukawa jiken shiryōshū*, No. 2 (Tokyo, April 1, 1954).

———. "Matsukawa jiken dai-ni-shin hanketsu zenbun" (Complete

Text of the Verdict in the Second Trial of the Matsukawa Case), *Matsukawa jiken shiryōshū*, No. 3 (Tokyo, March 30, 1954).

———. "Mujitsu no ronshō, Okabayashi shunin bengonin benron yōshi" (Proof of Innocence, the Brief of Chief Defense Attorney Okabayashi's Closing Address [in the Second Trial]), *Matsukawa jiken shiryōshū*, No. 4 (Tokyo, March 10, 1955).

———. "Ōta jihaku to sono kaibō" (The Ōta Confession and Its Dissection), *Matsukawa jiken shiryōshū*, No. 5 (Tokyo, June 1, 1955).

Suzuki Makoto, et al. *Matsukawa jiken jōkoku shuisho* (Matsukawa Case Jōkoku Appeal Documents) [Tokyo, September 1955]. Twenty-one volumes.

Matsukawa Jiken Bengodan Jōnin Sewa Kai (The Matsukawa Case Defense Attorneys' Standing Aid Association), ed. *Matsukawa jiken jōkoku-shin benron* (The Defense Arguments in the Appeal of the Matsukawa Case to the Supreme Court). Tokyo: Rōdō Jumpō Sha, 1959.

Saikō Saibansho (The Supreme Court). "Matsukawa jiken saikō saibansho hanketsu zenbun" (Complete Text of the [First] Supreme Court Verdict in the Matsukawa Case), *Jurisuto* (Jurist), September 1959. "Emergency Issue." Also printed in *Hōritsu jihō* (Law Review), September 1959, special issue; and in Matsukawa Jiken Taisaku Kyōgikai (Matsukawa Case Countermeasures Council), *Saikōsai hanketsu* (Supreme Court Verdict), Tokyo, 1959, "Matsukawa Shiriizu No. 4."

Sendai Kōtō Saibansho Dai Ichi Keijibu (Sendai High Court, First Criminal Affairs Division). *Matsukawa jiken sashimodoshi-shin kōhan kiroku* (Record of the Public Hearings of the Matsukawa Case Retrial) [Sendai, March 1960–August 1961]. Seventeen volumes.

———. *Matsukawa jiken sashimodoshi-shin kōhan shiryō* (Documentary Materials [Introduced during] the Public Hearings of the Matsukawa Case Retrial) [Sendai, 1961]. Fourteen volumes.

Sendai Kōtō Kensatsuchō (Sendai High Procuracy). *Kensatsukan iken yōshi* (Procurators' Brief) [Sendai, February 14–16, 1961].

Printed in Hōmushō Keijiyoku (Justice Ministry, Criminal Affairs Bureau). *Matsukawa jiken sashimodoshi-shin ronkoku* (The Procurators' Closing Address in the Matsukawa Case Retrial). Tokyo, May 1961. "Kensatsu Shiryō 113."

———. *Kensatsukan hosoku iken yōshi* (Supplementary Procurators' Brief) [Sendai, April 18, 24, 1961]. Two volumes. Mimeo.

Matsukawa Case Defense Attorneys' Unit. Four Special Documents "*Akama hikokura jihaku no nin'isei*" *kentō shiryō* (Documents for the Examination of "The Voluntariness of the Confessions Made by Akama and Other Defendants"). Reprint of the testimony of Police Inspector Tamagawa and others from the 22nd Session of the First Trial.

"*Suwa memo o chōten to suru hikokunin Satō Hajime no hachi-gatsu jū-go-nichi aribai no ronshō*" ("The Suwa Memo is Demonstrative Proof of the August 15 [1949] Alibi of Defendant Satō Hajime"). Defense Attorney's Brief, for presentation on April 3, 1961.

"*Honda hikoku no aribai*" ("The Alibi of Defendant Honda"). Defense Attorneys' Brief, for presentation on April 4, 1961.

"*Matsukawa senro han kara no bāru jizai-supana funshitsu no umu ni tsuite*" ("Concerning Whether a Crowbar and a Wrench were Lost from the Matsukawa Track Maintenance Crew's Shed"). Defense Attorney's Brief, for presentation on April 18, 1961.

Sendai Kōtō Saibansho Dai Ichi Keijibu. *Hanketsu shubun oyobi riyū no yōshi* (Brief of the Text of the Verdict and Its Reasoning) [Sendai, August 8, 1961]. Handwritten. Mimeo.

———. "*Matsukawa jiken hanketsu zenbun, sashimodoshi ato no dai-ni-shin hanketsu*" (Complete Text of the Verdict in the Matsukawa Case, The Verdict of the Retrial Following the [Supreme Court's] Referral Back Order), *Hanrei jihō* (Review of Leading Cases), No. 275 (November 11, 1961). Also printed in *Jurisuto*, No. 239 (December 1, 1961); and in Matsukawa Jiken Taisaku Kyōgikai, *Matsukawa muzai hanketsu* (The Matsukawa Not-Guilty Verdict), Tokyo, 1961. "Matsukawa Shiriizu No. 9."

Saikō saibansho (The Supreme Court). "Matsukawa jiken saishū hanketsu" (The Final Verdict in the Matsukawa Case), *Jurisuto*, No. 284 (October 15, 1973).

Matsukawa Jiken Zenkoku Renraku Kaigi (Matsukawa Case National Liaison Council). *Matsukawa jiken kokka baishō saiban hanketsubun* (Text of the Verdict in the Matsukawa Case State Compensation Trial) [Tokyo, 1969].

II. WORKS ON THE MATSUKAWA CASE

A. Books and Pamphlets

Aichi Ken Matsukawa Jiken Taisaku Kyōgikai (Aichi Prefecture Matsukawa Case Countermeasures Council). *Me de miru Matsukawa jiken; Akama jihaku o chūshin to shite* (The Matsukawa Case Before One's Eyes; According to the Akama Confession). Nagoya: Aichi Ken Kyōgikai, 1959.

Hirotsu Kazuo, et al. *Matsukawa jiken no uchisoto* (The Matsukawa Case Inside and Out). Tokyo: Hikari Shobō, 1959.

Hirotsu Kazuo. *Matsukawa jiken to saiban* (The Matsukawa Case and Trials). Tokyo: Iwanami Shoten, 1964.

———. *Matsukawa saiban* (The Matsukawa Trials). Tokyo: Chikuma Shobō, 1955, 1956, 1958. Three volumes.

———. *Matsukawa saiban no mondaiten* (Disputed Questions in the Matsukawa Trials). Tokyo: Chūō Kōron Sha, 1959.

———, Sata Ineko, Ikeda Michiko, Tsuboi Sakae, Matsuda Tokiko, et al. *Torimodoshita hitomi, Matsukawa no kazoku-tachi* (Their Loved Ones Returned, Matsukawa Families). Osaka: Daidō Shoin, 1959. The authors, besides Hirotsu, are all prominent left-wing women writers.

Japanese Government. Kokka Chihō Keisatsu Honbu Keiji-bu Sōsa-ka (National Rural Police Headquarters, Criminal Affairs Division, Investigation Section). *Matsukawa jiken no kenkyū* (A Study of the Matsukawa Case). Tokyo, 1953. "Criminal Police Materials Volume 15." "Internal Use Only."

Kanagawa Ken Matsukawa Tōsō Shi Hensan Iinkai (Kanagawa Prefecture History of the Matsukawa Struggle Compilation Committee) and Kanagawa Ken Matsukawa Jiken Taisaku Kyōgikai (Kanagawa Prefecture Matsukawa Case Countermeasures Council), eds. *Kanagawa ken Matsukawa tōsō shi* (History of the Matsukawa Struggle in Kanagawa Prefecture). Yokohama, 1964.

Matsukawa Jiken Bengodan Jōnin Sewa Kai (Matsukawa Case Defense Attorneys' Standing Aid Association). *Shin hannin tsuikyū no tame ni* (In Order to Catch the True Criminals). N.p., n.d. [1964]. Mimeo.

Matsukawa Jiken Bunshū Hensan Iinkai (Matsukawa Case Anthology Compilation Committee), ed. *Aijō wa kabe o tōshite, Matsukawa jiken no hikoku to kazoku no tegami* (Love Penetrates Walls, Letters Exchanged between the Matsukawa Defendants and Their Families). Tokyo: Aoki Shoten, 1954.

———. *Shinjitsu wa kabe o tōshite, Matsukawa jiken hikoku no shuki* (Truth Penetrates Walls, Writings of the Matsukawa Case Defendants). Tokyo: Aoki Bunko No. 153, 1953.

Matsukawa Jiken Shiryō Kankō Kai (Committee to Publish the Materials of the Matsukawa Case) and Matsukawa Jiken Taisaku Iinkai (Matsukawa Case Countermeasures Committee). *Matsukawa jiken no kakushin o tsuku* (Strike at the Core of the Matsukawa Case). Tokyo, July 20, 1954.

Matsukawa Jiken Taisaku Iinkai (Matsukawa Case Countermeasures Committee). *Matsukawa jiken, shinjitsu no shōri no tame ni* (The Matsukawa Case, For the Victory of Truth). Tokyo, 1954. "First Collection."

———. *Matsukawa, Shinjitsu to heiwa no tame ni* (Matsukawa, For Truth and Peace). Tokyo, 1956.

Matsukawa Jiken Taisaku Kyōgikai (Matsukawa Case Countermeasures Council), *Hōritsu wa ika ni magerareta ka* (How Was Justice Perverted?). Tokyo, n.d. [1959]. "Matsukawa Shiriizu No. 1."

———. *Kono jūsan nen* (These Thirteen Years). Tokyo, n.d. [1962]. "Matsukawa Shiriizu No. 12."

———. *Matsukawa jiken me de miru* (The Matsukawa Case Before One's Eyes). Tokyo, n.d. [1959].

———. *Matsukawa jiken, shinjitsu no shōri no tame ni* (The Matsukawa Case, For the Victory of Truth). Tokyo, n.d. [1959].

———. *Matsukawa jūgo nen* (Matsukawa Fifteen Years). Tokyo, 1964.

———. *Shin hannin wa dare ka* (Who Are The True Criminals?). Tokyo, n.d. [1959]. "Matsukawa Shiriizu No. 3."

———. *Suwa memo, kanken no shōko immetsu* (The Suwa Memorandum, Suppression of Evidence by Government Officials). Tokyo, n.d. [1959]. "Matsukawa Shiriizu No. 2."

———. *Tsukurareta shōgen* (Manufactured Testimony). Tokyo, n.d. [1960]. "Matsukawa Shiriizu No. 6."

———. *Yami ni kieta ku-nin* (The Nine Men Who Disappeared into the Dark). Tokyo, n.d. [1961]. "Matsukawa Shiriizu No. 7."

Matsukawa Jiken Taisaku Kyōgikai (The Matsukawa Case Countermeasures Council) and Matsukawa Undō Shi Hensan Iinkai (The Committee to Compile the History of the Matsukawa Movement), eds. *Matsukawa jūgo nen, Shinjitsu no shōri no tame ni* (Fifteen Years of Matsukawa, For the Victory of Truth). Tokyo: Rōdō Jumpō Sha, 1964.

Matsukawa Jiken Zenkoku Renraku Kaigi (Matsukawa Case National Liaison Council). *Matsukawa jiken kokka baishō saiban* (The Matsukawa Case State Compensation Trial). Tokyo, n.d. [1967].

———. *Ōta Shōji ikō shū* (Collected Posthumous Writings of Ōta Shōji). Tokyo, 1967.

Matsukawa Undō Shi Hensan Iinkai (The Committee to Compile the History of the Matsukawa Movement). *Matsukawa undō zenshi, taishū-teki saiban tōsō no jūgo nen* (Complete History of the Matsukawa Movement, Fifteen Years of Court Struggle by the Masses). Tokyo: Rōdō Jumpō Sha, 1965.

Matsumoto Seichō. *Nihon no kuroi kiri* (The Black Mist over Japan). Tokyo: Bungei Shunjū, 1962.

Murata Daizō, et al. *Matsukawa jiken wa kurisuchan ni totte nani o imi suru ka* (What is the Meaning of the Matsukawa Case for a Christian?). Miyagi Prefecture: Kirisuto-shin no Kyōkai, 1954.

Nakasone Yasuhiro, et al. *Warera Taishōkko* (We, Children of the Taishō Era). Tokyo: Tokuma Shoten "Human Books," 1961. Includes the autobiography of Satō Hajime, pp. 229–298.

Oda Takeo. *Shinjitsu no yukue, sabakareru hitobito* (Traces of the

Truth, The Accused). Tokyo: Geibun Shoin, 1957. Two volumes. A novel "inspired by the Matsukawa case."

Satō Hajime. Hikoku (Defendants). Tokyo: Heibonsha, 1958.

Sōhyō (The General Council of Japanese Labor Unions). Matsukawa jiken genchi chōsa no tebiki (Guidebook to the Matsukawa Case On-site Inspection). Tokyo: Matsukawa Jiken Genchi Chōsa Dan, 1957.

Toshimori Shigenobu. Akama jihaku (The Akama Confession). Tokyo: Moriwaki Bunko, 1959. A novel, with preface by Hirotsu Kazuo.

Uno Kōji. Yo ni mo fushigi na monogatari (The Strangest Story in the World). Tokyo: Dai Nihon Yūben Kai Kōdan Sha, 1953.

Yamada Seizaburō. Mahiru no ankoku, Matsukawa jiken (Darkness at Noon, the Matsukawa Case). Tokyo: San Ichi Shobō, 1956.

———. Nijū nin no hikokutachi (Twenty Defendants). Tokyo: Shindokusho Sha Shuppanbu, 1958.

———. Genba o mita hito; Matsukawa jiken no shin hannin wa dare ka (The Men Who Saw It Happen; Who Are the True Criminals of the Matsukawa Case?). Tokyo: Shunjū Sha, 1962.

Yamamoto Isamu and Suzuki Hisanori. Matsukawa jiken ni okeru kōhan tetsuzuki no un'yō ni kan suru kenkyū (A Study of the Courtroom Procedures Employed in the Matsukawa Case). Tokyo: Kensatsu Kenkyū Sho, 1952. "Kensatsu Kenkyū Sōsho 7." "Secret."

Yamamoto Satsuo, et al. Matsukawa jiken (The Matsukawa Case). N.p., n.d. Mimeo. Motion picture scenario.

Yoshihara Kōichirō. Matsukawa jiken no shin hannin (The True Criminals of the Matsukawa Case). Tokyo: San Ichi Shobō, 1962.

B. Periodicals

Asahi jānaru
"Tokushū: Matsukawa hanketsu o yonde" (Special Collection: On Reading the Matsukawa Verdict). Three articles. III:34 (August 20, 1961), 8–21.

Bungaku no tomo

Nose Katsuo, et al. "Hanketsu, Matsukawa jiken dai-ni-shin kōhan" (Verdict, the Second Trial of the Matsukawa Case). V:2 (February 1954), 1, 52–61.

Bungei shunjū

Kira Shunri. "Matsukawa jiken: kumei no shin hannin" (The Matsukawa Case: Nine True Criminals). XLIV:6 (June 1966), 276–287.

Chūō kōron

"Matsukawa saiban tokubetsu gō" (Matsukawa Trial Special Issue). No. 846 (November 1958), passim.

"Matsukawa jiken tokushū gō" (Matsukawa Case Special Issue). No. 860 (September 1959), passim.

Special Collection on the Verdict in the Retrial. No. 887 (October 1961), 90–132. Articles by Hirotsu Kazuo, Satō Hajime, Date Akio, and Ienaga Saburō.

Eiga hyōron

"Shinario: Matsukawa jiken, fuirumu ni yoru shōgen" (Scenario: The Matsukawa Case, Evidence through Film). No. 1 (January 1959), 116–134.

"Matsukawa jiken to sono shūhen no mondai" (The Matsukawa Case and the Problem of Its Locale). No. 3 (March 1961), 16–20.

Gunzō

Five Articles to Commemorate the Death of Hirotsu Kazuo. December 1968, 167–207.

Heiwa

Okabayashi Tatsuo. "Shin hannin wa ta ni iru Matsukawa jiken" (The Matsukawa Case, in which the True Criminals Have Escaped). No. 11 (1953), 24–34.

Hōgaku kyōshitsu

Uematsu Tadashi. "Akama jihaku to tento no iro, Matsukawa saiban kobore-hanashi" (The Akama Confession and the Color of the Tent, Scattered Comments on the Matsukawa Trials). No. 3 (March 1962), 124–125.

Hōgaku seminā

Gotō Shōjirō. "Matsukawa jiken sashimodoshi-shin, shōko no ne-

tsuzō to immetsu to" (The Matsukawa Case Retrial, the Fabrication and Suppression of Evidence). No. 59 (February 1961), 55–59.
Articles on Justice Shimoiizaka's dissent in the second Supreme Court verdict and an article by Gotō Shōjirō reviewing the problems of the case from the defense point of view. No. 92 (November 1963), 36–42.

Hōritsu jihō
"Matsukawa jiken hanketsu no hō-teki mondaiten" (Legal Problems of the Verdict in the Matsukawa Case). Six Articles. XXVI:7 (July 1954), 4–42.
"Saikōsai Matsukawa hanketsu hihyō" (Commentary on the Supreme Court's Verdict in the Matsukawa Case). Special issue (September 1959), passim.

Jinken no tame ni
"Matsukawa jiken tokushū" (Special Collection on the Matsukawa Case). No. 3 (October 1959), passim.
Ōtsuka Kazuo. "Matsukawa jiken in okeru shōko immetsu" (Suppression of Evidence in the Matsukawa Case). No. 5 (1960), 20–24.
Ueda Masayoshi. "Subete no shōko wa kenryoku hanzai o shōmei suru" (All of the Evidence Proves that the Authorities Committed Crimes). No. 10 (June 1961), 42–45, 59.
"Shiratori, Matsukawa jiken tokushū gō" (Special Issue on the Shiratori and Matsukawa Cases). Nos. 11 and 12 combined (April 1962), passim.

Jiyū to seigi
Ishida Tōru and Takezawa Tetsuo. "Matsukawa jiken no kokka baishō no seikyū" (Claims for State Compensation in the Matsukawa Case). XV:6 (June 1964), 14–17.
Ōtsuka Kazuo. "Matsukawa jiken ni okeru himitsu kōtsu ken no shingai" (Infringement of the Right of Secret Communication in the Matsukawa Case). XVII:1 (January 1966), 19–24.

Jurisuto
Hirano Ryūichi. "Matsukawa jiken no kyōkun" (Lessons of the Matsukawa Case). No. 50 (January 15, 1954), 1–4.

"Matsukawa jiken: haki-sashimodoshi hanketsu no imi suru mono" (Significant Aspects of the Reversal and Referral Back Verdict in the Matsukawa Case). Special extra issue (September 1959), passim.

"Matsukawa saiban no atoaji" (The Aftertaste of the Matsukawa Trial). No. 233 (September 1, 1961), 5, 70–92.

"Matsukawa jiken muzai hanketsu tokushū" (Special Collection on the Matsukawa Case Not-Guilty Verdict). No. 239 (December 1, 1961), passim.

"Tokushū: Matsukawa jiken saishū hanketsu" (Special Edition: The Final Verdict in the Matsukawa Case). No. 284 (October 15, 1963), passim.

Jurisuto bessatsu

Inoue Masaji, "Matsukawa jiken—haki-sashimodoshi hanketsu no kōsokuryoku" (The Matsukawa Case—The Binding Force of the Reversal and Referral Back Verdict). No. 3 (May 1965), 188–189.

Rekishi hyōron

"Matsukawa jiken to rekishigaku" (The Matsukawa Case and Historical Scholarship). Six articles. No. 52 (February 1954), 28–61.

"Matsukawa jiken to rekishigaku" (The Matsukawa Case and Historical Scholarship). No. 67 (June 1955), 20–30.

"Tokushū: Gendaishi to Matsukawa jiken" (Special Issue: Modern History and the Matsukawa Case). Six articles. No. 132 (August 1961), 1–53.

Articles by Nohara Shirō and Matsushima Eiichi on the verdict in the retrial. No. 134 (October 1961), 26–28.

Rekishigaku kenkyū

Suzuki Masashi, et al. "Matsukawa jiken to sono saiban" (The Matsukawa Case and Its Trial). No. 224 (October 1958), 38–53.

Miyagawa Torao. "Matsukawa tōsō ni tsuite" (Concerning the Matsukawa Struggle). No. 257 (September 1961), 39–41.

Sekai

"Matsukawa jiken o megutte" (Revolving Around the Matsukawa Case). Four articles. No. 86 (February 1953), 161–202.

Open letter from Hirotsu Kazuo et al., addressed to Judge Suzuki of the Sendai High Court, together with photos and two short articles. No. 96 (December 1953), 128–132.

"Jōkoku semaru Matsukawa jiken" (The Matsukawa Case Draws Near to Supreme Court Appeal). Three articles. No. 117 (September 1955), 114–144.

Hirotsu Kazuo. "Saiban to kokumin" (Court and Citizen). No. 145 (January 1958), 290–308.

————. "Tanin no jihaku to Matsukawa jiken" (Another Person's Confession and the Matsukawa Case). No. 156 (December 1958), 70–81.

Articles and photographs concerning the final not-guilty verdict. No. 215 (November 1963), 156–195.

Hirotsu Kazuo, "Matsukawa saiban ato ni nao kuyuru mono" (Things that Remain Obscure after the Matsukawa Trials). No. 225 (September 1964), 184–196.

Shin Nihon bungaku

Sata Ineko, "Matsukawa no koto sono ta" (Matsukawa Notes, and other Matters). No. 136 (November 1958), 172–177.

Three Matsukawa stories. No. 171 (October 1961), 177–187.

Sōzō

Article by Takeda Hisashi, a Matsukawa defendant, and reprints of court materials. No. 4 (n.d., c. 1953, mimeo.), 73–80.

Ushio

Articles and documents concerning the anonymous letters in the Kaji Wataru and Matsukawa cases. II:2 (February 1953), 62–72.

Zen'ei

"Matsukawa no shinjitsu" (The Truth of Matsukawa). No. 150 (January 1959), special issue, passim.

III. WORKS ON THE ERA OF THE MATSUKAWA CASE

A. Books

Aochi Shin. Gendaishi no magarikado (Turning Points in Modern History). Tokyo: Kōbundō, 1959.

Asahi Shimbun, Fukushima Bureau. Fukushima no jinmyaku (The

Pulse of Fukushima). Kōriyama: Takashima Shobō Shuppan-bu, 1967.

Fukuoka Takashi. *Ningen Matsumoto Seichō* (The Man Matsumoto Seichō). Tokyo: Taikō Sha, 1968.

Hara Toshio. *Nihon no saiban* (Japan's Courts). Tokyo: San'ichi Shobō, 1959.

Hironaka Toshio. *Sengo Nihon no keisatsu* (The Police of Postwar Japan). Tokyo: Iwanami Shinsho No. 684, 1968.

Ichinose Masayuki. *Nihon kyōsantō* (The Japanese Communist Party). Tokyo: Motomoto Sha, 1954.

Ienaga Saburō. *Saiban hihan* (Criticism of the Courts). Tokyo: Nihon Hyōron Shinsha, 1959.

Inomata Kōzō. *Teikō no keifu* (A Heritage of Resistance). Tokyo: Sakai Shoten, 1964.

Ishikawa Hiroyoshi. *Nihonjin no shakai shinri* (The Social Psychology of Japanese). Tokyo: San'ichi Shobō, 1965.

Japanese Government. Kōan Chōsa Chō (Public Security Investigation Agency). *Nihon kyōsantō o chūshin to shita naigai dōkō nempyō* (Chronological Tables of Foreign and Domestic Trends Centering Around the Japanese Communist Party). Tokyo: 1965 [1945–1963].

———. Kokka Chihō Keisatsu Honbu Keiji-bu Sōsa-ka (National Rural Police Headquarters, Criminal Affairs Division, Investigation Section). *Bōgaihan no sōsa* (Investigation of Sabotage Crimes). Tokyo: 1952. "Criminal Police Materials Vol. 10." "Internal Use Only."

Jiyū Hōsō Dan (League of Free Jurists). *Jiyū hōsō dan monogatari* (The Story of the League of Free Jurists). Tokyo: Rōdō Jumpō Sha, 1966.

Kainō Michitaka. *Hōritsu, sono hi sono tsuki* (The Law, Day by Day and Month by Month). Tokyo: Ichiryūsha, 1957.

Kawashima Takeyoshi. *Nihonjin no hō ishiki* (The Legal Consciousness of Japanese). Tokyo: Iwanami Shinsho No. 630, 1967.

Kobayashi Seiji and Yamada Akira. *Fukushima-ken no rekishi* (The History of Fukushima Prefecture). Tokyo: Yamakawa Shuppan Sha, 1970.

Kuroda Hidetoshi. *Shōwa genronshi e no shōgen* (Contributions Toward a History of the Press in the Shōwa Era). Tokyo: Kōbundō, 1966.

Mamiya Mosuke. *Hirotsu Kazuo, kono hito to no gojū nen* (My Fifty Years with Hirotsu Kazuo). Tokyo: Riron Sha, 1969.

Masaki Hiroshi. *Chikaki yori* (Near at Hand). Tokyo: Kōbundō, 1964.

———. *Yakai saiban* (The Yakai Trials). Tokyo: Chūkō Shinsho No. 189, 1969.

Mita Munesuke. *Gendai Nihon no seishin kōzō* (The Structure of Contemporary Japanese Values). Tokyo: Kōbundō, 1965.

Miyauchi Hiroshi, et al. *Sengo himitsu keisatsu no jittai* (Facts on the Postwar Secret Police). Tokyo: San'ichi Shobō, 1960.

Namba Hideo. *Kyūen undō monogatari* (The Story of the Relief Movement). Tokyo: Nihon Kokumin Kyūen Kai, 1966.

Nikkan Rōdō Tsūshin Sha (Labor Daily News Company), ed. *Sengo Nihon kyōsan-shugi undō* (The Postwar Japanese Communist Movement). Tokyo: Nikkan Rōdō Tsūshin Sha, 1955.

Ozaki Hotsuki and Yamada Munemutsu. *Sengo seikatsu bunka shi* (A History of the Postwar Culture of Daily Life). Tokyo: Kōbundō, 1966.

Shimoyama Jiken Kenkyū Kai (Association to Study the Shimoyama Case), ed. *Shiryō Shimoyama jiken* (Documents of the Shimoyama Case). Tokyo: Misuzu Shobō, 1969.

Shinobu Seizaburō. *Sengo Nihon seiji shi* (A History of Postwar Japanese Politics). Tokyo: Keisō Shobō, 1967. Volume III.

Takano Minoru. *Nihon no rōdō undō* (The Japanese Labor Movement). Tokyo: Iwanami Shinsho No. 303, 1958.

Ueda Seikichi and Gotō Shōjirō. *Ayamatta saiban, yattsu no keiji jiken* (Mistrials, The Eight Criminal Cases). Tokyo: Iwanami Shinsho No. 373, 1960.

Ushiomi Toshitaka. *Hōritsuka* (The Jurists). Tokyo: Iwanami Shinsho No. 751, 1970.

Yakai Case History Compilation Committee, ed. *Yakai jiken jūhachi nen* (Eighteen Years of the Yakai Case). Tokyo: Rōdō Jumpō Sha, 1969.

B. Periodicals

Asahi jānaru

Tanaka Kōtarō. "Saiban hihan o hihan suru" (Criticism of Criticism of the Courts). I:33 (October 25, 1959), 8–15.

Gendai

Matsumoto Seichō. "Saisetsu: Shimoyama kokutetsu sōsai bōsatsu ron" (Reexamination: The Murder Theory [of the Death] of Japanese National Railroads President Shimoyama). August 1969, 96–116.

Sekai

"Jihaku to wa?" (What is Confession?) No. 99 (March 1954), 89–182.

"Sengo jūshichi nen to Nihon no shōrai" (The Seventeen Postwar Years and Japan's Future). No. 200 (August 1962), special edition, passim.

IV. SPECIAL COLLECTIONS

Kokkai Toshokan, Shimbun Kirinuki Shitsu (National Diet Library, Newspaper Clipping Room). Matsukawa Case File. August 18, 1949–April 22, 1966. Eleven volumes. Microfilm.

Matsukawa tsūshin (Matsukawa Report). Tabloid newspaper of the Matsukawa Case Countermeasures Council. No. 19 (November 7, 1958). No. 20 (November 12, 1958). No. 21 (November 15, 1958). No. 24 (November 26, 1958). No. 25 (November 29, 1958). No. 146 (September 1, 1968). No. 147 (April 15, 1969). No. 148 (February 26, 1970). No. 149 (April 16, 1970).

Supreme Commander for the Allied Powers. Selected Archives. United States National Archives. Includes *History of the Nonmilitary Activities of the Occupation of Japan, 1945–1951.* Fifty-five volumes. Microfilm.

V. WORKS IN ENGLISH

Anderson, Joseph L., and Richie, Donald. *The Japanese Film: Art and Industry.* New York: Grove Press, 1960.

Bedford, Sybille. *The Faces of Justice*. New York: Simon and Schuster, 1961.

Dandō, Shigemitsu. *Japanese Criminal Procedure*. B. J. George, Jr., trans. South Hackensack, N.J.: Fred B. Rothman and Co., 1965.

Frank, Jerome, and Frank, Barbara. *Not Guilty*. New York: Doubleday, 1957.

Henderson, Dan Fenno, ed. *The Constitution of Japan, Its First Twenty Years, 1947–1967*. Seattle: University of Washington Press, 1968.

Japanese Government. Ministry of Justice. *The Code of Criminal Procedure of Japan*. Tokyo: Eibun Hōrei Sha, 1961.

————. *Criminal Statutes, Translation*. Tokyo: Ministry of Justice, n.d.

————. *The Penal Code of Japan*. Tokyo: Eibun Hōrei Sha, 1965.

————. The Supreme Court. *Courts in Japan*. Tokyo: The Supreme Court, 1965.

————. *Outline of Civil Trial in Japan*. Tokyo: The Supreme Court, 1963.

————. *Outline of Criminal Justice in Japan*. Tokyo: The Supreme Court, 1963.

Kennan, George F. *Memoirs (1925–1950)*. New York: Bantam ed., 1969.

Maki, John M. *Court and Constitution in Japan: Selected Supreme Court Decisions, 1948–1960*. Seattle: University of Washington Press, 1964.

Packard, George R., III. *Protest in Tokyo, The Security Treaty Crisis of 1960*. Princeton: Princeton University Press, 1966.

Packer, Herbert L. *The Limits of the Criminal Sanction*. Stanford: Stanford University Press, 1968.

Roth, Andrew. *Dilemma in Japan*. Boston: Little, Brown, 1945.

Scalapino, Robert A. *Democracy and the Party Movement in Prewar Japan*. Berkeley and Los Angeles: University of California Press, 1953.

————, and Masumi, Junnosuke. *Parties and Politics in Contemporary Japan*. Berkeley and Los Angeles: University of California Press, 1962.

————. *The Japanese Communist Movement, 1920–1966.* Berkeley and Los Angeles: University of California Press, 1967.

United States Army. *Reports of General MacArthur.* Washington: Government Printing Office, 1966.

von Mehren, Arthur T., ed. *Law in Japan.* Cambridge, Mass.: Harvard University Press, 1963.

Whittemore, Edward P. *The Press in Japan Today: A Case Study.* Columbia, S.C.: University of South Carolina Press, 1961.

Yamamura, Kozo. *Economic Policy in Postwar Japan, Growth Versus Economic Democracy.* Berkeley and Los Angeles: University of California Press, 1967.

Index